978 0436 46 6403

FILM CULTURE
An Anthology

CONTENTS

A section of illustrations follows page 214.

PREFACE

Magazines have been the bulwarks of polemical aesthetics in our times. Renato Poggioli, the theorist of avant-gardism, writes of "one of the external signs most characteristically avant-garde: periodicals of a group or movement; all of them were organs for a specific creative current and, especially, for a particular tendency of taste." To learn the character and to trace the evolution of a single such magazine, there is no better way than to peruse an entire "run" of its issues. Often, the least memorable, flimsiest articles provide an insight into the individuality of a publication that its "features" cannot reveal, especially, after a number of years; for, in a given period, several magazines share the best authors or compete for an author's best work. The peripheral pieces indicate the ideas and needs of individual editors.

This complicates the task of an anthologist who would collect the best of a periodical and still preserve a sense of its uniqueness. No anthology (the present volume included) can contain all the best and all the most characteristic of a magazine over many years. The present collection does not pretend to be comprehensive. It attempts to satisfy three needs. First, there is the need to bring back into print the crucial contributions to film criticism and aesthetics that have appeared in *Film Culture* since its inception, in January, 1955. Next, we have tried to document *Film Culture* as an organic entity, recognizing its various changes over the past fifteen years. Finally, we have designed the collection as a source book for readings in the avant-garde cinema, a field with which the magazine has come to be identified in the last decade.

Almost from the beginning, *Film Culture* has subtitled itself "America's Independent Motion Picture Magazine," indicating its critical attitude as well as its domain of interest. Jonas Mekas founded *Film Culture* not long after he came to the United States from Lithuania by way of postwar Germany. A formalist (and romantic) poet in his native language, he discovered the cinema in New York. In his initial editorial, he outlined the vision of a publication that would combine the interests and needs of film-makers and film viewers.

Today, the needs for a searching revaluation of the aesthetic standards obtaining both among film-makers and audiences and for thorough revision of the prevalent attitude to the function of cinema have assumed more challenging proportions than ever before. Cinematic creation tends to be approached primarily as a production of commodities, and large sections of the public—to whom film-going is still merely a mode of diversion—remain unaware of the full significance of filmic art.

The original editorial board contained Mekas's brother Adolfas, George Fenin, Louis Brigante, and Edouard de Laurot, a Marxist critic whose long theoretical articles dominated many of the early issues. Many foreign correspondents contributed articles and letters. Although it was oriented toward the European cinema, *Film Culture*, from its very first issue, focused critical attention on the embryonic "experimental" (as it was then called) cinema in America. Although it may have been a harsh critic of the avant-garde, *Film Culture* was the one place where it was taken seriously. The first chapter of this collection represents the initial position of the editors and contributors in respect to the avant-garde cinema. The final chapter is its complement, with recent sophisticated overviews of the American avant-garde in the context of film history and recent international achievements in the formal cinema.

Film Culture has never been solvent; in 1958, it collapsed as a monthly (it had been a bimonthly for its first eleven issues). Mekas wrote in the editorial of the last regular number (#18), the von Stroheim issue:

> For three years, we have been publishing in this country a periodical devoted to the advanced criticism of motion pictures—motion pictures as an art and as a social phenomenon. But as yet we have not had sufficient support on the part of the audience. There are not enough people in this country who realize that film is an art and that motion-picture fan-magazines are not enough. The institutions and foundations whose functions include the support of cultural activities have refused to help us, and, what is more, *Film Culture* has been asked to pay taxes! *Film Culture* has suffered the same sort of "men's stupidity" that killed Erich von Stroheim.
> Therefore, beginning with this issue, *Film Culture* will appear on an unperiodical basis, with selected collections of articles and essays on cinema—partisan-like, the most effective way at this juncture.

After that, *Film Culture* began to assume a new character. Mekas recognized the potential for an independent cinema in the United States and attempted to make the magazine a vehicle for its emergence. With the nineteenth issue, he initiated the Independent Film

Awards, given yearly (more or less) to call attention to the finest American films made outside of the commercial system.

Perhaps guided by the success of a group of French film-makers who had edited the magazine *Cahiers du Cinéma*, Mekas made his first film, *Guns of the Trees* (1960–61), with his coeditors Brigante, de Laurot, and Adolfas Mekas assisting him. The experience transfigured his vision of the cinema. In the first place, *Film Culture* immediately became a forum of ideas of economic alternatives to commercial production and distribution. At the same time, it rediscovered the native avant-garde cinema, which had existed for years without commercialization or concession.

In the eleven issues from 19 to 29, *Film Culture* gradually became the apologist of the New American Cinema (Mekas's term) of which it had once been so critical. Yet film has always perpetuated dualities and bifurcations. Film criticism can seem as schizophrenic as film production. As the magazine became the forum for an emerging avant-garde cinema, to which most other magazines had been and continue to be hostile or indifferent, it turned, simultaneously, from reviewing European films with an academic and intellectual viewpoint to demanding serious attention for the traditional output of Hollywood. Andrew Sarris, who had become an editor of the magazine, epitomized the American orientation with his special issue (#28) devoted to creating a hierarchy of Hollywood directors and summarizing their styles.

Even after the thirtieth issue, by which time it had become the quasiofficial magazine of the avant-garde film-maker, *Film Culture* continued to devote part of almost every issue to Sarris or other Americanist critics. In *Cahiers du Cinéma*, the dichotomy between the film-makers and the apologists of the commercial cinema was not great. In the first place, they were often the same persons. Secondly, as film-makers they were much more "commercial," certainly far less radical than the artists associated with *Film Culture*, and as critics of the traditional American film, they were seldom as enthusiastic as Sarris.

The presence of Andrew Sarris in the pages of *Film Culture* is complemented by that of Parker Tyler. Both began to write for the magazine soon after it was founded; both became frequent contributors during its transitional period in the early sixties; neither has contributed more than one article in the past few years, the magazine's most radical stage. Tyler gave measured support to the avant-garde film-maker during the period in which *Film Culture* was most critical and measured criticism as the editors became more fervid in their support of the movement. The articles of his we have selected represent a crucial station in the evolution of *Film Culture*. We would have included even more of his writings were they not all available in several recent editions of his essays.

The editors of *Film Culture* have at times devoted entire issues or large sections of an issue to a single topic. Sarris's critical index of American directors was one such issue; it has been omitted here because of its recent republication, in book form, as *The American Cinema*. Likewise, Seymour Stern's monumental study of D. W. Griffith's *The Birth of a Nation*, the first part of which filled issue 36, defies excerpting; and its complete version is immanent. We have attempted to encapsulate the issue (#18) devoted to Erich von Stroheim. From the volume of Stan Brakhage's writings *Metaphors on Vision* (issue 30), we have taken the introductory interview and the final chapter. The issue still remains in print but may soon be exhausted.

A copy of the cumulative index of *Film Culture* may be obtained free from *Film Culture*, Box 1499, G.P.O., New York, N.Y. 10001.

I am most indebted to Annette Michelson, the advisory editor in the film-book program at Praeger, for her encouragement and help in the preparation of this volume. Her careful reading of the manuscript guided me in making the final selection; what clarity and intellectual thrust there may be in my Introduction derive from her notes; the confusions are my own. It is a pleasure to have the opportunity to thank Malcolm Mills, who typed the manuscript, Valerie Curtis, who helped me proofread it, Susan Saunders, who made the initial index, and Gwen Thomas and Perlyn Goodman who helped me read the galleys.

The living authors have been most generous in allowing me to reprint their articles. I wish also to acknowledge Amos Vogel, who organized the symposium "Poetry and the Film" at Cinema 16, for his permission to reprint the transcription of that event, and E. P. Dutton & Co. for permission to use "The Cosmic Cinema of Jordan Belson" from Gene Youngblood's forthcoming book, *Expanded Cinema*.

The achievements of *Film Culture* reflect the spirit and genius of its founder and editor-in-chief, Jonas Mekas. I am grateful to him for allowing me to make this collection and for his consistent help and advice from its conception and throughout its production. Finally, I wish to thank my wife, who has willingly shared all my labors in making this book and seeing it through to publication.

P. ADAMS SITNEY

FILM CULTURE
An Anthology

To Jerome Hill

INTRODUCTION

A READER'S GUIDE TO THE AMERICAN AVANT-GARDE FILM

At its best, criticism can transfigure its object. The critic who illuminates the workings of the object of his criticism helps the reader to experience the object afresh in retrospect or upon subsequent encounter. On a lower level, the critic can *direct* the reader to a work he might not know or to a part of a familiar work he has overlooked and let him do the labor which leads to illumination himself. Much of the writing collected in this volume aspires to the higher level but must perforce function on the lower because of the relative obscurity of the films discussed.

While making this anthology, I was aware of the fact that it would be more immediately available to a reading public than the films upon which it concentrates: the New American Cinema. Therefore, an introductory essay to guide the reader through the complicated history of the avant-garde cinema in this country has been prefixed, although it never appeared as such in *Film Culture*.

I say "in this country," recognizing that film history has suffered more from the limitations of thinking in terms of national achievement than the history of any other modern art. Undeniably, there have been centers of activity; the avant-garde film surfaced simultaneously in Paris and Berlin in the early 1920's and developed in the former city throughout that decade. It faded in the 1930's to appear again, in full force, in California and New York at the end of World War II. The reasons for the hemispheric shift are simple. Nazism drove radical artists, the surviving Cubists, Dadaists, and Surrealists, to America where they found a provincial audience ready to look at, and assimilate, their works. So, when we speak of the American avant-garde film, we mean to encompass the German Hans Richter who taught and made cinema here, as well as Peter Kubelka who makes his films in Austria for a primarily American audience, and many others.

Without the sudden injection of European Modernism, there would have been no avant-garde art upsurge in America in the late 1940's. In the case of film-making, the fact that the new generation of film-makers clustered around the Art in Cinema film society in San Francisco and Cinema 16 in New York, where the older avant-garde films could be seen, indicates the directness of the tradition. Often, this radicalism in cinema has been too simply analyzed as a reaction to the stagnation of Hollywood. That was a historical factor, but not a dominating one. Perhaps the influence of Hollywood on the American avant-garde was simply negative; the exclusion of the possibility of finding creative work there saved many young artists years of wasted apprenticeship. Without a chance to make the kind of films they wanted to make commercially, they immediately set about doing what they could within the limitations of their circumstances.

Avant-garde film-making in the United States has never been a movement; the individualism of the artists prevented that. Yet there have been collective drifts, general tendencies (always with contemporary exceptions, of course), around which the film historian can structure his observations. As Ken Kelman pointed out in his 1964 survey of the New American Cinema for the *Nation* (May 13):

> Our current reduction of the totality of things is precisely what the New American Cinema is up against, and I would give cohesion to this cinema first in terms of its response to the prevalent modern superstitions. Again, I would not call it a movement so much as a release of energies, whose various aspects are related not so much by common purpose as by common necessity.

Through the work of the two film societies mentioned above and, later, through *Film Culture* and the Film-Makers Cooperative, avant-garde film-makers have been kept informed of each other's work. More than anything else, the reciprocity of information which all the contemporary arts share, has propelled change by keeping the avant-garde film community informed of the exhaustion of formal possibilities.

Two lines of development have persisted since the inception of the avant-garde cinema in Europe: the graphic and the subjective. Sometimes, these lines run parallel; sometimes, they overlap. The evolution of the graphic film has been calmer than the subjective; after the initial exploration of the flat surface and hard-edge forms, the graphic was vitalized by the development of the hand-painted film and quite recently has entered the area of imagery generated by computers and electrically modified (through television tape). The appearance of the flicker films (black and white or pure color alternations) bridges the division between animated and directly photographed film by its critical reduction of both to a common atomism.

A synoptic view of the history of the subjective film (for which specific examples follow) passes from the psychodrama, in which the film-maker acts out a Freudian situation in a symbolic landscape, to the mythopoeic film, where elemental and archetypal situations are elaborated in epic forms. At its most informal development, this genre manifested a period of anarchic picaresques.

A succession of plastic concerns attends upon this historical morphology. In the earliest period of the subjectivist film, the film-maker often acted the central role of his work, as a somnambulist or an entranced figure (Parker Tyler aptly called the genre "the Trance Film"). The primary material of these films, visually, are symbols, ominous objects in detail, since the film-maker as an actor cannot see the compositional field. In the picaresques, the actor (not the film-maker) becomes the central image. His gestures, often obscene, are the focus of directorial attention. Both the psychodrama and the picaresque are bas-reliefs, oblivious to spatial elaboration. In the mythopoeic film, one or a number of *personae*, abstracted and primitivized types, replace the somnambulist or anarchic hero; the essential visual dynamics are registered by the intricacies of montage.

The structural film has brought the redemption of deep space (and a corollary involvement with the flat, anti-illusionist screen). Before this plastic stage, which presupposed the disappearance of both the hero and the mythic *personae*, could be reached, the lyric film was essential, with its direct, *frontal* investigation of the film-maker's field of vision.

The succession of film-maker theoreticians within the American avant-garde begins with Maya Deren. Her statement at the Cinema 16 "Symposium on Poetry and the Film" articulates the subjectivist approach that dominated the avant-garde film until the middle 1960's. Her division of "vertical" and "horizontal" axes within narrative and dramatic structures, and her argument for purely "vertical" film poems, orients the avant-garde film as a vehicle for the manifestation of stream-of-consciousness and introspection in cinema.

In her own early work, as well as that of Markopoulos, Anger, Brakhage, Peterson, Broughton, and others, the formal representation of psychological states prefigured all other developments. From the end of World War II until late in the 1950's, psychodrama was by far the dominant genre of the "Experimental film," as it was then called. *Meshes of the Afternoon* (1943), Maya Deren's first film, reveals a simple chain of events—a woman (played by the film-maker) entering an empty house, observing the objects of the room, and taking a nap during which a man enters the house—in different aspects as the action is repeated with several variations. In each of them, symbolic dimensions of the objects in the room become progressively manifest and violent, climaxing in a suicide, the reality of which remains ambiguous.

In *At Land* (1944) and *Ritual in Transfigured Time* (1946) Deren formalized the principles of conscious disorientation of space and time that she had invented in her first film for a subjective effect. Her work evolved from the personal to the mythic, from a language of Freudian icons to Jungian archetypes; in so doing it rehearsed, in the 1940's, a progression that the avant-garde cinema as a whole was to make between the late 1950's and the early 1960's. I will return to this step later—a step that, incidentally, is anticipated within the filmographies of other film-makers.

In 1947, Kenneth Anger created a cinematic dream of homosexual encounters, *Fireworks*, which instantly made him the *enfant terrible* of the avant-garde. The episodes of his film are a tapestry of icons and symbols. The exaggerated offer of a "light" to a sailor against the painted backdrop of a bar, cruising cars at night, and muscle flexing exemplify the former; a Roman candle for a phallus and the equally phallic and ritualistic image of the hero crowned with a large Christmas tree and a burning candle atop it are extremes of the latter. The article by Mekas in the first chapter epitomizes the negative criticism Anger's radicalism, and that of his fellow avant-gardists, elicited at the time and for more than a decade later.

At this first station of the history of the avant-garde film in America the vital concerns of film-makers were symbolism, the subjective camera, and the representation of dreams. Sidney Peterson made two of the most sophisticated and witty films of the period, mixing formal commitment with psychological distancing. He had abstracted a methodology to make use of random objects for surrealistic comedies. As a teacher of film-making at the San Francisco Art Institute, Peterson had to use his students and make his academic situation the occasion for his art. His best works, *Mr. Frenhofer and the Minotaur* (1949) and *The Lead Shoes* (1949–50), employ anamorphic photography and themes compounded from diverse sources. *Mr. Frenhofer* combines the situation of Balzac's story "The Unknown Masterpiece" with the imagery of Picasso's "Minotaurachy," conjoined with a reading on the soundtrack of a serious parody of a Joycean monologue in the *persona* of an art student seduced by an elder artist. Two old English ballads and a diving suit which happened to be available were the source of *The Lead Shoes*, a hysterical study of incest and fratricide. In his article, "A Note on Comedy in Experimental Film," Peterson elaborates his involvement with the *process* of film-making, an involvement so intense that he was able to achieve a cinematic art despite the limitations of his pedagogic situation.

The subjective tradition in film has always intersected with the tradition of the abstract film, be it cinegraphic (that is, animated, hand-painted) or photographed. Both emerged out of the Modernist painting movements of the early years of this century: Dada, Surrealism, Cubism, and Constructivism. Viking Eggeling's *Diagonal Symphony* and Richter's *Rhythmus 21*, both from 1921, initiated the cinema of flat, nonobjective forms in movement. Man Ray employed both cinegraphic and subjective styles in his films *Return to Reason* (1924) and *Emak Bakia* (1926). Historically, these two aspects have always been related, sometimes overlapping in the works of individual film-makers.

In his interview, Harry Smith describes his involvement with the abstract film and the techniques he employed in making them. His works to date form an even more complete paradigm than Maya Deren's for the historical evolution of the American avant-garde film. The one phase he has not participated in is the psychodrama of the 1940's. Smith's earliest films (made throughout the 1940's) arise from the Bauhaus tradition of formal composition and illusory depth through color and shape. Smith's work is vitalized by a serious commitment to the textural surface of the film material itself (he paints, glues, scratches the raw material) for which his ability to invent and master graphic techniques distinguished him.

Between 1950 and 1960, Smith worked on a long animated film, literally a surrealistic cartoon of epic proportions. He has given us in this film a twentieth century inflection of "The Immortal Journey" —in the tradition of Dante, Milton, and Blake. By the time he finished the film, which is sometimes called *Heaven and Earth Magic* or *The Magic Feature*, the New American Cinema had entered its mythopoeic stage: film-makers who had worked in the psychodrama were elaborating epic myths—both classical and chthonian. His latest film, *Late Superimpositions* (1964), an auto-biographical fragment, brings us to the diary form which has been a major development of the late 1960's.

The animated film of the 1950's had both a kinetic and social manifestation. Robert Breer, working in the tradition of Eggeling, Richter, and Len Lye (who combined animated with photographed images in films such as *Trade Tattoo* [1927], has articulated a formal cinema based on the illusions and dissolutions of spatial complexes and on extreme speed of imagery. His film *Blazes* (1961) is made up of a hundred calligraphic images following one after the other in mostly single-frame shots; that is, twenty-four different pictures every second or one entire set of the hundred images in just five seconds. In *69* (1969), he systematically alternates abstract, linear forms, which affirm the flatness of the screen upon which they are projected with forms creating three-dimensional illusions and a sense of extreme depth in the screen. Breer's interest in spatial illusionism long antedates the recent emergence of that concern among those film-makers whom I have described as "Structuralist."

Gregory Markopoulos, working independently of Breer, developed a similar theory of speed and perception in his mythic narrative films, beginning with *Twice a Man* (1963). He expressed his meth-odology in a brief manifesto in *Film Culture* No. 30, "Towards a New Narrative Film Form," in which he wrote:

> I propose a new narrative form through the fusion of the classic montage technique with a more abstract system. This system involves the use of short film phrases which evoke thought-images. Each film phrase is composed of certain select frames that are similar to the harmonic units found in musical composition. The film phrases estab-lish ulterior relationships among themselves; in classic montage-tech-nique, there is a constant reference to the continuing shot; in my abstract system, there is a complex of differing frames being repeated.

In their socially oriented animation, the collage film-makers Stan Vanderbeek and Richard Preston use magazine cutouts for explicit and obtuse political satire. Vanderbeek's *Science Friction* (1958) shows preposterous objects and edifices, a religious tryptich, the

Empire State Building, lifting off like rockets out of their familiar backgrounds and landscapes. Bruce Conner, also a collagist, collected film clippings and reconstructed them to build a vision of human disaster (*A Movie*, 1958) or to express an equation between sexuality and war (*Cosmic Ray*, 1961).

The first New American Cinema Group represents an intersection of the lines of the American social documentary and the avant-garde psychodrama. It was as if the trauma dramas of Anger, Brakhage, etc., had found a social context. Of course, in the early 1960's, most of the members of the NAC Group considered themselves in direct opposition to the "experimental film" with its psychological orientation. They intended to offer a commercial alternative to the stagnant Hollywood cinema and made works inspired by the ideological concerns that produced the Beat movement. Yet, today, Mekas's *Guns of the Trees*, Cassavetes' *Shadows*, Alfred Leslie's and Robert Frank's *Pull My Daisy*, and Robert Frank's *Sin of Jesus* now seem to compose a late stage in the evolution of the American psychodrama.

The very last stage of the psychodramatic tradition was again unambiguously posited within the avant-garde: a picaresque cinema of anarchic nonsense, of sexual fantasy, of Zen, and of antiestablishment parody. The works of Ron Rice, Jack Smith, and Vernon Zimmerman, and the early works of Ken Jacobs represent this stage, which overlapped with, and was finally absorbed into, the mythopoeic cinema. In his article "Notes on the New American Cinema," Jonas Mekas captures the spirit and documents the phenomena of this moment in the history of the American avant-garde film. As a critic, Mekas has been most at home in his discussions of informal, Zen-oriented works; he is at his very best in this article and in his "Notes on Some New Films and Happiness."

While Brakhage was writing the essays that are collected in *Metaphors on Vision* (the introduction and final chapter are included in this anthology), he made a series of short films that define conclusively the lyrical in cinema. The lyrical is a specific film-linguistic person (in the grammatical sense) not to be confused with the general term "lyricism," which Mekas often uses to describe films; it is the artist addressing himself directly to his subject, the field of vision—a dialogue through the lens of the camera. In *The Dead* (1960), for instance, the film-maker, who makes his presence felt in the film implicitly through the movements of the hand-held camera, seeks and finds a visual image of "death," that complex of notions, fears, and philosophical reductions, in a superimposition and solarization of images from the Père Lachaise cemetery. This film, like the others he describes in the interview, represents the direct confrontation of the film artist with the visual world, a fruitful analysis without the mediation of actors or metaphors of sympathetic nature.

Window Water Baby Moving (1959) shows us not only the documented birth of Brakhage's first child, but the chain of attitudes and emotions the film-maker shared with his wife through her pregnancy and at the very moment of the birth. There is no contrivance in these lyrics. Everything is drawn from the world of sight; no images are set up to be filmed. The most artificial film Brakhage made during that period was *Mothlight* (1963), a collage in which real leaves and the real wings of dead moths were arranged on glue-covered strips of Mylar film, in rhythmic bursts meant to evoke the erratic flight and consummation-in-light of a moth.

Harold Bloom invokes the Jewish theologian, Martin Buber, and his essay "I and Thou" (in which the philosopher describes the ultimate and irreducible relationship between two entities), in defining the intensity of Shelley's confrontation with the objects of his consciousness. A like intensity obtains between Brakhage and the world he sees through the camera eye, which, in his theory, should be a mimetic extension of his own eye. Bloom also elucidated, in *Shelley's Mythmaking*, how mythopoeia grows out of the experience I have called the lyric. In Brakhage's case, the same development follows. Out of the series of short lyrics emerged his epic *Dog Star Man* (1960–65), called, in its most expansive form, *The Art of Vision*. The final chapter of *Metaphors on Vision* documents the genesis of mythopoeia out of the lyric experience, as Brakhage reveals his sources in recent American poetry (Olson, Duncan, Kelly, McClure).

In "Imagism and Four Avant-garde Films" I have outlined a set of intersections over a seventeen-year span between the contemporary nonnarrative film and the other arts, from various points in art history: Thus, Maya Deren, in 1943, cinematizes what she finds vital in contemporary dance (*Choreography for Camera*); Anger transposes the form of a baroque fugue to film (*Eaux d'Artifice*, 1953); Boultenhouse takes a Symbolist poem as his inspiration for *Handwritten* (1959); and Brakhage builds a ritual drama around the classical Noh and the poetic tradition of Ezra Pound, in *Dog Star Man: Part One* (1961).

The mythic film flourished between 1962 and 1965, when *Dog Star Man*, Anger's *Scorpio Rising*, Baillie's *Mass* and *Quixote*, Jack Smith's *Flaming Creatures* and Markopoulos's *Twice a Man* were completed. The entire span of film-making from the end of World

War II to the climax of the mythic period runs congruent to the reign of Abstract Expressionism in American art, as Annette Michelson was the first to point out in her seminal article "Film and the Radical Aspiration."

In 1965, when she made the speech out of which the article came, a new era was beginning for the American avant-garde film. In the films of Andy Warhol such as *Sleep* (1963), *Kiss* (1963), and *Eat* (1963), the aesthetics of the avant-garde tradition were challenged and successfully subverted. Warhol stands at a fulcrum point, as does Kubelka, an Austrian whose formidable work became known in America just at the crucial time when the Abstract Expressionist tradition was disintegrating. Out of their critical subversions of narrative- and lyrical-film forms, the structural film has emerged, applying the values previously held in the abstract or animated film to the deep space of photographic actuality.

This transposition of values also obtains for the animated or plastic film as exemplified by the work of Jordan Belson, whose abstractions have inherited the mythopoeic and cosmological impulse. The means of his achieving a visual cosmogenesis has not been a vibrant montage, but a reduction of imagery to undulating fields.

History demands a perspective which we do not yet have on the achievements of the late 1960's. Today the avant-garde film seems to be moving in several fragmented directions: The structural film (Snow, Landow, Frampton, etc.) and the diary (Mekas and the young erotic diarist Andrew Noren) are emerging forms that coexist with the latest developments in more established genres (the latest works of Brakhage, Kubelka, Anger, Markopoulos, etc.). A coherent idea of these very latest achievements has yet to arrive.

P. ADAMS SITNEY

ONE

THE FORMATIVE
YEARS, 1955-58

In its first stage, *Film Culture* was a general intellectual review of film, and, at times, television, with catholic interests in film history, theory, sociology, and economics. Since the editors believed in presenting an open dialogue on controversial issues, the magazine as a whole had no single polemical thrust.

The article by Jonas Mekas crystallizes the editorial attitude toward the American avant-garde cinema. It is answered, ideologically, if not directly, by the contributions from Hans Richter and Parker Tyler. Tyler's "Preface" later became a central essay in his book *The Three Faces of the Film*, which, for many years, has been the most competent study of the subjective film in English.

Film-historical studies have always been a vital part of *Film Culture*. The articles by Sarris and Michel and the four selections from the special issue on von Stroheim represent the best historical criticism from this period of the magazine.

Carl Th. Dreyer's letter answers an article by Guido Aristarco, *Film Culture*'s Italian correspondent, on the Venice Film Festival of 1955 in which the critic complained:

Yet, how much of contemporary Denmark, how many of the problems of its people are to be found in *Ordet?* Dreyer's position towards life and culture is undoubtedly anachronistic, as is that of Kaj Munk, the author of the drama from which the film was adapted. It is true that the still-recent tragedy of war, with its legacy of spiritual ruins, precludes any facile solutions that are not rooted in mysticism. Nevertheless, it is disconcerting to find Dreyer, in this atomic age synthesized by Einstein's equations, rejecting science for the miracles of religion.

THE FILM AS AN ORIGINAL ART FORM

BY HANS RICHTER

No. 1, January, 1955

The main aesthetic problem in the movies, which were invented for *reproduction* (of movement) is, paradoxically, the overcoming of *reproduction*. In other words, the question is: to what degree is the camera (film, color, sound, etc.) developed and used to *reproduce* (any object which appears before the lens) or to *produce* (sensations not possible in any other art medium)?

This question is by no means a purely technical or mechanical one. The technical liberation of the camera is intimately interrelated with psychological, social, economic, and aesthetic problems. They all play a role in deciding to what use technique is put and how much it is *liberated*. Before this fundamental matter, with its manifold implications, is sufficiently cleared up, it is impossible to speak of the film as an independent art form, even as an art form at all, whatever its promises might be. In the words of Pudovkin: "What is a work of art before it comes in front of the camera, such as acting, staging, or the novel is not a work of art on the screen."

Even to the sincere lover of the film in its present form it must seem that the film is overwhelmingly used for keeping *records* of creative achievements: of plays, actors, novels, or just plain nature, and proportionately less for the creation of original filmic sensations. It is true that the commercial entertainment-film uses many of the *liberating* elements, discovered since 1895 by Méliès, Griffith, Eisenstein, and others, leading toward an original cinematic form. But the general tendency of the film industry, as an economic institution, is the distribution of each film to a maximum number of people. This institution has to avoid moving away from the *traditional* forms of story-telling to which the maximum number of people are conditioned: the theater, with the supremacy of the actor, and the novel or the play, with the writer. Both traditions weigh heavily upon the film and prevent it from coming into its own.

David Wark Griffith forced the stage actor, as early as 1909, into mosaic-acting and broke up, in that way, the uninterrupted scene-acting of the stage actor into hundreds of separately acted scenes that assumed continuity only in the cutting room. His innovations of the close-up and the crosscutting of simultaneous events were revolutionary steps toward a filmic style. But when he broke with theater acting, he gave, involuntarily, an overwhelming influence back to the actor in the creation of the star. As star, the actor immortalized reproduction and dominated the film form once again.

The novel, on the other hand, has adapted itself in the last fifty years to the film. It has become increasingly image-minded. But its technique of psychological character-development, its style of story-telling—traditional properties of literature—dominate the film and make it, also, from this side, reproduction (of literary works, which were original art before they were *produced* in Hollywood, London, Paris, and Rome).

It does not concern us here that, in spite of dependency upon other art forms and in spite of the greater or smaller degree of reproduction, many films have shown exceptional qualities. It is known that the film industry has produced fascinating works, full of inventiveness, inspiration, and human values. The problem with which we are dealing here is the film as an original art form. *Good* and *bad* have no meaning as long as it is not clear upon what aesthetic fundamentals the film is supposed to be built.

The uncertainty of whether *film as such* (that is, the entertainment film) is essentially theatrical, literary, or fine art ends with the doubt in the minds of many sincere film-historians and -critics as to whether the film is, or ever will be, an original art at all! There is also another school of thought that defies the present form of the film altogether, in spite of its overwhelming success and powerful influence, rejects its values as social compensator in offering paradises, complete with gods and goddesses, and sees in it a grandiose perversion of the medium.

Between the two schools, I would prefer to say that the fictional film in its present form is a reproduction of several art forms mixed with original cinematographic elements. But the fact is that there are at least two film forms besides the fictional film that, less spectacular than Hollywood, are more cinematographic in the proper sense of the word.

Several times in the history of the movies, a revolt has temporarily broken the hold of the two traditional arts over the entertainment film. To state the two most important revolts: the post-revolutionary silent Russian film (*Potemkin*) and, after the liberation of Italy from Fascism, the postwar Italian film (*Paisan*). In both cases, the fictional film has turned from fiction to history and from theater style to documentary style in the use of natural setting, people not actors, and real events.

With the documentary approach, the film gets back to its fundamentals. Here, it has a solid aesthetic basis: in the free use of nature, including man, as raw material. By selection, elimination, and coordination of natural elements, a film form evolves that is original and not bound by theatrical or literary tradition. That goes of course, as much for the semidocumentary fictional film (*Potemkin, Paisan*), as for the documentary film itself. These elements might obtain a social, economic, political, or general human meaning, according to their selection and coordination. But this meaning does not exist *a priori* in the facts, nor is it a reproduction (as in an actor's performance). It is created in the camera and the cutting room. The documentary film is an original art form. It has come to grips with facts—on its own original level. It covers the *rational* side of our lives, from the scientific experiment to the poetic landscape-study, but never moves away from the factual. Its scope is wide. Nevertheless, it is an original art form only as far as it keeps strictly to the use of natural raw material in rational interpretation. The modern, more convenient technique of re-enacting factual scenes and events is sometimes not without setbacks, as it might easily introduce reproduction through the back door again: in reproducing enacted scenes.

The influence of the documentary film is growing, but its contribution to a filmic art is, by nature, limited. It is limited by the same token by which it has overcome the influence of the two old arts. Since its elements are facts, it can be original art only in the limits of this factuality. Any free use of the magic, poetic, irrational qualities to which the film medium might offer itself would have to be excluded *a priori* (as nonfactual). But just these qualities are essentially cinematographic, are characteristic of the film and are, aesthetically, the ones that promise future development. That is where the second of the original film-forms has its place: the experimental film.

There is a short chapter in the history of the movies that dealt especially with this side of the film. It was made by individuals concerned essentially with the film medium. They were neither prejudiced by production clichés, nor by necessity of rational interpretation, nor by financial obligations. The story of these individual artists, at the beginning of the 1920's, under the name of "avant-garde," can be properly read as a history of the conscious attempt to overcome reproduction and to arrive at the free use of the means of cinematographic expression. This movement spread over Europe and was sustained for the greatest part by modern painters who, in their own field, had broken away from the conventional: Eggeling, Léger, Duchamp, Man Ray, Picabia, Ruttman, Brugière, Len Lye, Cocteau, myself, and others.

The fact that it was nearly exclusively modern artists who represented this movement gives a hint of the direction in which the liberation of the film was sought. Already, in the 1910's Canudo and Delluc in France spoke of *photogenic* as the new *plastic* quality of the film medium. René Clair went further and declared film as a visual medium *per se*: "A blind man in a regular theater and a deaf mute in a movie theater should still get the essentials from the performance." The spoken word for the stage, the silent image for the film—those are the elements!

These artists discovered that film as a visual medium fitted into the tradition of the art without violation of its fundamentals. It was there that it could develop freely: "The film should positively avoid any connection with the historical, educational, romantic, moral or immoral, geographical or documentary subjects. The film should become, step by step, finally exclusively cinematography, that means that it should use exclusively photogenic elements" (Jean Epstein, 1923). Problems in modern art lead directly into the film. Organization and orchestration of form, color, the dynamics of motion, simultaneity, were problems with which Cézanne, the cubists, the futurists had to deal. Eggeling and I came directly out of the structural problems of abstract art, *volens-nolens* into the film medium. The connection to theater and literature was, completely, severed. Cubism, expressionism, dadaism, abstract art, surrealism found not only their expression in films but also *a new fulfilment on a new level.*

The tradition of modern art grew on a large front, logically, together with and into the film: the orchestration of motion in visual rhythms—the plastic expression of an object in motion under varying light conditions, "to create the rhythm of common objects in space and time, to present them in their plastic beauty, this seemed to me worthwhile" (Léger)—the distortion and dissection of a movement, an object or a form and its reconstruction in cinematic terms (just as the cubists dissected and rebuilt in pictorial terms)—the denaturalization of the object in any form to recreate it cinematographically with light—light with its transparency and airiness as a poetic, dramatic, constructive material—the use of the magic qualities of the film to create the original state of the dream—the complete liberation from the conventional story and its chronology in dadaist and surrealist developments in which the object is taken out of its conventional context and is put into new relationships, creating in that way a new content altogether. "The external object has broken away from its habitual environment. Its component parts had liberated themselves from the object in such a way that they could set up entirely new relationships with other elements"—André Breton (about Max Ernst).

The *external object* was used, as in the documentary film, as raw material, but, instead of employing it for a *rational* theme of social, economic, or scientific nature, it has broken away from its habitual environment and was used as material to express *irrational* visions. Films like *Ballet Mécanique, Entr'acte, Emak Bakia, Ghosts Before Breakfast, Andalusian Dog, Diagonal Symphony, Anemic Cinema, Blood of a Poet, Dreams that Money Can Buy,* and many others were not repeatable in any other medium and are essentially cinematic.

It is still too early to speak of a tradition, or of a style, comparable to those in older arts. The movement is still too young. There are, nevertheless, general traceable directions which cover a great deal of these efforts: abstract art and surrealism. Here in the United States is the work of the Whitney brothers and Francis Lee, the most characteristic of the one; the films of Curtis Harrington, Maya Deren, and Frank Stauffacher are examples of the other. There are many serious attempts but also many *followers* who use and abuse the sensations easily obtainable in this medium. Especially surrealism seems to offer a welcome excuse for the exhibition of a whole menu of inhibitions.

In England, France, Denmark, Holland, Belgium, experimental film groups of individual artists, mostly painters, have taken up the work begun by the avant-garde of the 1920's. They are following the only realistic line that an artist can follow: artistic integrity. In that way, a tradition, temporarily interrupted by the stormy political events in Europe has been taken up by a young generation, here and abroad. It is obvious today that this tradition will not be eradicated again but will grow. As small or as big as this movement becomes, it has opened a new road to film as an art form and has, as such, more than mere historical significance.

The stronger and more independent the documentary and the experimental film becomes and the more the general audience has occasion to see them, the more they will adapt themselves to a *screen style* instead of a theater style. Only after such a *transformation* of the general audience has taken place, the entertainment film can and will follow. At such golden times, film entertainment and film art might become identical.

characters or stories a larger, more human scope. "On the one side are produced private novels," wrote C. P. Snow recently,

> . . . with a readership of approximately one, which alone is treated as Art, and on the other side popular novelists give up the struggle for any glint of truth and get read in millions at the price of surrender to the mass media, the condensations, films, television. It is arguable that such polarization is the fate of all art in an advanced technological society. If it happens, and it may happen, we shall have committed cultural suicide.

This polarization, which C. P. Snow deplores in literature is, undoubtedly, reaching its climax in the motion pictures, too. On one side, there is Hollywood; on the other side, are the experimental film-makers. The middle, the largest area, the whole human reality, sung by the poets and painted on canvas from time immemorial—as the source of all art—is lying fallow.

THE CONSPIRACY OF HOMOSEXUALITY

If the man, the most frequent protagonist of American film poems, is presented as an unreal, frustrated dreamer, the woman here is usually robbed of both her true spirituality and her unashamed carnality. She is a white-dressed, unearthly, elusive symbol flowing dreamily along seashores (or sea-bottom), through bushes and upon hills (Deren, Harrington, Markopoulos, Broughton, Hugo, and so forth).

But it is the conspiracy of homosexuality that is becoming one of the most persistent and most shocking characteristics of American film poetry today. In these films, the protagonists are consistently exposed to physical and mental assault; they are a prey to the most ingenious forms of brutality, sadism, and masochism. The perversion of sex seems to be accepted by these film poets (in their films) as a natural way of life. This is, again, in parallel with what is going on in avant-garde literature. It is described by Hilton Kramer in his essay "The Abuse of the Terrible:"

> If we were to inquire into that vague personage who turns up everywhere in *The Roman Spring of Mrs. Stone*, now and then urinating in public or otherwise exposing his genitals at unlikely moments, we could expect to be put off with the assertion that he is a symbol. Of course! That is what a symbol has come to mean to a writer like Williams: some improbable character or action, preferably pressed to an extreme of violence, without motivations or credibility, and wholly exterior to whatever thin semblance of plot is holding the work together.

Thus, in line with this general tendency, there is not much difference between Mr. Bowles's hero driving a nail through the head of his companion and Kenneth Anger's, Peterson's, or Brakhage's sadistic or masochistic scenes. The claim of Parker Tyler that this is a "neo-surrealism" doesn't add anything to the clarification or justification of the substance of these films. For there is only a superficial and, therefore, most misleading resemblance between these films and the work of the great surrealists. The fundamental and decisive difference here is that a Rimbaud who aimed at "an intentional disordering of all the senses" derived his inspiration from a need to protest against "the accepted conventions and modes of grasping reality." Our film poets, however, attack and destroy reality itself and not a particular way of seizing it. Thus, being incoherent in their very intention, these films necessarily remain shallow and incomprehensible. It is not important to decide here whether or not these neurotic and homosexual poems can be called art. What I want to stress is that this art of abnormality is unmotivated, unresolved and lacks a moral dimension. One has to remember Kafka, Strindberg, or Dostoyevsky's Smerdiakov to realize what an artist can make of abnormality in a true work of art.

THE LACK OF CREATIVE INSPIRATION:
TECHNICAL CRUDITY AND THEMATIC NARROWNESS

Nevertheless, we can't deny a certain honesty to some of these films, particularly to those made by younger film poets. Although, in most cases, they do not succeed in becoming works of art, they still bear witness to the film poet's age, mentality, and inner state. However, even this spontaneous "self-revelation" is absent in the work of some more mature film makers. The supposed depth of Maya Deren is artificial, without the ingenious spontaneity which we find, for instance, in Brakhage's or Anger's work. For, if, on the one hand, the older generation lack perception and creativity proportionate to their experience, on the other hand, they also lack that youthful spontaneity that could, at least in part, compensate for their artistic impotence. Mechanical creation, without enough emotional content, results in films like *Jazz of Lights, Petrified Dog,* or in the intellectual formalism of Maya Deren. Or else, there is a tendency to indulge in the repetition of worn-out clichés and symbols exploited in the past either by themselves or by their predecessors. We witness an endless recurrence of such shots as walking up and down stairs, walking or running in slow motion, Greek statues, pillars, and so on.

More than that, most of these "experimental" films betray a conspicuous absence of artistic discipline, the *sine qua non* of any art. This, undoubtedly, could be remedied if their makers attempted to acquire a more solid technical and theoretical background, if they did not avoid frank and critical examination of one another's work, and, last but not least, if they strove after a clearer and deeper understanding of the function and mission of the artist. There is every reason to believe that, unless such fundamental changes in the approach to film art take place, the narrowness of the thematic range, the repetitiousness of visual symbols, the generally poor photographic quality, the lack of control of the sound track and color, the looseness in construction, the overburdening with poetical commentaries and similar symptoms, will continue to characterize our experimental-film production.

But, above all, these film poets lack what makes any art valuable to humanity: a deeper insight into the human soul, emotions, experiences, as related to the whole rather than to exceptional abnormalities. The creative intuition that would give the work a higher aesthetic and ethical quality, able to catch our imagination, thought, or feelings, is nowhere to be seen. Although some of the images in these films have a certain surface beauty, they do not reveal a deeper poetical reality behind them. And, if we would look into these films for moral values, we would find, paraphrasing John W. Aldridge's words on contemporary literature, that, if the struggle of the new film poets to make a dramatic affirmation of value could be plotted on a graph, the result would be a parabolic curve extending from the absolute zero of Maya Deren to the absolute zero of Stanley Brakhage.

CONCLUDING NOTES

The image of the contemporary American film poem and cineplastics, as briefly presented here, is decidedly unencouraging. However, the creative possibilities of these two forms are undeniable. Although the last decade did not contribute remarkable works to film art—say, of the depth and scope of *L'Age d'Or* or *Blood of a Poet*—it has helped to establish the film poem and cineplastics as definite film forms. It is for the film-maker of today and of the coming decade to strive to give it substance, scope, and importance.

If the above notes sometimes tend to be an attack on the film-maker's view of life or art (or lack of views, or superficiality of them), it is because I share the conviction with the leading artists of today and of the past that the content of a work of art is essential and dictates the technical and formal aspects of it. The task of a mature film-maker is, using Norman McLaren's words at the recent American Film Assembly, to achieve creative fusion of experiment with a social approach. To improve the quality of the American film poem, experiments should be directed not so much toward new techniques but toward deeper themes, toward a more penetrating treatment of the nature and drama of the man of our epoch. At the same time the work—virtues and failures—of the contemporary film poets and cineplasts should be studied and discussed among our film-makers and film society audiences. The contemporary experimental film should not be put in a small Hall of Fame, but should be looked upon more critically as a phase of preparation leading toward a more genuine and significant film art.

[What amazes me when re-reading (in 1970) this Saint-Augustine-before-the-conversion piece, is not the complete turnabout that I have traveled since then, but the fact that the tone, the thinking, and the argumentation of my essay of fifteen years ago are still used today by all the liberal and conservative critics to put down the avant-garde film-maker of 1970.—JONAS MEKAS.]

METAPHYSIC OF ORDET

A LETTER FROM CARL TH. DREYER

No. 7, 1956

The latest issue of *Film Culture* brings an article by Mr. Guido Aristarco about the Venice Festival. In his article, Mr. Aristarco mentions my picture *Ordet* understandingly and in detail. However, his concluding remarks are, "Nevertheless, it is disconcerting to find Dreyer, in this atomic age synthesized by Einstein's equations, rejecting science for the miracles of religion."

I am fortunate in that I can prove Mr. Aristarco wrong. As early as September 1954, when the film had not yet been completed, I was interviewed by the Danish State Radio, and, on that occasion, had the following to say.

Questioned about when I first had arrived at the idea of filming *Ordet* I replied:

It happened one evening twenty-two years ago, when I witnessed the first performance of *Ordet* at the Betty Nansen Theater. I was deeply moved by the play and overwhelmed by the audacity with which Kaj Munk presented the problems in relation to each other. I could not but admire the perfect ease with which the author put forth his paradoxical thoughts. When I left the theater, I felt convinced that the play had wonderful possibilities as a film.

When next questioned about when the manuscript had been written, I answered verbatim:

It did not happen until nearly twenty years later. Then I saw Kaj Munk's ideas in a different light, for so much had happened in the meantime. The new science that followed Einstein's theory of relativity had supplied that outside the three-dimensional world which we can grasp with our senses, there is a fourth dimension—the dimension of time—as well as a fifth dimension—the dimension of the psychic that proves that it is possible to live events that have not yet happened. New perspectives are opened up that make one realize an intimate connection between exact science and intuitive religion. The new science brings us toward a more intimate understanding of the divine power and is even beginning to give us a natural explanation to things of the supernatural. The Johannes figure of Kaj Munk's can now be seen from another angle. Kaj Munk felt this already, in 1925 when he wrote his play, and intimated that the mad Johannes may have been closer to God than the Christians surrounding him.

As will be seen from the above, I have not rejected modern science for the miracle of religion. On the contrary, Kaj Munk's play assumed new and added significance for me, because the paradoxical thoughts and ideas expressed in the play have been proved by recent psychic research, represented by pioneers like Rhine, Ouspensky, Dunne, Aldous Huxley, and so forth, whose theories, in the simplest manner, explained the seemingly inexplicable happenings of the play and established a natural cohesion behind the supernatural occurrences that are found in the film.

CITIZEN KANE: THE AMERICAN BAROQUE

BY ANDREW SARRIS

No. 9, 1956

The recent revival of *Citizen Kane* has not elicited the kind of reappraisal the occasion demands. It is too easy to dismiss *Kane* as a great film with the smug confidence that everything that is to be said about it has already been said. If nothing else, the fifteen years that have elapsed since its initial release should provide a new perspective. The fact that *Citizen Kane* still seems to be ahead of its time is as much an indictment of contemporary film-making as it is a vindication of the classic quality of its art. Stripped of its personal and topical sensationalism, the film has risen above the capricious attacks leveled against it fifteen years ago.

A great deal of the hostility aroused by *Kane* back in 1941 was directed at its youthful creator, Orson Welles. Many of his enemies have since been appeased by the simple fact that Welles has joined the mortal herd by getting fifteen years older. Others have come to admire his dogged professionalism in the face of disastrously inadequate financing and even personal injury as demonstrated by his recent performance of *Lear* from a wheelchair. Yet, though tempered by adversity and voluntary exile, the spectacular Welles personality still obscures the more substantial aspects of his genius.

On a less personal level, *Citizen Kane* disappointed many who were caught up in the portentous political atmosphere of 1941. Advance publicity had prepared many liberals for a savage political attack on William Randolph Hearst, one of the most prominent enemies of the New Deal. *The Grapes of Wrath* and *The Great Dictator,* both released in 1940, had made their stands at the barricades. Welles, himself, had recently mounted an anti-Fascist interpretation of *Julius Caesar* on the New York stage. The boycott of Welles and *Citizen Kane* by all Hearst publications further heightened the suspense of an impending collision between the *enfant terrible* of the left and the grand old man of the right.

When *Kane* finally appeared, it failed to justify all the ideological anticipation. Charles Foster Kane was not William Randolph Hearst in any "significant" sense. Welles and Herman J. Mankiewicz had merely borrowed biographical details, some virtually libelous, to fashion an intricate screen-play that posed a psychological mystery without advancing any cause.

After subtracting the criticism of the Welles personality and the criticism of the lack of ideology, all that is left and all that is relevant is the criticism of *Citizen Kane* as a work of art. To believe, as some do, that *Citizen Kane* is the great American film, it is necessary to produce an interpretation that answers some of the more serious objections to this film.

Citizen Kane has peculiar claims to greatness in that its distinctive merits are related to its alleged flaws. Adverse criticism of *Kane* is based mainly on three propositions: (1) Its narrative structure is unduly complicated; (2) its technique calls attention to itself; (3) its intellectual content is superficial.

If any one of these propositions is fully accepted, *Kane* falls far short of greatness. At first glance, all three points have some validity. The narrative zigzags and backtracks to its conclusion. The technique dazzles the eye and ear. No profound ideas are explicitly developed. A closer examination of the film, however, reveals an inner consistency of theme, structure, and technique. The implications of this consistency are crucial to any effective analysis of what *Citizen Kane* is really about.

Within the maze of its own aesthetic, *Kane* develops two interesting themes: the debasement of the private personality of the public figure and the crushing weight of materialism. Taken together, these two themes comprise the bitter irony of an American success story that ends in futile nostalgia, loneliness, and death. The fact that the personal theme is developed verbally while the materialistic theme is developed visually creates a distinctive stylistic counterpoint. Against this counterpoint, the themes unfold within the structure of a mystery story.

Charles Foster Kane dies in a lonely castle. His last word is "Rosebud." Who or what is "Rosebud?" This is the mystery of *Citizen Kane*. The detective is a reporter for a news service which produces *March of Time*-like newsreels. The suspects are all the persons and objects Kane encountered in his cluttered life. The clues are planted in the film on three occasions, but, unlike the conventional-mystery key, "Rosebud" is the answer to a man's life rather than his death. And since the intangible meanings of life end in the mystery of death, "Rosebud" is not the final solution but only the symbolic summation.

"Rosebud" is the means through which the past history of Charles Foster Kane is penetrated by the reporter-detective and the omniscient camera. Time is thrown back and brought forward in the four major movements of the film, the flashback-recollections of, respectively, Kane's banker-guardian, his business manager, his best friend, and his second wife. Each major flashback begins at a later point in time than its predecessor, but each flashback overlaps with at least one of the others so that the same event or period is seen from two or three points of view.

There is a fifth flashback—a newsreel of Kane's public career—which establishes the identity of Charles Foster Kane for the first time in the film. There is no transition between the opening scene of a man dying in a lonely castle with "Rosebud" on his lips and the startling appearance of the unframed newsreel. This is the first shock effect in *Citizen Kane*, and it has received undeserved abuse as a spectacularly devious method of narration. What has been generally overlooked is the great economy of this device in establishing the biographical premises of the film, without resorting to traditional montages of public reactions and telescoped historical events in the major movements of the story.

By isolating the newsreel from the main body of his film, Welles frees his flashbacks from the constricting demands of exposition, enabling his main characters to provide insights on the external outlines of the Kane biography. After the newsreel, the transitions are worked out very carefully through the logical movements of the reporter-detective. This shadowy, though thoroughly professional character links the present to the past in an interlocking jigsaw puzzle with one elusive piece—"Rosebud"—appearing only at the very end in the reporter's absence since his services are no longer needed.

The newsreel accomplishes more than a skeletal public biography of Charles Foster Kane. On a narrative level, it introduces Mr. Thatcher, Kane's banker-guardian, whose memoirs will provide the first personal flashback of Kane's life and the first significant clue to "Rosebud." The newsreel also produces a paradox that previsions the nonpolitical quality of the film. While Thatcher is telling a committee that Kane is a Communist, a speaker in Union Square attacks Kane as a Fascist. The elderly Kane tells newsreel audiences that he is and always has been an American. This is the first indication that Kane is not really committed to any cause but Kane.

The newsreel fades out; a sudden establishing shot picks up a darkened projection room. The first of the many disembodied voices in the film calls out from the darkness, and the shadow plot of *Citizen Kane* begins. A group of cynical newsmen discuss ways of pepping up the newsreel. The reporter is sent out to find the secret of "Rosebud." The semicolloquial dialogue is driven forth with relentless persistence from every direction. There is nothing profound or witty about any of it, but it moves quickly and economically.

The reporter begins his search, and the major movements of *Citizen Kane* begin. Through a hard, wide-angle lens, the reporter enters a cavernous museum, a dingy nightclub, a solidly upholstered office, a drab hospital ward, the gloomy mansion of Charles Foster Kane. The reporter's world is functional, institutional: an aging, weathered gateway to the life and time of Charles Foster Kane.

The sixth and last flashback of *Citizen Kane* offers the final clue to "Rosebud" and brings the reporter's quest to its unsuccessful conclusion. Interestingly enough, the three clues to "Rosebud" appear at times when Kane is being treated most remotely—in the cryptic death-scene in the beginning, in the unfriendly memoirs of his banker-guardian, and in the final flashback narration of a cynical butler. The narrations of his closest acquaintances yield no clues to the symbolic truth of his life. This is the ultimate confirmation of Kane's spiritual loneliness, and it is upon this loneliness that the mystery structure of the film is based.

The mystery of "Rosebud" is solved in a memorable manner. The reporter and his entourage have departed from the Kane castle. As the cynical butler is directing the disposal of Kane's "junk" into the furnace, a workman picks up a sled in routine haste and dumps it into the flames. The camera closes in on the surface of the sled and the name "Rosebud" as the letters are dissolving in liquid fire. The audience is given the solution with the added knowledge that no one living on the screen will ever know the secret of "Rosebud."

This solution has been attacked as a trick ending unworthy of its theme. Yet without this particular resolution, the film would remain a jumbled jigsaw puzzle. The burning sled is apt not only as a symbolic summation but also as a symbolic revelation. The reporter, the butler, the workman, the friends, the enemies, the acquaintances of Kane never discover "Rosebud" because it is lost amid the "junk" of Kane's materialistic existence.

Kane's tragedy lies in the inability of the props of experience to compensate for the bare emotional stage of his human relationships. Charles Foster Kane collected valuable treasures from all over the world, but his last thoughts were of a sled he used as a boy, before great wealth came into his life. At one point in the film, he tells his banker-guardian that he might have been a great man if he had not been so wealthy. "Rosebud" became the focal point of his nostalgia for a different turning point in his life. Kane's view of his own life is deterministic, and Kane's image throughout the film is remarkably consistent with this sense of determinism.

The apparent intellectual superficiality of *Citizen Kane* can be traced to the shallow quality of Kane himself. Even when Kane is seen as a crusading journalist battling for the lower classes, overtones of stiff self-idolatry mar his actions. His clever ironies are more those of the exhibitionist than the crusader. His best friend—a detached observer functioning as a sublimated conscience—remarks to the reporter that Kane never gave anything away: "He left you a tip." His second wife complained that Kane never gave her anything that was part of him, only material possessions that he might give a dog. His business adviser and life-long admirer expressed the other side of Kane's personality, when he observed that Kane wanted something more than money.

In each case, Kane's character is described in materialistic terms. What Kane wanted—love, emotional loyalty, the unspoiled world of his boyhood symbolized by "Rosebud"—he was unable to provide to those about him or buy for himself. It is, therefore, fitting that the story of Kane should begin with his lonely death and conclude with the immolation of his life symbol.

The technique of Welles and his photographer, Gregg Toland,

justifies the narrative structure. Apparently outrageous effects fall into place once the pattern of the film is discernible. *Kane* opens on a solid wire fence with a sign reading "No Trespassing." The camera moves up on a painted castle against a background of dark, brooding clouds. The same shots are repeated in reverse at the very end of the film. This initial and concluding clash of realism and expressionism flanks one of the most stylistically varied of all films.

The opening shots have been attacked as pretentious and the closing shots as anticlimactic. Yet, in a subtle way, the beginning and end of *Citizen Kane* suggest its theme. The intense material reality of the fence dissolves into the fantastic unreality of the castle and, in the end, the mystic pretension of the castle dissolves into the mundane substance of the fence. Matter has come full circle from its original quality to the grotesque baroque of its excess.

As each flashback unfolds, the visual scenario of *Citizen Kane* orchestrates the dialogue. A universe of ceilings dwarfs Kane's personal stature. He becomes the prisoner of his possessions, the ornament of his furnishings, the fiscal instrument of his collections. His booming voice is muffled by walls, carpets, furniture, hallways, stairs, and vast recesses of useless space.

Toland's camera setups are designed to frame characters in the oblique angles of light and shadow created by their artificial environment. There are no luminous close-ups in which faces are detached from their backgrounds. When characters move across rooms, the floors and ceilings move with them, altering the points of reference but never transcending them. This technique draws attention to itself both because it is so unusual and because it tends to dehumanize characters by reducing them to fixed ornaments in a shifting architecture.

Sound montage is used intensively within the flashbacks to denote the interval of time within two related scenes. A character will begin a sentence and complete it weeks, months, or years later in a different location. On occasion, one character will begin the sentence, and another will complete it in the same manner. This device results in a constriction of time and an elimination of transitional periods of rest and calm. Aside from the aesthetic dividends of pacing and highlighting, *Kane*'s sound montage reinforces the unnatural tension of the central character's driving, joyless ambition. In all respects, *Kane*'s technique is a reflection and projection of the inhuman quality of its protagonist.

One brilliant use of sound montage that has generally been ignored as a piece of aural gargoyle is the piercing scream of a parakeet that precedes the last appearance of Kane in the film. One flashback and several scenes previously, Kane and his second wife are arguing in a tent surrounded by hundreds of Kane's picnic guests. A shrill scream punctuates the argument with a persistent, sensual rhythm. It is clear that some sexual outrage is being committed. When the parakeet screams at the appearance of Kane, the sound linkage in tone but not in time further dehumanizes Kane's environment. In the baroque world that he has created, Kane is isolated from even the most dubious form of humanity.

Kane's lack of humanity is consistently represented in the performance of Orson Welles, who alters the contours of Kane's rigidity from youth to old age. As a young man, Kane is peculiarly joyless. A gala occasion is recalled in which Kane threw a party for his new writers hired away from a competing newspaper. A group of chorus girls come on the scene. Kane is thrown in their midst and begins cutting up. The scene is heavy with Kane's studied posturing as the life of the party.

The acting in *Kane* emerges as an elaborate arabesque of interrupted conversations, harsh dissonances, and awkward physical confrontations. Kane's world, peopled by Mercury Players, is tuned to the egocentric performance of Welles. Joseph Cotten, Everett Sloane, and Dorothy Comingore, as Kane's best friend, business adviser, and second wife, respectively, and the main narrators of the film, achieve a strident rapport with the demanding presence of Welles. The intense pitch of the acting charges each line of dialogue with unexpected meanings. The manner of expression often alters the verbal content toward a new level of self-conscious cynicism. In this, the acting evokes the intentional hypocrisy of the few protestations of principle that appear in the script.

Toward the end of his life, Kane reacts to the desertion of his second wife by wrecking the furniture in her room. Again, his violent actions are rigidly controlled by a chilling self-awareness. As he is completing his unduly methodical havoc, he comes upon a crystal paperweight in which a minute snow storm beats down on a miniature cottage. He speaks the name of "Rosebud" and walks past an array of guests across the path of endless mirrors and endless reflections of his image—mere repetitions of his ego without magnification. This is the final arithmetic of Kane's life, the last material accounting of his greatness.

Citizen Kane presents an intense vision of American life, distorting and amplifying its materialistic elements at the expense of human potentialities. The implied absence of free will in the development of Kane's character is thematically consistent with the moral climate of his environment. Kane's magnitude, unchecked by limiting principles or rooted traditions, becomes the cause of his spiritual ruin. Kane emerges as an extension of the *nouveau-riche* American seeking a living culture in the dead relics of the past. Striving desperately to transcend his material worth, Kane is victimized by the power his wealth possesses to alter the moral quality of his actions. In the end, everything has been bought and paid for, but nothing has been felt.

IN MEMORIAM OF DIMITRI KIRSANOV, A NEGLECTED MASTER

BY WALTER S. MICHEL

No. 15, December, 1957

I

A great artist and man is gone. Almost unknown in this country and forgotten in Europe, Dimitri Kirsanov was a poet who chose the cinema as his medium of expression and gave us, with *Ménilmontant, Brumes d'Automne* and *Rapt,* three of the most beautiful and intelligent films in the history of the cinema. He is neglected, partly because his films are poetry and do not fit the usual categories, partly because only one of them is easily accessible.

An admirer of his *Ménilmontant,* the only one of his films I had had an opportunity to see, I contacted Kirsanov in Paris two years ago. Incredulous that anyone should be interested in his films, he agreed to a meeting with Lotte Eisner and myself. This was followed by another and, later, by a screening of some of his recent short films. It was soon evident that here was a man of modesty, simplicity, and integrity. He seemed young and energetic. He talked of making a film in Spain, if plans, for once, worked out. News of his death came as a shock.

Kirsanov had come to Paris in 1919 and studied the cello at the Conservatory, acting as a stage extra and playing in an orchestra at night. His realization that "*le cinéma est un langage*" (quotations throughout this article are his own words) was sparked about 1921 by the Swedish film *La Montre Brisée*. During the next two or three years, he made his first two films: *L'Ironie du Destin* (1922–23), of which no copy exists, and *Ménilmontant* (1924), circulated by the Museum of Modern Art, New York. "Knowing nothing" about the technique of film-making, he hired an old cameraman Leonce Crouen, then out of a job. Crouen shot only the beginning of *Ménilmontant*, "everything which is in two dimensions." Then Kirsanov "took the camera off the tripod" and "shot the rest" himself.

On *Ménilmontant*, as he was always to do, Kirsanov worked alone. He stated definitely that he had not been in contact with either the French "avant-garde" or the Russian *émigrés*, with both of whom he is often associated. "Isolated then as now," making his elaborate dissolves and montages in the camera itself, he invented for *Ménilmontant* independently most of the techniques which were being developed at the same time or, later, by others better financed and more publicized.

Ménilmontant was followed, in 1926, by *Brumes d'Automne* ("put together according to musical formulae"), shown recently at the Museum of Modern Art, New York, and, in 1933, by *Rapt* based on the novel *La Séparation des Races* by C. F. Ramuz, also fortunately extant.

Ménilmontant and *Brumes d'Automne* had been brilliant, original, and mature, "independent" works. *Rapt,* one of the finest of all sound films, was the extension of these achievements into a full-length feature production with sound. One would think that, with the release of such a film, a rich career would have been opened to its creator. On the contrary, in the twenty-four years between *Rapt* and his death early this year, Kirsanov never again had the opportunity of directing a major film with any appreciable freedom. Thus has the cinema, stepchild of the arts, treated its masters ever since *Greed*.

Of the films he did make during these years—most of them short, low-budget productions—he showed me the three he liked best: *Arrière Saison*, *Mort d'un Cerf* and *Deux Amis*. These fairly recent films increase one's astonishment at the neglect of this fine artist, for all are accomplished and important and could be an inspiration to independent film-makers; but they are neither shown at festivals nor circulated by archives.

Of the other films he made during this period, he was highly critical. *Quartier sans Soleil* (1939) he called "very uneven, but interesting in parts"; three small musical films, which came next, "*gentil, pas plus*"; *Franco du Port*, "a gangster film, vulgar." The last was a partly commercial film as were the two following: *Faits Divers à Paris* and *Morte Moisson* (1949), both made with some government assistance and containing some interesting scenes that, it appears, he was permitted to write himself. Also included in his criticism was the early *Sables* (1926), which he condemned unsparingly as "*mauvais, puérile, stupide, joli*" and considers not his own film ("an imbecile wrote the story").

One feature-length film directed by Kirsanov after *Rapt* was *Le Crâneur*, a well-made thriller released in 1955. Stating that this was his first really commercial film, "made with cold reason, calculated for commercial success," he would not allow that there was anything good about it. When I pointed out a part I had liked, he shrugged it off, quite impatiently, with a "*c'est facile.*"

So ended the career of a great master.

In these conversations, Mlle. Eisner and I were the ones to be upset by the extent of his neglect. He himself was clearly no longer concerned—if he ever had been—with questions of recognition. All his thinking and energy seemed directed only toward the one end: creation. I think he would have gone anywhere on earth to make a film.

II

It is impossible to assess the achievement of Dimitri Kirsanov unless the use of the film medium as a poetic vehicle is properly appreciated. All extraneous considerations, those of sociological, political, or slice-of-life variety, must be forgotten. Kirsanov's films can be understood only in terms of themes and counterthemes, built up visually by artifice, that is, by nonnaturalistic means, using image, design, and metaphor. The camera, with all its possibilities and limitations, is supreme, but it is exploited only in so far as the adumbrations of the theme require and permit. The "story" is of the simplest nature, usually banal, a framework merely, but one that accommodates itself to the conception presented.

A study of Kirsanov's work from such a nonnarrative point of view is scheduled for future publication. In the present article, only a few introductory remarks on each of his most important films can be given.

Ménilmontant already exhibits in full maturity Kirsanov's ability as a photographer and editor. Cuts range in length from one frame (violence scenes) to over 600 frames (pan down from hotel window to dark door, where the camera stops while the couple enters; pan back up to window, now lighted, where the camera stops briefly; pan down again to door, where the camera stops while a newcomer arrives); motion within the frame may be so fast that it is blurred (violence scenes), or it may be completely still (successive stills while Sibirskaia sees the dead body of her father); lighting traverses the full range from dazzling to black; the camera may be stationary, or it may veer on top of a bus or swing over cobblestones.

But, always, the technique complements the image and mood. Always, theme and execution are matched. Nothing is "experimental" or *recherché* or "avant-garde." Kirsanov gives us a perfect rendering of poetic themes in a visual medium.

This is seen in its most obvious form in *Brumes d'Automne*, a film of a single mood conveyed through shots of rain and mist, through reflections in pools of the saturated earth, and by the measured stateliness of movement. Distorted autumn landscapes anticipate many of the gratuitous flourishes of later "experimental" film-makers, but here they are poetically justified as seen through the tears of Nadia Sibirskaia.

One of the most brilliant of cameramen and directors, Kirsanov is also one of the few film-makers who used sound creatively. This is clear from *Rapt*, with its triple counterpoint of music, and visual and stylized natural sound. The techniques used in this film are described in the articles by Honegger and Hoerée in *Revue Musicale*, December, 1934 (still some of the best writing on the subject of sound in film). A treatment of disorder and violence, *Rapt* has an abduction from an Alpine village and the consequent feud as its setting. It is characteristic of Kirsanov's method that the whole development is already summarized in the first few shots: In a tranquil setting with two men beside a stream, all in long shots, one of the men suddenly beats the water, splashing the other and disturbing the pastoral music. Playfulness supersedes stillness, in preparation for violence. The very last impression of the film is also reinforced by sound: the braying laughter of the village idiot over chords of music swelling to the finale. *Rapt* is a film of such magnificence that it must be classed as one of the three or four best sound films made. It would be flawless, but for the unaccountable intrusion in a few places of that affliction of the sound film, an excess of dialogue.

The same criticism may also be made of *Deux Amis,* based on the story by Maupassant. Though a fine achievement in acting and atmosphere, this is essentially a dialogue film.

Arrière Saison and *Mort d'un Cerf* are a return to the perfect collaboration between sound and image found in *Rapt,* only on the lesser scale necessitated by the more modest means then at the disposal of the director.

In *Arrière Saison* (1952), a woman leaves the lonely, boring life with her husband, a woodcutter, but returns on the following day. The mood is reminiscent of *Brumes d'Automne.* The sound track consists entirely of music, except for one brief interval: When the woman returns, the music is cut off abruptly and we hear the axes and shouts of the woodcutters in the distance. As she enters the house, the music resumes.

Mort d'un Cerf, a commissioned film, transforms the conventional events of a stag hunt into satire by witty use of cutting, sound, and silence. Some impressions of old prints of deer hunting lend a measure almost of elegance to the proceedings in the early scenes, although the arrival of the hunters by car is ominous. The ending shows the pack and hunters in full pursuit, accompanied by a crescendo of the music and hunting horns. Suddenly and abruptly, the music is cut off: The stag is seen standing still, surrounded by yelping dogs. In thudding anticlimax, the stag, standing thus at bay, is felled by rifle shots. The music resumes, the hunting horns building up to a great victory shout. Ladies munch sandwiches; the hunt is over.

While most of Kirsanov's films are at present extremely difficult of access, they could easily be made available to all those interested. One may hope that this opportunity will not be lost and that, as the finest tribute to a great director, his major *oeuvre* will be restored to circulation.

A PREFACE TO THE PROBLEMS OF THE EXPERIMENTAL FILM

BY PARKER TYLER

No. 17, February, 1958

The history of the Experimental (Avant-garde or Poetic) Film is a curious one that even possesses its Hollywood phase, when professional works with serious, as opposed to commercial, ideas decided, on their own and on very small budgets, to do imaginative work that used the camera the way a poet uses his pen: as an instrument of invention; it is significant that these professional workers were typically camera specialists, for the first step in visualizing the Experimental Film as a distinct reality is to conceive the proper role of the camera as a visual medium.

In the big industrial studios, the camera—now as large as a public monument—is a sort of gargantuan fetish, a Frankenstein's monster that can swallow and reproject vast panoramic spaces as on the new grandeur screens. So it is a fitting symbol of commerce. The Experimental camera is not at all like that, being as personal as a hunting rifle when compared to the collectiveness of a cannon on a battleship. If, in the art of painting, the brush is traditionally the indispensable instrument of work, in the art of film, this instrument is the camera. The commercial industry regards the camera only as a carry-all, an ingenious baggage compartment into which an art is stuffed and then purveyed in "magic reels" to be unloaded in theaters. Actually, the camera contains as many secrets of "significant form" as does a pencil, a brush, or, for that matter, the spout used by modern painters who pour their forms on canvas.

A standard technical book on the film by Raymond Spottiswoode is called A *Grammar of the Film*. Can one imagine a book called A *Grammar of Poetry* or of *Sculpture* or, even, *Playwriting*? No, one speaks of an "art," or, at the most rudimentary, a "craft," of the established aesthetic domains, as with Percy Lubbock's *The Craft of Fiction*. The "grammar!" This means the art is—and so it is here—in the kindergarten stage. Therefore, Jean Cocteau's kindly, paternally valid advice to a young film-maker who would take his art seriously is to equip himself with a small camera, go out into the world, and improvise. In view of all the factors enmeshed with the film craft, this ABC advice is very sound.

When one scrutinizes the basic craft of communicating meanings to the film medium—as opposed to just photographing, in the journalistic or subdocumentary sense—one sees that it is a problem held in some degree in common with *all* the arts to be classified as visual, with poetry in so far as it deals directly with images and, of course, with painting. As a total theatrical art, where the film combines with music and spoken dialogue, the auditory and literary enter the scheme; one deals with a theatrical spectacle of a given and complex kind. The movies, at this point in their artistic history, are all too much a synthetic art of an "easy," commercial type. To believe, however, that the film, at its mere appearance, automatically contributed an independent aesthetic dimension to the arts would be to believe that telegraphy as such contributed something independent to literature, or photography something independent to painting. It is true that we can conceive "telegraphic" literature and "photographic" painting: literally translated Oriental ideograms are a virtual telegraphese. But literature and painting, respectively, absorbed the technical innovations of the ideogramatic phrase and the instantaneously reproduced optical register of the photograph. When we deal with the film as such, we can see that, from the start, it has partially constituted a simple pictorial documentarism, a kinetic visual journalism and a kinetic visual science. But, in this regard, journalism and education have simply absorbed new techniques of expression, new channels of communication; no new dimension has sensibly been added thereby to a visual art. It remained for the aesthetic instinct animating all the arts to make the ultimate filmic contribution.

The one striking thing about the Experimental Film is that its practitioners, if gifted and sincere, automatically acquire a unique aura. This aura is nothing but the *independent* art of the film. Let us concede without quibble that some Experimentalists are naively misled, that some are even a bit opportunistic. It is so human and "traditional" to be opportunistic! Many film-makers, with a right intuition of the art whose essence is the replacement of words with vision, go astray or remain insignificant because, though their chosen path is a true one, they have more optimism than talent, more unsatisfied vanity than sturdy ambition. But there are those who fall by the wayside in every art—even, and *especially*, in the most popular, the most commercial, forms of an art. There is such a thing, however, as stick-to-itiveness, a first cousin to intuitiveness, and one will find that a young film-maker, once articulate as "having something to say," usually says it again, and more complexly, perhaps, says it better.

The first virtue of Film Experimentalists is the state known as radical, which only means, aesthetically speaking, being near the root of the matter, being close enough to understand and maneuver the root of the matter. In the very simplest sense, after certain technical rules of mechanics are grasped, all the Film Experimentalist does is translate his feelings into images *as though words did not exist*. This is what he must want to do, must aim at doing, must set up as ideal. Here the procedural question of the film script necessarily arises. There may be a shooting script—even a shooting script with poetic qualities such as Eisenstein wrote—but unless its words can be successfully translated into optical terms, it had better not exist at all.

The misfortune that befell the commercial film was, of course, the sound that became speech, actual words. It was a misfortune, however, only because the huge potentialities of the film as a visual medium had not been adequately—one should say *radically*—achieved before sound came and all too quickly triumphed. The history of the film art is a history of the corruption of an infant art before it had a chance to grow up; the stage play and the novel, the very media that intellectually and emotionally helped the movies develop beyond their primitive fairy-tale and vaudeville routines, also injected them with a virus of premature growth similar to the intoxication of Easter plants, which must be sold at once, before their glory perishes through the same intoxication that suddenly vitalized them.

For prestige, the early movies moved the Heaven of the stage play and the Earth of all literature. Commercial film, as partly a "poster" art, had to advertise famous Broadway successes, classic actresses—even Sarah Bernhardt—and literary classics as well as name novelists. For prestige or ballyhoo, whichever, the latest Cinemascope epic utilizes now the same prestige devices, but whatever the intrinsic artistic worth of prestige sources, they put no more than a deceptive gloss on the hybrid product of the film as it has evolved through its expanding technical phases to that synthetic sum of techniques, passing as the "film art," on popular screens today.

To get more people into the theaters—that is, to uproot them from their comfortable living-room chairs in front of the television screen—the movies have been overreaching the stage and novel to call upon the dynamic sensations of kinesthesia through the third-dimension effect and the illusion of being surrounded by the area of vision instead of, however cozily, being seated before it. In the case of Cinerama, the gimmick is to use the theater as a substitute for interior stations of actual flight—the airplane and the automobile or any rapidly moving vehicle—and to take the spectator to far places on a flying carpet of maximum illusion; thus, the Cinerama screen has two "arms" perpetually stretched out to lure the viewer into the illusion that he is experiencing a true third dimension because he seems to pass *through* it; that is, all the visual help possible to science is brought to bear toward the illusion of passage through space. Vain delusion! Because "italicized" physical passivity, in conjunction with illusory flight through space, merely isolates the watcher from "reality" without necessarily consolidating him with "dream." He exists only in a gelatinous state of wish fulfillment —like the man in the stratosphere who, for a while, was nowhere in particular.

The creation of space (a sense of dimension and all it may signify in terms of human and even superhuman experience) is, of course, an objective of all the arts, and each art has developed special means of attaining specific effects of "grand" space. The stage itself, in the hands of men such as Reinhardt, felt the need of involving the audience in the dramatic action as though the theater were a kind of church; hence, a spectacle such as *The Miracle*. This theater piece united the space of the spectator with that of the spectacle. The modern stage has utilized the aisles of the theater, and various stations in the theater, as well as specially constructed stairs, aprons, and ramps, to create the feeling of mobility, so that the spectator should feel the witnessed action more keenly by the sensation of being involved with it.

Now, whatever the technical virtues of such procedures, however mechanically clever and however much they may help weak productions of good plays and desperate productions of weak ones, the fact remains that the first law of projection exercised by a work of art is its appeal to the imagination and the sensibility. In other words, no matter what the means, the "space" ultimately created *is situated subjectively*; that is, it exists in the hearts and heads of the audience, and, if it doesn't, art has failed. But head and heart are not precisely the *nerves*. Unless the elaborate devices of mobility and depth allure, regardless of what art form be involved, assist serious motives in the makers and appeal to important feelings in the spectator, they are no more *aesthetically significant* than seeming to chute-the-chutes at Coney Island or fly over the Alps in a balloon while actually sitting in a theater before Cinerama or Todd-A-O screens.

I think the mobility theater, as a matter of fact, is a clever mechanical toy that can work both ways, for or against solid illusion, depending on exactly *what* is done, *when*, and *how*. As a modish aesthetic, a director may get away with it and, incidentally, add a little shock value—just as though the arm of your theater chair were suddenly to become electrified and give you a mild shock. I felt such a shock, with an accompanying puncture of illusion, when watching Tyrone Guthrie's Old Vic production of *Troilus and Cressida*, which played in New York recently. It was at the moment when Thersites, characterized as a cynical spot-photographer of the Nineties in Guthrie's modernization of Shakespeare, gets fed up with the Trojan War and its mock heroics and makes his escape up the aisle. On this occasion, it happened to be the aisle by which I sat, and I recall thinking, as he passed me, not of Thersites and what he meant to the action on the stage, but of the visible make-up of the actor playing the part and, thus, of the fact that he seemed really tall rather than illusorily tall. At this moment, everything either Shakespeare or the performance had tried to create went for nothing but a shock of dislocation. In a different way, the complex "depth," "space," and "mobility" theater of commercial movies accomplishes the same dislocation of illusion: a shock that may help would-be tourists to reconcile themselves to being in a New York theater rather than in Spain or Bali, but that amounts, by aesthetic computation, exactly to zero.

Such commonly available experiences as these emphasize but one point in relation to my theme: the whole shebang of the commercial film's "space devices" amounts to a pricked balloon when set next to the most elementary poetic step in an Experimental Film. Once this equation is understood and borne in mind, the virtues of the so-called professional as against the defects of the so-called amateur (or, as the professional world calls it, the arty) become radically compromised and subject to severe reversals of value. It is perfectly true that the Experimental Film also is immature, but it is honestly so, and its pretentiousness is the pretentiousness of raw youth, inexperience, and the subterfuges of a scarcity budget. On the other hand, the pretentiousness of the commercial film is that of success-intoxication, vulgar worldly sophistication, and being just purse-proud.

Experience can never help the commercial film. Quite the opposite —the more experience it has, the smugger it gets and the more careless of serious values. If it "succeeds," it sits on its laurels and expects to hatch more of the same; if it fails, it becomes hysterical and panicky and resorts to desperate measures in the direction of old-fashioned corn or new-fashioned gadgetry. Of course, there are always exceptional directors, exceptional actors, exceptional "art" films—but the vicissitudes attending genuine talent in the film world, if told truly step by step up to its status ten years after it first clicks, would make the blood run cold, if not also the hair stand on end. For one *Bicycle Thief*, there are ten *alleged* masterpieces of Italian Neo-Realism; for one *Cabiria,* sneered at by Bosley Crowther—the film critic for *The New York Times*—there are a hundred American, British, French, and Italian films that are no better than they should be, and yet many of which are greeted with smiles by the same and other Bosley Crowthers. I think a profound lesson lies in the following easily assimilated fable of fact:

Two of the most honest and artistically memorable films to come out of Hollywood were certainly von Stroheim's *Greed* and Huston's *Red Badge of Courage*; each remains, as is, a superior film standing out easily from the rank and file of commercial productions. But, even if Lillian Ross's damaging book on Huston's ordeal in making his film had not been written, the fact remains that, after their respective studios got through with these two movies and they were released, neither von Stroheim nor Huston would look at what had been made of the best, most serious effort of their respective careers.

Against the manifest vice of the commercial industry's bureaucratic editing and revamping system, the Experimentalist, merely by being in sole control (while perhaps working with one or two close collaborators), looms as Filmic Virtue incarnate. The Experimentalist's chief problem can hardly be the temptation to be popular, as is the commercial film-maker's; at the same time, now that film societies are growing so fast, the danger of such a temptation remains in the offing. When resisting a genuine vice, however, an artist may stumble on a virtue operating contingently as a "vice." Exhibitions of the definitely avant-garde category of Experimental Films are limited in scope by the presence of radical optical styles (such as the systematic distortion of anamorphic lenses) as well as of esoteric subject matter and approaches.

When assessing the "problems" of Experimental Film, it is important to remember that the phenomenon of the moving photograph appeared at a moment when there took place a radical change in aesthetic taste on the high level: when the Post-Impressionists, the Fauves, the Expressionists, and, then, the Cubists and the Futurists appeared in the visual medium of painting, and Symbolism and Surrealism rose up in literature. As a result, stage decor became symbolic, fantastic, and abstract, as these twentieth-century movements gained speed, in turn, influencing the visual style of such epoch-making films as *The Cabinet of Dr. Caligari, Berlin: Symphony of a City,* and *The Passion of Joan of Arc.* To be sure, those three films were primarily designed for popular markets, chiefly in Europe. But, already, several painters and poets, among them the poet-painter Cocteau and the photographer-painter, Man Ray, had essayed poems in plastic; that is, forms in motion, not as *things*, but as *forms* or *symbols*. Hence, in the very domain of the new visual art, "the movies," the twentieth-century struggle of painting and sculpture to dispense with naturalistic and classic forms found a potent ally in the radical inspiration of Film Experimentalists.

Basically, the legend that the commercial movies have gotten no further than nineteenth-century painting is true. Yet it is unfair to conclude, therefore, that photography as such invalidates the film as an art of creative caliber. Still artistically and creatively possible, it seems to me, are the visual novel and the visual fable; such, indeed, as Cocteau's myth films, which have influenced avant-garde film-making almost as much as his *Blood of a Poet.* But, beyond even that, the cinematic faculty as such is capable, as many more or less primitive experiments have shown, of producing the textures and the "significant" or irregular forms of modern painting itself; so far as they go, Norman McLaren's color abstractions set to music are ideal illustrations of what I mean, while Sidney Peterson's *Lead Shoes* has the best anamorphic photography I know. Thus, by being "radical," capable of sympathy with the newest styles of visual art, the movies possess, in the work of the Experimentalists, the one youthful factor that is not a symptom of arrested development, but, rather, one of much promise of fulfillment as an adult art.

Among real dangers to the Experimentalists' fire of youthful enthusiasm must be listed the temptation for *facile* emulation of forms and textures of modern painting, as though the film were mainly Abstract Art operating in the domain of movement. Here the very mid-century crisis of the visual arts comes into focus. What is the aesthetic future of the human image and of that surface representation of nature, which the photograph seems so eminently adapted to register? The link between the film and a "distortional" style such as Expressionism is plain enough and demonstrably evident: camera angle, exaggerated close-up, melted film, make-up, and decor are elements already used many times to the end of "Expressionistic" film. But if Expressionism is currently on the rise in painters' studios, it is so chiefly as the sheltered ally of all-powerful Abstractionism. At the same time, the very retrenchment of Abstractionism within Expressionistic, or what may be termed emotive, forms is most suggestive. Art must ever return so long as humanity remains human, to the emotional gesture, to the human image itself though it be reduced to hieroglyphics: to that "man" we see made of crossbars and circles in animated cartoons.

It seems not only the duty but the destiny of the Experimental, or Avant-garde, Film to use both surface nature and the literal human image as a vehicle of visual creation that eventually will reconstitute the lost supremacy of the hero of the nineteenth century. This will not mean a revival of the nineteenth century as such, but a mere reallocation of that cultural rhythm that has always taken place and that *will* take place so long as human civilization survives: a reappraisal of all tradition, including the modern, and a new criticism of the abstract style. Here is the value of the Experimentalist strategy: to be near the root of visual style itself; to sense, in the infinite possibility of distortion, a purely *expressive* means; to regard, in brief, the image distortion of a *Caligari* and the visual-angle displacement of a *Joan of Arc* (Dreyer) as a mere "grammar" of those formal inventions discussed in the books of great practicing craftsmen such as Eisenstein and Pudovkin.

Acquaintance with poetry and ritual has been encouraged in Experimentalism by such pioneering films as *Blood of a Poet, Andalusian Dog, L'Age d'Or,* and the American *Lot in Sodom.* Many valuable lessons have, thus, been learned even in the partial successes of young Film Experimentalists. Alliance with the art of dance has been as important as with that of painting, for, in dance, poetry and ritual contribute most of the style atmosphere . . . the formal, symbolic gesture, the image charged with complex relations so as to be a kind of living metaphor; such are the nude, basic implements in poetic film as well as in dance. The novel, despite James Joyce and the Surrealist movement, is still too realistic, having fallen back badly into stale nineteenth-century habits. This is part of the reason, doubtless, for the triumphant mediocrity of Hollywood and its international colleagues. "Fabulous" patterns of human behavior, of course, continue to inhere in the novel, and some contemporary young novelists have become aware of this, even apart from the special influence of Kafka's novels. Disguised fables, such as *The Bicycle Thief* by De Sica-Zavattini and *La Strada* and *Cabiria* by Fellini, have appeared in healthy distinction to the self-conscious "fabulizing" of Cocteau, which (as in *The Eagle with Two Heads*) slipped into a decadent romanticism unjustified by preciousness of taste. Very young Experimentalists, just arrived on the film scene, are aware of the fact that in the simplest forms of human behavior, such as the deathless theme of adolescent sex and its pristine discoveries, lie hidden some of the most indispensably meaningful patterns of legend, ritual, and myth.

Films by Experimentalists Sidney Peterson, Willard Maas, Stan Brakhage, Maya Deren, Curtis Harrington, and Kenneth Anger, though a significant style is attained in only a minority of their films, illustrate the profound situation of human emotion in the Initiation Rite, which is a lost tradition of fable except in poetry and dance, which themselves may tend to disguise its presence. Actually, the chief problem of Film Experimentalism is to find in ordinary behavior, where pure instinct is given the widest range and achieves the deepest sense of freedom, those prime sources of ritual and myth where humanity refreshes and revitalizes itself as in a mystic bath. The very fact that the Experimental Film uses, to begin with, the literal optical register, renders its most fertile opportunity to create extraordinary visions. To see the simple, the everyday, to see men and women as they are in mirrors, but illumined with inspiration, becoming rhythmic, behaving as if they were in dreamland rather than in the conscious, waking world . . . and to create the most startling transformations in things, and in time, as though such pro-cesses were "the order of the day" . . . this "magic" is the kinder-garten-stuff of Film Experimentalism. For all this to comprise more than a talented exercise, a stimulating blackboard lesson, film workers have to try very hard and must possess, to begin with, an innate gift for inventing with images and controlling the space in which images move of themselves and are moved by the camera; beyond this, in order to get something on film that is distinguished and memorable, film-makers must have something of their own to say: a personal message as well as poetic inspiration.

Naturally, a good deal depends on the amplitude of the mere mechanical means, the availability of technical equipment, which, in monetary terms, is extremely expensive and, even with the most discreet and canny usage, tends by its nature to be wasteful. This aspect of the problem is, to some extent, the responsibility of the Powers That Be and the well-wishing public of the Experimental Film. In all discouraging fact, there are far too few provisions in the charters of institutions of public benefaction covering film work, and, when these do exist, they cover uncreative, rather than creative work in the filmic medium. The bright solution of the Film Ex-perimentalist's problems, therefore, depends mostly on his own immediate skill and energy in demonstrating, with the limited means at his disposal, the inherent virtues of filmic creation.

THE MERRY WIDOW

INTRODUCED BY ERICH VON STROHEIM

No. 18, April, 1958

[The following text is a transcription of Erich von Stroheim's introductory remarks to a showing of *The Merry Widow* at the Palais des Beaux-Arts, Brussels, November 28, 1955. Jacques Ledoux of the Cinémathèque de Belgique, who has provided us with this text, writes: "You will see that it was an unprepared speech, thus full of hesitations; furthermore, it was typed by an employee who was satisfied in typing only what she heard."]

        I would like to introduce to you my friend, my collaborator, Denise Vernac . . . (applause) . . . It is always a very bad sign when a director has to speak before one of his own films . . . (laughter) . . . because he will be making excuses . . . and that is exactly what I want to do. I have many reasons for it and for asking your patience. In the first place, because I speak very poor French. Secondly, because this film, *The Merry Widow*, was made thirty years ago. It is a very long time. In those days, we did not have the techniques and equipment we have today, for instance, lighting, color, sound. . . . And then, this film that you are going to see, this copy is a . . . (Denise Vernac: "*Contretype*") . . . a *contretype* from a completely different version. This is a 16mm copy, and it will be projected on a regular-size screen and, for that reason, the images will not have the sharpness of focus. . . . Also, we don't have music. It was necessary, this very afternoon, to arrange something during the last two hours. In the old days, the MGM company had experienced composers who prepared scores for the theaters that had orchestras. The smaller theaters, naturally, had only pianos—that's all. Tonight, we have a very intelligent, extremely . . . (Denise Vernac: "able") . . . able musician who will do his best. . . .

Naturally, I like drama . . . tragedy. . . . But the producers do not like it. . . . They like only what brings money, and, in my youth, I hated money, although today . . . (laughter and applause). . . . Therefore, I never wanted to direct stories for infantiles like that . . . (laughter) . . . but because, before I embarked on *The Merry Widow*, I had made a great tragedy . . . when I say "great," I mean in length . . . (laughter) . . . and a great story . . . It was not my story this time—it was one of the greatest stories written by an American, Frank Norris, a student of Zola. And this film was, as the company said, a complete, a complete . . . (Denise Vernac: "fiasco") . . . fiasco . . . (laughter) . . . because it was not this company that gave me money to make the film but another one, which had supervised me during the shooting but which did not have a money interest in the film! It is very simple—the company did not give the film enough publicity and made it also into a financial fiasco probably. However, for me, it was a great success artistically. I had always wanted to make a great film, a good film and a long one, too, with an intermission—at a psychologically suitable moment—to give the audience time for dinner as the great Eugene O'Neill did in . . . (Denise Vernac: *Strange Interlude*) . . . *Strange Interlude*. He did it several years after me. I wanted to do it in *Greed*. . . . And I made the film. But it was too long for the producer, because he did not think about screening it in two sittings, as I did. So, the company hired a man who had never read Norris's book, did not know anything about my editing ideas, and was ordered to edit it . . . so he edited it . . . (laughter) . . . he edited it. . . . When, ten years later, I saw the film myself, for the first time, it was like seeing the corpse in a graveyard. I found it in its narrow casket among plenty of dust and a terrible stink . . . (laughter) . . . I found a thin part of the backbone and a little bone of the shoulder. And, naturally, I became sick, it made me very sick, because I had worked on this film for two years of my life, without any salary. Try to play this on your piano . . . (laughter) . . . Two years with a sick woman, with a sick child, very sick, with polio—and me, working without a salary on this film, for two years! At the end of the two years, I thought: If this film comes out the way I made it, I will be the greatest film director living. . . . But, when it was edited like this . . . and, after all this fiasco, imagine a producer coming to me and asking me to direct for him a film called *The Merry Widow*! He bought the rights to it for a great sum of money, dollars, not Belgian francs . . . and he had nothing for his money but the title, since the success of *The Merry Widow* was in its music. The story itself was ridiculous, or almost ridiculous. Naturally, I did not want to make it. And, besides, I had never had stars, because I don't like stars—both men and women stars. Particularly, women . . . (laughter) . . . because they have ideas. . . . When I direct, it is me who has the ideas. It is me who directs. So, to please me, the company forced me to accept two stars, not one. Two! . . . (laughter) . . . Mae Murray, who always played under the direction of her husband, a very great man, very great, six-feet-three, and a very gentle man. I could make a comparison between a Saint Bernard dog . . . (laughter) . . . She, herself, if I may say so . . . was very active, very agile, too active . . . (laughter) . . . So this *grand* man and this little woman . . . you know very well who won the battle . . . (laughter) . . . It was always Mae Murray, it was always she who won, and the big Saint Bernard did exactly what his wife told him to do. But it was very different with me, since I was not married to this woman . . . (laughter) . . . No. She was very gentle, but she had ideas . . . (laughter) . . . and, as I said before, I have ideas myself. So these two ideas . . . (laughter) . . . clashed. One time we had a terrible battle, during the embassy ball scene, and it was terrible because I had 350 extras in it who loved me very much . . . it was always the workers who liked me, not the producers —the workers . . . do you see the difference? . . . (laughter and applause). So this woman thought . . . it was after World War I . . . and she called me "dirty Hun" . . . Naturally, I did not like it, since I was born in Austria, in Vienna, and since she was born in Vienna, too. . . . (laughter) . . . As a matter of fact, she was born in Czechoslovakia, but, then, I did not see much difference

. . . (laughter) . . . and, since my workers, my extras understood that this meant the end, they took off their uniforms and threw them on the floor. . . .

I want to tell you a very, very strange story. You will permit me to sit down (he sits down on the podium). Thank you. Because this is a very strange story . . . (laughter) . . . I am very superstitious, also religious, and in many cases that goes together, as you know. I had troubles with Mae Murray, as I said before, and, also, troubles with electricity, lamps, with the helpers, with everybody. And it was strange, because it had never happened that way before. So, after the duel with Mae Murray, I was discharged by the company, but really . . . (laughter) . . . But I almost forgot to tell you my story. . . . Since I am very superstitious and a mystic, I used to visit a certain *voyeuse* (Denise Vernac: *"voyante"*) . . . *voyante* . . . (laughter). . . . So, before I started working on *The Merry Widow*, at the time when the company approached me, I naturally went first to my friend Madame Ora . . . (laughter) . . . She was an old woman, only an EAR, so I asked her what would be the outcome, should I make the film or not? She waited a little while, just enough to give the necessary weight, and said that I should "absolutely do it," because it will be a great feather in my hat . . . (laughter) . . . In California nobody wears a hat, and I did not have a hat—but she assured me of great success, a large feather, a beautiful plume in my hat, *bon*! So I started the film. I was discharged, and I came immediately, the first thing I did, to my adviser Madame Ora. I told her that I was discharged and that the president of the company had shown me the doors himself and that, in my turn, I'd given him a few words that he will never forget, and that I am in the street now. What should I do? And you have assured me that this will be a large feather in my hat! The Madame said to me: "Monsieur von Stroheim, I can't change my idea. You will continue tomorrow on *The Merry Widow*, you will direct it tomorrow, and it will be a great success, and it will be a great feather in your hat." I said, "Madame, you have not understood me correctly, I am in the street. . . ." (laughter) . . . "No, Monsieur, it is you who does not understand, it is you who does not understand. You will be continuing tomorrow morning." And this was at six o'clock in the afternoon. And she says to me, further, that now, this very moment, there are four or five men in my Los Angeles home waiting to see me . . . regarding tomorrow's work. I said, "But this is ridiculous, isn't it?" And she says, "They are in uniforms. . . ." (laughter) . . . And it was the time of prohibition in California, and I, like a good citizen, had plenty of whiskey in my house . . . (laughter) . . . and a few whiskeys in my car, just like that . . . (laughter) . . . That meant this . . . (laughter) . . . the years not in a private prison but on the island of Alcatraz . . . So I hurried home and, believe it or not, there were four men waiting and they were in uniforms. But they were not policemen but from the staff of the company, sent by the president himself to speak to me, to ask me to continue work on the film the next morning! That was too much . . . too strange. During the night, the president sent his men twice more, just to be sure that I would definitely be at work the next morning, at 8:30 —counting thirty minutes for the peace talks. . . . *Oui!* Madame Ora was right. I continued directing, it was one of the great successes of its time, and it was chosen by the critics of America as the best film of 1926. That, perhaps, is not such a great credit in itself, since, probably, the other films were very bad . . . (laughter) . . . At any rate, this film has made for its company 4½ million . . . though not for me. I had 25 per cent of it. How much do you think I received?

I thank you once more and ask you to have patience because the film is thirty years old, this print is only a 16 mm version projected on too large a screen, and I don't have the sound or the color or the Cinerama . . . I have nothing. And so I have made all the possible excuses that I could think of. All the good things in this film were made by me. The things that are no good in it were made by others. . . .

PORTRAIT OF AN ARTIST

BY RUDOLF ARNHEIM

No. 18, April, 1958

[When I wrote this article in Rome, almost a quarter of a century ago for the planned but never published *Encyclopedia del Cinema*, I surely did not expect that at its first publication it would serve as an obituary. (Erich von Stroheim died on May 12, 1957, after a long illness, in the castle of Maurepas, France.)—R.A.]

Von Stroheim is one of the great exceptional figures of American commercial film-making. By interfering with the business, he bestows on it, at the same time, some of the spiritual dignity it lacks otherwise. In Hollywood, the mechanization and commercialization of human creativity have been carried to the most violent consequences, not only because of the usual American thoroughness, but particularly because the tendencies of modern industry are applied here to the most recalcitrant product, namely, art. In Hollywood, therefore, the rebellion of a strong and exceptional personality against the rules and norms assumes gigantic dimensions. Millions of dollars are at stake, and the structure raised to protect these values is endangered when an individual artist insists on the freedom necessary for him to work according to his own standards. Chaplin can afford such freedom because his films are so successful commercially that any lavishness of the production is made up at the box office, whereas the success of a film by von Stroheim is always uncertain. Some of his works have exerted their fascinating power even on the masses. The exuberant strength of others could not be stomached by a public that is used to the mixture of moderate sweetness and moderate cruelty typically found in the average film fare.

The director and actor Erich von Stroheim is one of the three or four film artists whose work may be measured with the standards established by the traditions of the older arts. The contemporary scene, perhaps, does not as yet set these men off sufficiently against the many dozens of their talented colleagues, who at present are just as famous as they are; but as time passes they will stand out more and more—lonely figures, the heroes of film history, and their work will be held in esteem unless, indeed, the precious negatives will have fallen victim to stupidity and carelessness.

We all know von Stroheim personally. He is one of the few actors who incarnate a particular type so intensely that they hardly need to act; it is sufficient for them to appear. But is his type the image of a great artist? Piercing eyes, wily and evil, a brutal mouth, a bald head, and the bull neck of a boxer—a man who, according to the film chronicles, made good in Hollywood during the first World War by specializing in the stereotype of the sadistic German that was a stock in trade of propaganda movies; a nobleman, born in Vienna in 1888, an officer who had to leave the Austrian army, an immigrant who arrived in America in 1909, soldier, barkeeper, dishwasher, gardener, forester, stableman, acrobat, and, finally, movie actor.

In scrutinizing the expression of the man's head, we may come to remember that a polished intellect and refined sensitivity are not the necessary prerequisites of every artist. Sometimes, the wild fanaticism of an instinct-driven personality will hurl back into the world creatively shaped experiences whose images have been forged in the internal fire. One needs only to read about von Stroheim's method of work to understand that what impels him is an obsession rather than calculating reason. He works without any consideration of the taste or money of the employers on whom he depends; he is the most expensive, the most unmanageable director in all Hollywood; he consumes mountains of negative film and, after one or two years of desperate editing, turns up with a thirty-thousand-foot giant that does not fit the customary programs of the movie houses—films so unwieldy or so excessive in their consummation of horror that other directors are called in to "complete" them, to tone them down, and to cut them to size.

The original version of *Greed* required eight hours of projection time. His *magnum opus*, a monumental indictment of bourgeois society, was torn apart and sold as two films: *The Wedding March* and *Marriage of the Prince* (also known as *The Honeymoon*). *Merry-Go-Round* was taken away from him while he was in the midst of his work and given to the director Rupert Julian for speedier and more conventional completion. *Queen Kelly*—a film that, still unfinished, received its first public showing in Paris only recently—involved him in difficulties with the producer. He has worked for all the large companies: for Universal, for Metro-Goldwyn-Mayer, for Paramount, and for United Artists.

In Stroheim's films, one and the same instinctive compulsion determines every detail; hence, the consistency of his closed, singular world—the most impressive example of style and personal atmosphere that, apart from Chaplin and the Russians, the history of the motion picture has given us.

With grandiose one-sidedness, von Stroheim contemplates society through one of its segments. This segmentary world—to him, the whole world—is that of the army and the higher bourgeoisie in Imperial Austria. He hates that milieu and, at the same time, he loves it—as all great accusers seem to do with the objects of their wrath. He is a part of it while analyzing it as an outsider. He escaped from it across the ocean, but it never let him go. It has been said of him that he deals with outdated problems. Perhaps it is true that this particular nuance of vice and corruption, shielded by glamorous gentility, is no longer found in the image of our world, but the question that determines artistic validity is not whether a given setting exists, or continues to exist, but whether it is dramatic, that is, whether it embodies timeless conflicts.

Von Stroheim has aimed at the enduring core of human conflicts more determinedly than have most other film-makers. There is, for instance, the gruesome humor of an episode in *Foolish Wives* wherein an American officer stands stiffly, without making a move, after a lady drops her purse—an impoliteness that is explained later when we learn that the man has lost both arms in the war. In this example, utmost human helplessness conflicts not with an equally elemental force but with a superficial demand for good manners. Quite typically, von Stroheim shows the vital components of human nature engaged in a murderous fight against the shallow, but powerful, norms of a dying society. Tortured, suffering, rebelling creatures struggle with the ruthless exploiters of evil; and, interestingly enough, the creator of this world identifies himself with the evil, not the virtuous, powers. In two of his films, the villain is played by the actor Erich von Stroheim.

Von Stroheim exemplifies on the screen the contrast between the vicious nature of his characters and the beauty and honorable reputation of their external appearance. He, the pitiless seducer and profiteer, wears the immaculate uniform of the officer; if possible, full dress with gold braids and plumed helmet. His heroines are dolls of a more than American sweetness, bedecked with flowers and the bridal veil; but, in their pale eyes, are sleepless nights and the terrors of rape. Significantly, he often uses the theme of the limping woman on crutches. The crippled woman is more horrible than the crippled man, because the male represents the struggle of human impotence with all-powerful fate and, therefore, is ennobled rather than defaced by a scar or defect. Woman, however, symbolizes the remnants of the lost harmony and perfection left to man from the Creation. To see a beautiful woman mutilated is repugnant, because it is unfitting and meaningless, especially when the festively decorated groom, the officer, leads her down the aisle of a splendid cathedral, a sweet bride—limping all the way (*The Wedding March*). Only a great artist would thus throw into relief the pathetic frailty of the human race by contrasting it with a profusion of luxury.

Among the marginal figures of *Foolish Wives*, there are the armless veteran, already mentioned, and an old hag on crutches; also, among the children who gather around the gala coach, there is a little girl on crutches, singled out by the camera. In the same crowd of children, a small boy, as though by accident, amuses himself by wearing the steel helmet of the trenches. Thus, von Stroheim's style is manifest even in the anonymity of the "extras."

In *Greed* we get the symbolic illustration of a marriage gone to ruin: repulsive filth covers the bedroom, the washbasin is half broken, and, on the bed, a pale woman, her hair in a large matted mass, sits and rubs her hands with cold cream—smiling maliciously, like the devil rubbing his hands, pleased at his shrewdness in the accomplishment of some trick. In *The Wedding March*, there is a brothel scene in which two old drunks lie on the floor among squatting prostitutes. Barely able to talk, they, nevertheless, choose this moment to plan the marriage of their children. In *Foolish Wives*, love and loyalty take the shape of a miserable, exploited, apishly degenerate servant girl.

In the same film, we find one of those rare scenes in which the surface content of the story recedes and a primordial experience, or archetype, seems to become manifest. The villain, played by Stroheim, has rescued the wife of the wealthy American from a thunderstorm. She is drenched and has hurt her foot. They have found refuge in a mountain hut. As he approaches the sleeping injured woman, his uniform unbuttoned, a haggard monk, also seeking refuge, enters with a large dog. His dark, burning eyes are deeply set, and sharp wrinkles line his mouth. The monk neither says nor does anything. Having sought protection from the rain, he sits quietly on the bench and, with his immobile, uncanny glance, watches the moves of the seducer. After a long pantomimic passage, the villain reluctantly desists, curbed by the eternally watching countenance of Death, God, or the Devil.

A FOOTNOTE
TO FOOLISH WIVES

BY HERMAN G. WEINBERG

No. 18, April, 1958

No version of *Foolish Wives* is complete without the original titles written for it by Marian Ainslee in collaboration with von Stroheim himself. In these impressionistic captions, they evoked the mystery and glamour of the famous pleasure resort that was Monte Carlo in the era of its florescence at the turn of the century before World War I, when the art of living had been brought to its apogee. How to describe something that best described itself? Certainly, the realism with which this little artificial paradise at the time (1921) was reproduced by an ex-English Army captain, Richard Day, also in collaboration with von Stroheim, at Universal City in southern California, is historic. Nonetheless, such was the passion of this remarkable film's creator that nothing was left undone to give the spectator the fullest sense of what kind of world, in what kind of *milieu*, the story of *Foolish Wives* took place. This was not the Monte Carlo of *To Catch a*

Thief or *The Monte Carlo Story* or of any other film that ever hoped some of the fabled glamour of the Riviera would rub off on it. This is the Monte Carlo of the baroque Edwardian era before the lights of Europe began to go out on the eve of that great convulsion in 1914 that was to change the face of the world. (*Blind Husbands, The Devil's Passkey, The Merry Go Round, The Merry Widow, The Wedding March*, and *Queen Kelly* were all set in this period and in this *fin-de-siécle milieu*). Unhappily, only fragments of the stunning scenes that illustrated these titles (if you want to put it that way) remain in the several mutilated versions extant of this film and for some of the titles no scenes at all remain (such as all the opening scenes, the pigeon-shoots at the Sporting Club, the night street scenes, and so forth, but we do have a record of the titles to recall them and the unfathomable moments of rapture they were meant to evoke of a place that was once like Xanadu and that was mirrored with such poetry by the diamond-like translucent crystal of Stroheim's lens . . .

The opening title:

Monte Carlo—brine of the Mediterranean—breeze from the Alpine snows—roulette, trente et quarante, écarte—mondaines and cocottes—kings and crooks—amours, amours, and suicides—and waves and waves and waves!

Then:

Again, morning! Sun-drenched terrace-sapphire sea—all the world on a holiday—rifle fire—bleeding doves—brutality of men—and, still, the sun!

And night—mysterious and fragrant—bewitching, glamorous, enticing—the great enchantress of the world!

The barcarolle—perfume of night—murmur of waves—whispers and sighs and kisses . . .

Woman's vanity—flattery, subtle and insistent—busy husbands and idle, foolish wives . . .

Dense marshes, slimy, sombrous, betraying—then, night . . .

Evening, grateful, cool, caressing—lamps glow amid flowers—high-heeled slippers—froufrou of satins—muted violins—automobiles and the clatter of horses' hoofs . . .

Salon de roulette—the sound of rakes on green cloths and chips on chips—the rustle of paper money.

There were more, but that will give you an idea. Do you need sound for this? Or a screen the size of the Great Wall of China? Do you need Technicolor or anything else but imagination and a mind with which to accomplish the feat of imagination? Today's films make no demands on our capacities for imagination. We needn't meet them half-way; they go all the way, right into the depths of our popcorn boxes so that it's difficult to tell where the popcorn leaves off and the film begins.

In Japan, during any sort of performance on a stage, at a peak moment of the performer's art, members of the audience, in jubilation, will cry out the artist's name. It is a lovely custom and a tribute to the deep emotional sensitivity of the Japanese. I call out now— and for all time:

Von Stroheim!

COFFEE, BRANDY, & CIGARS XXX

BY HERMAN G. WEINBERG

No. 18, April, 1958

There's rosemary, that's for remembrance: pray you, love, remember . . . (Shakespeare: Hamlet)

Being some personal reminiscences of von Stroheim, recalled from memory . . .

To the Countess Maeterlinck: "I never took myself very seriously as an actor; as a director, yes—as an actor, no."

We were driving up Fifth Avenue on a rainy night—the long ribbon of green traffic lights suddenly changed to red, like a necklace of emeralds become one of rubies, reflected in the glistening asphalt. "That would make a nice shot in a film."

After sitting through all three acts of the play *Arsenic and Old Lace* in stone-faced silence, while all about him were laughing their heads off: "Oh, you know me—I don't find anything funny anymore."

To the query why he spoke his lines in French films so slowly and meticulously: "To stay on the screen longer."

Republic Pictures was always referred to as "Repulsive Pictures."

"Did you ever read Charles Fort's *The Book of the Damned?* You should, it's a remarkable book, all about natural phenomena the scientists can't explain. There are lots of things we have no explanation for. I believe in extrasensory perception and all that, I absolutely do."

He'd bought a car but never learned to drive it himself. "I can't think behind the wheel of the damned thing."

Trying to get him to deliver a promised article by press time for Klaus Mann's magazine *Decision* while touring one-night stands in *Arsenic and Old Lace* in the Midwest: "Unless the Holy Ghost comes down and writes the article for me, which, as you informed me, must be in Klaus Mann's hands in a week, I won't be able to contribute for the next number. That issue will greatly suffer through it, but it can't be helped."

Of von Sternberg: "A very cultured and intelligent director."

Of Lubitsch: "Lubitsch shows you first the king on his throne, then as he is in his bedroom. I show you the king first in his bedroom, so you'll know just what he is when you see him on his throne."

Of Jean Renoir: "The only man who can outdrink me."

At the "21" club in New York, Chaplin catches his eye—they smile, nod, hesitate . . . Who will defer to whom? As if there had never been any question about it, he gets up, excuses himself to us, and rushes over to Chaplin's table.

Whose work did he especially like in Hollywood? (The year is 1940). "Milestone, Ford, Victor Fleming, Capra, Lubitsch."

In Europe? "Renoir, Pagnol, René Clair, Eisenstein."

What American pictures? "*The Informer, Stage Coach, Of Mice and Men, Grapes of Wrath, Gone with the Wind, Mr. Deeds Goes to Town, Ninotchka, Our Town, The Biscuit Eater, Dead End.*"

European films? "*La Bandera, Les Bas-Fonds, La Chienne, La Grande Illusion, Sous les Toits de Paris, La Kermesse Héroique.*"

What projects would he like to do? "*The Diary of a Chambermaid* by Octave Mirbeau, *Les Civilisés* by Claude Farrère, *God's Little Acre* by Erskine Caldwell, certain stories by Maupassant, *Paprika* by myself."

What happened to *Walking Down Broadway?* "Sol Wurtzel, one of the chief moguls at Fox, did not understand the story or the picture. After it was finished, he had it rewritten, remade, and rebaptized. It came out as *Hello Sister!*—a 'B' picture. Sol Wurtzel wanted to prove to Winnie Sheehan that his (Sheehan's) judgment had been wrong in engaging me to direct during Wurtzel's absence. I happened to be in the middle of a feud between them."

He detested the German military roles of both world wars that economic necessity forced him to play. (There was one exception— von Rauffenstein in *La Grande Illusion*.) He found it ironic that, between the two world wars, he should have made an auspicious career as a director only to wind up playing the same antipathetic German officers he started out with, as if *Blind Husbands, The Devil's Passkey, Foolish Wives, Greed, The Merry Widow,* and *The Wedding March* had never happened.

When he threw a party, it was a real party—not a few miserable canapés, second-rate rye, and potato chips surrounded by a group of simpering, gushing hypocrites. I recall one in New York, replete with caviar, champagne, and sweetmeats galore to delight Heliogabalus, and a guest list as succulent. (Only Tom Curtiss, of the Paris *Herald-Tribune*, his long-time friend, mentor, and everything else good, including "father-confessor," outdid him once, in this respect, by throwing a party at the old Astor, designed to bring von Stroheim and Thomas Mann together as a prelude to discussions which he hoped would result in von Stroheim's filming *The Magic Mountain*. This was a wing-ding out of a Stroheim film, indeed.)

"*The Wedding March,*" said Erwin Piscator, "is like a novel by Balzac."

A picture postcard from Niagara Falls, during a visit there, inscribed, "So much water and no whiskey!"

A chain letter: "I am sending you this chain letter because I believe in Paul Kohner, my agent, and the guys listed ahead of him, Joe Pasternak, Robert Z. Leonard, etc., (as you can see, the sucker-list is pretty melodious) . . . and because I believe in you. . . ." (Someone must have broken the chain as he predicted it would be broken—but hope sprang eternal in those wonderful days . . .)

He wrote *Poto-Poto*, his African story, with Marlene Dietrich in mind to play the role of "Roulette" Masha, a flashy blonde who "works" the boats plying the Red Sea, taking on any gambler, staking herself against the cold cash of her partner. She loses a particularly high stake once to a degenerate African trader, who takes her back with him as his mistress to a steaming little green-hell up river on the East African coast. An expanded French translation of this story was recently published in Paris.

He directed a practical joke once on a young doctor friend who went calling on his girl, only to be met by another girl in his fiancée's apartment, who disclaimed all knowledge of the medico's inamorata, insisting it was *her* apartment. The strange girl, playing it straight-faced, had her sinister aspects, certainly, under the circumstances, but what gave the situation its most bizarre touch was the fact that, save for a pair of slippers (and smoking a cigarette in a long cigarette-holder), she conducted the entire conversation completely in the nude.

"R. H. Cochrane, vice-president in charge of publicity at Universal, after I finished *Foolish Wives,* thought its production cost of $735,000 was so close to a million that he decided to call it, for publicity purposes, the first million-dollar picture. Universal had put up an electric sign on Broadway, changed weekly as the production cost 'mounted.' They spelled my name in lights as '$troheim.' A lot of good that did me!"

He treasured a gold cigarette case that the cast of *The Merry Widow* gave him when the picture was finished, inscribed with all their signatures as an expression of their love for him.

When he was returning to France at the end of the war, a farewell party was held on the deck of the nondescript French freighter on which he was to voyage across, the big liners being not yet returned to passenger service. Turkey leg in one hand, bumper of scotch in the other, he grimly regarded a snarled coil of rope on the deck, a flagrant violation of one of the cardinal rules of the sea. "Just look at that," he said. "That would never happen on a German boat. Well, if you don't hear from me anymore, you'll know why." But he loved France and had only contempt for German junkerism.

How can one reminisce of von Stroheim and not also recall the role played by Denise Vernac after his first trip to France, when he was called over to appear in *Marthe Richard?* She came as a journalist to interview him and remained as his secretary, major-domo, and ministering angel, cushioning him against the "slings and arrows" of the world. Rarely, I think, has a woman exhibited such selfless devotion.

There never was a more valiant trio of "musketeers" than Denise Vernac, Tom Curtiss, and von Stroheim—whom Paris knew so well during the past decade.

He recalled his start in Hollywood when he, "Bull" Montana, and Lon Chaney used to walk each day to Universal City, seeking extra work. "Because of our combined overpowering handsomeness, we were known as 'The Three Graces.'"

Asked why he so often wore an armband of mourning in films in which he acted, he replied with a heavy sigh, "I don't know . . . *weltschmerz*, maybe."

He could think of the most startling things. "Did you ever make love in a steaming barn on a hot summer afternoon?"

By 1921, when the movies were still a wilderness, he had already directed three of the most sophisticated films ever made—*Blind Husbands, The Devil's Passkey,* and *Foolish Wives.*

"What were the lengths of your films as cut by you for their final versions and the actual lengths in which these films were released to the public by the producing companies?"

Answer:

Blind Husbands .... 9,000 ft. released in 8,000 ft.
The Devil's Passkey .... 12,000 ft. released in 12,000 ft.
Foolish Wives .... 21,000 ft. released in 14,000 ft.

The version at the Museum of Modern Art in New York is 7,000 ft.

Greed .... 24,000 ft. released in 10,000 ft.
The Merry Widow .... 12,000 ft. released in 11,000 ft.
The Wedding March .... 14,000 ft. released in 14,000 ft.*

He never won an Academy Award in Hollywood, either as actor or director, but France made him a Chevalier of the Legion of Honor.

His last screen role was as Beethoven in Sacha Guitry's *Napoléon* —fittingly, too, for what Romain Rolland once said of the master of Bonn was as applicable to von Stroheim: "Beethoven would not have been what he was were it not for his excesses."

Plagued by illness; doing one-night stands of *Arsenic and Old Lace*: ("I, who never could be sure of remembering two consecutive lines of dialogue!"); following up "leads" everywhere for a possible film role here, a possible directorial post there, most of which led up blind alleys; writing scripts, articles; beset by personal anxieties that would have tried the patience of Job—he, nevertheless, maintained touches of optimism amid the somber pessimism to which he had been brought by the chicanery that kept tripping him up. Despite that . . . he could close a letter jubilantly, as he did to me once, "Vivat . . . crescat . . . floreat!" Live, create, flourish!

He wanted to show that the whole world was kin, that there was good and evil everywhere, and not always where we would expect

---

* Von Stroheim was being generous—actually, according to the original script, there was more shot. The bordello scene, alone, was at least 1,000 to 2,000 feet longer than the released version. Also, this represents only the first part.

to find them, and, sometimes, in the most surprising places. Human nature was compounded of contradictory attributes, a fact which Dostoyevsky realized so trenchantly, and no von Stroheim character ever ceased for an instant to be a credible human being, whether cast in the role of hero or villain. A complete human being himself, with the wide latitude that this permits, he observed human frailty as he would observe it in himself, with irony or compassion, depending on the circumstances, but never losing his sense of humor, which was prodigious and, more often than not, withering. Round and round went the eternal game of lust that fascinated him as a scientist is fascinated by the development in research he is undertaking . . . lust for the things men lust for, the lust for money, for love, for youth, before which borderlines of nationality and caste crumble. Like Asmodeus, he soared over the rooftops of the world and peered into the windows, and what he saw there is partially discernible in the pitifully few fragments that were permitted to remain of his work by those whom he angered or made afraid. But he loved life, and it was this that the buffoons who tried to "put him in his place" did not understand, for how could they know that a man can have wings and rejoice only in the flight of his creative spirit?

TWO

THE NEW AMERICAN CINEMA

Between 1959 and 1963, it seemed, at least to the editors of *Film Culture*, as if a new cinema were about to emerge in the United States, a cinema of low-budget productions of high artistic interest, economically akin to the Off-Broadway theater, as it was then, or to the "new waves" in France, Italy, England, and Eastern Europe. This illusion lasted while Jonas Mekas, Shirley Clarke, Adolfas Mekas, Robert Frank, John Cassavetes, and a number of others were making their first feature films; it ended abruptly when they had completed them and were seeking distribution for them and financing for further projects. In the wake of this illusion, The Film-Makers Cooperative was born. Through it, the film-makers planned to distribute their own films and keep the income, minus a marginal percentage for operational costs. At this point, the low-budget film-makers joined forces with the "experimental" film-makers, who had no budgets at all. Within a year, it was apparent that the Film-Makers Cooperative could not bring in sufficient funds to keep a director working on a $25,000 budget; yet it could help to sustain the avant-gardists. Thus, *Film Culture* drifted from being the forum for low-budget film directors to that of the most radical innovators.

The articles in this chapter document the transition from the one position to the other. During the period under consideration, four Independent Film Awards were given (see Appendix A), and these form an accurate index to the evolving concerns of the magazine. Parker Tyler's article presents a critique of the first two awards.

Rudolph Arnheim's article is a transcription of an address he gave, at Cinema 16, on the death of Maya Deren. Miss Deren, who called her own films "chamber films," championed, through her Creative Film Foundation, the cause of film experimentation. Shortly after her untimely death, which became a rallying point for independent film-makers, the Film-Makers Cooperative was founded.

The reader will find it interesting to compare Jonas Mekas's "Notes" with his article written eight years earlier, excerpted in the previous chapter.

A CALL FOR A NEW GENERATION OF FILM-MAKERS

BY JONAS MEKAS

No. 19, 1959

The establishment of the Independent Film Award marks the entrance of a new generation of film-makers into American cinema.

The time has long been ripe for it. We had expected it to happen with the breaking up of the Hollywood monolith into small, independent film companies. But our hopes proved to be only wishful thinking. Most independent companies soon became small Hollywoods in themselves.

The only independent artist left in dramatic feature film, Orson Welles, is constantly being bended down and butchered, as he was in *Touch of Evil*.

The only free film-making being done was in the short experimental film. However, lately, it, too, has become sterile and has been frozen into a genre. Film experimentation has degenerated into "making experimental films."

Still, experimental film-makers (and such artists as Orson Welles) kept the spirit of free cinema alive in America. We praise them not so much for their achievements as for the course they have faithfully followed.

However, to break the stifling conventions of the dramatic film, the cinema needs a larger movement than that of the experimental film-makers.

We think that such a movement is about to begin.

The first signs of a larger stir up are visible. Several dramatic films, some already completed, some about to be finished in coming months—films such as John Cassavetes's *Shadows,* Morris Engel's *Weddings and Babies,* Alfred Leslie and Robert Frank's *Pull My Daisy,* Edouard Laurot's *Sunday Junction,* and Jerome Hill's *The Sand Castle,* to mention only a few—clearly point up a new spirit in American cinema: a spirit that is akin to that which guides the young British film-makers centered around Free Cinema, a spirit that is being felt among the French film newcomers such as Claude Chabrol, Alexandre Astruc, François Truffaut, Roger Vadim, Georges Franju, and a spirit which is changing the face of the young Polish cinema.

Basically, they all:

mistrust and loathe the official cinema and its thematic and formal stiffness;

are primarily preoccupied with the emotional and intellectual conditions of their own generation as opposed to the neorealists' preoccupation with materiality;

seek to free themselves from the overprofessionalism and over-technicality that usually handicap the inspiration and spontaneity of the official cinema, guiding themselves more by intuition and improvisation than by discipline. (As the postwar emergence of neorealism freed cinematography from the conventions of studio lighting, thereby coming closer to visual truth, so the new generation of film-makers may eventually free direction, acting, and sets from their dead and commercial conceptions and go on to seize the truth of their experiences and their dreams.)

Obviously, this is not what the "professionals" want. These film-makers will be severely criticized and, perhaps, even accused of betraying cinema. However, they come closer to the truth with their nakedness than the "professionals" with their pretentious expensiveness.

It is wrong to believe (Cocteau said it long ago) that good films can be made in 35mm only, as it is wrong to believe that only the 16mm experimental film-makers can be really free.

John Cassavetes's film *Shadows* proves that a feature film can be made with only $15,000. And a film that doesn't betray life or cinema. What does it prove? It proves that we can make our films *now* and by *ourselves*. Hollywood and miniature Hollywoods of our "independents" will never make *our* films.

A $15,000 film is financially unbeatable. Television cannot kill it. The apathy of the audience cannot kill it. Theatrical distributors cannot kill it. It is free.

Therefore,

it is time to bring our film up to date. Hollywood films (and we mean Hollywoods all over the world) reach us beautiful and dead. They are made with money, cameras, and splicers, instead of with enthusiasm, passion, and imagination. If it will help us to free our cinema by throwing out the splicers and the budget-makers and by shooting our films on 16mm as Cassavetes did, let us do so.

Our hope for a free American cinema is entirely in the hands of the new generation of film-makers. And there is no other way of breaking the frozen cinematic ground than through a *complete* derangement of the official cinematic senses.

FOR AN UNCONTROLLED CINEMA

BY RICHARD LEACOCK

No. 22–23, Summer, 1961

In 1908, a newsreel was made showing Tolstoy talking to petitioners on the veranda of his home at Yasnaya Polyana. And though it is a remarkable sight, how frustrating that one cannot hear what he is saying to these people! And herein lay the problem. How could you record human relations without that uniquely human means of communication—speech?

The art of the cinema was to develop for a good half of its life so far without speech. Four films are reasonably typical of this period: *Potemkin*, *The Kid*, *Nanook*, and *The Eternal Triangle* (starring Mary Pickford). Most people will agree that *Potemkin* is fascinating but very odd when one looks at it today; *The Kid* and *Nanook* work perfectly and seem strangely contemporary; and *The Eternal Triangle* appears utterly ludicrous. Yet I think it is the latter film that is the grandmother of what we consider the normal theatrical film of today.

Potemkin represents one of the most exciting developments in the history of film. A film form was developed that was in effect a marvelous visual language. A great amount of attention has been paid to these techniques, which came to be called 'montage.' A body of theory did grow up around montage, and it did seem to many that film-making was coming of age and would, henceforth, have an elegant theoretical base to lean upon. Pudovkin wrote *Film Technique* and Eisenstein wrote *Film Sense*, which gave what appeared to be a *general* approach to film-making.

However, when sound-on-film made its appearance, an appalling fact became very evident—one no longer needed a visual substitute for speech. Theories die hard, and there are still many film theoreticians who cling to the "golden age of film-making." Perhaps they should look again at Pudovkin's first sound film to see how empty this new situation left him. To quote Roberto Rossellini: ". . . in the silent cinema, montage had a precise meaning, because it represented language. From the silent cinema, we have inherited this myth of montage, though it has lost most of its meaning."

There was one ancient art form that lent itself perfectly to the silent cinema and that, of course, was pantomime (in all its forms, including slapstick). It didn't really matter how the filming was done so long as you could see the pantomime. *The Kid* is still running all over the world. It needs no words and has no "foreign versions." The pantomime artists of this period achieved a worldwide following that has probably never been equaled.

Ever since the invention of the "talking picture," it has been blithely assumed that films are an extension of the theater in that you cause a story to be acted out before an audience (the camera) under controlled conditions. Control is of the essence. The lines are written down and learned by the actors, the actions are rehearsed on carefully selected or constructed sets, and these rehearsals are repeated over and over again until the resulting scene conforms with the preconceived ideas of the director. What horror. . . . None of this activity has any life of its own. If anything, it has far less "spirit" than a production in a theater, because the tyranny of technique is far greater than in the theater. True, if you rented an empty theater nothing would happen of itself . . . no play would spontaneously take place . . . but, as a play is prepared, it does seem to take on some life of its own, partly because its form emerges during rehearsals. Whereas a film succumbs to the tyranny of Production Efficiency and is torn to fragments to make things more convenient for the camera. If two utterly unrelated scenes are to be made in the same locale, they will be made consecutively, even though they will end up at opposite ends of the picture and require completely different emotional responses from the actors.

In a recent interview with the late André Bazin, Jean Renoir complained: ". . . in the cinema at present, the camera has become a sort of God. You have a camera, fixed on its tripod or crane, which is just like a heathen altar; about it are the high priests—the director, cameraman, assistants who bring victims before the camera, like burnt offerings, and cast them in the flames, and the camera is there, immobile—or almost so—and, when it does move, it follows patterns ordained by the high priests, not by the victims." Both theater and the vast bulk of film-making as we know it are the result of control by these "high priests," and it is not surprising to note that many of our leading film directors divide their time between the theater and motion picture production.

Many of us have, like Renoir, become ". . . immensely bored by a great number of contemporary films." If we go back to the earliest days of cinema we find a recurrent notion that has never really been realized, a desire to utilize that aspect of film that is uniquely different from theater: to record aspects of what did actually happen in a real situation. Not what someone thought should or could have happened but what *did* happen in its most absolute sense. From the four examples I gave, *Nanook* comes closest to it, and it is for this reason that it will never be outdated. However, it too was limited by the lack of sound.

As far back as 1906, Leo Tolstoy noted: ". . . It is necessary that the cinema should represent Russian reality in its most varied manifestations. For this purpose Russian life ought to be reproduced as it is by the cinema; it is not necessary to go running after invented subjects."

Here is a proposal that has nothing to do with theater. Tolstoy envisioned the film-maker as an observer and, perhaps, as a participant capturing the essence of what takes place around him, selecting, arranging but never controlling the event. Here, it would be possible for the significance of what is taking place to transcend the conceptions of the film-maker, because, essentially, he is observing that ultimate mystery, the reality. Today, fifty years after Tolstoy's death, we have reached a point in the development of cinema where this proposal is beginning to be realized.

THE FIRST STATEMENT OF THE NEW AMERICAN CINEMA GROUP

No. 22–23, Summer, 1961

THE GROUP

On September 28th, 1960, a group of twenty-three independent film-makers, gathered by invitation of Lewis Allen, stage and film producer, and Jonas Mekas, met at 165 West 46th Street (Producers Theater) and, by unanimous vote, bound themselves into a free open organization of the new American cinema: The Group.

A temporary executive board was elected, consisting of Shirley Clarke, Emile de Antonio, Edward Bland, Jonas Mekas, and Lewis Allen.

The participants at the meeting of September 28th were:

Lionel Rogosin (*On the Bowery; Come Back, Africa*);
Peter Bogdanovich (*The Land of Opportunity*, in preparation);
Robert Frank (*Pull My Daisy; The Sin of Jesus*);
Alfred Leslie (*Pull My Daisy*);

Edouard de Laurot (*Sunday Junction; The Quarantine*, in preparation);

Ben Carruthers and Argus Speare Juilliard (actors in *Shadows* and *Guns of the Trees*; their first feature, *Sunday*, in preparation);

Jonas Mekas (*Guns of the Trees*);

Adolfas Mekas (*Hallelujah The Hills*, in preparation);

Emile de Antonio (film distributor);

Lewis Allen (producer, *The Connection*);

Shirley Clarke (*Skyscraper; Bullfight; The Connection*);

Gregory Markopoulos (*Psyche; Charmides; Lysis; Serenity*);

Daniel Talbot (manager, The New Yorker Theater);

Guy Thomajan (a feature in preparation);

Louis Brigante (*Hot Damn, Uncle Sam!*, in preparation);

Harold Humes (*Don Peyote*);

Sanders Brothers—absent—(*Time Out of War, Crime and Punishment, U.S.A.*);

Bert Stern (*Jazz on a Summer's Day*);

Don Gillin (film distributor and producer);

Walter Gutman (producer);

Jack Perlman (theatrical and film attorney);

David C. Stone (producer);

Sheldon Rochlin (a feature in preparation);

Edward Bland (*The Cry of Jazz; The Hero*, in preparation).

FIRST STATEMENT

In the course of the past three years we have been witnessing the spontaneous growth of a new generation of film-makers—the Free Cinema in England, the Nouvelle Vague in France, the young movements in Poland, Italy, and Russia, and, in this country, the work of Lionel Rogosin, John Cassavetes, Alfred Leslie, Robert Frank, Edward Bland, Bert Stern, and the Sanders brothers.

The official cinema all over the world is running out of breath. It is morally corrupt, aesthetically obsolete, thematically superficial, temperamentally boring. Even the seemingly worthwhile films, those that lay claim to high moral and aesthetic standards and have been accepted as such by critics and the public alike, reveal the decay of the Product Film. The very slickness of their execution has become a perversion covering the falsity of their themes, their lack of sensitivity, their lack of style.

If the New American Cinema has until now been an unconscious and sporadic manifestation, we feel the time has come to join together. There are many of us—the movement is reaching significant proportions—and we know what needs to be destroyed and what we stand for.

As in the other arts in America today—painting, poetry, sculpture, theater, where fresh winds have been blowing for the last few years—our rebellion against the old, official, corrupt, and pretentious is primarily an ethical one. We are concerned with Man. We are concerned with what is happening to Man. We are not an aesthetic school that constricts the film-maker within a set of dead principles. We feel we cannot trust any classical principles either in art or life.

1. We believe that cinema is indivisibly a personal expression. We, therefore, reject the interference of producers, distributors, and investors until our work is ready to be projected on the screen.

2. We reject censorship. We never signed any censorship laws. Neither do we accept such relics as film licensing. No book, play, or poem—no piece of music needs a license from anybody. We will take legal actions against licensing and censorship of films, including that of the U.S. Customs Bureau. Films have the right to travel from country to country free of censors and the bureaucrats' scissors. United States should take the lead in initiating the program of free passage of films from country to country.

Who are the censors? Who chooses them, and what are their qualifications? What's the legal basis for censorship? These are the questions that need answers.

3. We are seeking new forms of financing, working toward a reorganization of film investing methods, setting up the basis for a free film industry. A number of discriminating investors have already placed money in *Shadows, Pull My Daisy, The Sin of Jesus, Don Peyote, The Connection, Guns Of The Trees.* These investments have been made on a limited partnership basis as has been customary in the financing of Broadway plays. A number of theatrical investors have entered the field of low-budget film production on the East Coast.

4. The New American Cinema is abolishing the Budget Myth, proving that good, internationally marketable films can be made on a budget of $25,000 to $200,000. *Shadows, Pull My Daisy, The Little Fugitive* prove it. Our realistic budgets give us freedom from stars, studios, and producers. The film-maker is his own producer, and, paradoxically, low-budget films give a higher return margin than big-budget films.

The low budget is not a purely commercial consideration. It goes with our ethical and aesthetic beliefs, directly connected with the things we want to say, and the way we want to say them.

5. We'll take a stand against the present distribution-exhibition

policies. There is something decidedly wrong with the whole system of film exhibition; it is time to blow the whole thing up. It's not the audience that prevents films like *Shadows* or *Come Back, Africa* from being seen but the distributors and theater owners. It is a sad fact that our films first have to open in London, Paris, or Tokyo, before they can reach our own theatres.

6. We plan to establish our own cooperative distribution center. This task has been entrusted to Emile de Antonio, our charter member. The New Yorker Theater, the Bleecker Street Cinema, the Art Overbrook Theater (Philadelphia) are the first movie houses to join us by pledging to exhibit our films. Together with the cooperative distribution center, we will start a publicity campaign preparing the climate for the New Cinema in other cities. The American Federation of Film Societies will be of great assistance in this work.

7. It's about time the East Coast had its own film festival, one that would serve as a meeting place for the New Cinema from all over the world. The purely commercial distributors will never do justice to cinema. The best of the Italian, Polish, Japanese, and a great part of the modern French cinema is completely unknown in this country. Such a festival will bring these films to the attention of exhibitors and the public.

8. While we fully understand the purposes and interests of unions. we find it unjust that demands made on an independent work, budgeted at $25,000 (most of which is deferred) are the same as those made on a $1,000,000 movie. We shall meet with the unions to work out more reasonable methods, similar to those existing Off-Broadway—a system based on the size and the nature of the production.

9. We pledge to put aside a certain percentage of our film profits, so as to build up a fund that would be used to help our members finish films or stand as a guarantor for the laboratories.

In joining together, we want to make it clear that there is one basic difference between our group and organizations such as United Artists. We are not joining together to make money. We are joining together to make films. We are joining together to build the New American Cinema. And we are going to do it together with the rest of America, together with the rest of our generation. Common beliefs, common knowledge, common anger and impatience binds us together—and it also binds us together with the New Cinema movements of the rest of the world. Our colleagues in France, Italy, Russia, Poland, or England can depend on our determination. As they, we have had enough of the Big Lie in life and in the arts. As they, we are not only for the New Cinema: we are also for the New Man. As they, we are for art, but not at the expense of life. We don't want false, polished, slick films—we prefer them rough, unpolished, but alive; we don't want rosy films—we want them the color of blood.

TO MAYA DEREN

BY RUDOLF ARNHEIM

No. 24, Spring, 1962

There is a photograph of Maya Deren, so striking and so well known that some of us think of it when we think of her.* It is taken from a scene of her film *Meshes of the Afternoon* and shows a girl looking out through a window. Those who knew her recognize her, and yet the image is not really she. Her face is transformed into photographic matter— a transformation made possible by one of the two great miracles of photography. What are these two miracles?

Through one of them, the noisier and more spectacular of the two, objects become capable of imprinting their own authentic images upon the sensitive emulsion. It is owing to this miracle that even now, after her death, we can see the figure of Maya Deren recorded with the authenticity of a fingerprint and that, indeed, she can be present among us with an almost physical immediacy.

* See fifth page of photographic insert in this book.—PAS

This miracle of photography, however, is essentially materialistic. There is another, quieter, but more magical, one, which is that of the transformation of reality accomplished by the medium itself. While photographs earn gratitude by preserving corporeal appearance, we admire the new technique even more for its being able to dematerialize the familiar face of the girl into a precise shape of transparent whiteness. We see her dark hair disappear in the reflections of the trees on the window pane. That window pane itself is not present. It is made visible by the girl's raised hands pressing lightly against it, against something that is not there. This transformation is the true miracle of the photographic image; and Maya Deren was one of its most delicate magicians.

Of crude magicians, we have had many. Some call themselves surrealists, although, instead of going beyond reality, they merely add a few tricks to it. They take hold of the top hat and the rabbit, and a combination of top hat and rabbit is all the magic they have to offer. Others—the expressionist kind of miracle worker—have invaded our prosaic space with wild make-up and crooked scenery. Maya Deren had little patience with either technique. She insisted that the true magic of the photograph in motion is more than a reshuffling of raw material, more than a masquerade. And she, who could be energetic to the point of violence when she fought for her ideas, had the sensitive fingers and eyes of a surgeon, when it came to shaping her photographic visions without hurting the tissues of the physical surface.

What does she show us? What was she after? She was one of the artists and thinkers who speak of the great paradox of our time; who say that, although our civilization has come closest to penetrating the secrets of inorganic and organic matter, we are less familiar with the world of tangible things than any human tribe has ever been. And, thus, in Maya Deren's films, the familiar world captures us by its pervasive strangeness. The white hands press against a window pane that is not there. The human body drifts through weightless space. Geographic distances give way to new visible connections. There is no practical plot to these films. When two faces look at each other, two minds call on each other. When an actor or dancer walks across the screen, he travels the path of his life's journey. The staircase turns in symbolic space, and a seated woman winds the thread of a hank of wool fatefully.

Do these pictures show us more than the alienation of the familiar? Are they simply the ghosts of a world that has died on us? I would not undertake to make the happenings in these films explicit through words. Nor do I believe that they were verbally explicit in Maya's own thoughts, articulate though she was. What we can assert is that the sequences of her images are logical. They are neither arbitrary nor absurd. They follow the letter of a law we never studied on paper; but, guided by our eyes, our minds conform willingly.

Maya Deren was always interested in ritual. She went to Haiti in search of the remnants of a culture in which the symbolism of the human gesture and of the space in which the body moves was still standardized by what psychologists call "consensual validation." We, in the New York of the twentieth century, no longer profit from that sort of consensus. Our common standards are reduced to the practical. But we are still accessible to a picture language that, half-shrouded in personal meanings, half-revealed by common sensation, can call upon us, distant though the caller may be.

NOTES ON THE NEW AMERICAN CINEMA

BY JONAS MEKAS

No. 24, Spring, 1962

Ever since the article on the Cinema of the New Generation appeared in these pages two years ago (No. 21), there has been continuous discussion on the subject of the new American cinema. Fresh material for this discussion was provided by the Spoleto Film Exposition, Summer, 1961, which was devoted exclusively to the American independent film-makers and was the most representative program of their work assembled for public scrutiny until now.

Since there has been much misunderstanding concerning this new cinema, it is timely to present a fuller and firsthand investigation of the ideas, styles and achievements of this new cinema; to inquire into the motivations behind it; to attempt to describe what the new artist feels, how his mind works, why he creates the way he does; why he chooses his particular style to express the physical and psychological realities of his life.

I shall try to understand the new artist instead of telling him what to do. I will leave it for the critics to erect abstract theories and judge the work of the new artist from behind the stools of Culture. I don't want any part of the Big Art game. The new cinema, like the new man, is nothing definitive, nothing final. It is a living thing. It is imperfect; it errs. Nevertheless, it is the artist, with all his imperfections, who is the antenna (e. pound) of his race, not the critic. All a critic can do is to try and understand the artist, interpret him, explain the state of society through the works of its artists—and not vice versa. This is where our critics fail unanimously.

"Painting—any kind of painting, any style of painting—to be painting at all, in fact—is a way of living today, a style of living, so to speak."

—WILLEM DE KOONING

"A poet is the combined product of such internal powers as modify the nature of others; and of such external influences as excite and sustain these powers; his is not one, but both. Every man's mind is, in this respect, modified by all the objects which he ever admitted to act upon his consciousness; it is the mirror upon which all forms are reflected, and in which they compose one form. Poets, not otherwise than philosophers, painters, sculptors, and musicians, are, in one sense, the creators, and in another, the creations, of their age. From this subjection the loftiest do not escape."

—PERCY BYSSHE SHELLEY, Preface to
Prometheus Unbound

PART ONE

Helen Levitt, James Agee, Sidney Meyers. From the Studios into the Streets.

In the Street (shot in 1948, edited in 1951), by Helen Levitt, Janice Loeb, and James Agee, a documentary shot in the streets of New York, and *The Quiet One* (1949), by Sidney Meyers, a story about a lonely, psychologically disturbed Negro boy, are two films that can be considered the forerunners of the low-budget independent film and the beginnings of a new film style, something that has been often called the New York film school.

Both films dealt with realistic subject matter, both used non-actors; both were shot on actual location, often with concealed cameras. And they both had a spontaneity of action and camera that was very different from their documentary predecessors (Willard Van Dyke, Paul Strand, Pare Lorentz) and the experimental films made at about the same time in New York and San Francisco. Whereas the experimentalists such as Maya Deren, Willard Maas, Hans Richter, and Sidney Peterson were concerned with the exploration of the subconscious, with the development of a universal, abstracted film poetry, free from time and place, this other group of film-makers were interested in exploring their world in a more prosaic and realistic manner, right here and now.

It is a mistake for the critics to treat these film-makers as a conscious anti-Hollywood movement. Like the experimentalists, these "stream-of-life" film-makers did not band together to fight Hollywood. These were single individuals who were quietly trying to express their own cinematic truth, to make their own kind of cinema. Needless to say, on aesthetic grounds, they were dissatisfied with the Hollywood style and its themes. In their own films, they wanted to break away from the closed circle of "cinema as a profession," they wanted to make films in a more personal manner. They were not exactly clear how to go about it. However, one thing was clear: They had to move out, no matter where, and learn from actual experience. The low budgets, the small crews, and the visual and technical roughness imposed by the new and unpredictable shooting circumstances, served as an impetus in freeing their work from the conventional, overused visual and dramatic forms, and also forced them to search for new angles, and in a new light.

Stylistically and thematically, *In the Street* and *The Quiet One* seemed to indicate the proper direction for the new experiments. They perfectly complied with the proposition of James Agee, the man who contributed much to the formulation of an aesthetic basis for the New York film school:

"The films I most eagerly look forward to will not be documentaries but works of fiction, played against and into and in collaboration with unrehearsed and uninvented reality."

Morris Engel. The Low-Budget Feature.

In *The Little Fugitive* (1953), a story about a little boy's adventures in Coney Island, Morris Engel pushed the low-budget techniques further into the dramatic film. With sure skill, he used the New York background to convey the humor and the poetry of everyday life. He made a low-budget film that was suitable for a large commercial market and, thus, once and for all, destroyed the

$1,000,000 production-cost myth. Shot on a $50,000 budget—in Hollywood it would have cost ten times more—this film, more than any other, contributed to the growth of low-budget independent feature production in America.

In *Lovers and Lillipops* (1955) and *Weddings and Babies* (1958), Morris Engel expanded his experiments to the camera and sound track. He improved and used with great success the portable camera and the new synchronous sound recording units. Ricky Leacock, himself an explorer of new camera techniques, said: "Morris Engel's camera was almost totally uninhibited by the usual complications of changing position. It was able to go anywhere with a minimum of preparation and delay. I had the feeling that the camera was able to catch subtleties in the acting that are usually lost under normal conditions of shooting. *Weddings and Babies* is the first theatrical motion picture to make use of a fully mobile, synchronous sound-and-picture system. It should be of enormous interest to film-makers, because it is precisely in this area that the greatest undeveloped potential of the film is to be found."

Morris Engel also experimented with a plotless, episodic story construction. His films were freer from imposed dramas than those of other film-makers of the time. Engel concentrated on recognizable, everyday incidents and situations, on basic character relationships, relying much on improvisation, contributing to the destruction of the literary and theatrical conventions in cinema. The importance of Morris Engel films will grow with time—his films being irreplaceable documents of midcentury America. The faithfulness of their detail, the purity of their style, and the objectivity of the camera work sets them apart from other entertainment films of the period.

Lionel Rogosin. Social Engagement.

With *On the Bowery* (1956) and *Come Back, Africa* (1958), Lionel Rogosin brought to the independent cinema a strong note of social consciousness. The first film was a plea for Manhattan's skid-row; the second film, in Rogosin's own words, "is concerned essentially with human conditions as they exist in the Union of South Africa under the ruthless policy of the present regime. Art may be indefinable," he continues, "but for me it is important to do something significant. The form must grow from the subject matter and from our times. The artist must be engaged in his times in the strongest way possible."

Formally, one of Rogosin's contributions to the new cinema was an effective dramatization of reality, the use of real-life scenes in an organized, planned drama. This blending of the documentary with the dramatic enabled him to record the truth of the situation through the lips of the people who actually live in that situation themselves, and to create a drama that was effective on its own terms.

Lionel Rogosin writes about his method:

> To capture reality spontaneously and to give it life, more is involved of course than simply casting people of the milieu. They must be allowed to be themselves, to express themselves in their own manner but in accordance with the abstractions and themes which you as the director must be able to see in them. This is something quite different from traditional script writing, in which the ideas and abstractions are essentially the writer's, with professional actors portraying those ideas and abstractions through their personality. The final product of such films is far removed from the reality of the society portrayed, although it may be highly satisfactory as a drama of symbolic ideas in which plot, dialogue, and actors are primarily devices for describing the writer's ideas and themes. But for expressing the inner life of people in a particular milieu, I believe the method I followed in my films is a deeper and truer one.

Cassavetes. The Improvisation.

Shadows (1958), a workshop project coordinated by John Cassavetes, carried the improvisation techniques in a fictional dramatic film to new heights.

The content sought by Cassavetes and his actors was no longer the surface realism alone, which was well explored by Morris Engel and the neorealists. For the new cinema, *Shadows* represented a turn inwards—a focusing upon psychological realities. The little bits of plot were used only as loose frameworks to explore and exhibit the actors' own emotions, attitudes, remembrances, reactions. Hence, a correct comparison of *Shadows* to Chekhov's writings. The actors and the director improvised as they went along, searching into their own experiences, listening, without forcing, without dramatizing. It is this immediacy of the dramaless, beginningless, and endless episode which is the most important aspect of *Shadows*. The true value of the "immediacy" being not its realism, but its cinematic properties. The film's rhythm, its temperament is not that of the ideas in it, but, primarily, that of the people in it, their faces, their movements, their tone of voice, their stammerings, their pauses— their psychological reality as revealed through the most insignificant daily incidents and situations.

Without knowing it, Cassavetes and his actors created a work that moved freely in what Siegfried Kracauer has called "camera reality"—a film free from literary and theatrical ideas. And it is precisely this "undramatic," "unintelligent," "amoeba-like" camera reality that provokes the most criticism from the old school of critics. One could, in fact, write a long discourse called "In Defense of Stupidity in Cinema," or "The Wisdom of the Camera Reality," or "The Difference Between Literary- and Camera-Intelligence."

Sidney Meyers. The Naked Camera Eye.

The Savage Eye (1959), by Sidney Meyers, Ben Maddow and Joseph Strick, concentrated mainly on camera-eye techniques. Their camera, like that of Dziga-Vertov's thirty years ago in Russia, watched and recorded contemporary American life. There was one essential difference, however, between Dziga-Vertov and Sidney Meyers. Vertov photographed the typical aspects of Soviet life, attempting to reveal the sensations of the usual, ordinary events of the day, whereas Meyers chose the atypical, the sensational, the exceptional. Sidney Meyers's camera eye is cynical, cold. He laughs at the tragic and the sad with the same detachment that he laughs at the evil, corrupt.

Despite this, The Savage Eye remains a tour-de-force lesson in camera-eye techniques. It was this camera-eye technique, but with a more subjective, personal attitude on the part of the film-maker, that was developed to perfection by Ricky Leacock during the last few years, revolutionizing much of the independent film-making in America.

Ricky Leacock. New Documentary Frontiers. Revolution of the Camera.

Cuba Sí, Yankee No (1960), Primary (1960), Eddie (1960), by Ricky Leacock, assisted by the brothers Al and David Maysles and Don Pennebaker, demonstrated anew the immense capabilities of the camera to record life, its poetry and its prose—a fact often forgotten since Lumière took his first street shots.

The experiences of Morris Engel with the portable synchronous sound camera, contributed much to this new development. During the past two years, this equipment is being constantly perfected and the experiments have been continuing. These experiments enabled Leacock to reduce the shooting team to one man—the film-maker himself is now the director, cameraman, and, often, sound man, all in one. The film-maker now can go everywhere, watch the scene unobtrusively and record the drama or the beauty of what he sees, all in perfect sync and color.

Today, there is a bustle of young film-makers everywhere in

America, working on low-budget, independent productions, like never before. There is a feeling in the air that cinema is only beginning, that now cinema is available not only to those who possess a high organizational and group-work talent, but also to those poets who are more sensitive, but often uncommunal, who prefer privacy, whose powers of observation and imagination are most active in privacy. An entire area of subject matter, untouched by cinema, is opening before the film-maker—an area into which he can delve and come up with a new and deeper contribution to the sum total of human experience.

The attitude and the working methods of the new documentary film-makers are best described by Ricky Leacock himself:

> Tolstoy envisioned the film-maker as an observer and perhaps as a participant capturing the essence of what takes place around him, selecting, arranging but never controlling the event. Here it would be possible for the significance of what is taking place to transcend the conceptions of the film-maker because essentially he is observing that ultimate mystery, the reality. Many film-makers feel that the aim of the film-maker is to have complete control. Then the conception of what happens is limited to the conception of the film-maker. We don't want to put this limit on actuality. What's happening, the action, has no limitations, neither does the significance of what's happening. The film-maker's problem is more a problem of how to convey it. How to convey the feeling of being there.

Leacock's Camera and the Dramatic Feature

During the last few months, Leacock has turned his interest toward the dramatic feature. We'll soon be able to see the first results. In his first feature length documentary, *Eddie* (it is also known under the title *On the Pole*), Leacock has already demonstrated the virtues of his approach. *Eddie* is not the usual type documentary. It is a documentary drama. We follow the protagonist, we live with him, we get to know him, we identify with him. But we know all the time that he is not acting his life for the camera (as did the shepherds for Vittorio de Seta in *Banditi a Orgosolo*) —the camera is only a stranger, catching, unobtrusively, glimpses from his life. Using this same technique—leaving the camera completely alone, an independent observer—the acted film drama may gain a new and much-needed freedom, a freedom toward which cinema is desperately reaching, as exemplified through such films as *Breathless*, *Chronique d'un Été*, and *Shadows*. The creative function of the cameraman will play a much greater role in this new type of film-making. As a matter of fact, the director will have to become his own cameraman. It is not at all surprising, therefore, that the Nouvelle Vague directors, more author-conscious than Hollywood, have been the first ones to invade Leacock's 43rd Street studio to get acquainted with the new techniques. Leacock's studio suddenly has become a sort of crossroad of the world for the new cinema.

Meanwhile, on their own, below 43rd Street, the students of Ricky Leacock are pushing documentary film-making into various unexplored directions.

Dan Drasin. Burton Brothers.

In *Sunday* (1951), Dan Drasin's uninhibited camera, zooming in and out and around the action, caught the clash between the folk-singers and the police in New York with an immediacy and aliveness seldom seen in the documentary film or television. Drasin was greatly assisted by his ignorance of certain professional techniques which would have hampered his freedom. He came to cinema completely free of professional inhibitions. He moved with his zoom freely, against all textbook rules, not afraid of shaky movements or garbled sounds. The shooting circumstances didn't even permit much time for perfectionism. He lost the slickness but he gained the truth, both in sound and image.

AFTER SEEING *SUNDAY*

THE FINAL DEFENSE OF THE AMERICAN IS HIS INTEGRITY, HIS HUMANITY, ITS FLOWERING IS IN HIS CONSCIOUS WILLINGNESS TO DEFEND BOTH, FREE AS MAN & ARTIST.

THIS FILM IS THE CLEAREST ILLUMINATION OF THE BASIC AMERICAN CONFLICT, THE CLASH BETWEEN UNFEELING, BRUTAL, SELF-RIGHTEOUS AUTHORITY & THE MOST HUMAN, UNIVERSAL AMERICAN ASPIRATIONS, THE ULTIMATE LIBERATION OF THE AMERICAN SOUL.

THE FOLKSINGERS ARE AMERICA, THE ARTISTS ARE AMERICA, AMERICA IS PEOPLE, NOTHING MORE OR LESS.

GOD BLESS THE PEOPLE SINGING, SPEAKING, WALKING, TALKING, SCREAMING, HURTING WITHIN THIS FILM, FREE!

GOD BLESS THE PEOPLE WHO MADE THIS FILM, THE ARTIST UNSEEN, AMERICA WILL TAKE CARE OF THE OTHERS.

BOB KAUFMAN

However, like Cassavetes before him, Drasin seems not to be aware of the true meaning of his own achievement. He is not consciously aware of the true success and the meaning of his film. "As the event fades into the past, I reflect more and more on what a piece of cinema *Sunday* might have been had I, as editor, been less impregnated with the reality of the *event*, and more concerned with the *idea* and the *cinematic* reality. I will probably never make another film like *Sunday*," writes Drasin in a postscript to the film, not realizing, that this "*idea* and the *cinematic* reality" would have thrown his film back into the literary. The true *cinematic* reality and *idea* was caught in *Sunday* precisely because of his impregnation with the reality of the event. Without it, the film wouldn't exist. Drasin, the artist "unseen" (b. kaufman) was right.

Michael Burton and Philip Burton followed the same direction in their documentary on the Un-American Activities Committee, *Wasn't That a Time?* (1961). Their approach to the new style and the new techniques, however, was a more conscious act. The theme of their film called for the elimination of the formal documentary approach. The sense of informality achieved in *Wasn't That a Time?* was neither an accident nor an abstract game in the new style—it was chosen consciously. The free informality of the film was posed against the abstract formality of the government machine. The camera showed us the casual, insignificant moments in the lives of the three protagonists, stressing the everyday, the informal against the official and the formal. The tears rolling down the face of Barbara Sherwood are the first real tears cinema has seen—tears which make the staged film drama look insignificant, pretentious, small.

What is most admirable in the work of Leacock, Maysles, Drasin, and Burton is their complete freedom of movement. One could say that only now is the camera becoming conscious of its steps. Until now, the camera could move only in a robot-like fashion, on pre-planned tracks, and along indicated lines. Now it is beginning to move freely, by itself according to its own desires and whims, tracing its own steps. Cinema is groping, cinema is going through its own Actors' Studio period—mumbling, stammering, searching.

Robert Frank. Alfred Leslie. Further Explorations of Improvisation.

Turning from the documentary to the fiction film—*Pull My Daisy* (1959), by Robert Frank and Alfred Leslie, a spoof on the beat generation, a nonsense comedy, blended most perfectly the elements of improvisation and conscious planning, both in camera work and directing. The plotless episode has never been more eloquent than it is in this film. That feeling of "being there," of which Leacock speaks in connection with the documentary, was achieved in this fictional film to the highest degree. Its authenticity is so effective, its style so perfect, that the film has fooled even some very intelligent critics: They speak about it as if it were a slice-of-life film, a piece cut out from the raw stream of life, a documentary. Instead of criticizing the film, they criticize the beat generation. The film's amazing sense of style and form escapes through their fingers like a fluid—it is almost invisible, transparent. No other film ever said so much, and in such a pure and condensed manner, about the man of the beat generation.

In *The Sin of Jesus* (1961), Robert Frank continues his documentation of the soul of modern man. Formally, the film is an attempt to merge the best of the old with the best of the new cinema. It can be much criticized on these grounds. Despite its formal faults, the presence of the director is unmistakable.

"If your aim is high, it should be you that comes through the most," says Robert Frank. The self-expression of an artist, however, is a universal act, it expresses a universal content. This is what the modern artist is doing in his "useless," "shapeless," "meaningless" work. The lonely woman's desperate and recriminatory cry in the dark, doomed, and desolate fields of New Jersey expresses the despair of our own existence—or, should I say, the American existence Anno, 1961. One could say, perhaps, even more: that this pessimism, this desolation, or doom, or despair revealed in *The Sin of Jesus* is the inner landscape of the twentieth-century man, a place that is cold, cruel, heartless, stupid, lonely, desolate—this landscape emerges from Robert Frank's film with a crying, terrifying nakedness. Robert Frank is here as much a documentarist as Robert Flaherty was in *Nanook*.

Shirley Clarke. The Connection.

It is a similar spiritual landscape that Shirley Clarke is painting in her first feature, *The Connection* (1961). Again, one could criticize the film on formal grounds, its use of Pirandelloisms, which are more suitable for the stage than the screen. However, such criticism can not minimize the importance of this film as an attempt to put across on the commercial screen the new content, the new reality. The play has been molded into a strong cinematic unity with a single-mindedness of style that makes it merit an important place in the annals of independent cinema. Whether you take it as a piece of "magic realism," the American version of *Waiting for*

Godot, or just a simple parable about a group of junkies waiting for a fix—the film remains a unique achievement.

Guns of the Trees. Elimination of the Plot. Film as an Emotional Statement.

In my one film, *Guns of the Trees* (1961), I attempted to break away from the last remnants of the traditional manner of story telling, using single, disconnected scenes as parts of an accumulative emotional fresco—like an action painter uses his splashes of paint. The film departs from realism and attempts to reach into the poetic. At a certain point, if one wants to reach down into deeper truths, if one wants to speak indirectly, one has to abandon realism and enter the regions of poetry.

The new content asks for a new mode of artistic expression. The artist is beginning to express his anxiety and discontent in a more open and direct manner. He is searching for a freer form, one that allows him a larger scale of emotional and intellectual statements, explosions of truths, outcries of warnings, accumulations of images— not to carry out an amusing story but to express fully the tremblings of man's unconscious and to confront us, eye to eye, with the soul of modern man. The new artist is not interested in entertaining the viewer: He is making personal statements about the world today.

Vanderbeek. Preston. Social-Political Satire. Protest Films.

In this context, I should mention the work of Stanley Vanderbeek and Richard Preston, two foremost satirists of the new cinema. During the last three years, they have produced a number of short films that, in a free, plotless manner, sharply comment on various aspects of contemporary American life. Nothing is spared—the arts, the sciences, the press, television, housewives, presidents, sex. Both use collage and assemblage techniques; both are ingenious manipulators of everyday imagery; both are perfect masters of their medium. Unlike the surrealists of the 1920's, who expressed their dissatisfaction in personal, often indecipherable imagery, these satirists use the everyday objects and textures of modern America as their vocabulary. They are not entertainers; nor are they story tellers. They are, rather, modern clowns who splash their discontent and their irony into the face of the public. Their style, like that of other modern artists, is a result of an exploded emotion, an act that couldn't be kept back any longer.

Says Preston:

I have been in the pillory for years, but now, with the aid of film, I have managed to wriggle one arm free. With this good arm, I can catch and hurl back some of the garbage that has been thrown at me. And, by garbage, I mean the lies, the distortions, the hypocrisies that are the manipulators' weapons. In short, through film, I have discovered power. The will to have power is good only when it is directed to power over things . . . steel, stone, paints, film. It is evil when it is directed to the control and manipulation of other men.

And says Stanley Vanderbeek:

The purpose of "poetic-political" satire in my films is to attack some of the aspects of the superreality that has been so hastily, carelessly built around us. It seems desperate and peculiar that, today, we have so few comic and comic-tragic spokesmen to jibe at the massive, involuntary joke of living in a monolithic society and statistical age. If my films have a social ambition, it is to help disarm the social fuse of people living with anxiety, to point out the insidious folly of competitive suicide (by way of rockets). I am trying to evolve a "literagraphic" image, an international sign-language of fantasy and satire. There is a social literature through filmic pantomime, that is, nonverbal comedy-satire: a "comic-ominous" image that pertains to our time and interests that Hollywood and the commercial film are ignoring.

In this respect, a significant development is the increasing number of *protest* documentary films. To mention some of the most significant:

Edward Bland's *Cry of Jazz* (1958), a thesis film about the position of the Negro in America today;

John Korty's *Language of Faces* (1961), an antiwar film, based on the peace vigil in front of the White House;

Polaris Action (1962), a group project, edited by Hilary Harris— an antiwar film;

The already mentioned Dan Drasin's *Sunday* and the Burton brothers' *Wasn't That a Time*—two films on freedom of speech.

Notwithstanding the statements of some foreign and local critics who reproach the independent film-maker for what they call his escapism, the American cinema has never been so deeply grounded in reality, reacting to it, expressing it, and commenting upon it. All film-makers discussed in this survey take their content and their form from the most direct stream of modern life.

Brakhage. Breer. Menken. The Pure Poets of Cinema.

Robert Breer, Stanley Brakhage, and Marie Menken, thematically and formally represent, in the new American cinema, the best of the tradition of experimental and poetic cinema. Freely, beautifully, they sing the physical world, its textures, its colors, its movements; or they speak in little bursts of memories, reflections, meditations.

Unlike the early avant-garde films, these films are not burdened by Greek or Freudian mythology and symbolism; their meaning is more immediate, more visual and suggestive. Stylistically and formally, their work represents the highest and purest creation achieved in the poetic cinema.

It was a short film by Stanley Brakhage, *Desistfilm* (1954)—still one of the most influential of all modern American films—that started the stylistic revolution that has now reached the documentary and is beginning to be noticeable in the commercial dramatic film. (Truffaut kicks and shakes his camera in *Jules et Jim* to destroy static, "professional" smooth pans and tilts.) Very few other film-makers have been as preoccupied with style and techniques as has been Brakhage. Ironically enough, it is Brakhage who is usually picked up by the old school critics when they need an example of bad style and bad techniques. They couldn't have chosen a more fallacious example, for Brakhage is truly one of the virtuosos of modern cinema.

Some of Brakhage's attitudes toward film style and techniques can best be illustrated through his own writings:

> So the money vendors have begun it again. To the catacombs then, or, rather, plant this seed deeper in the underground beyond false nourishing of sewage waters. Let it draw nourishment from hidden, uprising springs channeled by gods . . . Forget ideology, for film unborn as it is has no language and speaks like an aborigine— monotonous rhetoric . . . Abandon aesthetics . . . Negate techniques, for film, like America, has not been discovered yet, and mechaniza-tion, in the deepest possible sense of the word, traps both beyond measuring even chances . . . Let film be. It is something . . . becoming.
>   . . . somewhere, we have an eye capable of any imagining. And then we have the camera eye, its lenses ground to achieve nineteenth-cen-tury Western compositional perspective (as best exemplified by the nineteenth-century architectural conglomeration of details of the "classic" ruin) in bending the light and limiting the frame of the image just so, its standard camera and projector speed for recording movement geared to the feeling of the ideal slow Viennese waltz, and even its tripod head, being the neck it swings on, balled with bearings to permit it that *Les Sylphides* motion (ideal to the con-templative romance) and virtually restricted to horizontal and vertical movements (pillars and horizon lines) a diagonal requiring a major adjustment, its lenses coated or provided with filters, its light meters balanced, and its color film manufactured to produce that picture postcard effect (salon painting) exemplified by those, oh, so blue skies and peachy skins.
>   By deliberately spitting on the lens or wrecking its focal intention,

one can achieve the early stages of impressionism. One can make this prima donna heavy in performance of image movement by speeding up the motor, or one can break up movement, in a way that approaches a more direct inspiration of contemporary human eye perceptibility of movement, by slowing the motion while recording the image. One may hand hold the camera and inherit worlds of space. One may over- or under-expose the film. One may use the filters of the world, fog, downpours, unbalanced lights, neons with neurotic color temperatures, glass that was never designed for a camera, or even glass that was, but that can be used against specifications, or one may photograph an hour after sunrise or an hour before sunset, those marvelous taboo hours when the film labs will guarantee nothing, or one may go into the night with a specific daylight film or vice versa. One may become vice versa, the supreme trickster, with hatfuls of all the rabbits listed above breeding madly. One may, out of incredible courage, become Méliès, that marvelous man who gave even the "art of film" its beginning in magic.

In his latest film, *Prelude* (1961), Brakhage achieves a synthesis of all his techniques. In this film of exquisite beauty, the images become like words; they come back, in little bursts, and disappear, and come back again, as though in sentences, creating visual and mental impressions, experiences. Within the abstract context, the flashes of memories of a more personal and temporal nature appear, always in a hinting, oblique, indirect manner—the images of foreboding clouds, memories of the atom bomb, endless cosmic spaces, dreams and fears that constitute the subconscious of modern man. If the contemporaneity of the other film-makers discussed here is very real, emotional, raw, and still a part of our daily experience—in *Prelude* (as in the work of Robert Breer and Marie Menken), this contemporaneity is abstracted, filtered, it becomes a thought, a meditation occurring in a world of its own, in the world of a work of art.

Brakhage, from a letter to a friend (1958), before beginning his work on *Prelude:*

I am now considering a second feature-length film, which will dwell cinematically upon the atomic bomb. But, as *Anticipation of the Night* is a work of art rather than an indictment of contemporary civilization in terms of the child, so too my prospective film will dream upon the bomb, create it out of, as I envision it, an almost Spinozian world of mathematical theory, visualize the flowering of its form in relation to the beautiful growths as well as to those more intellectually parasitic, and, in the wake of its smoke, deal with the devastation it leaves in the human mind, rather than material devastation, the nightmare and also the "devoutly to be wished" that it engenders, ergo, religion—the end, the resolve with death.

There are only one or two other film-makers working today who can transform reality into art as successfully as Brakhage, Breer, and Menken. A landscape, a face, a blotch of light—everything changes under their eyes to become something else, an essence of itself, at the service of their personal vision. To watch, in Brakhage's *Whiteye*, a winter landscape transform itself, through the magic of motion, temperament, and light, into pure poetry of white, is an unforgettable experience.

Ron Rice. Vernon Zimmerman. The Poetry of the Absurd.

The *Flower Thief* (1960), by Ron Rice, and *Lemon Hearts* (1961), by Vernon Zimmerman, are two of the latest and most successful examples of post-*Pull My Daisy* cinema. Both are made with the utmost creative freedom, with the utmost disrespect for the "professional" camera, plot, character conventions. They merge and combine the spontaneous cinema of *Pull My Daisy*, the freedom of the image of Brakhage, the "uncleanliness" of action painting, the theater of Happenings (Kaprow) and the sense of humor of Zen. Their imagination, coming from deeply "deranged" and liberated senses, is boundless. Nothing is forced in these films. They rediscover the poetry and wisdom of the irrational, of nonsense, of the absurd—the poetry that comes from regions that are beyond all intelligence, the regions of *Zéro de Conduite*, of *Fireworks*, of *Desistfilm*.

Nevertheless, the materials with which they create are embedded in reality. Didn't Rimbaud write his *Illuminations* out of the burning, intensified reality of his own life? Such are the lives of the modern film poets. With their own lives, they create a "cinema reality" that is tense to the point of explosion. In a sense, they don't have to "invent"; they just have to turn the camera upon themselves, or upon their close friends, and it explodes into the pyrotechnics upon which no imagination could improve.

Ode to the Eye

About that time it was decided by the Gods that reality was more important than creation. The reality of anything moves the spirit more than artificial attempts to create motion where there is static.

A drunkard struggling in the alley to remove the cap from the wine bottle strikes the emotions with more force and meaning than any logical sequence of staged events that don't have the fibre of life.

Any scene, no matter what, can evoke more of man to believe and feel than a parallelism which contains logic without reality.

It is better to film anything that is living and real than to film ideas of what should, or might be, real.

Ron Rice

The Others

The few films discussed here indicate the main tendencies of the so-called new American cinema. There are other films which, in one way or another, also have contributed to the growth of the new cinema, and they should be mentioned in any survey of this kind: George Stoney's *All My Babies* (circa 1953); Bert Stern's *Jazz on a Summer's Day* (1959); Jerome Hill's *The Sand Castle* (1960); Peter Kass's *Time of the Heathen* (1961); Gregory Markopoulos's unfinished film *Serenity* (1961); Ricky Carrier's *Strangers in the City* (1961); Irving Kershner's *Stakeout on Dope Street* (circa 1958); Stanley Kubrick's *Fear and Desire* (circa 1953); Denis and Terry Sanders's *Time out of War* and *Crime and Punishment, U.S.A.* (1959); John Frankenheimer's *The Young Strangers;* Tom Laughlin's *The Proper Time* (1960); Curtis Harrington's *Night Tide* (1961); Alexander Singer's *A Cold Wind in August* (1961); Leslie Stevens's *Private Property* (1960); Allen Baron's *Blast of Silence* (1961)—and a few others. Some of these constitute what might be called the "experimental" or "fringe" Hollywood; others are works of young new directors who are trying to find themselves. One could find much unfulfilled exciting promise among these films. I should also mention the experimental film-makers, such as Charles Boultenhouse, Gregory Markopoulos, Carmen D'Avino, Hilary Harris, whose work I did not have space enough to discuss but whose contribution to the independent cinema is of great importance.

The independent film-maker is now at a stage where he feels himself entirely free from the bonds of Hollywood; only now he is becoming truly independent and only now can he say the whole truth and nothing but the truth, be it his personal truth or a social, communal truth—he can say it as freely as the poet with his typewriter. The first phase of the independent cinema is coming to an end, and one can state firmly that it has liberated the film-maker, it has given him self-confidence, and, at the same time, it has created a series of films that are both documents of man's spirit and works of art—films that can serve as an inspiration and a reminder of standards.

PART TWO: A FEW STATEMENTS ON THE NEW AMERICAN ARTIST AS A MAN

Like the new poet, the new film-maker is not interested in public acceptance. The new artist knows that most of what's publicly said today is corrupt and distorted. He knows that the truth is somewhere else, not in *The New York Times* and not in *Pravda*. He feels that he must do something about it, for his own conscience, that he must rebel against the tightening web of lies.

Some writers from home and abroad have accused the new artist of nihilism and anarchy. The American artist could sing happily and carelessly, with no despair in his voice—but then he would reflect neither his society nor himself, he would be a liar like everybody else. With man's soul being squeezed out in all the four corners of the world today, when governments are encroaching upon his personal being with the huge machinery of bureaucracy, war, and mass communications, he feels that the only way to preserve man is to encourage his sense of rebellion, his sense of disobedience, even at the cost of open anarchy and nihilism. The entire landscape of human thought, as it is accepted publicly in the Western world, has to be turned over. All public ideologies, values, and ways of life must be doubted, attacked. "Smell it and get high, maybe we'll all get the answer that way! Don't give up the ship!" exclaims Allen Ginsberg. Yes, the artist is getting high on the death of his civilization, breathing in its poisonous gases. And yes, our art definitely suffers from it. Our art is "confused" and all that jazz, jazz, jazz (taylor mead). But we refuse to continue the Big Lie of Culture. To the new artist the fate of man is more important than the fate of art, more important than the temporary confusions of art. You criticize our work from a purist, formalistic, and classicist point of view. But we say to you: What's the use of cinema if man's soul goes rotten?

Stan Brakhage:

> *It seems to me that the entire society of man is bent on destroying that which is alive within its individuals (most contemporarily exemplified by the artist), so that presumably the society can run on and on like the machine it is, at the expense of the humans composing it. I have felt this both personally and in objectively watching the lives of others alive in their struggles, and most particularly in observing the death of the average human being insisted upon by the society at the time of that human being's adolescence.*

Dick Preston:

> *Artists, poets, film-makers: It is you who are the last inheritors of the world's conscience, the visionaries and prophets of the twentieth century. The voices of our "leaders" are as sound tracks in reverse. The parliaments and the churches of men preach dissension and confusion.*

PART THREE: SUMMING UP. CONNECTING THE STYLE WITH THE MAN.

Thus, we can say, that the new independent cinema movement—like the other arts in America today—is primarily an existential movement, or, if you want, an ethical movement, a human act; it is only secondarily an aesthetic one. But then one could say that all art in all times has been, primarily, an existential act. Even when our films seem to be utterly detached from reality, like the works of Robert Breer, or Brakhage—they come from a dissatisfaction with the static, outdated concepts of life and art. One could say that there is a *morality in the new*.

A Side Note on the Morality of the New.

One may wonder, sometimes, why I am so obsessed with the new, why this hatred for the old.

I believe that true wisdom and knowledge are very old; but this wisdom and this knowledge have been covered with layers and layers of static culture.

If we know anything about man, it is this: He must be allowed to fulfill his own life, to live his life as fully as possible. The cul-de-sac of western culture is stifling the spiritual life of man. His "culture" is misleading his thoughts and his intuitions. My position is this: Everything that keeps man in the molds of Western culture prevents him from living his own life. Surely, one of the functions of the artist is to listen to the true voice of man.

The new artist, by directing his ear inward, is beginning to catch bits of man's true vision. By simply being *new* (which means, by listening deeper than their other contemporaries), Brakhage and Breer contribute to the liberation of man's spirit from the dead matter of culture; they open new vistas for life. In this sense, an old art is immoral—it keeps man's spirit in bondage to Culture. The very destructiveness of the modern artist, his anarchy, as in Happenings, or, even, action painting, is, therefore, a confirmation of life and freedom.

A Note on Improvisation

I have heard too often both American and foreign critics laugh at the words "spontaneity" and "improvisation." They say this is not creation, that no art can be created "off the cuff." Need I state here that such criticism is pure ignorance, that it represents only a snobbish, superficial understanding of the meaning of "improvisation?" The truth is that improvisation never excludes condensation or selection. On the contrary, improvisation is the highest form of condensation, it points to the very essence of a thought, an emotion, a movement. It was not without reason that Adam Mickiewicz called his famous Konrad Walenrod soliloquy an improvisation. Improvisation is, I repeat, the highest form of concentration, of awareness, of intuitive knowledge, when the imagination begins to dismiss the prearranged, the contrived mental structures, and goes directly to the depths of the matter. This is the true meaning of improvisation, and it is not a method at all; it is, rather, a state of being necessary for any inspired creation. It is an ability that every true artist develops by a constant and life-long inner vigilance, by the cultivation—yes!—of his senses.

A Note on the "Shaky Camera"

I am sick and tired of the guardians of Cinema Art who accuse the new film-maker of shaky camera work and bad technique. In like manner, they accuse the modern composer, the modern sculptor, the modern painter of sloppiness and poor technique. I have pity for such critics. They are hopeless. I would rather spend my time in heralding the new. Mayakovsky once said that there is an area in the human mind that can be reached only through poetry, and only through poetry that is awake, changing. One could also say that there is an area in the human mind (or heart) that can be reached only through cinema, through that cinema that is always awake, always changing. Only such cinema can reveal, describe, make us conscious, hint at what we really are or what we aren't, or sing the true and changing beauty of the world around us. Only this kind of cinema contains the proper vocabulary and syntax to express the true and the beautiful. If we study the modern film poetry, we find that even the mistakes, the out-of-focus shots, the shaky shots, the unsure steps, the hesitant movements, the overexposed and the underexposed bits, have become part of the new cinema vocabulary, being part of the psychological and visual reality of modern man.

The Second Note on Improvisation

It was in his quest for inner freedom that the new artist came to improvisation. The young American film-maker, like the young painter, musician, actor, resists his society. He knows that everything he has learned from his society about life and death is false. He cannot, therefore, arrive at any true creation, creation as revelation of truth, by reworking and rehashing ideas, images, and feelings that are dead and inflated—he has to descend much deeper, below all that clutter, he has to escape the centrifugal force of everything he has learned from his society. His spontaneity, his anarchy, even his passivity are his acts of freedom.

On Acting

The fragile, searching acting style of the early Marlon Brando, a James Dean, a Ben Carruthers is only a reflection of their unconscious moral attitudes, their anxiety to be—and these are important words—honest, sincere, truthful. Film truth needs no words. There is more truth and real intelligence in their "mumbling" than in all the clearly pronounced words on Broadway in five seasons. Their incoherence is as expressive as 1,000 words.

The young actor of today doesn't trust any other will than his own, which, he knows, is still too frail and, thus, harmless—it is no will at all, only the distant, deep waves and motions and voices and groans of a Marlon Brando, a James Dean, a Ben Carruthers, waiting, listening (the same way Kerouac is listening for the new American word and syntax and rhythm in his improvisations; or Coltrane in his jazz; or De Kooning in his paintings). As long as the "lucidly minded" critics will stay out, with all their "form," "content," "art," "structure," "clarity," "importance,"—everything will be all right, just keep them out. For the new soul is still a bud, still going through its most dangerous, most sensitive stage.

Closing Remarks

Several things should be clear by now:

The new American artist can not be blamed for the fact that his art is in a mess: He was born into that mess. He is doing everything to get out of that mess.

His rejection of "official" (Hollywood) cinema is not always based on artistic objections. It is not a question of films being bad or good artistically. It is a question of the appearance of a new attitude toward life, a new understanding of man.

It is irrelevant to ask the young American artist to make films like those made in Russia or France or Italy; their needs are different, their anxieties are different. Content and form in art cannot be transplanted from country to country like beans.

To ask the American artist to make "positive" films, to clean out —at this time—all the anarchic elements from his work, means to ask him to accept the existing social, political, and ethical order of today.

The films being made by the new American artist, that is, the independents, are by no means in the majority. But we must remember that it is always the few, the most sensitive ones who are the spokesmen of the true feelings, the truths of any generation.

And, finally, the films we are making are not the films we want to make forever, they are not our ideal of art: These are the films we *must* make if we don't want to betray our selves and our art, if we want to move forward. These films represent only one specific period in the development of our lives and our work.

I can think of various arguments the critics or the readers of these notes may throw against me or against the young American artist of today as he is described here. Some may say that he is on a dangerous road, that he may never get out of his confusion in one piece; that he may succeed in destroying everything, that he will have nothing new to offer in its place, etc. etc.—the usual arguments that are thrown against anything young, budding, unknown.

I, however, I look at the new man with trust. I believe in the truth (victory) of the new.

Our world is too cluttered with bombs, newspapers, TV antennae —there is no place for a subtle feeling or a subtle truth to rest its head. But the artists are working. And, with every word, every image, every new musical sound, the confidence in the old is shaken, the entrance to the heart is widened.

Natural processes are uncertain, *in spite of their lawfulness. Perfectionism and uncertainty are mutually exclusive.*

Research without mistakes is impossible. All natural research is, and was, from its very beginning, explorative, "unlawful," labile, eternally reshaping, in flux, uncertain and unsure, yet still in contact with real *natural processes. For these objective natural processes are, in all their basic lawfulness, variable to the highest degree, free in the sense of irregular, incalculable, and unrepeatable.*

WILHELM REICH
(*Orgonomic Functionalism*)

FOR SHADOWS, AGAINST PULL MY DAISY

BY PARKER TYLER

No. 24, Spring, 1962

I can hear some of my readers: Here's that Heavy Culture Man again! Right, man. And it's not going to let up as long as there's a drop of think in me. All my opportunities for joining literary cliques have been passed up or automatically short-circuited, opportunities that began appearing about 1927. I myself have little taste for large organization. Charles Henri Ford and I made a sort of two-man team on View, 1940–47, but, although View is kindly remembered in some quarters, Ford and I were never really indigenous to the New York milieu. I daresay this beginning is more self-conscious than it ought to be, but observation of the milieu over many years has given me the impression that the grammatical first-person no longer denotes egocentrism so much as do certain transports of self-forgetfulness, where identification with others—in fact, with almost anything—requires a minimum of cerebral effort; *unconscious* identification is the preferred blessing. Then you owe nobody, not even yourself, anything. The point of this sermon is at hand in the two films that I wish to put in a new light.

First, *Shadows* is *not* part of the Beat da-da-da. Beatism is a wee, wee cult with a public-relations palate as visible as that of the wolf when he impersonated Little Red Riding Hood's grandmother. *Pull My Daisy*, one of its sugar-capped teeth, focuses on a tendency with its roots in the international avant-gardism of the 1920's. The most striking thing about the modern school from which *Pull My Daisy* stems is its lack of historical consciousness in its own field: its obvious debt (incarnate in Jack Kerouac) to a bagful of Dada and pre-Dada, Surrealism, Gertrude Stein, Ernest Hemingway, Scott Fitzgerald, e. e. cummings, and Henry Miller. The grabbing is as big as the bag. One might even, on heavier thought, add to the above list. Kerouac's personal contribution, the sound track, which is the purely literary facet of *Pull My Daisy*, reeks of the *recherché*. Oh, Kerouac has a knack! But so has Danny Kaye—it's just a case of different fields. The very fact that the film grew from Kerouac's unproduced play, *The Beat Generation,* and that it became, in many ways, a designing improvisation, points straight to what I mean.

A few professional critics saluted the authenticity of *Pull My Daisy* with familiar, quotable clichés. "Fresh," for example. The film's as fresh as a frozen green pea, which, of course, in a manner of speaking and after all, is an authentic green pea with a relatively new unfreshness. Pompous acclaim of mere authenticity is one of the great moral and intellectual failings of our time: a time drunk on the sweet fragrance of statistics. Some inconsequential, undesirable, and tainted things are habitually "authentic." Hitler was authentic, and so was Stalin. Concentration camps, like riots and demonstrations, are as authentic as American reform legislation. They're the tit-for-tat known historically as the dialectic. Well, then, everything is in its way authentic, even the atom bomb—with the single exception (if Allen Ginsberg, as quoted by Jacques Barzun, is to be believed) of man himself. Man is "obsolete." In the mouths of men, this puts every authenticity in question, and, sure enough, Ginsberg is made to say in *Pull My Daisy*: "Bishop, are holy flowers holy?" Aside from questions, the only remaining authenticity is a sort of deaf-mute atavism, problematically blind.

Objectively, it can be insisted, Beatism is a collective form of authenticity. One can't deny its existence or that its existence has a joy of its own. (Yeah, man—to be a bit obsolete.) But "joy?"

I'd like to correct the word from my corner. Euphoria, I think, is the antithesis of *angst*. Yet the Beat collective naturally escapes definition. Its pleasure, like its pain, its *angst*, like its euphoria, show through like the latest juvenile delinquent to be technically embarrassed by the public spotlight. What accounts for this quality? A built-in nonself-criticism, defying criticism by anyone or any standards. Grim or gory (by token), carefree, airy, ecstatic, blah, or flat-footed, in bad taste or ephemerally inspired, professionalized or "at home," it's to be enjoyed because it "had to be," and if not enjoyable, it's you who don't "belong," not it. *Lebensraum*, at a minimum. That is: *Shantih*.

If, despite orders from headquarters, the sun of history still shines, it is possible to conclude that the Beat canon is a sort of art-processing derived from thought-smashing. Kerouac's script for *Pull My Daisy* (printed in paperback) ends: "Hello, gang./Da da da da da/And they're going dada da da dada da da da. . . . Let's go. 'sgo, sgo. . . . Off they go." To interpolate an addendum before the silence: "Ta ta. Goonight. Goonight. Good night, ladies, good night, sweet ladies, good night, good night." To let it settle: "Datta. Dayadhvam. Damyatta." I forgot to add T. S. Eliot to the above list. *He* knew where all that stuff came from. Kerouac and his gang aren't aware of Eliot's presence; at least, they're trying to forget it, as they try to forget the presence of those others. In any case, other presences (as per Beat) are irrelevant. The world is for the eternally young, etc., etc., etc. One may note that, when the Surrealists made automatic texts a method, however, they were *getting away from* Eliotism, not being fed at its breast.

To put in a word for historical consciousness in the arts, no one was more historically conscious than the highly distinguished Alfred Jarry, creator of "Ubu." The avant-garde impulse, nevertheless, began finding history irksome, for reasons best known to itself, and, having gone through the wringers of Dada and Surrealism, its free speech has become, at last, less the artist's privilege than the soap-boxer's arrogation. The spotlight of publicity has always been something the Belligerent Bohemian needed like a warm bath: It's quieting (at first, anyway). The film camera, in such cases, is a pretty good substitute for a warm bath. *Pull My Daisy* was meant to document the performances supposedly going on in the tenement-like homes the impoverished Beats have made, statistically, into their Waste Lands. The film is a contemporary version of everything colloquial in Eliot's poem: The poet-witness is set off against the common people and their poverty on grounds where he is, of course, an ambiguously welcome trespasser. The scene witnessed by the camera eye in *Pull My Daisy* is as old as the location of the Province-town Theatre. Never before today has bohemian revolt been con-sidered so ofay—and never before, consistently, has the outcast tramp-poet been so much a theatrical charade. *Pull My Daisy* is an audio-visual paean to this fact. I don't think *this* authenticity can be denied. Yet by an obscure act of will, the Beats *have* cut off historic consciousness. None of them is quite so anonymous as the late, un-lamented John Rose Gildea, and none of them—unless I am far, far wrong—will end up like Maxwell Bodenheim.

To me, the look of the pressure on literature and its history, which has made the Beat fission possible, is, whether on page or film reel, a flotsam of literary tags unstably imbedded in an inde-scribable jelly of content. Sassy youth, moral anarchism, cadged wine and beer (see soundtrack) are as much window-dressing as anything else. Specific literary effort sometimes rises above them. The best contribution to the paperback text of the film is not in the film itself. This is the amusingly pornographic song of the same title by Kerouac and Ginsberg; though rather static, it has a real literary imagination. With one line sourly bowdlerized, an actress sings two partial stanzas in the film. The way Hollywood-type cen-sorship creeps in here is like the odor of the casting office that con-nects the dramatis personae of *Pull My Daisy* with the dramatis personae of Shaw's Salvation Army play. Compassing the world of the "Salvation Army," the Frank-Leslie-Kerouac film has the same holier-than-thou cynicism. Aren't the Beats the "Salvation Army" of the avant-garde? *Damyatta*, ineffably. Somehow, too, the film's persons seem to have been filtered into the vicinity of contemporary Tenth Street through Arthur Millerism or latter-day Clifford Odet-ism.

I believe that no grain of such affiliations (quite innocent, of course, for everything Beat is innocent) adheres to *Shadows*, so that any mentioned connection between the two films seems unfortunate and inauthentic. If they can be classed together, it is only on the loosest level of current film conventions. In fact, the shots in *Pull My Daisy* are more self-consciously "art photography" than anything in *Shadows*. This loosest level, I suppose, may soon get to be called the Flow of Life Film, something making that notable flow more *comme ci, comme ca*, than does the *Nouvelle Vague*, which, to be readily marketable, had to make raw sex and other popular con-ventions a part of the flow. Surely, some foreign directorial talent has mined poetry from this very flow—and erotic poetry—but the comparative value of such achievements is eminently arguable. Let that point, however, pass.

Shadows has been surprisingly well appreciated while mostly for the wrong reasons. One wrong reason is its superficial technical kinship with *Pull My Daisy* and the documentary film. No one, I believe, except the author of an article on Cassavetes in a small West Coast film magazine, has noticed the relation between the method of *Shadows* to that of Chekhov in his plays and especially his short stories. *Shadows* approaches its subject with the same casual directness as Chekhov his subjects; it punctures life, as it were, the skin of life, and, as the bleeding goes on, vanishes before the outflow is stanched. The American literary tradition echoing Chekhov is Sherwood Anderson more than Hemingway, and that very talented short-story writer, Eudora Welty. This is the basic style that Cassavetes instinctively followed. It takes a few characters and reveals their life situation; the situation moves behind the veil of full consciousness, and yet it communicates. Orson Welles and Jean Renoir are among the very few commercial directors of note who have used techniques homogenizing plot, character, social scene, and ordinary talk into one unified, if baroque and only partly intelligible, surface. The relation of this effect to the way dialogue is employed in *The Waste Land* is close. Life is a surface that, from this viewpoint, is tantalizingly inarticulate, laced with enigmas of sound and sight, fleetingly submerged in its own volubility, retreating (when least expected) into symbolic idioms.

This stylistic trait is clearly related to modern ambiguity in the arts. Meaning lies behind meaning, consciousness within consciousness. You have to catch their contact on the move. Everything in *Pull My Daisy* steers, willy-nilly, toward the self-consciously literary, at times the arty. Without pause, its gab unwinds from the reel created by this much practiced self-consciousness. The characters in *Shadows* are not puppets of such literary lazy-daisiness, trademarked by every artistic movement in the first half of the century. However, *Shadows* does suffer from Village tradition of sitting around and bee-essing (I follow the bowdlerizing trend) as a form of passive, futile protest against having nothing else to do; thus, when something *is* done, it may well be catastrophic. In *Shadows*, the passage taking place in the garden of the Museum of Modern Art should be clipped from the film; it's bloodcurdlingly gauche and irrelevant to the theme. I fancy it's masochistic, perhaps some penance imposed by Cassavetes on himself, or else his sadistic exploitation of the masochism he found emerging from the film's fringe-of-culture milieu: highbrow chatter forces its way to the surface of a party scene and "modern art" reproductions stare disconcertingly from casually encountered walls.*

All *that* belongs to the naïveté of the milieu Cassavetes is portraying; it is not the meat of the matter. The *meat* is solely the meaning inherent, and poignantly inherent, in human relationships. I believe these relationships have been discussed by reviewers only on a superficial plane because, in a day of racial integration, the theme is a very tender one.† That this "tenderness" has its own ambiguity is part of *Shadows's* accomplishment. The dark, African-type big brother, mothering, fathering, and otherwise coddling his white-looking younger half-brother and half-sister, is martyred not by their dependence on him, but by their urgent temptation to find love and fulfillment by passing for white. This may be a delusion on their part, a delusion of youth, of inexperience, even of a lack of intelligence; it becomes real, nevertheless. If the younger brother's climactic reaction against the "color" atmosphere of the party in his home is basically an incestuous emotion he has for his sister (which is a possible motivation), the indisputable truth is that, in effect, it is a protest—however transitory, however unconscious—against the Negroid itself. This is a daringly candid element of Cassavetes's story. Ostensibly, he developed the action with his actors' help; they themselves felt, or had empathy for, the feelings of the fictional persons. The three leading roles are first-rate performances by any standard, on Broadway or off, and have the best virtues of so-called Method acting. The crowded scene where the big brother (a jazz musician) is discussing business with his agent, while simultaneously his brother tries to get some money out of him, is a miracle of polyphonic, polyvisual style.

The crisis is precipitated when the young girl goes to bed with a young white man. It is the most natural sort of sexual incident in the world. They fall hard, and the affair immediately looks serious. Almost at once, then, he discovers her Negroid strain, when her dark half-brother surprises them in her apartment. Instinctively revolted, the white man shows it and is ordered to leave the house by the

* Editor's note: Curiously enough, both of these scenes did not appear in the first version of *Shadows*; they were shot later and included in the second version, which was released commercially and which Mr. Tyler is discussing here.

† In a quotation from the very end of the script of *Shadows* (*Sight and Sound*: Summer and Autumn, 1959), Jonas Mekas reveals that Cassavetes consciously wrought his film's situation, and yet, for their part, commentators tended not to "follow the script."

girl's big brother. She morally sides with her dark brother, accepting as fatal her allegiance to his race and personal gratitude to him. Bolstered by a certain moral horror of her lover's racial prejudice, her gratitude seems the deciding factor. But, obviously, she is shattered; her future looms empty; she feels a prisoner in a debt of blood and honor casting a shadow over her life. The play between skin color and mood in the action and the film's title is another of its scanted merits. One feels, as everything drifts into stalemate, that, inside the three people, a perfectly private agony is growing—an agony that shows its stripe when the younger brother strikes a black girl who makes up to him at a party given at his home, is roughed by his big brother, and rushes out.

Told in its offhanded, somewhat deceptive way, *Shadows* could have been the opposite of delicate. But Cassavetes had a saving intelligence for what he was doing. He possesses a film sense and human tactfulness, a feeling for the inner person's dignity and the facts encompassing it. So many would like to have this quality today, and it is often imputed with insufficient evidence. Yet I know of no film, but *Shadows,* that offers it in so precise and ample, truly considered, a form. It is much superior to any other film I know with a common racial dilemma for its major theme. As a jazz musician, the black big brother is far from brilliant; this fact alone is an inspired touch of candor: He has only creature kindness to offer for admiration. Whatever personal "talents" may lie in the younger brother and sister seem to have been muffled by racial and personal allegiance, fostered to some extent by their economic dependence on their brother. All this is brought to the breaking point by the girl's love affair. She has always known she could "pass," but she keeps to a mixed society, being drawn away from it on an occasion when a boy friend takes her to the party where she meets her lover-to-be. After the scene where her lover is shown the door, there remains only the painful birth of the whole situation's insolubility. True to their big brother, each passing black or at least "neutral" while looking white, neither girl nor boy feels free. New tenderness for the girl is awakened in her big brother after her disastrous affair; without admitting it to himself, he begins to divine the rock-bottom plight of her feelings. She longs to pass for white, to leave the marginal world where her big brother must stay. Does she have incestuous feelings for her white-looking brother? Perhaps. Probably he does for her. At any rate, it seems as much his sympathy for her as awareness that his dilemma is like hers that causes his wild outbreak and his fight with his brother.

And where does he work off his shame—his shame at feeling revolt against part of his blood, at striking the Negress, at his inability to solve his dilemma? In brute action, of course, in the gang action when he and his "white" buddies flirt with some other fellows' girls and get beaten up in an alley. If we decide that this is, in one respect, his "black" masochism, I don't think the conclusion is offensive; it is simply true, and *Shadows* is its medium. It may not be final, this masochism. At the very end, the boy splits from his friends to let his agony purge or despoil him in isolation. Is he really alone? This is part of the Chekhovian suspense ending.

Shadows is subtle—and everything could have been expected of it but subtlety! Why not subtlety? The point has nothing to do with the film's style or its subject matter. The appearance of a film-maker of power and insight, one with this fresh and difficult sense of style and the courage to reveal human depths raw with controversy was, on the face of things, highly improbable. Perhaps *Shadows* could be better edited. I don't even know if I saw the "better" version of it. But such questions are here the nuances of artistic virtue. Cassavetes had his insight, his inspired theme, and made them work together with his actors and his medium. . . . To let the material speak for itself! To show life "as it is!" Never to impose artificial, shopworn patterns on human behavior! All these ideal goals are claimed for the documentary school of film-making. They are all very well, and yet, as hundreds of films attest, they can, at times, produce hollow shells, pretentious banalities, an arbitrary flattening of the life dimension, a perverse shunning of all depth of feeling and idea.

I'm afraid that the documentarists and the flow-of-lifers may consider my attribution of subtlety to Cassavetes's film (especially as I construe its meaning) as some sort of smear, something for him and the supposed tendency represented by his film to repudiate. However that may be, I am glad I could present my argument in this particular form in this particular place. My desire—wistful as it must be—was to demonstrate that a presumed art-style film, *Pull My Daisy*, placed next to a presumed documentary-style film, *Shadows*, can reverse these classifications; the former's pretensions are futile and unfresh, far removed from life's center; the latter's achievement is misunderstood, fresher and more important than anyone seems to have felt, and close to life's center. And I think that time (if it's any good any more) will prove this.

To the above, I can add my genuine surprise that Cassavetes's film made for Paramount, *Too Late Blues* (released in New York as this issue of *Film Culture* is about to be set up), sustains nearly all the original and interesting qualities of *Shadows*, even if we see them, as it were, in the disguise of certain commercial formulas. This disguise betrays itself in the fact that here, unlike *Shadows*, the actors do not invariably get contact with Cassavetes's intentions, whether because of the studio shooting schedule or their individual resistance, I am not in a position to know. Discounting the lesser cooperation by the actors (observable most in Stella Stevens, who is still brilliant in spots), *Too Late Blues* remains earmarked as a Cassavetes work, worthy of the most earnest attention. I should say altogether that Cassavetes remains the only individual now preoccupied with big films who strictly confines himself to being an expert in *human* rather than *public* relations. This goes for the flashy new crop of foreign directors with very, very few exceptions.

The "popular" elements witnessed in *Shadows* are likewise in *Too Late Blues*: unblunted (here very promiscuous) sex; a whopping scene of brute violence; the exact realism of the complex surface offered by life as it is lived: the cross of talk and behavior, as well as the ambiguity of moral currents; the timidity and plotting of people puzzled by themselves and shy of outright commitment. However, one of the surprising things in *Too Late Blues*, which is the partial odyssey of a jazz band leader and composer with delusions of grandeur, is how much people *do* come out in the open when the fat is in the fire of interpersonal relations. I am sure all the film's scenes were deliberately, professionally rehearsed, yet many have the effect of using hidden cameras and hidden microphones—so cannily, so uncompromisingly does Cassavetes get his grip on his material. Perhaps he exaggerates! Most interesting artists in the world have "exaggerated." I still maintain that such extravagance is based on the most intelligent observation of human beings to air itself these days in film studios.

Critically speaking, I should wish *not* to seem to exaggerate. But, placed against the film's demerits, its virtues, I think, shine out irresistibly. For once, the saturating light of bold studio photography is justified by the force of what is being seen and heard; it is vulgar, it is stupid, it is often corny—just like the characters themselves. Yet Cassavetes has that subtle detachment from the nature of his material that defines the truthfulness of mere reporting or comic-strip populism. When he makes the hero (played with inspiration by none but Bobby Darin) balmy with love, obsessively self-starred, maddened, corruptible, cowardly, cynical, brutal and brutally sentimental, it seems not "for effect" but from respect for the human facts. In all his characters—including the band leader's vindictive, incredibly hard-shelled agent—we see head on (in pitiless, breathtaking close-ups of faces and speeches) the automatic reflexes of daily, hourly emotions. "This is my view of life, my view of myself," each individual bursts out, "take it or leave it!—meaning *me!*" Human beings slip from kindliness and romantic softness into unconcealed anger, cruelty and cynicism, without realizing, apparently, that transitions are taking place. This is a sizable contribution to naturalizing the film's imaginative view of contemporary life. Will Hollywood annihilate this extraordinary talent—that is, will Cassavetes *let it* be annihilated? That remains to be seen. Cassavetes is his own "new wave." He is bound to reach a crest with his next couple of films.

THREE

THE COMMERCIAL CINEMA AND THE AUTEUR THEORY

In "Notes on the *Auteur* Theory in 1962," Andrew Sarris defines his critical method and outlines a new orientation for serious film viewing. The film-maker Charles Boultenhouse directly opposed Sarris's essay with his article, "The Camera as a God." He offers a vision of the film-maker/cameraman as a lyricist confronting his material with religious, ritualistic intensity as an antidote to the anonymity of production Sarris extols in Hollywood.

The articles by the playwright Ken Kelman on the work of Carl Dreyer, and the poet Michael McClure's paean to Jayne Mansfield exemplify the tendency in *Film Culture* to encourage and publish writers in other genres to study particular manifestations of the cinema that interest them.

NOTES ON THE AUTEUR THEORY IN 1962

BY ANDREW SARRIS

No. 27, Winter, 1962–63

> I call these sketches Shadowgraphs, partly by the designation to re-
> mind you at once that they derive from the darker side of life, partly
> because, like other shadowgraphs, they are not directly visible. When
> I take a shadowgraph in my hand, it makes no impression on me,
> and gives me no clear conception of it. Only when I hold it up oppo-
> site the wall, and now look not directly at it, but at that which
> appears on the wall, am I able to see it. So also with the picture I
> wish to show here, an inward picture that does not become percep-
> tible until I see it through the external. This external is perhaps not
> quite unobtrusive, but, not until I look through it, do I discover that
> inner picture that I desire to show you, an inner picture too delicately
> drawn to be outwardly visible, woven as it is of the tenderest moods
> of the soul.
>
> SØREN KIERKEGAARD, in *Either/Or*

An exhibitor once asked me if an old film I had recommended
was *really* good or good only according to the *auteur* theory. I ap-

preciate the distinction. Like the alchemists of old, *auteur* critics are notorious for rationalizing leaden clinkers into golden nuggets. Their judgments are seldom vindicated, because few spectators are conditioned to perceive in individual works the organic unity of a director's career. On a given evening, a film by John Ford must take its chances as if it were a film by Henry King. Am I implying that the weakest Ford is superior to the strongest King? Yes! This kind of unqualified affirmation seems to reduce the *auteur* theory to a game of aesthetic solitaire with all the cards turned face up. By *auteur* rules, the Fords will come up aces as invariably as the Kings will come up deuces. Presumably, we can all go home as soon as the directorial signature is flashed on the screen. To those who linger, *The Gunfighter* (King 1950) may appear worthier than *Flesh* (Ford 1932). (And how deeply one must burrow to undermine Ford!) No matter. The *auteur* theory is unyielding. If, by definition, Ford is invariably superior to King, any evidence to the contrary is merely an optical illusion. Now what could be sillier than this inflexible attitude? Let us abandon the absurdities of the *auteur* theory so that we may return to the chaos of common sense.

My labored performance as devil's advocate notwithstanding, I intend to praise the *auteur* theory, not to bury it. At the very least, I would like to grant the condemned system a hearing before its execution. The trial has dragged on for years, I know, and everyone is now bored by the abstract reasoning involved. I have little in the way of new evidence or new arguments, but I would like to change some of my previous testimony. What follows is, consequently, less a manifesto than a credo, a somewhat disorganized credo, to be sure, expressed in formless notes rather than in formal brief.

I. AIMEZ-VOUS BRAHMS?

Goethe? Shakespeare? Everything signed with their names is considered good, and one wracks one's brains to find beauty in their stupidities and failures, thus distorting the general taste. All these great talents, the Goethes, the Shakespeares, the Beethovens, the Michelangelos, created, side by side with their masterpieces, works not merely mediocre, but quite simply frightful.
—LEO TOLSTOY, *Journal*, 1895–99

The preceding quotation prefaces the late André Bazin's famous critique of "*la politique des auteurs*," which appeared in the *Cahiers du Cinéma* of April, 1957. Because no comparably lucid statement opposing the *politique* has appeared since that time, I would like to discuss some of Bazin's arguments with reference to the current situation. (I except, of course, Richard Roud's penetrating article "The French Line," which dealt mainly with the post-*Nouvelle Vague* situation when the *politique* had degenerated into McMahonism.)

As Tolstoy's observation indicates, *la politique des auteurs* antedates the cinema. For centuries, the Elizabethan *politique* has decreed the reading of every Shakespearean play before any encounter with the Jonsonian repertory. At some point between *Timon of Athens* and *Volpone*, this procedure is patently unfair to Jonson's reputation. But not really. On the most superficial level of artistic reputations, the *auteur* theory is merely a figure of speech. If the man in the street could not invoke Shakespeare's name as an identifiable cultural reference, he would probably have less contact with all things artistic. The Shakespearean scholar, by contrast, will always be driven to explore the surrounding terrain, with the result that all the Elizabethan dramatists gain more rather than less recognition through the pre-eminence of one of their number. Therefore, on balance, the *politique*, as a figure of speech, does more good than harm.

Occasionally, some iconoclast will attempt to demonstrate the fallacy of this figure of speech. We will be solemnly informed that *The Gambler* was a potboiler for Dostoyevsky in the most literal sense of the word. In Jacques Rivette's *Paris Nous Appartient,* Jean-Claude Brialy asks Betty Schneider if she would still admire *Pericles* if it were not signed by Shakespeare. Zealous musicologists have played *Wellington's Victory* so often as an example of inferior Beethoven that I have grown fond of the piece, atrocious as it is. The trouble with such iconoclasm is that it presupposes an encyclopedic awareness of the *auteur* in question. If one is familiar with every Beethoven composition, *Wellington's Victory*, in itself, will hardly tip the scale toward Mozart, Bach, or Schubert. Yet that is the issue raised by the *auteur* theory. If not Beethoven, who? And why? Let us say that the *politique* for composers went Mozart, Beethoven, Bach, and Schubert. Each composer would represent a task force of compositions, arrayed by type and quality with the mighty battleships and aircraft carriers flanked by flotillas of cruisers, destroyers, and mine sweepers. When the Mozart task force collides with the Beethoven task force, symphonies roar against symphonies, quartets maneuver against quartets, and it is simply no contest with the operas. As a single force, Beethoven's nine symphonies, outgun any nine of Mozart's forty-one symphonies, both sets of quartets are almost on a par with Schubert's, but *The Magic Flute, The Marriage of Figaro,* and *Don Giovanni* will blow poor *Fidelio* out of the water. Then, of course, there is Bach with an entirely different deployment of composition and instrumentation. The Haydn and Handel cultists are moored in their inlets ready to join the fray, and the moderns with their nuclear noises are still mobilizing their forces.

It can be argued that any exact ranking of artists is arbitrary and pointless. Arbitrary up to a point, perhaps, but pointless, no. Even Bazin concedes the polemical value of the *politique.* Many film critics would rather not commit themselves to specific rankings ostensibly because every film should be judged on its own merits. In many instances, this reticence masks the critic's condescension to the medium. Because it has not been firmly established that the cinema is an art at all, it requires cultural audacity to establish a pantheon for film directors. Without such audacity, I see little point in being a film critic. Anyway, is it possible to honor a work of art without honoring the artist involved? I think not. Of course, any idiot can erect a pantheon out of hearsay and gossip. Without specifying any work, the Saganesque seducer will ask quite cynically, "Aimez-vous Brahms?" The fact that Brahms is included in the pantheon of high-brow pickups does not invalidate the industrious criticism that justifies the composer as a figure of speech.

Unfortunately, some critics have embraced the *auteur* theory as a short-cut to film scholarship. With a "you-see-it-or-you-don't" attitude toward the reader, the particularly lazy *auteur* critic can save himself the drudgery of communication and explanation. Indeed, at their worst, *auteur* critiques are less meaningful than the straight-forward plot reviews that pass for criticism in America. Without the necessary research and analysis, the *auteur* theory can degenerate into the kind of snobbish racket that is associated with the merchandising of paintings.

It was largely against the inadequate theoretical formulation of *la politique des auteurs* that Bazin was reacting in his friendly critique. (Henceforth, I will abbreviate *la politique des auteurs* as the *auteur* theory to avoid confusion.) Bazin introduces his arguments within the context of a family quarrel over the editorial policies of *Cahiers.* He fears that, by assigning reviews to admirers of given directors, notably Alfred Hitchcock, Jean Renoir, Roberto Rossellini, Fritz Lang, Howard Hawks, and Nicholas Ray, every work, major and minor, of these exalted figures is made to radiate the same beauties of style and meaning. Specifically, Bazin notes a distortion when the kindly indulgence accorded the imperfect work of a Minnelli is coldly withheld from the imperfect work of Huston. The inherent bias of the *auteur* theory magnifies the gap between the two films.

I would make two points here. First, Bazin's greatness as a critic, (and I believe strongly that he was the greatest film critic who ever lived) rested in his disinterested conception of the cinema as a universal entity. It follows that he would react against a theory that cultivated what he felt were inaccurate judgments for the sake of dramatic paradoxes. He was, if anything, generous to a fault, seeking in every film some vestige of the cinematic art. That he would seek justice for Huston vis-à-vis Minnelli on even the secondary levels of creation indicates the scrupulousness of his critical personality.

However, my second point would seem to contradict my first. Bazin was wrong in this instance, insofar as any critic can be said to be wrong in retrospect. We are dealing here with Minnelli in his *Lust for Life* period and Huston in his *Moby Dick* period. Both films can be considered failures on almost any level. The miscasting alone is disastrous. The snarling force of Kirk Douglas as the tormented Van Gogh, the brutish insensibility of Anthony Quinn as Gauguin, and the nervously scraping tension between these two absurdly limited actors, deface Minnelli's meticulously objective decor, itself inappropriate for the mood of its subject. The director's presentation of the paintings themselves is singularly unperceptive in the repeated failure to maintain the proper optical distance from canvases that arouse the spectator less by their detailed draughtsmanship than by the shock of a *gestalt* wholeness. As for *Moby Dick*, Gregory Peck's Ahab deliberates long enough to let all the demons flee the Pequod, taking Melville's Lear-like fantasies with them. Huston's epic technique with its casually shifting camera viewpoint then drifts on an intellectually becalmed sea toward a fitting rendezvous with a rubber whale. These two films are neither the best nor the worst of their time. The question is: Which deserves the harder review? And there's the rub. At the time, Huston's stock in America was higher than Minnelli's. Most critics expected Huston to do "big" things, and, if they thought about it at all, expected Minnelli to stick to "small" things like musicals. Although neither film was a critical failure, audiences stayed away in large enough numbers to make the cultural respectability of the projects suspect. On the whole, *Lust for Life* was more successful with the audiences it did reach than was *Moby Dick*.

In retrospect, *Moby Dick* represents the turning downward of

Huston as a director to be taken seriously. By contrast, *Lust for Life* is simply an isolated episode in the erratic career of an interesting stylist. The exact size of Minnelli's talent may inspire controversy, but he does represent something in the cinema today. Huston is virtually a forgotten man with a few actors' classics behind him surviving as the ruins of a once-promising career. Both Eric Rohmer, who denigrated Huston in 1957, and Jean Domarchi, who was kind to Minnelli that same year, somehow saw the future more clearly on an *auteur* level than did Bazin. As Santayana has remarked: "It is a great advantage for a system of philosophy to be substantially true." If the *auteur* critics of the 1950's had not scored so many coups of clairvoyance, the *auteur* theory would not be worth discussing in the 1960's. I must add that, at the time, I would have agreed with Bazin on this and every other objection to the *auteur* theory, but subsequent history, that history about which Bazin was always so mystical, has substantially confirmed most of the principles of the *auteur* theory. Ironically, most of the original supporters of the *auteur* theory have now abandoned it. Some have discovered more useful *politiques* as directors and would-be directors. Others have succumbed to a European-oriented pragmatism where intention is now more nearly equal to talent in critical relevance. Luc Moullet's belated discovery that Samuel Fuller was, in fact, fifty years old, signaled a reorientation of *Cahiers* away from the American cinema. (The handwriting was already on the wall when Truffaut remarked recently that, whereas he and his colleagues had "discovered" *auteurs*, his successors have "invented" them.)

Bazin then explores the implications of Giraudoux's epigram: "There are no works; there are only authors." Truffaut has seized upon this paradox as the battle cry of *la politique des auteurs*. Bazin casually demonstrates how the contrary can be argued with equal probability of truth or error. He subsequently dredges up the equivalents of *Wellington's Victory* for Voltaire, Beaumarchais, Flaubert, and Gide to document his point. Bazin then yields some ground to Rohmer's argument that the history of art does not confirm the decline with age of authentic geniuses like Titian, Rembrandt, Beethoven, or nearer to us, Bonnard, Matisse, and Stravinsky. Bazin agrees with Rohmer that it is inconsistent to attribute senility only to aging film directors while, at the same time, honoring the gnarled austerity of Rembrandt's later style. This is one of the crucial propositions of the *auteur* theory, because it refutes the popular theory of decline for aging giants like Renoir and Chaplin and asserts, instead, that, as a director grows older, he is likely to become more profoundly personal than most audiences and critics can appreciate. However, Bazin immediately retrieves his lost ground by arguing that, whereas the senility of directors is no longer at issue, the evolution of an art form is. Where directors fail and fall is in the realm not of psychology but of history. If a director fails to keep pace with the development of his medium, his work will become obsolescent. What seems like senility is, in reality, a disharmony between the subjective inspiration of the director and the objective evolution of the medium. By making this distinction between the subjective capability of an *auteur* and the objective value of a work in film history, Bazin reinforces the popular impression that the Griffith of *Birth of a Nation* is superior to the Griffith of *Abraham Lincoln* in the perspective of timing, which similarly distinguishes the Eisenstein of *Potemkin* from the Eisenstein of *Ivan the Terrible*, the Renoir of *La Grande Illusion* from the Renoir of *Picnic in the Grass*, and the Welles of *Citizen Kane* from the Welles of *Mr. Arkadin*.

I have embroidered Bazin's actual examples for the sake of greater contact with the American scene. In fact, Bazin implicitly denies a decline in the later works of Chaplin and Renoir and never mentions Griffith. He suggests circuitously that Hawks's *Scarface* is clearly superior to Hawks's *Gentlemen Prefer Blondes*, although the *auteur* critics would argue the contrary. Bazin is particularly critical of Rivette's circular reasoning on *Monkey Business* as the proof of Hawks's genius. "One sees the danger," Bazin warns, "which is an aesthetic cult of personality."

Bazin's taste, it should be noted, was far more discriminating than that of American film historians. Films Bazin cites as unquestionable classics are still quite debatable here in America. After all, *Citizen Kane* was originally panned by James Agee, Richard Griffith, and Bosley Crowther, and *Scarface* has never been regarded as one of the landmarks of the American cinema by native critics. I would say that the American public has been ahead of its critics on both *Kane* and *Scarface*. Thus, to argue against the *auteur* theory in America is to assume that we have anyone of Bazin's sensibility and dedication to provide an alternative, and we simply don't.

Bazin, finally, concentrates on the American cinema, which invariably serves as the decisive battleground of the *auteur* theory, whether over *Monkey Business* or *Party Girl*. Unlike most "serious" American critics, Bazin likes Hollywood films, but not solely because of the talent of this or that director. For Bazin, the distinctively American comedy, western, and gangster genres have their own mystiques apart from the personalities of the directors concerned. How can one review an Anthony Mann western, Bazin asks, as if it were not an expression of the genre's conventions. Not that Bazin dislikes Anthony Mann's westerns. He is more concerned with otherwise admirable westerns that the *auteur* theory rejects because their directors happen to be unfashionable. Again, Bazin's critical generosity comes to the fore against the negative aspects of the *auteur* theory.

Some of Bazin's arguments tend to overlap each other as if to counter rebuttals from any direction. He argues, in turn, that the cinema is less individualistic an art than painting or literature, that Hollywood is less individualistic than other cinemas, and that, even so, the *auteur* theory never really applies anywhere. In upholding historical determinism, Bazin goes so far as to speculate that, if Racine had lived in Voltaire's century, it is unlikely that Racine's tragedies would have been any more inspired than Voltaire's. Presumably, the Age of Reason would have stifled Racine's neoclassical impulses. Perhaps. Perhaps not. Bazin's hypothesis can hardly be argued to a verifiable conclusion, but I suspect somewhat greater reciprocity between an artist and his *zeitgeist* than Bazin would allow. He mentions, more than once and in other contexts, capitalism's influence on the cinema. Without denying this influence, I still find it impossible to attribute X directors and Y films to any particular system or culture. Why should the Italian cinema be superior to the German cinema after one war, when the reverse was true after the previous one? As for artists conforming to the spirit of their age, that spirit is often expressed in contradictions, whether between Stravinsky and Sibelius, Fielding and Richardson, Picasso and Matisse, Chateaubriand and Stendhal. Even if the artist does not spring from the idealized head of Zeus, free of the embryonic stains of history, history itself is profoundly affected by his arrival. If we cannot imagine Griffith's *October* or Eisenstein's *Birth of a Nation* because we find it difficult to transpose one artist's unifying conceptions of Lee and Lincoln to the other's dialectical conceptions of Lenin and Kerensky, we are, nevertheless, compelled to recognize other differences in the personalities of these two pioneers beyond their respective cultural complexes. It is with these latter differences that the *auteur* theory is most deeply concerned. If directors and other artists cannot be wrenched from their historical environments, aesthetics is reduced to a subordinate branch of ethnography.

I have not done full justice to the subtlety of Bazin's reasoning and to the civilized skepticism with which he propounds his own arguments as slight probabilities rather than absolute certainties. Contemporary opponents of the *auteur* theory may feel that Bazin himself is suspect as a member of the *Cahiers* family. After all, Bazin does express qualified approval of the *auteur* theory as a relatively objective method of evaluating films apart from the subjective perils of impressionistic and ideological criticism. Better to analyze the director's personality than the critic's nerve centers or politics. Nevertheless, Bazin makes his stand clear by concluding: "This is not to deny the role of the author, but to restore to him the preposition without which the noun is only a limp concept. 'Author,' undoubtedly, but of what?"

Bazin's syntactical flourish raises an interesting problem in English usage. The French preposition "de" serves many functions, but among others, those of possession and authorship. In English, the preposition "by" once created a scandal in the American film industry when Otto Preminger had the temerity to advertise *The Man With the Golden Arm* as a film "by Otto Preminger." Novelist Nelson Algren and the Screenwriters' Guild raised such an outcry that the offending preposition was deleted. Even the noun "author" (which I cunningly mask as "*auteur*") has a literary connotation in English. In general conversation, an "author" is invariably taken to be a writer. Since "by" is a preposition of authorship and not of ownership like the ambiguous "de," the fact that Preminger both produced and directed *The Man with the Golden Arm* did not entitle him in America to the preposition "by." No one would have objected to the possessive form: "Otto Preminger's *The Man with the Golden Arm*." But, even in this case, a novelist of sufficient reputation is usually honored with the possessive designation. Now, this is hardly the case in France, where *The Red and the Black* is advertised as "un film de Claude Autant-Lara." In America, "directed by" is all the director can claim, when he is not also a well-known producer like Alfred Hitchcock or Cecil B. de Mille.

Since most American film critics are oriented toward literature or journalism, rather than toward future film-making, most American film criticism is directed toward the script instead of toward the screen. The writer-hero in *Sunset Boulevard* complains that people don't realize that someone "writes a picture; they think the actors make it up as they go along." It would never occur to this writer or most of his colleagues that people are even less aware of the director's function.

Of course, the much-abused man in the street has a good excuse not to be aware of the *auteur* theory even as a figure of speech. Even on the so-called classic level, he is not encouraged to ask "Aimez-vous Griffith?" or "Aimez-vous Eisenstein?" Instead, it is which Griffith or which Eisenstein? As for less acclaimed directors, he is lucky to find their names in the fourth paragraph of the typical review. I doubt that most American film critics really believe that an indifferently directed film is comparable to an indifferently written book. However, there is little point in wailing at the Philistines on this issue, particularly when some progress is being made in telling one director from another, at least when the film comes from abroad. The Fellini, Bergman, Kurosawa, and Antonioni promotions have helped push more directors up to the first paragraph of a review, even ahead of the plot synopsis. So, we mustn't complain.

Where I wish to redirect the argument is toward the relative position of the American cinema as opposed to the foreign cinema. Some critics have advised me that the *auteur* theory only applies to a small number of artists who make personal films, not to the run-of-the-mill Hollywood director who takes whatever assignment is available. Like most Americans who take films seriously, I have always felt a cultural inferiority complex about Hollywood. Just a few years ago, I would have thought it unthinkable to speak in the same breath of a "commercial" director like Hitchcock and a "pure" director like Bresson. Even today, *Sight and Sound* uses different type sizes for Bresson and Hitchcock films. After years of tortured revaluation, I am now prepared to stake my critical reputation, such as it is, on the proposition that Alfred Hitchcock is artistically superior to Robert Bresson by every criterion of excellence and, further, that, film for film, director for director, the American cinema has been consistently superior to that of the rest of the world from 1915 through 1962. Consequently, I now regard the *auteur* theory primarily as a critical device for recording the history of the American cinema, the only cinema in the world worth exploring in depth beneath the frosting of a few great directors at the top.

These propositions remain to be proven and, I hope, debated. The proof will be difficult because direction in the cinema is a nebulous force in literary terms. In addition to its own jargon, the director's craft often pulls in the related jargon of music, painting, sculpture, dance, literature, theatre, architecture, all in a generally futile attempt to describe the indescribable. What is it the old jazz man says of his art? If you gotta ask what it is, it ain't? Well, the cinema is like that. Criticism can only attempt an approximation, a reasonable preponderance of accuracy over inaccuracy. I know the exceptions to the *auteur* theory as well as anyone. I can feel the human attraction of an audience going one way when I am going the other. The temptations of cynicism, common sense, and facile culture-mongering are always very strong, but, somehow, I feel that the *auteur* theory is the only hope for extending the appreciation of personal qualities in the cinema. By grouping and evaluating films according to directors, the critic can rescue individual achievements from an unjustifiable anonymity. If medieval architects and African sculptors are anonymous today, it is not because they deserved to be. When Ingmar Bergman bemoans the alienation of the modern artist from the collective spirit that rebuilt the cathedral at Chartres, he is only dramatizing his own individuality for an age that has rewarded him handsomely for the travail of his alienation. There is no justification for penalizing Hollywood directors for the sake of collective mythology. So, invective aside, "Aimez-vous Cukor?"

II. WHAT IS THE *AUTEUR* THEORY?

As far as I know, there is no definition of the *auteur* theory in the English language, that is, by any American or British critic. Truffaut has recently gone to great pains to emphasize that the *auteur* theory was merely a polemical weapon for a given time and a given place, and I am willing to take him at his word. But, lest I be accused of misappropriating a theory no one wants anymore, I will give the *Cahiers* critics full credit for the original formulation of an idea that reshaped my thinking on the cinema. First of all, how does the *auteur* theory differ from a straightforward theory of directors. Ian Cameron's article "Films, Directors, and Critics," in *Movie* of September, 1962, makes an interesting comment on this issue: "The assumption that underlies all the writing in *Movie* is that the director is the author of a film, the person who gives it any distinctive quality. There are quite large exceptions, with which I shall deal later." So far, so good, at least for the *auteur* theory, which even allows for exceptions. However, Cameron continues: "On the whole, we accept the cinema of directors, although without going to the farthest-out extremes of the *la politique des auteurs*, which makes it difficult to think of a bad director making a good film and almost impossible to think of a good director making a bad one." We are back to Bazin again, although Cameron naturally uses different examples. That three otherwise divergent critics like Bazin, Roud, and Cameron make essentially the same point about the *auteur* theory suggests a common fear of its abuses. I believe there is a misunderstanding here about what the *auteur* theory actually claims, particularly since the theory itself is so vague at the present time.

First of all, the *auteur* theory, at least as I understand it and now intend to express it, claims neither the gift of prophecy nor the option of extracinematic perception. Directors, even *auteurs*, do not always run true to form, and the critic can never assume that a bad director will always make a bad film. No, not always, but almost always, and that is the point. What is a bad director, but a director who has made many bad films? What is the problem then? Simply this: The badness of a director is not necessarily considered the badness of a film. If Joseph Pevney directed Garbo, Cherkassov, Olivier, Belmondo, and Harriet Andersson in *The Cherry Orchard*, the resulting spectacle might not be entirely devoid of merit with so many subsidiary *auteurs* to cover up for Joe. In fact, with this cast and this literary property, a Lumet might be safer than a Welles. The realities of casting apply to directors as well as to actors, but the *auteur* theory would demand the gamble with Welles, if he were willing.

Marlon Brando has shown us that a film can be made without a director. Indeed, *One-Eyed Jacks* is more entertaining than many films with directors. A director-conscious critic would find it difficult to say anything good or bad about direction that is nonexistent. One can talk here about photography, editing, acting, but not direction. The film even has personality, but, like *The Longest Day* and *Mutiny on the Bounty*, it is a cipher directorially. Obviously, the *auteur* theory cannot possibly cover every vagrant charm of the cinema. Nevertheless, the first premise of the *auteur* theory is the technical competence of a director as a criterion of value. A badly directed or an undirected film has no importance in a critical scale of values, but one can make interesting conversation about the subject, the script, the acting, the color, the photography, the editing, the music, the costumes, the decor, and so forth. That is the nature of the medium. You always get more for your money than mere art. Now, by the *auteur* theory, if a director has no technical competence, no elementary flair for the cinema, he is automatically cast out from the pantheon of directors. A great director has to be at least a good director. This is true in any art. What constitutes directorial talent is more difficult to define abstractly. There is less disagreement, however, on this first level of the *auteur* theory than there will be later.

The second premise of the *auteur* theory is the distinguishable personality of the director as a criterion of value. Over a group of films, a director must exhibit certain recurring characteristics of style, which serve as his signature. The way a film looks and moves should have some relationship to the way a director thinks and feels. This is an area where American directors are generally superior to foreign directors. Because so much of the American cinema is commissioned, a director is forced to express his personality through the visual treatment of material rather than through the literary content of the material. A Cukor, who works with all sorts of projects, has a more developed abstract style than a Bergman, who is free to develop his own scripts. Not that Bergman lacks personality, but his work has declined with the depletion of his ideas largely because his technique never equaled his sensibility. Joseph L. Mankiewicz and Billy Wilder are other examples of writer-directors without adequate technical mastery. By contrast, Douglas Sirk and Otto Preminger have moved up the scale because their miscellaneous projects reveal a stylistic consistency.

The third and ultimate premise of the *auteur* theory is concerned with interior meaning, the ultimate glory of the cinema as an art. Interior meaning is extrapolated from the tension between a director's personality and his material. This conception of interior meaning comes close to what Astruc defines as *mise en scène,* but not quite. It is not quite the vision of the world a director projects nor quite his attitude toward life. It is ambiguous, in any literary sense, because part of it is imbedded in the stuff of the cinema and cannot be rendered in noncinematic terms. Truffaut has called it the temperature of the director on the set, and that is a close approximation of its professional aspect. Dare I come out and say what I think it to be is an *élan* of the soul?

Lest I seem unduly mystical, let me hasten to add that all I mean by "soul" is that intangible difference between one personality and another, all other things being equal. Sometimes, this difference is expressed by no more than a beat's hesitation in the rhythm of a film. In one sequence of *La Règle du Jeu,* Renoir gallops up the stairs, turns to his right with a lurching movement, stops in hop-like uncertainty when his name is called by a coquettish maid, and, then, with marvelous postreflex continuity, resumes his bearishly shambling journey to the heroine's boudoir. If I could describe the musical grace note of that momentary suspension, and I can't, I might be able to provide a more precise definition of the *auteur* theory. As it is, all I can do is point at the specific beauties of interior meaning on the screen and, later, catalogue the moments of recognition.

The three premises of the *auteur* theory may be visualized as three concentric circles: the outer circle as technique; the middle circle, personal style; and the inner circle, interior meaning. The corresponding roles of the director may be designated as those of a technician, a stylist, and an *auteur.* There is no prescribed course by which a director passes through the three circles. Godard once re-marked that Visconti had evolved from a *metteur en scène* to an *auteur*, whereas Rossellini had evolved from an *auteur* to a *metteur en scène*. From opposite directions, they emerged with comparable status. Minnelli began and remained in the second circle as a stylist; Buñuel was an *auteur* even before he had assembled the technique of the first circle. Technique is simply the ability to put a film to-gether with some clarity and coherence. Nowadays, it is possible to become a director without knowing too much about the technical side, even the crucial functions of photography and editing. An expert production crew could probably cover up for a chimpanzee in the director's chair. How do you tell the genuine director from the quasichimpanzee? After a given number of films, a pattern is established.

In fact, the *auteur* theory itself is a pattern theory in constant flux. I would never endorse a Ptolemaic constellation of directors in a fixed orbit. At the moment, my list of *auteurs* runs something like this through the first twenty: Ophuls, Renoir, Mizoguchi, Hitchcock, Chaplin, Ford, Welles, Dreyer, Rossellini, Murnau, Griffith, Stern-berg, Eisenstein, von Stroheim, Buñuel, Bresson, Hawks, Lang, Flaherty, Vigo. This list is somewhat weighted toward seniority and established reputations. In time, some of these *auteurs* will rise, some will fall, and some will be displaced either by new directors or rediscovered ancients. Again, the exact order is less important than the specific definitions of these and as many as two hundred other potential *auteurs*. I would hardly expect any other critic in the world fully to endorse this list, especially on faith. Only after thou-sands of films have been revaluated, will any personal pantheon have a reasonably objective validity. The task of validating the *auteur* theory is an enormous one, and the end will never be in sight. Mean-while, the *auteur* habit of collecting random films in directorial bundles will serve posterity with at least a tentative classification.

Although the *auteur* theory emphasizes the body of a director's work rather than isolated masterpieces, it is expected of great direc-tors that they make great films every so often. The only possible exception to his rule I can think of is Abel Gance, whose greatness is largely a function of his aspiration. Even with Gance, *La Roue* is as close to being a great film as any single work of Flaherty's. Not that single works matter that much. As Renoir has observed, a director spends his life on variations of the same film.

Two recent omnibus films—*Boccaccio '70* and *The Seven Capital Sins*—unwittingly reinforced the *auteur* theory by confirming the relative standing of the many directors involved. If I had not seen either film, I would have anticipated that the order of merit in *Boccaccio '70* would be Visconti, Fellini, and De Sica, and in *The Seven Capital Sins* Godard, Chabrol, Demy, Vadim, De Broca, Molinaro. (Dhomme, Ionesco's stage director and an unknown quantity in advance, turned out to be the worst of the lot.) There might be some argument about the relative badness of De Broca and Molinaro, but, otherwise, the directors ran true to form by almost any objective criterion of value. However, the main point here is that even in these frothy, ultracommercial servings of entertainment, the contribution of each director had less in common stylistically with the work of other directors on the project than with his own previous work.

Sometimes, a great deal of corn must be husked to yield a few kernels of internal meaning. I recently saw *Every Night at Eight*, one of the many maddeningly routine films Raoul Walsh has directed in his long career. This 1935 effort featured George Raft, Alice Faye, Frances Langford, and Patsy Kelly in one of those familiar plots about radio shows of the period. The film keeps moving along in the pleasantly unpretentious manner one would expect of Walsh until one incongruously intense scene with George Raft thrashing about in his sleep, revealing his inner fears in mumbling dream-talk. The girl he loves comes into the room in the midst of his unconscious avowals of feeling and listens sympathetically. This unusual scene was later amplified in *High Sierra* with Humphrey Bogart and Ida Lupino. The point is that one of the screen's most virile directors employed an essentially feminine narrative device to dramatize the emotional vulnerability of his heroes. If I had not been aware of Walsh in *Every Night at Eight*, the crucial link to *High Sierra* would have passed unnoticed. Such are the joys of the *auteur* theory.

THE CAMERA AS A GOD

BY CHARLES BOULTENHOUSE

No. 29, Summer, 1963

In ancient times, anything from trees to the wind was thought to be inhabited by spirits. Many of these spirits ultimately became gods. This metamorphosis was the result of the ministration of priests, magicians, and sorcerers (the artists of those times), who discovered the potential of the spirits by intuition and perfected them through ritual. Robert Graves has reminded us that Phoebus Apollo began as a mouse demon.

The good film-maker is he who is engaged (consciously or unconsciously) in preserving and perfecting the demon in the camera; the very best film-maker is he who is engaged in transforming the demon into the god. I am sure you will see that an idea so theological as this will probably make out experimental film to be positively sacred in character and commercial film rather blasphemous. You will be right.

The commercial film, however, is being well spoken of these days. An effort is being made to bestow on it a kind of authenticity, which, I believe, is an absurd thing to try to do. There are two assertions that I think are particularly wrong: One is that commercial film is a natural kind of Pop Art; the other is that commercial film conceals a director of such creative intensity that he can be regarded as an author (in the higher sense).

I. SNAP, CRACKLE AND POP

Let us first consider movies as Pop Art. Said without sneers, this means that Hollywood is the Original Pop Art and is GREAT because IT IS what IT IS. Gorgeous flesh and mostly terrible acting! Divine! Campy dialogue and preposterous plots! Divine! Sexy fantasy and unorgasmic tedium! Divine!

Now the significance of such a cinema is centered entirely upon the sensibility of the person experiencing it. When Parker Tyler wrote about basically bad films that were also basically fantastic, he transformed them into something more than they appeared on the surface. As Paul Goodman said, "Parker Tyler reacting to a Hollywood movie is a better movie than they ever dreamed of there. . . ." Furthermore, Mr. Tyler wrote playfully and consciously. He never regressed to the teenage responses that now appear in serious magazines.

The question of Hollywood in relation to all of us was very clearly raised at the 1961 Creative Film Foundation evening at Cinema 16, when the painter and film-maker Alfred Leslie, taking issue with the derogatory remarks made about Hollywood, went to the microphone to announce that he liked Hollywood films and always had. Although the late Maya Deren, chairman of the evening, rose in full and splendid fury and offered rebuttal (as did Shirley Clarke), neither pointed out the following: that, even though Alfred Leslie enjoyed Hollywood films, when it came to making a film (*Pull My Daisy*), neither the standards nor methods of Hollywood were used. In a sense, we all grew up on Hollywood, and, for many of us, our first experiences of the Marvelous is enshrined in the tacky trappings of Hollywood glamor. But, at the same time that these films aroused, they also failed to satisfy. Hollywood is the tease of all time. See how its seething teenage adorers long for the corny fantasy to turn into pornography. Reflect that it never will. Think how pornography would fulfill Hollywood. Remember that it never will. No ritual orgy will be set off by a modern King and Queen of the May. The gods of the teenagers will not strip and copulate. Thus, the only thing that could save the Pop Art of Hollywood is precisely what will not occur. The teenagers of all ages who worship its fetishes will never be satisfied; nor will the Demon of the Camera, bored almost cross-eyed by the miles of Nothing pasing before it into Oblivion.

II. "AUTHOR, AUTHOR!"

Another strategy to give prestige to the commercial film is the claim that directors can be artists and, indeed, unbeknownst, actually have been artists all along; that, in developing their craft, they have been developing style and, in discovering their own styles and methods, have developed the art of the film as a whole. I find this a particularly depressing idea because, originating in France, where it has a certain plausibility, it has been applied to Hollywood, where it has very, very little. The Hollywood director is usually surprised to discover that his "art" has been taken seriously; this is because he had never been serious about "art" as such. His first concern has been to make his film as exciting as possible in order to keep the customers coming to see it, so that the investment would be protected—yield a profit.

A Hollywood director, plainly speaking, is a craftsman using all his skills to protect an investment by making as large a profit as possible. If his skills and devices are repeated and developed to the point where they can be identified, this does not make him into an artist. I must say that, though I have never invested in a commercial film, were I to do so, I would absolutely insist that the director protect my investment to the utmost of his abilities. It is not surprising that, if many successful Hollywood directors are terribly, terribly old, it is because the banks trust them, and, clearly, the banks are correct. One cannot help sympathizing with those men who now spend what euphemistically are known as the golden years out in the hot sun, still directing westerns in some godforsaken spot on the planet.

When it comes to the total work of these efficient, imaginative craftsmen, one must simply face the facts. Their films cannot be studied as a developing revelation of artistic intention, not because their skills did not develop, but because they never had a single artistic intention and it is pointless to pretend that they did. In a recent issue of *Film Culture*, a preposterous comparison was made between the anonymity of the Hollywood craftsmen and the anonymity of the creators of the great cathedrals. The comparison is absurd because the intentions of the cathedral builders and the Hollywood directors are opposed. The great cathedrals were dedicated to the glory of God, which (it is my pleasure to remind those whose minds it has escaped) is an exalted and exalting thing to have done. It is no matter that the burghers of the medieval towns were enthusiastic supporters of those enormous and expensive enterprises, because they knew the cathedrals meant pilgrims and pilgrims meant business; the point is, the vast cathedrals in themselves, *for* themselves, were vast and vibrant with their dedication to the great idea of immortality. Hollywood, on the other hand, becomes aware of exaltation only in the last few moments of a picture—where it takes on the form of a particularly repellent musical climax—and is dedicated to a particularly empty idea: Entertainment must be superficial distraction.

In the world of Hollywood, it would be a waste of time to study the techniques of the best directors—barring the exceptional aforementioned case, where one's living depends on one's sound investments. Critical analysis is, therefore, quite irrelevant. For the critic, the study of film style ought to be restricted to those directors who are genuine "authors" (it is no accident that the greatest of them have written scripts of their own: Eisenstein, Welles, Pagnol, Cocteau, Fellini, Antonioni, and so forth). The truth is that the commercial director should have the proper and honest reward of being credited with a job well done rather than wear the dubious appellation of "artist."

The demon in the camera, however, likes the *"auteur"* theory because the demon wishes it were true. When this theory is applied to the films of those to whom it is usually applied, it is confused because it doesn't remember those cases, or remembers them only vaguely, as in an interminable daydream. Even after seeing such film works anew, the demon does not remember them because they have merged so hopelessly with the endless miles of other commercial films that all seem interchangeable and unchanging—indistinguishable and undistinguished.

III. NOT JUST AN EXPERIMENT

The experimental film has a wonderful way of persisting. Someone or other always seems interested in looking at them. Always there seems someone new who wants to decipher the enigmas and blazons of Cocteau; to analyze the dreams of Maya Deren; to soar into the flying signs and symbols of Stan Brakhage; to—but rather than seem to promote all this, I prefer to analyze. The experimental film is not just an experiment in the scientific sense, but it does resemble science in that each of its films are stages in the study of the Being of the

Camera. Since Poe, all the arts have tended to evolve an almost scientific attitude toward the given nature and Being of their own materials. All the arts are, thus, engaged in testing, and film especially so. All the arts are also engaged, in Wallace Stevens's phrase, in making "Notes Toward a Supreme Fiction." Film especially so. I advocate, in an analytical spirit, that the Supreme Fiction wants the Camera to be a God.

DREYER

BY KEN KELMAN

No. 35, Winter, 1964–65

[The article has been revised for this republication, and an appendix concerning Dreyer's last film, *Gertrud*, has been added.—PAS]

The most striking aspect of the recent Dreyer retrospective at the Museum of Modern Art was that, until the last rich four films, there was little formal distinction, but, on the other hand, strong thematic relationship between more and less mature work. *The Parson's Widow* was as far, stylistically, from the final films as the other early ones were but still stood as good in its own right.

As for that last quartet, it became clear that the purest and fullest expression of life-long themes occurs in the very latest ones, sort of summings up: *Day of Wrath* and *Ordet* (*The Word*). So, I will focus on those two, developing others in the dark and light of *Day of Wrath*, and ending, as the series did, with *The Word*.

The President was Dreyer's first film—not the least pleasing visually, but the least personal. Still, there are many anticipations of what is to follow. The setting of romantic episodes in a rowboat on a lake—beautifully photographed—is a device later used more elaborately in *Day of Wrath*. The intercutting of the hero being honored, with his daughter preparing to escape prison, is quite in the straightforward style of all such passages in later Dreyer. And the concept of honor and duty versus nature and love—along with that of the hypocrisy that results from attempting both to save face and to have heart—can already be detected in this rather conventional melodrama of a respectable father who betrays his trust out of compassion for his disreputable daughter.

Leaves from Satan's Book follows the theme of betrayal throughout the ages, in four separate stories, a procedure (un)inspired by Griffith's *Intolerance*. The prime betrayal, however, is that of a most promising title by a tedious movie. There is no intercutting of the various episodes, as with Griffith, and probably just as well, since Dreyer has never cared much for editing pyrotechnics—which, however, are the main interest of *Intolerance*, and utterly lacking in *Leaves from Satan's Book*.

Little remains to comment on, except suggestions throughout of the Dreyeresque themes of desire in conflict with duty and masked by hypocrisy (especially in the Inquisition sequence), and natural love opposed to ideals (especially in the 1918 Finland episode). The irony of the function of evil is superficially treated in the frame story of Satan's reluctant career of tempting man on earth; a concept expressed at its fullest in *Ordet*. But, apart from isolated gorgeous shots, it is hard to conceive of *Leaves* being Dreyer.

The Parson's Widow is most refreshing, the best of the early films, funny, touching, the real revelation of the retrospective. Of all the pre-*Passion* pictures, it is the only one where the major later themes are found with some definition. Here we have the first clear confrontation in Dreyer of the forces of life and death. For the two young lovers, life is just a gambol, until the boy wins the job of parson with a joyous, vital, affirmative sermon, as opposed to the torpid, gloomy talks of his rivals. The parson's ancient widow goes with his position, though; and when the youth drunkenly accepts both, we have the first instance in Dreyer of the opposition and suffocation of youth by age (which later becomes a recurrent motif), as well as a fully developed case of socially imposed duty conflicting with natural love. These ideas are consummated and elevated in the end of *The Parson's Widow*, where the old lady, who has outlived three husbands, confronted with the fact of young love, bids goodbye to the creatures of her farm, and all things of the earth she loves. (Animals are strongly associated with physical life *per se* in *Day of Wrath* and *Ordet*.) After some few hints of the goodness and wisdom in an austere, domineering, and comical character, she finally becomes a figure of poignancy that almost wells up to tragic proportions. Thus, in this third film of Dreyer, age yields gracefully, graciously to death, and leaves life to youth. Later solutions will not be so simple, but the matter is already stated unmistakably.

Expression through action itself is here, as in the other early work, predominant over more purely formal means. Nevertheless, there are distinct formal properties in the stately gait of the ancient widow as opposed to the caperings of the young people; and her dark clothing and regulated household is a contrast, as in *Day of Wrath*, to the sunny countryside where the lovers meet.

Noteworthy are two scenes unique in Dreyer. One is quite phallic, where the hero wiggles his finger through a cloth being woven on the other side, not by his girlfriend as he thinks, but by a shocked old maid who grabs his member and yells for help. The other is a burlesque foreshadowing of horrors of future films, when the young man masquerades as a demon, grotesque to the point of absurdity, to scare the old lady out of his life, and maybe even hers. The monster's foot-long claws and fangs, ludicrous enough, are complemented by an impish face on his backside; and, of course, the plan fails. It is not through evil, mock or otherwise, that rigid authority is dissolved —but only through love. (The prime parable of this is the corruption of Anne in *Day of Wrath*.)

The splendid *Parson's Widow* makes its immediate successors all the more disappointing. *Love One Another* contains Dreyer's most complicated plot (a difficulty compounded for us by lack of English titles). It does seem that the narrative technique is flawed, though, since the images themselves fail so often to give even a trace of what is going on. The struggle of love in a repressive society is central here as in later work; and the brutality of the mob scenes anticipates that in the *Passion of Joan*, as well as the violence in *Vampyr* and *Day of Wrath*. To add at least a pinch of praise, Dreyer elicits excellent acting, as always.

Of the fairy tale *Once Upon a Time* only a fragment exists. The Museum pamphlet refers to it as a finished work of which most has been lost, but there sometimes seem to be two or three takes of the same action, indicating rushes. What was shown was really not very promising and makes me suspect that Dreyer just abandoned the project.

Mikael is the only Dreyer film with a distinctly upper-class milieu, and the combination of lavish interiors with a melodramatic story makes for an extremely "stagey" quality. At least in the other melodramas, contrivances of plot are more or less balanced or obscured by straightforwardness of settings; but here all is artificial. It is a deliberate choice to express the atmosphere of suffocating luxury in which the artist-hero lives; and, indeed, this movie is all shot in interiors, the only case where Dreyer provides only the merest glimpse of nature, the outdoors. The effect is not altogether fortunate, as I have mentioned. I am sure that the absence of English titles did special injury to this theatrically conceived film, since the precise points of tension and climax needed for dramatic realization cannot be made through synopsis alone, but require the lines themselves. Still, there is, to the naked eye, not much formal interest or plastic beauty in *Mikael*.

Its highlight is when Dreyer creates an ingenious interplay between the artist, his audience, and his painting. These shots of the hero posed before his unveiled picture, of a suffering Titan, so that his own form is composed in that image to balance the other heroic figure, build a passage of real visual impact.

In another way, the film bears its maker's stamp more strongly, for, with the old artist trying to hold onto his young male model Mikael, we recognize a constant theme of Dreyer, that of youth up against age. And the typically abrupt intercutting of the artist on his deathbed with young Mikael on his love(life) bed, as the old man calls for him in vain, is a resolution much like that of *The Parson's Widow*, though markedly less serene.

Master of the House is probably the master's least remarkable feature film (the shorts are not quite worth discussing). The imagery never possesses the power or glory that even in Dreyer's poorer works shows in random redeeming shots. The story is not only melodramatic, but predictable and ordinary; though the situation of repressive dogmatic authority crushing love and life may be faintly related to themes in other films.

The caged bird, which the oppressed wife dotes on and the tyrannical husband dislikes to the point of menace, is a motif implying the impingement of free life, appearing again in *Vampyr*; and is a distant relative of the birds in *The Passion of Joan*, as well as *Ordet*. And the clock, its pendulum ending in a heartshape, the "beat" of which is started again when the wife returns to her repentant spouse, is a direct ancestor of the timepiece in *Ordet*.

The final work that marks Dreyer's early period is *The Bride of Glomdale*, a pleasant undistinguished romance. The use of wheatfields for love scenes is later found in *Day of Wrath*; and the story of young lovers forbidden by parents to marry has some similarity to *Ordet*. The lack of emotional charge in *The Bride* is plainly indicated by the fact that the climax is a suspense sequence where the hero is being swept toward a waterfall; an episode of purely superficial excitement obviously suggested by the perils of Gish in Griffith's *Way Down East*, but not cut nearly as well.

With the next work, *The Passion of Joan of Arc*, there occurs a most striking change in both the film-maker's style and his intensity of thematic concentration. A few potent shots in previous movies hardly promise the unique and brilliant imagery that here bursts forth frame after frame. Chiefly striking earlier were lushly lit views of lakes and trees; now there is almost no nature, but empty sky; and mostly stark interiors, with all picturesqueness sacrificed for all intensity's sake. The framing of characters in bare space before neutral walls or skies represents both a compositional innovation and a device whereby the depicted historical events and personages are lifted out of their time and place, so their impacts and passions are felt, immediate and ageless. The basic pictorial principle of *Joan* is that the eye should be undistracted from the passion itself.

Also in this film appears, just as suddenly, another device henceforth typical of Dreyer, the long-drawn pan shot, which precisely does render the action with a panoramic sense. Influence of the German moving-camera school can be detected here, as in the even more unexpected zoom shots. The rapid back-and-forth camera movements, used on the mouths of shouting characters to evoke visually the air-splitting noise, are especially reminiscent of such shots as the zoom to the eavesdropping ear in *Variety*. Most obviously novel, however, are the shots of soldiers, and of their dispersing the aroused populace, shown upside down. Such portrayal of evil—which, for Dreyer, is the denial of life—as the reverse of natural process is later found in the inverted images of Absalon, Inger, and David Gray, who die unnatural deaths in *Day of Wrath*, *Ordet*, and *Vampyr*; as well as in the upside-down shadows which play in the last.

The new resources Dreyer employs are part of a summoning up of powers to express, for the first time, in depth and fullness, those themes most closely approached in *The Parson's Widow* and, elsewhere, merely hinted at. Dreyer's old camera techniques, editing, and imagery genre were bound up with a kind of narrative form, and, indeed, a type of vision, too literary and literal for the further development of his ideas.

The vision of Joan is inspired or demoniac. Her passion is observed with clinical detail in the sharp-etched, stark compositions, the many relentless close-ups. But this is also *loving* detail, for Joan is the first of Dreyer's possessed, a lineage which may be traced through the victims of *Vampyr* to Anne in *Day of Wrath* and Johannes in *Ordet*; characters who work out their passions throughout the process of their films with peculiar intensity and directness, so that identification with the director himself is implicit.

This passion charges ideas already familiar from earlier films. The frictions between freedom and authority; between love (here, of God) and repressive custom; between youth (Joan states at the start that she is nineteen) and age (all the clerics except the few who side with her are distinctly old, if not ancient); between duty (to her ideals) and love (of life); and, ultimately and essentially, between life (for which Joan struggles) and death (which her opponents impose); all existed before, but never before struck fire.

Joan herself catches fire, bears fire to her people from her God, and is bared to the core of burning soul and body by her flames. Inner fire let out, heavenly fire on earth, turn out to be all-consuming. But that is her self-fulfilment. She is tempted by the flowers of life (the only "nature" in this film), and horrified by the skull, too recent; but seeing her crown of thorns swept up as trash, she realizes her destiny.

Symbols, of the concrete metaphorical kind, are more numerous in *The Passion of Joan* than anywhere else in Dreyer. Apart from the phallic finger and heart-shaped pendulum-weight, I recall none earlier. In this alone, the artist's departure, the newness of levels he travels, becomes conspicuous. Besides the fire and flowers and thorns, Dreyer employs: a crosslike shadow cast by a windowpane framework, which consoles Joan in prison, and is obliterated by the Inquisitor, who steps into the light and whose purpose is in fact to trick Joan into recanting; an infant being suckled, connoting life, and similar in image and function to a shot in Pudovkin's earlier *Mother*, though also analogous to the cross which the heroine clutches to her breast for spiritual succor at the stake; birds which fly off as the fire starts, heralding Joan's final victory and the liberation of her soul; and the smoke from the fire, which incites the people to rebel, shrouding them as well as their saint in its oppressive darkness.

The irony of the deathly smoke issuing from Joan's immortal fire is one element in a complex of tensions between life and death. There is no intrinsic contradiction between love of life and love of God, but Joan is constrained by man-made institutions to choose one or the other. When she recants, the crowd celebrates her fleshly salvation, in a scene intercut, as baldly as Dreyer always does, with Joan's hair being shorn and her thorny laurels thrown away. Life itself becomes a mockery, for death is now the saint's natural course—which is indicated in the people's grotesque antics and contortions as they frolic carnivally beneath the gallows. The crowd, which sides with Joan, learns, though, through English spears and maces, that the life of the spirit in their world means the death of the body. Not until twenty-five years later, does Dreyer show us another kind of world.

Vampyr transpires in no *earthly* world at all; but clearly in the realm of absolute vision. *Vampyr* is a veritable initiation into the mysteries of death. It fits the form of what Parker Tyler has called trance-film, the prototype of which is *Caligari*: in which an essentially passive hero experiences events which function primarily as manifestations of the unconscious. Dreyer goes so far as to exaggerate the unearthliness of landscape and characters, "spiritualizing" all in twilight and mystic air, so all perception is as through a glass darkly; as if there were a distance greater than space between this region and our mortal eyes. Moreover, the characters' movements are automatic and fated, as though the real actors were invisible forces; and their voices float so hollow and distant on the soundtrack as to hardly belong to the speakers, rather suggesting disembodied spirits.

The shading of *Vampyr* is awfully fine, since the action itself is treated matter-of-factly even when bizarre, and the point of view is never fantastical but literal and realistic. Indeed, there appears to be a more or less traditional and coherent story, with the implicit promise that all may be explained. But it never is. Causal connections between events are deviously lacking, and stranger powers rush into the vacuum. Logic is undermined, and the "plot" can be followed at best with the aid of our most hidden resources. This subversion of "reality" reaches its climax toward the end, when the scene of David Gray finding the bound heroine is repeated exactly, a visual echo and more, the very ghost of event.

By such ellipsis and abstraction, Dreyer relates crucial *emotional* images without adequate *reason*; creating an apparent reality as immediately convincing as dream, but as ultimately elusive. Thus, the viewer is truly taken in. And not only are we involved in the structure of dream which is the film; the characters are entranced within the trance. So we experience "the strange adventures of David Gray" the way *he* does; and the crucial vision of evil and death which he suffers, his own funeral, we see right along with him, through his eyes, staring up out of the coffin.

The whole film becomes ultimately the kind of dream-vision had in "primitive" cultures, whether induced by solitude, hunger, or drugs; a revelation of the terrible secrets of existence, often in the form of a journey, an adventure of the dreamer's spirit in other worlds or underworlds. In this case, the matter of life and death is epitomized in the figure of the vampire. Through experience of this *tremendem*, David Gray is shocked to awareness and pressured to pass from innocence and ignorance to consciousness of forces that must be confronted. First he—or his spirit—shrinks from the horror, then investigates it, and finally resists it. And, as I mentioned, Dreyer subtly brings us right along on this rite of passage into the dark world and back.

An early image, of a reaper and his scythe in silhouette, graphically establishes *Vampyr*'s preoccupations. The death-scented smoke from *Joan of Arc* seeps into this film as a thick mist pervading the whole landscape. There is not a sunny frame in the whole movie. Even when the hero and heroine get across the Stygian waters, the picture does not appreciably brighten, as they walk through tall trees arranged in disquieting symmetry, straight row after row. But youth and love do survive and escape age and death, the land of the old, the old Count, the old servants, the old doctor and old vampire who drain the life-blood of the young (as the old doctor bled and weakened Joan).

And death again, as it did for Joan, has its salubrious side. It is a deliverance for the Count and the bedridden girl, animated as they are by evil spirits. On the other bony hand, it is unnatural and horrible for the hero, David Gray, as he is borne, alive and healthy, but trancefixed, in a coffin toward his grave.

So Dreyer's old themes operate in a very new way in *Vampyr*. And other changes accompany those in plot and character conception. Camera movement is less insistent and consistent than in *Joan*, and the imagery is a blend of that film's abstraction with the picturesque qualities of earlier work. Most notable as technical departure is Dreyer's only use ever of superimposition, to create shadows which leave bodies and return, as well as transparent spirits; supernatural effects to reinforce the other strangeness. The soundtrack is quite successful in this too, with its precisely eerie music; and the strange noises which serve as characters' voices, from the canine growls the old villain intermittently emits, to the weirdly distant, unearthly tones of David Gray's love. A poignant touch occurs when the hoarse

voice of the possessed girl alters, at the moment of her final liberation, to the pure high pitch of the ethereal heroine.

A very special film, obscure enough in origin, though a little is lit
up by tracking traces of its literary basis. Dreyer took, it looks like,
whatever appealed to him, I mean, struck his fan(ta)cy, out of a
collection five stories wide by Sheridan Le Fanu, titled *In a Glass
Darkly*. Thus, from *The Familiar*, comes the concept of a malevolent
being that materializes as a bird; from *Mr. Justice Harbottle*, a procession emerging from a closet (the peg-legged henchman comes out
of the clock in *Vampyr*); from *The Room in the Dragon Volant*,
the hero, fully conscious, lying helpless and immobile in a coffin
gazing upwards; and, from *Carmilla* (the basis of Vadim's *Blood
and Roses*), the vehement passion of the girl vampire for her female
victim. The apparent randomness of selection does indicate how
much *Vampyr* is imagined rather than thought-wrought.

Other influence, specifically Griffith's, may be discerned in the
film's finale. The situation of a villain meeting his death in a granary,
buried under heaps of cascading flour, is the same as the conclusion
of *A Corner in Wheat*. The machinery which grinds out doom here
is much like the torture apparatus in *Joan of Arc*, with its inexorable
wheels, and the wheel again turns, less elaborate and abstract, in the
inquisition of the witch in *Day of Wrath*.

The conclusion, with good triumphant and evil destroyed, would
be more comforting were it the integral function of a complete
process; and not the fluke of a fanciful providence and literal *deus
ex machina*. But the happy end is just a fragment of a figment of
fantasy, and the afterimage of the whole is disturbing, a dark taste
in the eye.

But not so black as *Day of Wrath*'s. Insofar as *Vampyr* is a horror
and/or fantasy film, it constitutes escapist entertainment. Insofar as
it is what Parker Tyler calls "trance film," the horror is definitely
imagined rather than grounded in any real world. Such colorful
buffers and morbid distractions as *Vampyr* does offer give way in
Day of Wrath to relentless investigation.

The picture largely proceeds as an inquiry, on the part of the
artist as well as his characters. It begins with the detection and trial
of the old witch Marthe and continues with the suspecting and
ultimate testing of Anne. As Dreyer before used the pressures of a
trial to squeeze out the utmost and innermost resources of a character, and then used the abnormal powers of evil to grind characters
to sheer spirit before those forces ground down themselves, here, he
compounds the two motifs of trial and magic into an uncannily

oppressive atmosphere, which suffocates the heroine until she must gasp out her darkest secrets.

More is revealed than Anne's guilt; a whole social system built on the skeleton of death is probed to the bone. Against this, against age, rigidity, and, indeed, the dead, is pitted, as in *Joan of Arc* and *Vampyr*, the strivings of young love.

Plot here is, in complete reversal of *Vampyr*'s form, tightly knit in inexorable causality. The absolute logic of an ossified, severely formal society becomes fateful. Among those obsessed with death, the truly alive can only be distrusted. Anne is altogether too vivacious to accept. Her stirrings or life are not only conspicuous but disruptive. Absalon's mother reacts severely to this annetidote for the sickness unto death that is her life; perceiving sensibly enough that her son's young wife does not measure to community standards, let alone achieve the proper mundane solidity she herself has, the efficient, dutiful homemaker. The mercurial Anne eludes the mold of her culture.

Here the dead dominate all. The shade of Anne's witch-mother tones the beginning of the film, as her husband's does the end. Due to the first deceased, Anne is suspected of supernatural powers, and she herself suspects she may have them; due to the second, she is suspected of committing the crime (and she herself also suspects this). She seeks to emerge from the shadow but lives in the valley of death. Her only light is her husband's son. With Martin, she blooms; she appears in the brightest scenes, among quivering leaves and waving grain. But, when Absalon dies and the air is further polluted, the fertile nature of their joys becomes darkened with the thick mist of *Vampyr*.

"Life must be secretive to survive," goes one of Absalon's lines. He himself has trespassed, saving Anne's mother to have Anne, with which the old witch accuses him to save herself, but only succeeds in heightening his guilt. The secret makes him morbid and solitary, all the unhappier for Anne. Then her guilt for Absalon's death replaces his as a central motive.

And, as the father once said, when Anne asked to stay with him that night, after the witch was caught, "No, I must commune with myself"; so the son now says, when Anne asks, "Shall I keep watch with you?"—"No, I should like to be alone." Her secret is as needed for survival and as destructive of life, of love, as that of Absalon. Anne does join Martin keeping watch and swears her innocence over Absalon's corpse; at which Martin hesitantly must swear his allegiance to her. But, at the funeral, Absalon's mother stands up with all the force of her terrible faith—a hooded figure filling the screen with black—does her awful, lawful duty, and denounces her daughter-in-law. And Martin puts the dead between him and Anne, switches sides. And Anne admits her witchery.

Law and duty serve death and are imposed by the old. Absalon took a young wife, gave her no child, wants life but cannot make it, is even incapable of comforting her with human tenderness. When Anne trembles at the pursuit of old Marthe, her husband clasps his hands in prayer, and she falls into Martin's arms. As the old woman screams at the stake, Absalon prays, and the frightened Anne is comforted by Martin's caresses. Absalon tries "to be young with the young," but they go off to the woods and leave him to his musty study. Anne's duty is against her nature, all nature. Her husband's uneasiness with nature is brought to a climax in the storm through which he struggles home. This is a parallel in reverse to scenes before, for here he is outdoors while the lovers are inside; but the skies are now dark, while it is lighter in the house. Nature is alien to Absalon, and the gentle breeze that lulled the lovers becomes a raging gale around him. (The menacing sound of wind heard by Absalon's family recurs in *Ordet* during the fatal birth, suggesting nature turned hostile; and also, in the chill moving air, the idea of deathly spirits.)

So, the old, too, grasp at life as best they can. The aged witch is, indeed, the character who most vehemently cries out for life. Of course, she also collects charms from under the gallows, and says, "There is power in evil." Marthe's evil is, paradoxically, innocent compared to those who persecute it. Under their stress, she no longer trusts in evil or is familiar to death, but simply clings to life tooth and nail. This relationship to physical life is expressed when she escapes from her cottage, groping her way through the sheep. Anne and Martin frolic briefly with a goat during one of their idylls; and no other characters are seen with animals. Dreyer's relationships are all precise: As life and nature are alien to Absalon and beautiful to Anne, they are a desperate need for old Marthe. She uses nature as a refuge when life is almost lost, a fact exactly rendered both in her escape among the animals and in her clinging for support to the fences of the fields. Absalon leans, likewise, during the storm, for he, too, is old and lost. Only the young lovers move with grace and confidence in natural surroundings; though always crosscut with contrasting scenes of Absalon's guilty brooding, Laurentius's dying, and, finally, the deathwatch of Absalon's mother.

In this film, then, Dreyer, more than ever, opposes death to life.

Before, the lethal stake was, at least on one level, a deliverance, for Joan, and for the victims in *Vampyr*; but here it means stark destruction to the old witch who raves in no ecstasy but terror. Yet the smothering vapor, of *Joan*'s burning, of *Vampyr*'s woods, of the final rustic tryst of Anne and Martin, does mystify this agonizing scene so the smoke becomes incense, as the choir sings angelically. And we may precall the Doctor's remark to the grieving Mikkel in *Ordet* (the Doctor, who so carefully puts on rubber gloves before touching Inger and who so meticulously wipes his hands when he is through): "Remember, Borgen, there may be great beauty in pain"—a comment that does as little to relieve Mikkel's anguish as the singing soothes Marthe's. The aesthetic aspect is undeniable though and emphasized in Absalon's record of the event, that the witch was burnt "on this very beauteous day." It also appears in a precise metaphor: The boy singers (again the motif of youth ruled by the old) are first shown, being conducted in the *Dies Irae*; then, their voices are heard, while the image is just the choir master's *shadow* on the sheet of music. Thus, beauty soars in a song of death led by an actual shade. (If the spirit of death is thus rendered, note that, as Anne wills Martin to come to her, with the magic of life and love, a glow illuminates her.)

So, even in *Day of Wrath*, there is something to be said for the powers of darkness, for death itself, for the whole morbid mystique that infects the society depicted. In Marthe's death, horror did mingle with beauty. Yet her prosecutor, Laurentius, dying after her curse, does not expire, as we might expect, in cold light or darkness, but in a gentle glow. He dies well, as Absalon remarks. This serene scene is lyrically intercut with the lovers drifting on the lake; which is not merely a contrast, thematically, but a harmony, emotionally. In a similar way, the communion of the two death-ridden men over the cup is paralleled by the earlier drinking of Anne and Martin together from a spring. Death and age, too, have their rights and proper rituals, their beauties. They may be fitting and even noble, so long as they do not violate nature. Laurentius, dying, has the grace to doubt the justice of Marthe's doom and to accept his own fate with the dignity and wisdom his austere faith does here provide.

This demonstrates ironically well that the only real peace, the only ecstasy that does not burn into dirty choking smoke, in the world of Laurentius and Absalon, is that of death. The "flame" of life Martin and his father see in Anne's eyes becomes, by the alchemy of death, the wild fire of possession that burned about Joan of Arc. Anne herself is ultimately forced to take the only possible peace, as she took the only possible passion. That adultery is not her real sin; it never seriously disturbs her or Martin. But, when she invokes the powers of evil and death, she accepts the very values she hates, she turns truly guilty. Martin may be right after all to abandon her—a witch. The powers of life are defeated, the passion of Anne is over.

The end of Ordet is also a funeral, but with its processes absolutely in reverse to those in Day of Wrath. Ordet, in fact, is quite different from any other Dreyer film. While The Passion of Joan proceeds by abstraction and intensification of a historical world, Vampyr by variations on a dream world, and Day of Wrath by conjuring up the spirit of a dead world, Ordet is the re-creation of our own world.

"Re-creation"—to fully understand the implications here of the word, we must consider the forces at work. Death itself is present, palpably so in the visions of Johannes; though its human adherents are no longer vampires or inquisitors, but the members of a gloomy religious sect led by Petersen the tailor. Explicitly opposed to them is farmer Borgen's group, who stress fulfilment rather than denial; and Borgen's vital, very pregnant daughter-in-law Inger is full-blown life incarnate. The third force we do not encounter until the conclusion, though it is often mentioned throughout—true faith, absolute faith. Without this, neither sect can win, over the other, or win the other over. So their arguments are merely circular.

But their leaders must confront each other about a very real problem. Borgen's son Anders and Petersen's daughter Anne want to marry. After considerable maneuvering, the expansive old farmer yields; but Petersen is rigidly opposed. He hums dreary hymns as he sews, keeps his meek Anne like a bird in a cage, and leads the small congregation in his home in sententious confession and mournful song. As old Borgen and Anders approach, their cart is seen in the ripe fields and, then, in the tailor's house, heard beneath his arid sermon. Dreyer visually elaborates this auditory contrast between the lovers and the deniers of life with standard complementary themes of his; when the boy and girl are sitting at either end of a table, between them is her old mother with her bible—age and dogma interfering with youth and nature. There is a related image among the singers of a young boy wedged between two old worshippers, evidently relatives who have dragged him to the service.

At the end of this sequence, when religious differences have destroyed any hope of the marriage, Borgen and Petersen further reveal themselves under pressure of another crisis; the news over the phone of Inger's peril in childbirth seems to Borgen terrible, faith-shaking; and to Petersen, providential, a warning to the sinner to repent. Thus, the two men and their groups are even more definitely aligned with life on the one hand and death on the other.

But the picture is not so black and white as that. This is most tangible in the quality of its light. In the indoor Inger scenes especially, there is a feeling of the buoyance of air. The atmosphere never possesses the oppression of *Day of Wrath*, the murkiness of *Vampyr*, the harsh clarity and contrasts of *Joan of Arc*. There is none of the smoke or fog of the three previous films. The search episode toward the end is dark, but not threatening; and the death scenes have solemn chill and cold illumination, but not a tomb-like air. The atmosphere, realized through light, is one of serene lucidity.

For all is part of a pattern, the dark of which is death. Inger's serves to reconcile the feuding families, as well as to shock Johannes back to sanity. Such small miracles are explicable in terms of the normal forces of life and death. The big miracle requires the extraordinary power of faith.

This power is preached by Johannes throughout. But his ecstasy is mad; as he ascends the hill to speak, the white wash flutters like false angels, spectacular and disturbing. (The second scene with the hill is a direct parallel, but without the wash, just the bare poles that held the clothesline. The apocalyptic frenzy is ended.) Johannes is not a false prophet so much as half a one; his vision is only clear in one direction, and, though he may be "closer to God," as Inger says, he is also too far from the earth, his passion is unnatural. In his tremendous scene with little Inger, Johannes suggests that it might be better to have a mother in heaven than on earth—which idea she naturally rejects. His alienation is manifest in an awkward, shambling gait, uncoordinated gestures, an abstract facial expression, a high, monotonous, faraway voice—as if he does not belong on earth —the severest kind of *unbalance*. And in Johannes's sermon on the hill, he is framed against only the sky; we sense his feet are not on earth; while old Borgen and Mikkel watch from down below, half-hidden by the wheat which grows about them. They are perhaps too much of the earth. (Borgen's earthiness is epitomized when he goes for consolation to sit with his pigs, as the worldliness of the Vicar and the Doctor are evoked in their mutual partaking of coffee and cigars while discussing religion.)

But the balance of worldly and godly is ultimately achieved, along with that of life and death, by faith, which embraces all. When Johannes collapses during his abortive revival of Inger, falling on her bed at the foot in reverse of her position at the head, and is carried off motionless, it is the death of the madman-Christ; and when he reappears at the funeral, the door he slowly opens is like a coffin lid being raised. Johannes returns, resurrected—his *body* rejoined with his *spirit*, again *balanced*—just when Inger's coffin is about to be finally sealed. And, through him, and little Inger's faith, her mother is brought back to life—her *spirit* reanimating her *body*. It is this union that Dreyer's previous heroines Joan and Anne could not have; they were forced to sacrifice one for the other (as for the wispy girl in *Vampyr*, there is not much sense of her wish being solid in the first place). And the spirit of old Borgen is charged, and Mikkel's too, with the faith that bore the miracle and now is born of it.

Ordet progresses by many paths toward that conclusion. The struggle between life and death is never more explicit in Dreyer than in the childbirth sequence—until the end itself. Inger's giving birth is in the tradition of other scenes where physical stress is part of the process of losing life: Joan's bleeding, David Gray's transfusion, Marthe's torture. It is a crisis and a test. Indeed, as *The Passion of Joan* was a trial of faith (and of the deliverance Joan believes in) and *Day of Wrath* a trial of magic (and of the faith it destroys, between Martin and Anne), so, the whole of *Ordet* is a trial of faith and its miracles.

Twice, in fact, there occur camera movements analogous to the long pans during the trials in *Joan* and *Day of Wrath*. The first shows the morose singers of Petersen's sect (who are intercut with Inger's labor, to signify the forces opposed); and the second, the lively singers of Borgen's group, not rigidly posed, darkly lit, or severely rendered as are the figures in the previous three instances. These latter hymners are assembled at Inger's funeral, but good-spiritedly accept death as a meaningful, natural aspect of life. Their treatment by the camera suggests the comparison (or trial) of their faith with that of the other sect, as well as the whole background of trials in Dreyer's work.

And the ultimate test soon comes. All converges toward the bare room where Inger's corpse lies; the parlor so full of warmth before, now stripped of its furniture and decorations, and bathed with strange twilight or dawn light. It is as stark as the place of Joan's or Marthe's trial or the room of Absalon's coffin. It is a place for final recognitions. To this place all come; here all assemble at last. Through the wheatfields is borne Inger's coffin (fields are a motif repeated in *Ordet* much as the countryside in *Day of Wrath*); through the archway come the Petersens, among chickens that flutter with stirrings of life and vague intimations of what is to happen; through the door comes Johannes. All are drawn to this ultimate place. In front of the empty wall, in pure, abstracted space, the confrontations, recognitions, resolutions take place. Old Borgen meets Johannes and Petersen in peace. His son is sane; Anne and Anders may marry—two small wonders have come to pass. Death has, thus, served life.

Now faith must prove itself. A horse whinnies outside, with perhaps a sensing of powers in the air, perhaps the suggestion of an apocalyptic trumpet call; and, certainly, this is another association of animals with elemental life. For Johannes receives the true word to speak, and Inger's hands tremble into movement.

Hands, which feel life, by which the things of the earth become tangible: so, Inger ties old Borgen's hands with yarn when she advocates Anders's marriage; so, the Doctor puts on his gloves before the birth; so, Anders takes Anne's hand when Petersen has given her; so, the child takes Johannes's as they pray for her mother to live. And the camera itself caresses the objects and creatures of *Ordet*, glides through the air to make it tangible. The camera moves to impart a fullness, roundness of life to its subjects, as when it turns full circle around Johannes telling little Inger he will bring her mother back to life. The camera searches out space, touching lovingly upon all details as it travels to capture an act or gesture. Thus Dreyer's sensibility, his own feeling for physical creation is impressed upon the film.

His machine is more than humanized, though. The camera moves with a fourth force—besides those of life, death, and faith—fate. A process hinted at in *Joan of Arc* and *Vampyr*, more noticeable in *Day of Wrath*, becomes, here, unmistakable. Slowly, surely, the camera often moves to *anticipate* what happens; moves to a window that is to be looked out, moves to a door before a character enters, moves to an object about to be used. Thus, a sense is conveyed that all is somehow predestined. Dreyer himself is responsible, he has created the world of *Ordet*, its actions and its pattern; and, with the camera, he expresses his absolute power over that world.

This is not obvious until the end, which is not credible in terms of real, off-screen life. Of course, the message is: If we had faith, such things could really happen. But we do not; so the miracle is clearly, purely, just a creation of Dreyer's. The world we could recognize so far as ours, becomes, at the end, absolutely his. Dreyer resurrects Inger. As god of her world, he has that power. On another level, he is only an instrument, as the camera is his, of a force that claims his own faith and possesses him. This power charges the camera to move and, in its relation to the events of the film, takes on the guise of destiny.

So, after all the years and all the triumphs of death, now, with this one scene, the balance is restored, the energies of nature, love, life, so long pent up, find irresistible release, with all the force of fate. Inger rises, dazed, and presses her open mouth all along Mikkel's face. The hunger for the flesh, for life itself, denied and thwarted by so many forms of death in a generation of films, at last is satisfied.

Anders starts the clock again, which Mikkel stopped when Inger died. It ticks, the silence is over and seeing the pendulum's beat we may remember the one in *Master of the House*, which had as its weight a heart.

Johannes prayed, "Grant me—the word." The word was the speech of faith needed to resurrect Inger. But there is another "word." Mikkel speaks it, and Inger, in his embrace, repeats it, the last sounds of *Ordet*. The word is "life."

APPENDIX: DISILLUSION—SENSES OF *GERTRUD*

Gertrud is like one of those old, slow, gloomy Scandinavian sex movies before they discovered flesh; like a theater melodrama eternalized on film; like a Bergman picture minus chic; except, as a dear friend of mine remarked, it takes forever—a scale on which all love becomes a movement toward salvation.

All the formalities are religiously observed in *Gertrud*—so rigorously that it becomes clear they are the mere tense surface of life. The time of the film swallows all words, and runs strong between, deep beneath all gestures. These are not merely the petty social formalities, but art, marriage, rank, morality, fame, and, indeed, the accustomed ideas and ideals of man. Success in these is shown to have no power against the ultimate failure.

The characters talk to each other, according to the conventions of speech, only a bit more so. They speak a little too deliberately, and looking past each other. Their isolation is clear. And it is clear that they are never talking about the real issues, but using speech as a habitual indirection, a way of brushing things they cannot come to grips with; and, finally, their speech possesses a ritual opacity: It is the series of symbols and expressions with which man clothes himself to take on personality and to live (act a life) on the way to his definitive death. This is not so much a film on the difficulty of communication, as on the difficulty of existence.

All the people of *Gertrud* have the same sense, manifest in various ways, that they are not living the real life. They have intimations of what a mere show it is that passes for reality, that nothing they do is any less vain than the procession of students and the speeches honoring the poet—ostentation, acting, the merest illusion.

All are profoundly, precisely disillusioned. The process of *Gertrud* is the baring of painful partial truth after truth, with no prospect of full revelation. Gertrud's husband is continually disillusioned by her, though it is obvious how he creates over and over the illusions she must destroy, from her first hint of leaving to her final admission that she loved him "in a way." Her old lover, the poet, is disillusioned by what he discovers of the past, but mainly because of the hopes of her he maintains, which are plainly doomed to failure. Her young lover, the musician, the object of her own illusion, is ironically enough quite disillusioned from the start and, indeed, goes on to show that the absence of illusion means defeat—at least when it is not founded in truth and consciousness, but only in muddled despair. Gertrud herself is most thoroughly and systematically disillusioned. The poet disillusioned her once, and for all time, so it seemed; so, she was able to enter into a conventional, good, realistic marriage with no nonsense, no illusions; and yet the composer revived love in her, that love that must mean (dis)illusion, being an absolute passion directed toward a mutable creature.

Dreyer is most pointedly revealing in *Gertrud* why love on this earth must fail. It is always partial, always conditional, of a particular place and time. Yet the characters grasp at it as their redemption from what they stare at past each other—nothing, eternity. Sometimes the sense of reality's unreality, of nothing, seizes them. Gertrud's husband muses on it all seeming like a dream, as he rides back from the opera. She herself disquiets her young lover, toward the crowning of his desire, by murmuring of life as "a dream, a long dream"; and, just after this, she undresses as he plays his nocturne, and only her shadow can be seen—an ironical image of life as dream indeed.

We create our own worlds, Dreyer shows, in *Day of Wrath*, where human belief creates life in its images, and in *Ordet*, where human faith overcomes the "natural," the "real." The people of *Gertrud* exist in a godless, rational world, where they are still driven to seek solace and hope and grace, irrationally, in love. But the stark reality of illusion, of the emptiness of the worldly show, stares them in the face, stares from their faces, all the time. They tremble with doubt and mortality, and only Gertrud has the strength to face it all directly. She who will not compromise, who will settle for no less than the absolute in love, must find the absolute elsewhere.

At the end we find her, at home in aloneness, cherishing memories (not so much with regret or nostalgia for past lost reality, as with aesthetic or philosophic appreciation for beautiful illusions), having found no belief, no greater love, no final truth; resigned and even serene in her disillusion, meditative and almost saintlike in her austere isolation. Gertrud practices a religious discipline, but she has no faith. The world is as nothing, but there is nothing to fill that vacuum. Gertrud has achieved her absolute, a relative, but no more, of absolution. The last shot of *Gertrud*, held interminably, is of an empty room, a closed door.

DEFENSE OF JAYNE MANSFIELD

BY MICHAEL McCLURE

No. 32, Spring, 1964

This essay was written before the death of Marilyn Monroe, the Perfect Mammal—and I send her my farewell in another book . . .

I.

Jayne Mansfield is a member of a black American tradition that stretches from Poe to her—and includes Thoreau and many known and unremembered beings. —I said that to Henry Miller. He was drinking, and I was high on mountain air. I was serious, and we discussed it; he told me he likes Sophia Loren most, and the conversation drifted to other things. Since that night, I've thought of what I said. I wasn't able to see my dark tradition clearly again and brooded on it. Miller said he thought Jayne Mansfield synthetic and contrived.

There's no more contrivance to Jayne Mansfield than there is to Thoreau or Poe. I'm not speaking of her art as actress. I speak of her as a being. Thoreau and Poe are similar creatures—they capture human imagination by their *existence*. That they catch thought doesn't mean they are synthetic or contrived. I think the three have a secret darkness in common.

I only think of her physical beauty. With Poe, we speak of the beauty of his physical mind, and, with Thoreau, we think of the physiology of his desire for freedom.

A blackness and sexuality and mystery cloudily surrounds all lambs of this world—there is an intense secrecy beneath everything soft. This is not purely an American thing—tho we see much of it here —there is an alienation of creature from creature on our continent, and it fosters mysteries. The great French poet Antonin Artaud is one of the lambs of Europe.

While talking to Henry Miller, Artaud came up. I asked Miller about Artaud because I knew they had met in Pairs . . . it was so natural to go from Jayne Mansfield to Artaud—it was like continuing a conversation about a secret host of this world.

There is nothing more synthetic in the body of Jayne Mansfield than there is in the writing or brain of Artaud. Artaud is a warchief of history as well as a lamb. Artaud is as real a warchief as Crazy Horse, and Jayne Mansfield is as much a black lamb as Artaud. Artaud fought for eternal truth and beauty and the immortality of his supermasochistic soul. We only dimly know and faintly guess for what Crazy Horse died—his mind is a foreign universe forever closed. (What sight of American mountains and bison did he envision over Custer's corpse?) I know that Artaud is a lamb and a warchief, and I know Jayne Mansfield is at least a lamb. My eyes and body tell me she is a lamb. If she were contrived, her capturing of my love would be more strange. In the dark tradition, it is possible that the most sure members are not conscious of the mystery they carry in their physique or words.

The tradition of blackness is a heritage of health carried unconsciously by innocents. The darkness is *Love* that is driven undercover into their bodies or souls and spirits. It makes them darkly luminous. They are the carriers of a lost and necessary health that is desired by those they attract. The innocents, the lambs, that carry darkness must be understood and loved!

Poe, Thoreau, Mansfield are trappers of men's imaginations— whether they do it by bodies of words on the page or by lovely gestures.

How does the lover of every spring flower, awaiting the specific day of each blossoming, become driven to write on civil disobedience?

How does a poet of such fine sensibility as Poe's become involved with the music of decay? His sensibility is lamblike. (Read *The Narrative of A. Gordon Pym*.) Poe's love of clarity and science fastened on more than the decor of love-of-death; his secret writings are a view of the universe that he came to by inspired and idealistic thought. The true black that lies unnoticed in so many beings is healthiness and a striving for health—it is the desire to see, be, speak, and disobey.

The importance of a work of art notwithstanding (Jayne Mansfield leaves no works of art), there is a great importance to each dark being.

Marlon Brando is singular, but he does not contain blackness. He enacted our desire to act, and we trembled. Brando and Jayne Mansfield are both temporal—and Artaud, Poe, Thoreau are immortal. All of them cause us to tremble. There are always overlappings of mortality and immortality, and art and being and being and art . . . it cannot be unraveled because it need not be. There's a secret: *We are all creatures of talents and qualities*—some humans attract our imaginations because of a darkness that they glow outwards, and we long for it.

Jayne Mansfield draws by the black mystery of her physical presence. I know it is a soundness and a wholesomeness I see in her, and I admire it. It is strange that men put down her health—it is so mysterious and dark, because it is suppressed by most who have it.

Surely most loving men would want Jayne Mansfield's love. In Latin America, crowds shout for the sight of her breasts, and she shows herself.*

Jayne Mansfield is ambitious—how black and simple and lovely her ambitions are. How straight she must be with herself sometimes! She looks so sane! There's something clean and simple about ambition—about having your body and winning with it.

The artist may be a catalyst, but how can he work, what may he work with, without the sight of the talents and qualities and mysteries of men and women? How few show themselves as simply as Jayne Mansfield. Perhaps all suppressions are related—and much beauty is a luminescence of the darkly unseen. But that is not a reason to hide—it is a reason to bring to light—there will always be a new beauty recoverable! Where are the bones of Crazy Horse?

* Why do we cover women's breasts. . . ? They haven't always been hidden. The reasons are not moral but economic and sexual. I'd rather see breasts—it would wake a rolling splashing cataract of economic and social doubts—and it would be beautiful. —An awakening of honesty and tenderness.

Jayne Mansfield's secret and her darkness and her wholesomeness are her sexuality. Thoreau's mystery was his health, too—his desire to expand and disobey and withdraw at the pleasure of his own dilation and longings. Thoreau and Mansfield are dark because both must hold within what they should be free to display—it is only dark because it is undercover. The abundance of darkness manifests itself upon the face of Mansfield and the pages of H. D. Thoreau. What mass of Thoreau's thoughts and feelings are left unsaid? . . . What he didn't say is nearly apparent.

Darkness is upon Jayne Mansfield's face and her arms and fingers. Even there, she must hold back to pass censors and creators of suppression. Sexuality is plainly black and mysterious in itself. Sex in darkness and sex in light is always black. We live in an age that darkens sex and often brings hunger to the fields of plenty.

The Greeks, responding to the universe, were lovers of sleek and firm flesh—it was at hand for them—for eye, for touches, for kisses and garlands. They loved exaggeration of sexuality—they consecrated temples to the breasts and buttocks of Venus. They loved the supernaturality of huge breasts, and they were intent on the loveliness of buttocks. They would believe that the torso and limbs and smile of Jayne Mansfield are supernatural.

If Jayne Mansfield's body is Spirit, and I think that it is true of all, then she is supernatural! Her breasts and beauty and body are to be admired. Jayne Mansfield and all lovely sexual beings are held back to a half sexuality and they may not achieve completed voluptuousness. There is health in her that is half manifested—but that is not her fault; *she tries*. She is blocked from completion and fulfillment.

Athens would worship her as Buenos Aires did—or more, Athens would make statues of her.

The secret and mystery of Jayne Mansfield is apparent to the puritanic—the blackness is obvious. She wears the black fur of her body and is crowned by whiteness.

The fame that she has is accounted to the shameless wet-mouthedness of her beauty—but I mean that, too . . . it's part of her mystery and supernaturality . . . the blackness of her health catches at us in our dreams.

Give Jayne Mansfield roses and lilies, and rare honey and juice of apricots and liquors more secret than drambuie and the whitest, most perfect bread. Let Anacreon praise her, and the scholars in two thousand years shall argue whether the verses are silver or golden. She is a dark creature—let the words that come from her lips be remembered; perhaps if she is *cherished*, then words of unearthly wisdom will accompany her beauty. We must not imagine what she is or expect what she is. Leave her to BE and show us her supernaturality.

Free Jayne Mansfield and let her wholly manifest herself! What may she show us of love?—she who is by exaggeration of body and spirit so much a creature of love!

That which is beautiful is not synthetic, tho it must sometimes come out on a field of falseness—she was borne into it by her body. Let the darkness out to the light . . .

II. MANSFIELD & HARLOW

> *Oh, lamb, lamb, could I but remember*
> *the poem I wrote for you*
> *in the book that now lies burnt.*

Jean Harlow, I didn't destroy the poem I wrote for you. And you don't need a defense.

Jayne Mansfield you are THE BLACK. Jean Harlow, you are *La Plus Blanche*—the most white. Marilyn Monroe is THE MAMMAL. Jayne Mansfield alone needs protection and a champion—but you are all creatures of love.

Jean Harlow, were you a better actress than Mansfield or Monroe? . . . I only saw you twice. Once in a film, you stepped between Laurel and Hardy in a hotel lobby—you glided between the thick and thin of comedy like a woman of velvet between two shadows. I was stirred as they were—and they didn't put it on. I saw part of *China Doll*—I couldn't watch it, even for your sake, or, *for* your sake, I wouldn't watch it. But I hoarded pictures of you . . . they are locked tight in my brain. I have never found a biography of you (—nor of Lana Turner, tho I've read some of her love letters in the newspapers, and they should be printed as a tribute to the warmth of women.) I don't care if you could act or not. I fell in love with you in a half minute—your greatness of being brings about love. Some see you as tough whore or nymph—but they see you with the same eyes. You are a unity!

●

I wrote the poem with a still of her profile before me, but it was not her face that caused me to feel loveliness—the sight of her walking came to my eyes. When she stepped, Jean Harlow did not touch the earth—but she did touch it—and she didn't pretend that her toes were not there on it. She passed by with liquid sexual grace of a woman. She didn't take the grace-pose an actress makes before the camera for a million million admirers in futurity. She moved and smiled with the whiteness of life, and she turned to stare! The still photo pictures only her face and a sensitive sleekness to eye, to chin, and to gaze—and a yearning in her neck and shoulder.

A poem I wrote for Jayne Mansfield, and burned was caused by a photo I saw of her. She lay naked with a towel over her buttocks. She looked up, smiling her lovely smile of huge lips and white teeth. Her enormity and supernaturality stretched out upon the boardwalk like a mysterious fleshly first-aid kit of love . . . She had some good thing that was badly needed, and she gave it freely. It seemed that what she had—her medicine—was more than aid; it must also be a challenge. To love Jayne Mansfield would be to find the supernormal in yourself—to reply to her love. And is not that supernormal a true norm? She seems like a red-cross lamb of love with darkness gleaming through delicacy, slim arms, and huge bosoms, into the sunlight. In another snapshot, she holds a tiny teddy bear to her breasts—its nose presses through the opening of a transparent negligee to her nipples—while she looks down smiling with her platinum hair piled up on her head like a waif. And I've seen stranger pictures, too. I like her eyes. I always wonder what she *might* do in life—if she were free to do it. What public demonstration or celebration of love would she make from her blackness if she were free to do it?

Jean Harlow is the whole moist woman and white beast—she seems only to bring simple love—she is sophisticated, and the love is still simple—she wants to bring and receive pleasure with pointed highlights of emotion. Though one is black and one is white, neither Mansfield nor Harlow would injure or tear at a lover. Jean Harlow makes no challenge—she asks for a partner and protector, and, though her body is spiritual, she longs with a soul we all understand. The breasts and vast smile of Jayne Mansfield are a meat-spirit that we can barely conceive of.

The sight of Jean Harlow, womanly and striding, makes gentle concussions that become immortal statuaries in the memory. The appearance of Jayne Mansfield is a sexual occasion. She does not disguise the event; she makes it for us. She does all that can be done with an instant of speech or photograph—sexuality flows from her in undulant and almost comic fullness and implies what is still there. She seems to mock herself with good humor and surplus. It is wrong to think the dark tradition is without humor or is full of gloom—Poe is one of the comic writers . . . even *Walden* has humorous passages. And why is Mark Twain immortal?

Would a small child seeing Jean Harlow in a film remember? Or would he think, in his simpler world, that all women are like Harlow—or that they should be. Jean Harlow has a gift of common and almost perfect love—there is nothing *unattainable* in her. She has a shadowiness—but it is the darkness of a comedy that depends on a higher vision of her soul—her sexuality is white and simple and not dark. Harlow has no *demand* or ecstasy of the flesh—but she searches for feeling and has a gift of intense and gentle pleasure. I think a child *might* remember Mansfield more . . . in the night.

Perhaps Harlow is most to the man or youth who has suffered from love.

And there is Marilyn Monroe, who is a classical balance of men's desires; she is the most understandable, for she contains all—she is no specialist but a perfection—she is understood at once, but the understanding is not casual. Monroe is neither black nor white—she's rosy.

Harlow shows the simple greatness of women—she is an embodiment of simplicity and flow of pleasure. There are more beautiful *eyes* than Harlow's—but there is no more beautiful creature.

Mansfield brings to memory faces and bodies of childlike challenging sexual ecstasy. But should it be challenge? Harlow makes me think of tender pleasures without threat. There are huger breasts than Jayne Mansfield's—but there are few beings like her, and the others hide their blackness behind a cold face.

Let us give honor to beauty in all beings and set men and women free, so they may make their secret selves apparent. Let's not block Jayne Mansfield's unmade acts of sexual and voluptuous greatness, nor any other creature's. What would be the fulfillment of any person's qualities and talents? The Greeks were wise with their beauties and praised supernaturality and naturality alike—and loved women's flesh. Let all beauty be named and recognized as beauty.

A Lover would not deny the blackness of Jayne Mansfield—even tho he prefers his own madonna. To deny is to cancel a part of what love may be. I'm tired of voices of definition and denial.

The dark quality of Mansfield in each being should be cherished —even when there is only a trace—and she flows with it. Harlow and her quality are loved. We will carry Jean Harlow into space, and Mansfield is still among us. For truth, there must be liberty of all loves.

Man, free thinker, are you really solitary, reasoning
On earth where life shakes everything?
Your liberty is disposal of your forces
But the Universe is absent from your resolutions.

Respect an active spirit in the beast.
Each flower is a spirit-genius locked to Nature.
A love mystery lives in metal.
All is sensate! And everything is mighty on your
    being.

Beware in the blind wall a prying stare.
Matter is equipped with a voice!
—Don't make it serve a single impious use!

Often in a dark being lives a hidden god.
And like a newborn eye, covered by lids,
A pure spirit rises under the skin of stones.

Gérard de Nerval

An eternal love-shot lies in all that's modern, and the hallucinations of pure beauty are as sizeless as a universe. Man and woman and child know their loves and hungers, and the irises and constellations are one thing. Cuba, and anger, and gold will not change or become less warm by lies.

Blackness, sexuality, and freedom must not be denied in any shape—or they wither. Love and the Mysterious knock at the door! To deny any beauty is to deny a part of liberty—but everyone is free to do that. To deny any beauty is to deny a part of truth AND ALL DARK WHITE LOVELINESS!

FOUR

THE AMERICAN
AVANT-GARDE

The articles in this chapter are introduced in the "Reader's Guide to the American Avant-Garde Film" (page 3).

POETRY AND THE FILM: A SYMPOSIUM

WITH MAYA DEREN, ARTHUR MILLER, DYLAN THOMAS, PARKER TYLER. CHAIRMAN, WILLARD MAAS. ORGANIZED BY AMOS VOGEL

No. 29, Summer, 1963

[On October 28, 1953, Cinema 16 held two sessions of a symposium with Maya Deren, Parker Tyler, Dylan Thomas, and Arthur Miller. Willard Maas acted as chairman. The following excerpts make up about one half of the symposium. Ideas repeated for the second audience and personal introductions of the panel make up, for the most part, the missing half.]

Maas: In a prepanel discussion earlier this week with the majority of the panel, we decided that maybe the best way to start this discussion would be to try to have the members of the panel outline . . . some of the basic aesthetic principles of the poetic film; and, therefore, I think I would like to call on Mr. Tyler first. . . .

Tyler: Thank you. My thought was that the question, rather than the assumption, by which the symposium will proceed tonight is that of what poetry, in and outside the film, actually is. Perhaps it would be necessary, for such a demonstration, to conceive the question at the start, and honestly, as faced with the two horns of a dilemma. Now that dilemma is: On the one hand, there's the *theory* of poetry, its possibilities as such in the film medium, and on the other hand the *practice* of poetry, as concentrated in the avant-garde film. It should be hoped that we don't snag on either of these but will steer a just course between them. Now I thought we might get an over-all picture of the field to be surveyed, and to that end I'd like to give you a memorandum, so to speak, of the types of poetical expression that do appear in films today; that is, these expressions may be whole or fragmentary, they may be pure or impure, but at least they exist, and they are to be recognized as such. Now, poetical expression falls rather automatically into two groups: that is, poetry as a visual medium and poetry as a verbal medium, or, in a larger sense, as auditory, and that would, of course, include music. We might well begin with some of the shorter films that concentrate on poetry as a visual medium, and this, of course, leads right to Cocteau's *Blood of a Poet*, and to Buñuel-Dali's *Andalusian Dog*, and to Watson's *Lot in Sodom*. All these are classics now, and they emphasized a surrealist poetry of the image and gave rise to schools and styles of avant-garde all over the world. Cinema 16 patrons are familiar with some of these outstanding works—those of Maya Deren, of James Broughton, of Kenneth Anger, of Curtis Harrington. All these film-makers concentrated on what might be called pure cinema—entirely without words as a rule, although sometimes with music. Then to go back (after all, the avant-garde movement in poetry in America goes rather far back, at least to the 1920's) I know there was a type of film which got the name of cine-poem, and these films were impressionistic, but they concentrated on pictorial conceptions of city life, of nature, and, importantly, they stressed abstract patterns. Then, of course, there's the poetry of painting in motion—the pure abstract film—which also has a considerable history (there are Norman McLaren, the Whitney brothers, and many others). Then, also as a candidate in this list (perhaps disputable, but at any rate certainly worth mentioning), a school of naturalistic poetry of which Robert Flaherty was the pioneer. And we presume that his films can be considered integral without the commentary. And, finally, I would include the dream and hallucination sequences, with sound effects sometimes, that appear in commercial films.

Now poetry as a visual-verbal medium: We have the fantasy films of Jean Vigo (these films are primarily visual); and we have the avant-garde films that are set to poems or to poetic prose (those of Sidney Peterson, of Willard Maas, of Ian Hugo); then there's what I would term the "severe formalism" of Sergei Eisenstein, whose montage borders on pure poetry. There are, of course, the Cocteau myth films: *Beauty and the Beast, The Eternal Return,* and *Orpheus.* And we might also include a special class of naturalistic poetry documents, such as *The River* and *The Blood of the Beasts* . . . of course they had commentary. And, then, to conclude, the fifty-fifty fusion; that is, Shakespeare's plays, Eliot's *Murder in the Cathedral,* and the numerous operas that have been filmed. Now these are, admittedly, only the main leads of a very broad field, indeed. Many definitions are required in order to isolate the poetic content and the poetic potentialities in these various manifestations . . . Above all, there's the indications of value that have to be made. I'm sure that the members of the panel, including myself, have a number of significant distinctions and perhaps even more important opinions on these aspects.

Maas: Well, Miss Deren, will you take over from there?

Deren: I'm going to do something I think is a bit risky, and that is to go a little bit into the question of what is poetry, and what distinguishes what we would call poetry from anything else, because I think that only if we can get this straight, can we sensibly discuss poetry in film, or the poetic film, or anything else. Now I say that it's risky, because this is a subject that has been discussed for many, many centuries, and it's been very difficult to pin down. But the reason I'm going into it is not because I think distinctions are important as formulae and as rigidities, but I think they're important in the sense that they give an audience, or any *potential* audience, a preparation, an approach, to what they're going to see. In the sense that if they're thinking they are going to see an adventure film, and if they are confronted with a poetic film, that's not going to go very well. I don't think one is always predisposed toward poetry; the whole notion of distinguishing and, if you will, labeling things is not a matter of defining them so much as a matter of giving a clue to the frame of mind you bring to them. In other words, what are you going to be watching as this unrolls? What are you going to be listening for? If you're watching for *what* happens, you might not get the point of some of the retardations because they're concerned with *how* it happens. Now poetry, to my mind, consists not of assonance; or rhythm, or rhyme, or any of these other qualities we associate as being characteristic of poetry. Poetry, to my mind, is an approach to experience, in the sense that a poet is looking at the same experience that a dramatist may be looking at. It comes out differently because they are looking at it from a different point of view and because they are concerned with different elements in it. Now, the characteristics of poetry, such as rhyme, or color, or any of those emotional qualities which we attach to the poetic work, also may be present in works which are not poetry, and this will confuse us. The distinction of poetry is its construction (what I mean by "a poetic structure"), and the poetic construct arises from the fact, if you will, that it is a "vertical" investigation of a situation, in that it probes the ramifications of the moment, and is concerned with its qualities and its depth, so that you have poetry concerned, in a sense, not with what is occurring but with what it feels like or what it means. A poem, to my mind, creates visible or auditory forms for something that is invisible, which is the feeling, or the emotion, or the metaphysical content of the movement. Now it also may include action, but its attack is what I would call the "vertical" attack, and this may be a little bit clearer if you will contrast it to what I would call the "horizontal" attack of drama, which is concerned with the development, let's say, within a very small situation from feeling to feeling. Perhaps it would be made most clear if you take a Shakespearean work that combines the two movements. In Shakespeare, you have the drama moving forward on a "horizontal" plane of development, of one circumstance—one action—leading to another, and this delineates the character. Every once and a while, however, he arrives at a point of action where he wants to illuminate the meaning to *this* moment of drama, and, at that moment, he builds a pyramid or investigates it "vertically," if you will, so that you have a "horizontal" development with periodic "vertical" investigations, which are the poems, which are the monologues. Now if you consider it this way, then you can think of any kind of combination being possible. You can have operas where the "horizontal" development is virtually unimportant—the plots are very silly, but they serve as an excuse for stringing together a number of arias that are essentially lyric statements. Lieder are, in singing, comparable to the lyric poems, and you can see that all sorts of combinations would be possible.

It seems to me that in many films, very often in the opening passages, you get the camera establishing the mood, and, when it does that, cinematically, those sections are quite different from the rest of the film. You know, if it's establishing New York, you get a montage of images, that is, a poetic construct, after which what follows is a dramatic construct that is essentially "horizontal" in its development. The same thing would apply to the dream sequences. They occur at a moment when the intensification is carried out not by action but by the illumination of that moment. Now the short films, to my mind (and they are short because it is difficult to maintain such intensity for a long period of time), are comparable to lyric poems, and they are completely a "vertical," or what I would call a poetic construct, and they are complete as such. One of the combinations that would be possible would be to have a film that is a dramatic construct, visually, accompanied by a commentary that is essentially poetic; that is, it illuminates the moments as they occur, so that you have a chain of moments developing, and each one of them is illuminated. It's things of this sort that, I believe, occur in the work of Mr. Maas, who has done that to a certain extent in his last film, *Image in the Snow*, where the development of the film is very largely "horizontal," that is, there is a story line, but this is illuminated constantly by the poetic commentary so that you have two actions going on simultaneously. Now this, I think, is one of the great potentials of film and something that could very well be carried and developed much further, and I think that one of the distinctions of that film and also of *Geography of the Body*, is that it combines these principles. I think that this is a way of handling poetry *and* film, and poetry *in* film . . . I don't know how the other people feel about it.

Maas: Well, Mr. Thomas, being a poet, what do you feel about it?

Thomas: Well, I'm sure that all Maya Deren said was what I would have said, had I thought of it or understood it (*laughter and slight applause*). I was asked, on the side, whether that meant that I thought that the audience didn't understand what Miss Deren was saying. I'm sure they did, and I wish I was down there. But it sounds different from that side, you know. Now I'm all for (I'm in the wrong place tonight) . . . I'm all for horizontal and vertical (laughter), and all for what we heard about in the avant-garde. The only avant-garde play I saw in New York was in a cellar, or a sewer, or somewhere (laughter). I happened to be with Mr. Miller over there. We saw this play going on . . . I'm sure it was fine. And, in the middle, he said, "Good God, this is avant-garde." He said, "In a moment, the hero's going to take his clothes off . . ."

Maas: Did he?

Thomas: He did. (*Laughter.*)

Maas: All to the good.

Thomas: But I don't know. I haven't a theory to my back, as they say. But there are, all through films that I've seen all my life . . . there have always been . . . bits that have seemed to me . . . Now, this is a bit of poetry. They might have been in the UFA films or something that I saw as a child. Or somebody coming down some murderous dark, dark, silent street, apart from the piano playing. Or it might have been a little moment when Laurel and Hardy were failing to get a piano up or down a flight of stairs. That always seemed to me the poetry . . . when those moments came. Well, I have to go a step beyond those UFA films, now, to the non-silent films. In the best of those moments, the words seemed to fit. They were really the right words, even though the right word might only be a grunt. I'm not at all sure that I want such a thing, myself, as a poetic film. I think films, fine as they are, if only they were better! And I'm not quite sure that I want a new kind of film at all. While I'm recharging an almost empty mind with an almost empty battery, perhaps Mr. Miller would say something. (*Applause*.)

Maas: Well, I don't think I'll let it go at that, Mr. Thomas. Surely you must realize that the film is a popular medium, and you, more than anybody else, have tried to bring poetry to the public from the platform. Don't you think, in the popular art, in the way that the Elizabethan theater was a popular art, don't you think it would be possible in some way to weld poetry to the film? Do you think that it's just a verbal thing? That it would not be possible in the way that Elizabethan drama somehow welded language to the film?

Thomas: Well, just as a poem comes out . . . one image makes another in the ordinary dialectic process (somebody left out the word "dialectic," well I may as well bring it in, you know). So, as in a poem one image breeds another, I think, in a film, it's really the visual image that breeds another—breeds and breathes it. If it's possible to combine a verbal image to a visual image in this sort of horizontal way, I'd rather see horizontal films, myself. I like stories. You know, I like to see something going on (laughter and applause).

Maas: I shouldn't be saying anything; I'm the moderator. So, Mr. Miller, you talk about it.

Miller: Well, there've been about forty different ideas that have come across this table. It seems to me that to create a poetic film is, at bottom, the same problem as the drama presents when you contrast what is normally called naturalism with what is generally called a poetic drama. The only criticism I would have of such a discussion as this is that it is not tied to what anybody wishes to say. If I'm speaking to you now with a reasonable amount of confusion, I will sound confused, and I will speak in this tone of voice. If, on the other hand, I was clearly imbued with something very emotionally important to me, I would start speaking in a different rhythm. I would possibly use some images and so forth, so that to speak in the blue without reference to our lives, without references really to the age in which we live, about this problem is an endless talk. Ah, that's the first place. On the question of technique, there's one obvious thing to me: The motion picture image is an overwhelming fact; it is different from any other experience we have in the arts because it is so much larger than we are. The possibility for the poet or the writer to tell a story or to transmit an emotion in their films, it seem to me, is contained within the image, so that I'm afraid, even though I'm much in sympathy with Willard's desire to join poetic speech with images, that, possibly, in the long run, it will be discovered to be a redundancy—that the poetry is in the film just as it is in the action of the play first. I was gratified to see that the poet's poet, T. S. Eliot, not long ago said as much, that, after pushing the drama around on his desk for many years, he had come to the conclusion that if the structure of the drama was not complete and beautiful, nothing he could do in the way of technical manipulation of words could get him out of the hole. I think, at bottom, that the structure of the film is the structure of the man's mind who made it, and if that is a mind that is striving for effect because it is striving for effect, the film will be empty, however interesting it happens to be on the surface. If it is a mind that has been able to organize its own experience, and if that experience is cohesive and of one piece, it will be a poetic film. Mr. Thomas has said, as (Mr. Tyler) has said, too, that the commercial film is full of poetic things because, at certain moments, in almost any poor structure, certain accidental qualities come into synchronization, so to speak, where, as in life sometimes, one needs only to drop a package of cigarettes, and the world explodes. Symbolic action is the point of all organization in the drama as well as in the film. To get back to the first proposition again . . . I think that it would be profitable to speak about the special nature of any film, of the fact of images unwinding off a machine. Until that's understood, and I don't know that it's understood (I have some theories about it myself), we can't begin to create, on a methodical basis, an aesthetic for that film. We don't understand the psychological meaning of images—any images—coming off a machine. There are basic problems, it seems to me, that could be discussed here. I've probably added no end to the confusion, but that's what I have to say at the moment. (*Applause.*)

Maas: Well, it seems to me that we have to start thinking about the image—the visual image and the verbal image. Can they be welded in some way?

Miller: I think that the basis for my remarks is perhaps almost physiological. I think that the reason why it seems to many of us that the silent film is the purest film and the best is because it mimics the way we dream. We mostly dream silent, black and white. A few of us claim to dream in technicolor, but that's disputed by psychologists. It's sort of a boast: Certain people want to have more expensive dreams . . . I think that the film is the closest mechanical or aesthetic device that man has ever made to the structure of the dream. In a dream, montage is of the essence, as a superimposition of images in a dream is quite ordinary. The cutting in a dream is from symbolic point to symbolic point. No time is wasted. There is no fooling around between one important situation and the most important moment in the next situation. It seems to me that if we looked at the physiology of the film, so to speak, and the pyschology of the film, the way it actually turns off the machine, we begin to get the whole question of style and the whole question of aesthetics changing when one sees it that way. In other words, sound in films and speech seem, perhaps, like the redundancy they so often are in films. I'll just leave it at that for the moment; maybe somebody else will have something to say about it.

Maas: Maya, I'm sure you have something to say about it.

Deren: If everyone will forgive me, Mr. Miller has made several references to "the way it comes out of the machine," he obviously hasn't made a film because first you have to put it in the machine, and that's awfully hard. It does begin before the machine. And it begins in the mind of the creator. And your reference to montage, and so on, is, if I may be permitted to return to my "vertical"— that is, the relationship between the images in dreams, in montage, and in poetry—is . . . they are related because they are held together by either an emotion or a meaning that they have in common, rather than by the logical action. In other words, it isn't that one action leads to another action (this is what I would call a "horizontal" development), but they are brought to a center, gathered up, and collected by the fact that they all refer to a common emotion, although the incidents themselves may be quite disparate. Whereas, in what is called a "horizontal" development, the logic is a logic of actions. In a "vertical" development, it is a logic of a central emotion or idea that attracts to itself even disparate images which contain that central core, which they have in common. This, to me, is the structure of poetry, so that, for example, you could have a dramatic development, in the sense of a "horizontal" development, for a while, as I said, in Shakespeare, and let us take the monologues where, in a poetic or a "vertical" structure, he brings together all various images that relate to the feeling, let us say, of indecision. Now what I mean there by being essentially a "horizontal" development, is that it would have sufficed for Hamlet to say, "I can't make up my mind," and that's all, and that would not have affected the drama of the play, do you see? The poetic monologue there is, as it were, outside it or built upon it as a pyramid at that point as a means of intensifying that moment in the "horizontal" development. That is why film, I believe, lends itself particularly to the poetic statement, because it is essentially a montage and, therefore, seems by its very nature to be a poetic medium.

Miller: That's why I'm wondering whether the words are at all necessary, you see. Because the nature of the thing itself is so condensed. It would be like adding music to Hamlet's soliloquies.

Deren: May I answer that? The words are not necessary when they come, as in the theater, from what you see. You see, the way the words are used in films mostly derives from the theatrical tradition in which what you see makes the sound you hear. And so, in that sense, they would be redundant in film if they were used as a further projection from the image. However, if they were brought in on a different level, not issuing from the image, which should be complete in itself, but as another dimension relating to it, then it is the two things together that make the poem. It's almost as if you were standing at a window and looking out into the street, and there are children playing hopscotch. Well, that's your visual experience. Behind you, in the room, are women discussing hats or something, and that's your auditory experience. You stand at the place where these two come together by virtue of your presence. What relates these two moments is your position in relation to the two of them. They don't know about each other, and so you stand by the window and have a sense of afternoon, which is neither the children in the street nor the women talking behind you but a curious combination of both, and that is your resultant image, do you see? And this is possible in film because you can put a track on it.

Miller: I understand the process, but you see, in the drama there was a time, as you know, when action was quite rudimentary, and the drama consisted of a chorus which told the audience, in effect, what happened. Sometimes, it developed into a thespian coming forward and imitating action such as we understand action today. Gradually, the drama grew into a condition where the chorus fell away, and all of its comment was incorporated into the action. Now for good or ill, that was the development of the drama. I'm wondering now whether it's moot, whether it's to any point, to arrange a scenario so that it is necessary (and if it isn't necessary, of course it's aesthetically unwarranted) for words to be added to the organization of images, and whether that makes it more poetic. I don't think so. I can see the impulse behind it, but it seems to me that if it's a movie, it's a movie.

Maas: Well, doesn't it seem to have something to do with who is going to make this film? Is it going to be the man who has a poetical idea at the beginning, who then decides to work with a film director on this thing? Or is the poet going to work on it himself? Through words or through nothing, but just through a poetical idea, which is both visual and verbal at the same time? If he is going to work with a director, he is going to have to be terribly close to that director. He may as well be the same person. Then you have to have a poet who can also make a film.

Thomas: Oh, I think that's absolutely true—or you could work very closely with someone who knew film technique to carry it out. But I think the poet should establish a scenario and a commentary that would do that as well. And he may as well star in it as well.

Maas: Miss Deren has played in her own films, and I think she played in them because she couldn't get people to do the things that a director asks people to do unless they pay them ten thousand a week. I know that for myself, because I'm working on a new poetic film with Mr. Ben Moore, another poet; we found that he had to play the leading role because nobody would go through the trouble to do it. You see, you're not going to get commercial people to do this. What I am interested in at the moment is Mr. Miller's idea about film, and I'm afraid, Mr. Miller, that I think that you think that it must always be a drama. Then if it is a drama, is there not a difference between prose drama and poetic drama? There is certainly a difference between Shakespeare and even Ibsen. Don't you think so?

Miller: I wasn't thinking only of the drama. Of course, there have been poetic pictures made, as you know, which are silent. I suppose most of them, as a matter of fact, are not dramas. But my preference is toward drama because I'm primarily interested in action. It seems to me an aesthetic impurity to introduce words into a picture of any kind. I was against, as a whole, the idea of spoken pictures, anyway. It simply attests to the poverty of imagination of screenwriters that they need the words, and to the poverty of the imagination of the audience that it demands the words. I don't think that it has anything to do remotely with real films. The words came in because the movies came after the theater, and the first people who moved into the movies were theater people, and the first commercially made films were, many of them, simply filmed plays. There's no relationship between the theater in that sense, and the films, for the simple reason I return to—a technical, physiological reason, and that is, that you're looking at an image many, many times larger than yourself, and that changes everything. It is a redundancy to add to that image, it seems to me. I just hope that your ambition to add words to film is not because you love words so much (which you should because you are a poet). I wouldn't want to interfere. I think that what you would say in words should be said instead in images.

Maas: Well, you must realize that there is a difference between Shakespeare and, let us say, any dramatist of repute. And there is a difference within poetic language, is there not?

Miller: There is, of course. The difference, however, is not of the same quality as the difference between words in a movie. The whole posture of the Elizabethan drama, so to speak, is larger than life as opposed to the modern drama, which is trying to be about the same size as life. Well, the movie starts out that way. It's almost impossible, as you know, to photograph reality in pictures and make it come out reality. I know that people have tried with cameras to destroy the . . . this leads to a humorous remark. I was involved with a director once who wanted to make pictures in New York that would look real. They photographed and photographed, and it ended up looking glamorous, no matter how deep down into the East Side they went. (*Laughter.*) They tried to dirty the film and do everything they could do to it. And I kept telling him that what was required was an organization of an idea to make this look like the East Side. My point is that, in the Elizabethan drama, it takes an effort of aesthetic will to raise life larger than it is on the stage. As soon as you point a camera at anything, it's no longer real.

Maas: Mr. Tyler, I don't want to answer this. You ought to say something. You must have been thinking a lot.

Tyler: We *are* snagged on the horns of a dilemma in a way, although I'm sure we've covered a lot of ground. I think one of the most interesting things is the shape and the character of these horns —that is, Miss Deren, who is a professional artist in the poetic film, started out by using a rather complex, a rather difficult, technical vocabulary in order to describe her theory about what she does. Now that's perfectly all right. But it struck Mr. Thomas as not precisely all right, and he then proceeded to talk about his very spontaneous reactions to films in terms of what he thought was poetic in them, various little incidents, certain aspects, just points of emotion. And then Mr. Miller took over and started to talk about dreams and the pure medium of the film. Now the fact is that both these gentlemen—both of whom are professional writers, and one a professional poet—expressed the very view of life, the cinematic attitude toward life that Miss Deren and a number of other film-makers started out with and, in this primitive way, are simply reflecting, perhaps, the first stage of her development when she had the impulse to make poetic films—that is, to create meaningful images through the medium of moving photography. Now, it becomes the problem, especially here tonight, as to why she started out by using a very difficult vocabulary, a technical vocabulary, to express a sort of intellectual specialty in the way she regarded her art. As a matter of fact, the surrealists started out by excerpting parts of commercial films, jumbling them up, and making little poems out of them. It is simply a question of the editing, the montage, as Mr. Miller intelligently hinted a moment ago, a question of integrating a series of photographs, of spontaneous shots into a form, a shape, and then you have something. That is, you have a feeling about reality—which is what art is. So I think that the rudimentary ground is present; that is, poetic film means using the film as a conscious and exclusive means of creating ideas through images. As for poets and other artists collaborating with film-makers, the method of Eisenstein was one of strict collaboration in a technical sense. It was also one of literature in that he wrote out very elaborate, very detailed scripts, action for action, shot for shot, beforehand, and then, when he was in the field, since he was an artist, he remained open so that his technical advisors were always listened to. It was a question of using an original script, which was really literature, which was written as a starting point and, out of this kind of literature, creating a film. Certainly, among big film-makers and artists who created full length films, and films that were commercially distributed, Eisenstein was, in the history of films, the most conscious artist. So it seems to me just a little strange that Mr. Miller, in particular, being a dramatist, should take a purist point of view toward the film. I mean, that's his privilege, if he feels that way. But the hard part, at least to me, is that this is the way that the little film-makers, the poets of the film such as Miss Deren, feel—this is their approach to life. So now I don't know where we are! It's a question of what role literature, what role verbal poetry, should have in film. I don't know why Mr. Thomas and Mr. Miller should insist, and I'm waiting to find out if they will insist, why poetry as literature should not, or cannot, collaborate with poetry as film.

Deren: I wish mainly to say that I'm a little bit flabbergasted at the fact that people who have handled words with such dexterity as Mr. Thomas and Mr. Miller and Mr. Tyler, should have difficulty with such a simple idea as the "vertical" and the "horizontal" (applause).

Thomas: (*aside*) Here we go up and down again.

Deren: These seem to me the most elementary movements in the world and really quite fundamental.

Maas: I don't think you ought to get vulgar.

Deren: That has really flabbergasted me to the extent that I am unable to develop the idea any further . . . I don't see anything so difficult in the notion that what I called a "horizontal" development is more or less of a narrative development, such as occurs in drama from action to action, and that a "vertical" development such as occurs in poetry, is a part of plunging down or a construction that is based on the intent of the moment, so that, for example, from a short story, one should be able to deduce the life of the hero before and after. In other words, the chosen moment should be of such significance that one can deduce all history from it. So, in a poem, in a way, from the emotion one can particularize to the incidents that might contain it, whereas in a drama, one generalizes the emotion from the particular instant. That is, the actions of the drama may not be personally known, but one generalizes the emotion that comes from it, and then it becomes possible to identify with it as a generalized emotion. I still don't know what's so difficult about those two differences, and I think I'd like to hear something from the floor myself.

Miller: Let me just say, I didn't intend to make it so difficult; it isn't. It's just not separate. There is no separation in my mind between a horizontal story and the plumbing of its meaning in depth. (*Applause.*)

Maas: Well, surely, Mr. Miller, you must see the difference between presenting something by words or dialogue, as you do and I do and Mr. Thomas does, and presenting something by the visual image. Now Ezra Pound said, in a definition of the image, that it is an emotional and intellectual complex caught in an instant of time. It's a very direct and quick way of saying things, a lyric way of saying things, whereas the way a dramatist says things is by putting the characters that speak back and forth in conflict. We know that you can't have any sort of situation, poetic or otherwise, without dramatic conflict. I agree with that, but it's quite different in developing a narrative action from presenting it imagistically and quickly, and I think in the film you can do that. You can do it by word; you can do it by visual image, and by the combination of the two, which is a very complicated thing. Though mentioned, no one here tonight has talked very extensively about Jean Cocteau's *Blood of a Poet*. Anybody who sees that, sees the perfect welding of the two. It can be done. Though he is the father of the poetic film, Jean Cocteau does not have many forebears. Still, I know there is a technique that could be done, and is essentially different, I'm afraid, from one of presenting things imagistically and presenting them narratively, and by statement and by dramatic action. There's a great difference there.

* * *

Miller: (*answering a question from the floor*) To hell with that "vertical" and "horizontal." It doesn't mean anything. (*Applause.*) I understand perfectly what it means, but the point is, if an action is worth anything emotionally, it proceeds to get deeper into its meaning as it progesses, as it reveals. The whole intent of any good playwright is to construct such action as will finally achieve the greatest depths of meaning. So that it is simply a question of, here again, an image, which is, in one case, when you speak of "vertical" and "horizontal," rather mechanical. And I'm sure the lady didn't mean it that way, and that's why it was taken so absurdly. But it isn't absurd; it's just that they aren't separated in any way. A perfectly prosaic play, as we all know, can sometimes arrive at a point which creates a very high poetic feeling. Now, it's a different problem; you have the whole question of verse structure and so on. But the verse structure will never come without that plumbing, without that going deep. You can't implant it on a vacuous piece of material. My only point is that it's of one piece. The technique cannot be used simply because one wishes to use it. (*Applause.*) It's all a question of the degree. But you might say that the best example of the relationship between words and action is that while we're talking here, all these people are walking out. (*Laughter, applause.*)

Maas: We spent most of our time talking about what Miss Deren called "vertical" and "horizontal." I think in a way she was talking about narrative and lyric. Is that right?

Deren: Yes. The gentleman who brought it up, brought up the question here as to the fact that he thought poetry and film were different ways of doing the same thing. That is why I went into the whole nature of what I call the poetic structure, because I believe that this poetic structure can be present in any one of the forms. For example, in dance, you would have a narrative ballet or you would have an essentially lyric ballet; or you might have a *pas de deux*, in it, which was an exploration of a moment that occurred. The *pas de deux* is over, and you go back to the line of your plot. So that I'm not thinking of the poetic structure as referring to poetry simply as a verbal form; I'm thinking of it as a way of structuring in any one of a number of mediums, and (I think) that it is also possible to make the dramatic structure in any one, or that it is also possible to combine them. When Mr. Miller says he doesn't think they are different, it is another way of saying that they can be combined, in which sense he is contradicting his rather purist insistence that they should not be combined. To me, this comes out a contradiction. I think that they can. Now I am speaking for a combination, although personally, in my films, there has not been such a combination. I'm speaking of other films and of the way poetry occurs in them, either as an image—the sudden development of a poetic image, which you might have in a dream sequence of a film that was otherwise narrative in its structure, and the whole narrative stops while the hero has a dream which illuminates the particular moment in the story, and then he goes back to the narrative, somebody wakes him up or something like that, and you go on with the narrative development. It's this sort of nightmare that was present in *Death of a Salesman*, which was a moment in which, in effect, the action almost stopped, and you had this poetic illumination of the moment.

Miller: That's a good point because I know something about that. You see, that's precisely the point; it didn't stop. It never stopped. This has been confused with a flashback. It was never a flashback. The design of that play is concurrent stories. Now we can get right to the movie, and here's a good example. I am wedded to action; I can't bear "narrative drama." It's to me an impossibility; it bores me to tears. There's a difference between narrative and dramatic, obviously. Now the place that you would speak, I presume, of the "vertical" investigation, let's call it, is in those sections of the play where the man goes back into time. To be sure, the present moment vanishes in the sense that he goes back in time, but every word that is in those memories changes the situation that will arise as soon as those things are over. They are not, in other words, excursions, for the sake of reaching outside the structure of the play to bring in some information. They are incorporated, completely wedded to the action. They *are* action. Now the only argument I have here at all, and the reason I have a feeling that verse, possibly, doesn't belong in the movies, is that if you have on the screen an image . . . an image is a bad word because it seems static . . . an action. Now it can be an action that is seemingly real or a fantastic one. And then, on top of it, you have an unseen narrator who is speaking —I'm afraid that the spoken word will be a kind of narrative, or lyrical, nondramatic verse. And that is going to stop the motion of the motion picture. And I'm against that. I think it's an intrusion on the medium. That's all I mean, I'm speaking for an organic art, that's all. (*Applause.*) . . . There's a good example in the making of the movie of *Death of a Salesman*. This was a very fascinating problem, and it is right to the point here. On the stage, it seemed perfectly all right to most people that the man should move into his memories which were evoked by the action in the present. I didn't like the script of the movie, and I quarreled very much with it. One would think, offhand, that it would be much easier in a movie to dissolve the present, because the very word dissolve is so natural to the camera and simply throws the man into the past. When the present was dissolved, the meaning of what happened in the past was less. And the reason for it was that, on stage, you had the present with you all the time. We couldn't remove the set. The man had his dreams in relation to the real set that he was standing on, so there was a tension involved. There was, in other words, a reproduction of reality, because when we talk to ourselves on the street, the street is still there, and we don't vanish in thin air. But, in the movie, they made the terrible mistake of evaporating his sur-roundings, so that he was thrust completely into his dream. And what happened was: It became a narrative. The conflict was that this man—after all, it's not quite as bad to talk to yourself when you're alone in the desert as it is when you're standing in front of a girl at Macy's counter—that has an entirely different meaning. In one case, the man can be quite balanced; in the other case, he begins to look as though he's losing his balance. This, to my mind, is an analogy between anything that stops action, that is bad in a picture. I think, in the movie of *Death of a Salesman*, the action was stopped because the visual thing that kept the tension of those memories was evaporated. And I'm afraid that the same thing would happen with speech in a picture.

IMAGISM IN FOUR AVANT-GARDE FILMS

BY P. ADAMS SITNEY

No. 31, Winter, 1963–64

The image is not an idea. It is a radiant node or cluster; it is what I can, and must perforce, call a VORTEX, from which, and through which, and into which ideas are constantly rushing.
—Ezra Pound, in *Gaudier-Brzeska*

A few months ago, Ken Kelman and I were outlining our still unwritten "interpretive history of the experimental film," *The Sliced Eye*. I was trying to find fresh categories for that mode of film-making and remembered that Stan Brakhage once mentioned in speaking of his *Dog Star Man: Part 1* that he had been inspired by Ezra Pound's concept of Imagism: that images are not decorations and that one central image can motivate an entire poem. Brakhage had clarified what he meant by connecting it very specifically with the making of his film, but I was excited about the possibility of relating his ideas to avant-garde film-making in general. I recalled the leap through space in Maya Deren's *Choreography for Camera*, the transformation of woman into fountain in Kenneth Anger's *Eaux d'Artifice*, and the moment of artistic inspiration seen as the slam of a poet's fist in Charles Boultenhouse's *Handwritten*. I realized that the single-central-image film played an important part in the historical and aesthetic development of the American avant-garde cinema.

Kelman was quick to detect the academic stench. I too felt the category, which had six or seven examples then, was rather forced. We discussed the films, and as Curtis Harrington's *On The Edge* and Willard Maas's *Mechanics of Love* dropped out, the idea of the central-image film became more reasonable. I took consolation in Pound, again from the marvelous *Gaudier-Brzeska* memoir: "Imagisme, in so far as it has been known at all, has been known chiefly as a stylistic movement, as a movement of criticism rather than of creation. This is natural, for, despite all possible celerity of publication, the public is always, and of necessity, some years behind the artists' actual thought."

To begin with the simplest and earliest example—Maya Deren's *Choreography for Camera*. The camera pans past a dancer in the woods only to encounter him again before that pan has stopped. He dances from the woods into a living room and then an art museum in one fluid movement. He spins around and *leaps*—we see him float into the air and glide through it, his leotard black against a grey sky—landing back in the woods in squatting position, surveying landscape from the vantage point of a hill. The action is simple and unified: It is a slow-motion running jump through irrationally connected spaces within a more or less rational time.

There is a metaphor in the film of no special importance in the appreciation of the total work but nonetheless relevant to what I will say about metaphors in other central-image films. Just before the dancer leaps out of the museum, there is a closeup of his spinning head. In the corner of the screen there is also an Indian statue, a Janus-headed bodhisattva. The implied metaphor identifies the dancer, whose twirling head seems to face all directions at the same time, with the statue and relates to the theme of the ambiguity of space (here, direction). More important than the force of the metaphor itself is that it is a "compositional" metaphor—one made by framing rather than by interrupting the action/image with superimposition or intercutting.

* * *

There is a film by Kenneth Anger, *Eaux d'Artifice*, close to the spirit of *Choreography for Camera* but different in several notable ways: (1) It is in color, whereas *Choreography* was in black and white; in fact, it is the most remarkable and simplest use of color I have ever seen in the movies. Everything is deep blue (the film was shot on black and white stock and printed blue)—everything, that is, except a tiny spot of green light seen just before the end of the film. Anger, who calls this spot "the night moth," painted it on by hand. His casting the entire film in a cool blue was ingenious and tasteful, but when he climaxed it with the green light—a masterpiece! (2) Maya Deren's human figure is unmistakably a dancer, and his movements are classically choreographic. She uses the camera for the advantage of the dance. On the other hand, Anger's single character is a woman in a Baroque gown complete with an elegantly plumed headpiece, whose movements are natural. The "balletlike" structure of *Eaux d'Artifice* is a result of photography and editing and not "pas de deux" (as Deren calls her method) between the camera and its subject. (3) The most important distinction—*Eaux d'Artifice* does not feature its protagonist in every shot as *Choreography* did. There is the same simplicity and fluidity of action, but the camera repeatedly turns away to view other sights. The setting is an elaborate Baroque labyrinth, and the film's first image is of a fountain with its waters falling in slow motion. Throughout the film, there are various fountains, streams, and gargoyles as well as the fleeing woman. Yet the study of her "flight" is *always* the central objective of the film. (4) A Vivaldi fugue accompanies the film (*Choreography* is silent), and the montage of water, woman, and gargoyles matches the rhythms of the music.

At this point, I should insist that Anger's film is not a mechanical "visualization" of a piece of music: It is a visual fugue. The Vivaldi is not synchronized with the pictures but acts in counterpoint to them, emphasizing the type of visual form—directing the eye to it—without determining it. To return to my analysis—even though water and gargoyles appear on the screen as much as the woman does, her flight is the central image of the film. The pace of the montage and the music, combined with those glimpses the film-maker does give of her hurrying down flights of stairs, make the intensity of her emotional state clear at every given moment, regardless of the specific image on the screen. In other words, as she walks gracefully past a grove of trees, we see shots of water moving in slow motion and leisurely dollies towards the stone faces . . . as she scurries along, the camera zooms across the labyrinth with rock-steady quickness . . . when she runs, Anger shows the crest of a fountain briefly; there is a rapid zoom at a gargoyle . . . and so on in contrapuntal patterns. When the material has been developed, repeated, and interwoven mosaically to such an extent that a viewer might wonder, "What can he possibly do next with those few images?" a climax occurs: The night moth appears in front of the woman (perhaps that was what she was fleeing or pursuing). The resolving chord is metamorphosis —*she becomes*, dissolves into, *a fountain*, its highest geyser taking the exact shape of her plume.

The movement of the camera and the movement within the still frame is always subtle, always graceful and correct, beautifully, not mechanically, correct. The perfection of *Eaux d'Artifice* cannot be overemphasized: The blue tone, the music, the montage moving from slow to rapid without ever suggesting the frantic, all contribute to make a simple visual image—a woman becomes a fountain—one of the most finely wrought in avant-garde cinema.

* * *

There can be Imagist films in which no human being appears, but, for the purpose of this paper, I have considered them a separate or sub-class. The two films discussed above and the two yet to be considered, *Handwritten* and *Dog Star Man: Part 1*, show the human in action. In all these films, there is an overt or implied attitude towards the human body; in fact, I take it as an axiom of the category that there be an "anatomical" theme. If the camera is to concentrate on a single human and one significant action (that is, a complex of his movements), how is a statement about the body avoidable? Deren made a paean to its strength and grace, suggesting that it was the one constant in a world of changing space and time. Anger took an opposite position and showed its Heraclitan mutability in a static landscape. In Boultenhouse and Brakhage, the ideas about the body are more overt and not nearly so clear cut. Both film-makers are *so* concerned with anatomical questions that it is nearly impossible to give a simple résumé of their attitudes.

* * *

In *Handwritten*, a man reads a Mallarmé poem, drinks a cocktail, and begins to contemplate his hand. His thoughts build to a dizzy climax at the height of which his daemon takes possession of him and he smashes the glass top of his cocktail table. Despite the overall simplicity of this nine-minute film, it is infinitely more intricate than either Deren's or Anger's film.

Most of the complexity of *Handwritten* comes from interrelationships between the central image and (1) the poetry spoken on the sound track and (2) the rapid-fire intercutting of various images parallel to, or metaphorically connected with, that image/action. Even before the titles, Boultenhouse states a major theme. The poet says, "Man's first instrument of communication was a hand. . . . His first word was a hand made out of a cry." On the screen, there is a static image of a paleolithic drawing of a hand. The concept of a primordial fusion of hand and word is reinforced by the next image, that of the title itself: *Handwritten*.

In order to do justice to the multiple levels of meaning in *Handwritten*, each image should be analyzed in terms of several themes. I will try to weld together a hodgepodge of thematic allusions as they relate to the one image at the core of the film. Following the titles, the protagonist, whom I have called the poet (he is played by the film-maker), appears, dressed in black, reading in a black room. I stress the blackness because Boultenhouse stresses it; the super-realism of black and white in this color film is perhaps the most important theme after the central "visualization of the creative impulse becoming manifest."

There is a close-up of the poet's face, then his eyes, suggesting his thoughts are about to be exposed. His voice is heard, though his lips do not move: "Once I held a *white* bird in my *hand* . . . I studied its speckled wings . . . I deciphered its markings." (Italics mine.) The film-maker intercuts shots of Mallarmé's words splattered on the pages of his "A Throw of Dice Will Never Abolish Chance." There are implied metaphors—wing-page: markings-words. Such visual/verbal tension, more technically known as "vertical montage," is maintained throughout the film.

The page turns, and, as its shadow falls across the new page on which the words

"watching

doubting"

appear. He says: "The bird watched me, doubted me, spreading its wings with an indifference *shadowed* in mystery." The allusions to the Mallarmé poem give me the most trouble here, because I do not feel competent to write about the poem as a work in itself. It is a piece of shaped verse with words spread about on twenty-two pages in various kinds and sizes of type. The typography coupled with the denotation of the words suggests ships tossing on a billowing sea, thoughts in the mind, and stars in the sky. Anyone unfamiliar with the poem is not handicapped in his viewing of Boultenhouse's film; for the most important ideas and images of the poem are clearly expressed in film form.

The camera is back on the poet's face. His words, "The bird will prophesy," introduces the theme of *time*. All the themes are converging, and the meaning of the central image, especially its climax (the smashing of the table, yet to be seen) can be found. The spiritual and intellectual traditions of the past—the paleolithic drawings and the pages of a dead poet's poem—act upon our poet and will have their force in the future, in his work. Since the filmic image cannot show explicit past or future, only various qualities of the present (that is, every image's *being there*—on the screen—implies its taking place *now*), past and future are outside of the central visual image and must be distinguished by the sound track.

He explains the prophecy and, in so doing, includes the theme of words: "How all words shall alter. How all words shall be cast into oblivion." The word "cast" generates two images on the screen: *white* dice with black markings falling through the air, and then *black* dice with white markings being shaken by a *hand*. The word "dice" from the first page of the poem appears on the screen. The trembling hands of the poet make the letters of the book dance on the screen. He extends the ideas of prophecy and blackness-whiteness as he says: "How all white words shall be made black. How all black pages shall be made white. And yet!"

This jumble of critical prose should not give the impression that *Handwritten* is a hopelessly obscure crossword puzzle. The most marvelous quality of Boultenhouse's film is its clarity and direct use of vision. On one viewing the central image is pellucid. The poet's sense that he is pregnant with an *opus* is shown not only clearly but violently.

It might be said that the Imagist films are remarkable among avant-garde works for their lack of obscurity—at least on the primary visual level. Imagist films have a simple structure, a pattern in the shape of a human gesture, and all the complexities are allowed or helped to spring from that image. It happens faster than prose can describe it, faster even, at times, than the words of a poem.

Returning to the film, I can say that the description above might be artificially categorized as the "literary inspiration" section. The poet then puts down the book and contemplates his hand. His language no longer suggests the future. He is aware of his present state, his anatomy. He cries: "Notice! Notice in the nowing now! Tense in the present . . . my hand! Not the fish fin or bird's wing it might have been, but my hand—what it is *now!*" He reaches for a cocktail (white or clear). As he drinks it, the camera catches his reflection off the glass top of the cocktail table (black). There are bits of shaped verse placed under the glass of the table. The act of drinking—accompanied with the line, "The deep now of incommunicable communion," and with the oriental music of Teiji Ito—is a natural function of the ritual aspect of *Handwritten*. The image of the maturing creative impulse is a *rite*, as Boultenhouse makes it. It is impersonal, without character, and for all artists everywhere.

The poet is standing, slowly raising his hand high in the air and proclaiming: "A scene! . . . A scene of pulse and impulse . . . unseen the fountain of blood running dry, unseen the hand feeling hollow with stars." When he lies supine staring up at his hand, the entire room starts to spin. "This is the womb of the turning blood," he says, "bleeding round and round under the bandage of the skin." Close-ups of the poet waving his head are intercut with the spinning room. Is it really spinning or is it moving only in his imagination, consciously and physically induced?

Suddenly the film-maker repeats in flashes the opening images of paleolithic hands. He combines them with images of a living hand tracing the outline of another hand on a wall. In other words, there are staccato interruptions of an ancient cave-drawn hand and a set of living hands *making it new*. Lights sweep over the poet's face a few times transforming him from a marble mien to living flesh. He rises and raises his fist above his head—in the gesture, shots of him nude are intercut with those of him in his black clothes in such a way that the act of lifting the fist is continuous and uninterrupted although the "lifter" changes. (Mallarmé wrote:

"ancestrally not to unclench his hand

contracted
above his worthless head")

He slams his fist on the cocktail table, destroying the old and making a new pattern in one act. The camera zooms back and forth above the shattered glass as if the hand had an eye. It dollies up to and away from the resting hand ten times, objectifying the pulsing of blood and the waves of pain. The voice announces: "The demented energy . . . still reverberating from the pulse that created it." In close-up, the camera moves across the broken glass, glimpsing the words underneath. The tracing of hands is seen again. It is completed, and the hands are removed. The work is finished! The poet ends the film with: "The hand like a cry . . . the cry like a hand. The stars are not ours. All words are flesh."

Handwritten is a chamber film—a diagram of the making of art out of the complex of an experienced "now." As a ritual, it is universal. Yet it is also consciously a little film made "In honor of broken glass," as the poet says. It is the work of a man who understands Mallarmé's conclusion: "All thought emits a Throw of Dice."

* * *

Maya Deren introduced metaphor through a framing device. Boultenhouse took more liberties with the single image than she did. He interrupted it with foreign material (the drawings, dice, and so forth), with shots so brief that the main gesture is never forgotten. It is as if he were squeezing an image in sideways without using up time. Cocteau carried this to an extreme in *Blood of a Poet* by interrupting a shot of a falling tower with his entire film and letting the tower complete its fall an hour later. Stan Brakhage edited *Dog Star Man: Part 1* with as much foreign material as could possibly be included without usurping the center of the film from the central image of a woodsman climbing a mountain, moving two steps forward and one step backward. I always come away from that film feeling that that central image could not have been extended a shot further without the whole structure of the film falling apart.

Pound again, in the *Gaudier-Brzeska* memoir, which anyone seriously interested in Brakhage ought to read, writes: "I am often asked whether there can be a long imagiste or vorticist poem. The Japanese, who evolved the hokku, evolved also the Noh plays. In the best Noh the whole play may consist of one image. I mean it is gathered about one image. Its unity consists in one image, enforced by movement and music." Brakhage has called his film "A Noh drama in slow motion!" (I'll go into the definition of Vorticism later; for insomuch as there is a distinction between Imagism and Vorticism, *Part 1* is Vorticist.)

In one sense, *Part 1* is an antithesis to *Prelude*. In *Prelude*, Brakhage built a pyrotechnics of split-second montage with as much varied material as he could *force into* a half hour. *Part 1* is a *tour de force* of the least and most thematically similar material *stretched out to* a half hour. The unusually great number of fades in and out in *Part 1* are a key to its structure. The film organizes itself in waves. Or to expand an analogy of Jonas Mekas's, if *Prelude* is a collage of images joined together as if they were words in a sentence, then *Part 1* must be an *opus* of film "paragraphs." The paragraph analogy is a guide to the grouping of images within the film, yet something must be said of the organization of the "paragraphs" themselves. Perhaps a musical analogy is appropriate: I can think of nothing it resembles as much as sonata-allegro form. There is a rather clear-cut exposition of themes, a long and difficult-to-divide development, which makes up more than two-thirds of the film, and a definite finale (though not a recapitulation in the usual sonata-allegro sense, but then *Dog Star Man: Part 1* is a movie, not a piece of music).

The opening shots articulate the themes of place and plastic design. Planets become clouds, which sweep in fast motion down from the Rocky Mountains. Fire swallows itself (backwards motion) into frost on a window pane, later becoming the white disk of the sun. The mountain has been placed in the universe and in every image the perpetual transformation of triangle into circle and *vice versa* has been maintained. (Gaudier-Brzeska begins his "Vortex" statement with: "Sculptural energy is the mountain." He ends it three pages later with: "We have crystallized the sphere into the cube, we have made a combination of all the possible shaped masses —concentrating them to express our abstract thoughts of conscious superiority. Will and consciousness are our *vortex*.") The next "paragraph" of eight shots continues the triangle-arc metamorphoses and introduces the protagonist, Brakhage himself as the *Dog Star Man*, a woodsman with a beard down to his chest and his hair below his shoulders. In blue, pink, and brown, in long shots, mediums, and closeups fading into one another, he struggles up the snow-covered mountain, falls, gets up, struggles a little further. . . .

A greenish shot of the Dog Star Man turning in his sleep introduces the first doubts of the "reality" (that is, Is it a dream?) in this heavily epistemological film. How such a shot, related to the central-image in so indirect a way, can occur in *Part 1* is relevant to my comparisons with other Imagist films. For the most part, fades in or out, sometimes accompanied with periods of black or white leader, phrase subsections of the film. Brakhage established a definite, though not mathematical, rhythm, and, by maintaining the expected pulse and color-tone, but positing a foreign image, he does not destroy the central-image unity.

The sleeper fades into the arc of the moon, which, in turn, fades into the first section in which "subjective" shots occur. By "subjective" I mean shots as if through the eyes of the Dog Star Man as he climbs the mountain. They are hand held and impressionistic. Since no cinematic quotation marks (yet) exist to distinguish the camera as an impersonal eye from the camera assuming the dramatic persona of a protagonist's eye, it is difficult to be precise always in dividing the objective from the subjective. Perhaps this is best for the sake of a poetic ambiguity in film. Best or not, it is a fact.

In the visual "paragraph" just mentioned there is another positing of place and elements—blue water, blue clouds introduce a blue-filtered objective shot of the DSM inching up the mountain. Objective shots recur among subjective ones of the sun, leaves, snow, and various blurs. The visions through the DSM's eyes change to shots of what is behind his eyes—his internal organs, tissues, the blood stream.

Part 1 is "about" the DSM climbing the mountain and its total implications, including the mountain itself, its place in the universe, the snow, the trees, even the sun, which illuminates them all and makes possible the filming. The section just described is the exposition of the man as a totality; that is, his outward appearance, what he sees and thinks, and his physiology. There are a few shots that do not fit this human triptych—for instance, a hand-held shot of the DSM's forehead, something he could not possibly see. But that should be a stumbling block only to those who demand that vision fit their preconceptions. I am trying to offer some concepts about a given vision. If they fit exactly, it wouldn't be as good a film. Pound notes the third commandment of the Imagist faith: "As regarding rhythm: to compose in the sequence of the musical phrase, not in the sequence of the metronome." Interpret it widely.

As the film proceeds towards its middle, the phrasing becomes less obvious. The first two paragraphs were distinct: They are the exposition proper. The exposition of the objective-subjective-internal Dog Star Man theme, though, blends into its own development-by-variations. The sequence becomes retrogressive, moving from the abstract to the concrete—moving from blurs to the sun and eventually back to three fades (each filtered differently) of the objective view of the DSM in slow motion. Just before a black silence, which marks the beginning of the main development, there is a shot functionally related to that of the sleeper. It is a closeup of bodies probably in intercourse. I explained how the shot of the DSM sleeping fit the form of the film because of the fade rhythm. This shot fits because of its use of the triangle in plastic design. The internal composition in terms of triangles and arc (the screen itself being the square of Cézanne's three elements) cannot be overemphasized. It is equally as important as the over-all sonata-allegro pattern and the rhythmic uses of fades and leaders. The intercourse shot fits, formally, because Brakhage lit it with a distinct triangle of light. I have devoted a paragraph on this and the sleeper shot not because they are so important in themselves (although they are very beautiful compositions) but because they are the outstanding examples of how the film-maker weaves countless shots, not natural parts of the central-image, into the texture of *Dog Star Man: Part 1.*

In the development proper, the image and associated concepts of the dog, the snow, and the barren trees, which were only incidental during the exposition of themes, come to the fore for a minute or so, generate metaphysical and physical observations, and fade again. As more and more impressionistic camera work is used, Brakhage achieves a uniquely cinematic tension. There is the dual realization that a particular shot is meant to suggest what the DSM is seeing, and yet that same shot is an obvious "camera trick." For instance, the DSM sees the mountains writhing against the sky. The effect is wrought by a flagrantly obvious twisting of an anamorphic lens. Two of Brakhage's most ardent viewers find this recurring shot the most distracting in his film. Their uneasiness is a testament to the film-maker's achievement. He can present a subjective vision, while insisting that the same shot is also camera work—*which it necessarily is.* The violation of the dramatic illusion always jars an audience. This is especially true of *Prelude* and *Part 1* of *Dog Star Man*, where the violation is not an interruption for comic or dramatic effect that can be immediately dismissed: It is an integral part of the epistemology of a film that questions the nature of art and reality. The same kind of tension occurs in countless ways. Shadows spread across the mountain in accelerated speed and flames swallow themselves in backward motion. And always Brakhage presents a purely sensuous visual image working faster than the intellectual tension.

When the subtheme of trees, branches, boughs, and so on, has its development, several flashes of a flying axe and of the DSM chopping seem enigmatic. Brakhage once outlined the plot of the entire epic to me, and a synopsis will clear this and many other problems. The *Prelude* contains a staccato accumulation of images from all of the following four parts. It is structured as a dream with two scenes projected simultaneously. *Part 1* is the winter section. The DSM slowly struggles up a mountain, carrying his axe and accompanied by his dog. In *Part 2* (spring), he reaches the top of the mountain and struggles with, and throws down, a dead white tree. His biography and that of his family will be paralleled to his fight. *Part 3* (summer) —In a context of his sexual fantasies, he will chop up the tree. *Part 4* (fall)—The Fall of Man will be depicted in terms of the DSM's fall down the mountain into winter again. The shots of chopping described above then have a double significance in the form. (1) They contribute to the totality of the central image; that is, there *are* trees on the mountain, and the DSM *is* a woodsman. (2) They foreshadow the dead white tree and its destruction. Likewise, those few shots in *Part 1* that seem only remotely related to the central image (such as the backwards motion of a childbirth, or the DSM writhing in the nude) fit the "intellectual" pattern of the film better when they are thought of in terms of themes that will be dominant later.

The further I get into the development section the less precise my analysis must become. In each image, several themes find their beginning, middle, or end. There is also a greater visual ambiguity. In the center of the film, the shots get shorter, the phrasing by fades and leaders less frequent, and the nonobjective flashes more regular. Brakhage even photographs previously articulate images of trees, falling snow, hair, and the body through a prismatic lens to establish a metaphor with occasional occurrences of a stained glass window. Negative images appear, but only of the protagonist. With them, comes all the associated metaphysics of "the negative of a man." Since I am unable to give an exhaustive analysis of the development, I will leave it with the scattered theme-plucking above.

I come back to Pound for a distinction in Imagist theory, which is also a distinction between *Dog Star Man: Part 1* and the three films discussed before it. He defined Vorticism in *Gaudier-Brzeska*:

> Every concept, every emotion presents itself to the vivid consciousness in some primary form. It belongs to the art of that form. . . . It is no more ridiculous that a person should receive or convey an emotion by an arrangement of shapes, or planes, or colours, than that they should receive or convey such an emotion by an arrangement of musical notes.

He is getting at a concept of vortex as "the point of maximum energy. . . . that there is a point at which an artistic impulse is visceral and abstract and can be realized in any of the arts. Vorticism is art before it has spread itself into flaccidity, into elaboration and secondary application." The distinction is in power. Vorticism is Imagism with primitive concentration.

Of the four Imagist films discussed, only *Dog Star Man: Part 1* is clearly Vorticist. *Choreography for Camera* and *Handwritten* are not as intensely cinematic, the former is filtered through the dance, the latter through poetry. It is difficult to categorize *Eaux d'Artifice:* It might fall in either section. *Part 1* is not only Vorticist in its force, it is *mythopoeic.* Mythopoeia is the often attempted and seldom achieved result of making a myth new or making a new myth. Before *Dog Star Man,* I didn't believe mythopoeia was a cinematic possibility. There is a shot, in the middle of the main development section, of the DSM exhausted by his fight with the mountain, staggering across a screen artificially elongated by an anamorphic lens. For me, that shot more than any other expresses the monumental nature of the conflict. The mountain is the DSM's White Whale, and Brakhage presents both the protagonist and antagonist in micro- and macrocosmic perspective. I am coming to believe that mythopoeia implies a kind of literary (and now filmic) Vorticism–plus, of course, a substantial load of guts. One literary critic defined mythopoeia in terms of Buber's "I and Thou"; that is, the opposing forces become so urgent that they cease to be an It and become Thou, all that is other embodied in one. The primitive encounter of a single man with a real mountain and the secondary conflict between vision and reality are so vivid in *Part 1* that it is a Vorticist film, and the Buberian terms are not extravagant.

On the most vital level, the level of direct eyesight, *Dog Star Man: Part 1* has a pulse of its own that reinforces the rhythm of its subject. The viewer must inch up the mountain of film images falling and climbing simultaneously, must feel the recurring heartbeat, see the sun, feel the cold of the snow, *participate in the hallucination.* That is the point of the development section: to put the guts mentioned above into the struggle, to show the whole of it in a score of ways, to extend the material until its reality becomes questionable and then, in the finale, extend that question to hysteria.

The development gradually glides into the finale, and it isn't until the film is over that a clear division can be made. The last part of the development is a meditation on snow. The falling snow becomes the smoke of a forest fire; the DSM shakes snow off the branches as he clears his way with his axe; there is a single-frame animation of snow crystals. This visual "paragraph" leads into the finale and gradually the precision of the opening groupings returns.

The coda of Brakhage's latest film, *Mothlight,* offers an interesting comparison to the end of *Part 1.* In *Mothlight,* Brakhage placed bits of moth wings, flowers, seeds, etc., between two layers of Mylar editing tape to produce what is probably the first film collage. After a master print was made, Brakhage sent the original strips to his friends. I am holding the coda to it now. It opens with a few splatters of fibers and moth wings separated by an inch or so of blankness. The particle sections are about a foot and a half long. After the last foot of wings, there are three inches of blankness, then three wings, a foot of blankness, and finally a single wing. Brakhage likes to end his films this way: A splatter of images punctured by a silence, and, as the image material grows slimmer, the silences get larger.

There are six separate phrasings of images in the finale of *Part 1*. The first begins with the DSM in slow motion climbing up a slight incline with the dog moving easily by his side. As the finale progresses, he seems to move slower and slower. Appropriately, by the end, he has almost stopped. He climbs from the other side of the screen at the same incline, and then falls. Brakhage shows flashes of his face in falling, followed by a shot of his heart. A black silence.

The second phrase is only two shots: The DSM climbing at a forty-five degree angle, and a subjective shot of him falling. Then whiteness. The next section is again at a forty-five degree angle of a fall. It is cut short, as the dog begins to move. Blackness is followed by internal tissues intercut with Greek columns. The fallen DSM in negative struggles to get up amid orange flashes.

The fourth "paragraph" is the most crucial in the finale. The DSM makes his way up a sixty degree incline. The film-maker has forced the viewer back to the tension between eye and camera vision. Is the mountain just a tilted camera? The next shot, a seventy degree slope, answers affirmatively. The dog, with magnificent grace, easily glides up to his master's side proving the camera tilt. Whiteness fades into black. In the fifth phrase, the protagonist is lying in the snow, first in positive, then in negative. He pulls himself up a ninety degree cliff of snow. Brakhage is not willing to let us escape with the easy realization of camera trickery. He admits it subtly (through the dog's leap) and then overcomes it openly. A long period of whiteness follows, and then the sixth phrase, a single shot. It is a microscopic one of the blood stream in its natural two-steps-forward–one-step-backward motion. How much of this is camera magic? Obviously none! In the union of physiology and natural choreography, I'll end. Beyond this, there is the mythopoeic power, and that must be *seen*.

INTERVIEW WITH STAN BRAKHAGE

BY P. ADAMS SITNEY

No. 30, Fall, 1963

Brakhage: I can remember when I got married, many of my friends who had been waiting for me to transform into a homosexual were bitterly disappointed, frustrated, and considered that, by their mythos of what the artist was, I was completely through. It wasn't all just their personal wants, but it was in respect to the mythos. A married artist was an incomprehensible thing to many friends, artists working in film and other mediums. They were referring to a whole mythos that passes most clearly through Jean Cocteau in *Orpheus*, that is, that moment where the whole film unreels itself and Orpheus is cast back into the arms of Eurydice, and he himself as poet, deeper than social-conscious poet, is completely destroyed. That mythos has been one of the most dominant in this century, and I had to cope with that at a time when the total form-structure of my work had changed completely when *Anticipation of the Night* was made. That was, in one sense, to be my last film. I had seen myself, cast before where I was as a human being, as leading to inevitable suicide through another contemporary myth. Certainly by the age of 26, I was getting too old to still be alive and around and fulfilling the myth of myself. *Anticipation of the Night* was the vehicle out.

Sitney: Do you mean you were actually going to kill yourself at the completion of the film?

I didn't think this through consciously. Occurrences that happened afterwards made it clear that's what I'd intended. For months, I'd been getting more and more ill with neurotic diseases, some of them, like asthma, which had a long history in my life, and others that were completely new. At that time the fourth and fifth fingers of my left hand, that is the marriage and death fingers, were completely crippled with arthritis; I couldn't move them, I was practically on a cane (at the age of 26, mind), I was defeated in all searches of love, trying to reach out of myself, except in relation to film. Even the drama structures of film were collapsing around me, like old walls that I could no longer inhabit. There was a reach out, but when those walls fell, it seemed as if there was nothing but night out there, and I then thought of all my life as being in anticipation of that night. That night could only cast one shadow for me, could only form itself into one black shape, and that was the hanged man. That is the shadow seen on the wall at the end of *Anticipation of the Night*. I had kept saying for months, without ever questioning why, that I would shoot the hanged man sequence spontaneously. On the one hand, I was hyperediting the film, that is, pitching more of the forming into the editing process than any film I had made up to that time. On the other hand, I was saying, "When I come to the hanged man sequence, I'll shoot it spontaneously. I will go out and put a rope around my neck and photograph as the feelings arrive and just attach that section on to the end of the film." I didn't really become aware of what I had intended until months after our marriage.

Did you get married while the film was still being made?

I was still editing the film, specifically the birth-of-the-child sequence in which the child is made out of abstractions, that is, water abstracted, the rose as a concept of prismatic light breakings, etc.; in other words, the child is formed completely out of mythic elements. Right at that moment something, physically in myself, was wrenching out to another being, Jane, at a moment when she, for similar reasons in her own life, was completely open-ended; that is, ready for suicide. She reached to me, and we had a beginning, finding expression in immediate sex love, but with enough power open-ended re: sex-death, that Spanish tradition, that we had something to go on with. The conscious mind wasn't aware of this for some time.

A month after we were married, I was out on the front lawn with Jane, whom I wasn't yet seeing deeply beyond sex desire, and I was putting a rope around my neck and standing up on a kitchen chair in a suburb of Denver with all the neighbors gathering on porches to wonder what that madman was up to now. Those neighbors had seen me set a rosebush on fire and photograph it with upside-down camera. (The image was too myth-structured, too unreal to me, to be used in *Anticipation of the Night*: It had to be made more out of eye sources.)

Anyway, neighbors were gathering, watching me putting rope around my neck and photographing my shadow against a wall. There was no need for the kitchen chair: My shadow was never seen below the waist. And out of my nonrecognition of where I actually was as a total being, I was trying to re-enact, dramatize, or, in some sense, fulfill my own prophesy that I must die by hanging, and I was trying to realize what I had intended.

So there I was on a chair with rope around neck photographing and, then, fortunately a friend dropped by and was also watching the process, and I handed the camera to Jane and said, "Well, that's that," meaning I'm finished, and without realizing or remembering that the rope was around my neck, stepped off the chair and swung in midair for a few seconds, was grabbed by the friend, put back up on the chair, and suddenly had the full realization of what had been intended. I was sure that I had intended for months to finish the editing of *Anticipation of the Night* up to that point, go out into the yard, climb up on a chair camera in hand, jump off the chair, and while hanging run out as much film as I could, leaving a note saying, "Attach this to the end of *Anticipation of the Night*."

I had to re-enact some semblance of this intention. This is particularly appropriate to my idea (as expressed in *Dog Star Man: Part 1*) of the rhythm of life being such that you could paraphrase it in two steps forward and one back. That instant, when I didn't realize where I actually was in relationship to Jane, and where we were going with new form, was the back step. I had to step back, that is, take my fall—rope around neck and all, and pitch myself into a close proximity with death, to realize what had been intended. At that point, I was not really seeing Jane or what we had, the strength of love, and what it could build: She was the person who received the camera when I said, "Well, that's that!" Or the person who was thought of as just doing the housework or as only in bed with sex the touchstone of something flowering between us that would be the growth up and out; but everywhere else we could not see each other, and this nonseeing, which many share during the first months of marriage, became so crucial that I felt out of absolute necessity we had to film.

One day in midst of a quarrel, I felt the necessity to take the camera and photograph her again and again. I grabbed the lights and began letting her face emerge in and out of black and white flashes in order that as much as I could see be immediately pitched into expression. I moved the light with one hand—painting her image as it moved over her and away into darkness—and photographed her with the other hand.

Was Wedlock House: An Intercourse *the film being made?*

Yes. At a crucial moment out of some graciousness that I did not fully comprehend; (I kept feeling a little guilty wondering what Jane's view of me would be). I sensed that my view, or what I would cast upon her, was becoming too dominant. So I handed her the camera, and she took it very quickly. We were trying to re-enact the quarrel, trying to comprehend it.

You were acting?

We started by acting, but, as we began passing the camera back and forth, the quarrel was pitched onto a visual level. Jane didn't have much technical knowledge of the camera, but enough to make it possible for her to control it out of her anger and determination to grasp those images, that is, her view of me, and retain them for me to look at later. Her images came out of such a quality that they could actually cut back and forth with mine. She too grabbed the light, as I had done, and began taking up the same form of painting-in my image with moving light source, she automatically grasped what my style was on a feeling level, and went right on with her version of it. This was the first time we were both photographing; I photographing her, she me, but in relation to the form that was springing out of me. We got glimpses of each other, in flashes of moving light, as if emerging out of long hallways in sheer darkness. All the quarrels we were having at that time became pitched on that visual level. You do not need to know this, of course, to see *Wedlock House: An Intercourse*.

It is extremely interesting to Jane and me that her face changes so much through that film, and it changes always in reference to women I had known previously. At certain moments, she looks like the girl in *Interim*; at certain moments, like the girl in *Desistfilm*; at certain moments, like girls that weren't in any of these films; and, at some moments (shudder), like my mother (bless her). The amazing thing was that, without will, and with the light being moved interpretively faster than the brain could move, I was capable of forcing, by those movements, her face into a variety of contexts, which were actually what was standing between me and my being able to see her as she was then. Her pictures of me related to pictures of her brother and other men that she had known. As a matter of fact, I was wearing a cast-off Army shirt of her brother's. This was one of her strongest images of him in that film. She was not conscious of this. The viewer, not having known, would not realize this by looking at the film and those images. But this is how we were astonished and kept tabs of the formal integrity that was passing between us. The next step was to take this material and edit it.

We were so shocked by seeing the footage that we suddenly had an intense realization of what we had to cope with as human beings to make our love grow together and be more than something that could flower in a dark bed where nothing more than body material was accessible for its pure sensual growth. That's what I mean when I say sex is a touchstone, but not a foundation. The crudity of trying to make sex a foundation would be like trying to take the Blarney stone and make it the foundation for Babylon; you know, horrible. Foundation has to spring new at each moment from each happening. Cornerstone of any foundation or structure always, whether it's for one person, or two people, has to be supporting where they are at each moment. So we had to keep "making it new" in the pitched structure we had in mind as to where we were going. That it always be new, with its cornerstone supporting the moment where we were, however hard it was to make it tangential to that moment and where we thought we were going. I started editing *Wedlock House* months later. We had moved from Denver to Princeton, N. J., and it took me months to accept that footage as being material for a balanced work of art.

Looking at the images and getting only horror, I was afraid of editing, afraid that I would be performing some black-magic act, cursing what little chance we had for making a love structure out of our life together. For months, I resisted, resisted. I struggled with that footage trying to edit it, you know, trying to get it balanced. Finally, I gave up and said, "If horror is what it is, then

I will go straight into it." It was like breaking through a sound barrier: Suddenly, the total beauty of what happened to us right straight off the battle ground of our lives was what was structured and made true scenes in these flashes.

The last shots give a clear sense of where we were when I was editing that film. I had been capable of editing all those images so they expressed, first Jane's parental love, then her romantic relations, then her sex relations, and my own also, and interrelated them and finally brought those image-material faces, hers and mine, to the point where it was close to the way we saw each other when I was editing the film, which was months after it was shot. Jane was involved in the editing, too: I would ask specific questions as to what she saw in this facial feature of mine, always referring her to my images, not to my view of hers. I drew statements out of her that structured the work so that the quarrel would be totally fair. Then comes the finished work, which, in photography and in spirit, is so dependent on her view of me and the things she said about my images that it was something like a collaboration; that is, her view of me and mine of her finally meshed so carefully and so closely together that it does tend to be a balance, not collaborative, but true.

The film ends with an intercourse scene. How does that fit in?

That was the whole other level of it. There were the faces, the movements through the hallways, the dramatic action, the quarrel and the coffee-cup scene, and then always interspersed and intercut with this was *Intercourse*, that being to me the course, the way of the course; intercourse. Sex, which was the thread that seemed to hold the whole tapestry together, was always weaving in and out. It held together precisely to the extent that all intercourse scenes remained distinct from dramatic scenes. It became like warp-woof. You can call intercourse warp or woof, whichever you like, but whatever it is, the dramatic scenes are the other. The beauty of the ending is that, previously, every moment the film moves out of intercourse scenes into drama scenes of quarrels, or searches, etc., it does so by way of plastic cutting on a single part of the body, but, at the end of the film, Jane's face goes to pure white, and the intercourse emerges out of white, making the most total plastic cut in the film.

Your next film was Cat's Cradle, *wasn't it?*

Cat's Cradle was next shot, but not next edited. The next edited was *Window Water Baby Moving*. Cat's Cradle presented a crucial problem because then, Jane, like most young people, had an image of what marriage was, which was very uninteresting to her. I had a concept of what marriage was that was struck off of the marriage of two close friends of mine, James Tenney and Carolee Schnee-mann, who had married shortly after the making of *Loving*, in which I had seen them as ideal lovers. So they were heavily in-volved in the mythos of film-making by way of *Loving*, and the love they had found for each other and the marriage they had made was an idealized one. Fool that I was, like many young husbands are, I felt an urgency to take Jane into a relationship with them, that is, went to visit them in Vermont and stayed two very disturbing weeks with them, where naturally Jane, not sharing my mythos of marriage, and certainly not by way of another man and woman, resisted all of that concept tremendously. I was trying to take an ideal form and strike a marriage thereoff, like taking a cookie shape and making cookies.

There was a fantastic level of sarcasm, particularly between the two women. Women are always great in this area, you know, re-sisting each other by way of fantastic allusions, of which men, if they don't listen carefully, are never aware. And I was trying so hard to relate to Jim as man that there are images in *Cat's Cradle* in which you can't tell whether it's Jim or myself you are looking at, even though he had a beard and I didn't. How do you explain that kind of visual magic? I was trying to superimpose Jane in relationship to Carolee Schneemann and failing miserably on all counts. The touchstone of this seemed to be that the cat belonging to Jim and Carolee happened to come into heat right after we arrived and shockingly enough remained in heat all the time we were there. So the cat became the source of sex objectivity, and I didn't see it symbolically any more. I didn't have time to fool around with symbols, and I didn't have enough film to waste trying to create symbolic structures. I had to move right into the shape/ form of what was developing straight off the cat. That cat became a source of hyperforms and a touchstone visually and formally of everything else that happens in the film. Since I did not have time to bother about casting dramas, I began shooting very short shots, which interrelated total scenes. I had to get an image, an *idée fixe*, out of the way so I could see what was not on the surface, and so we could go on. Then Jim and Carolee could go on unhindered by the myth, and we could all be friends; but there was a tre-mendous battle that had to take place first.

But the film itself doesn't express very much of the battle. I mean I didn't see it in the film.

Well, you see, that would be hard for me to disengage myself from, I am so aware of the battle that was struck off from it. But people tell me that it is very lyrical, and I think it is probably a song that uses all this material that was so painful to deal with at the time for making a tone poem that struggles to contain a sense of separation. A key phrase to it, which I discovered later, was Freud's quotation that Durrell uses in the preface to *Justine*. Freud wrote in a letter, "I am accustoming myself to the idea of regarding every sexual act as a process in which four persons are involved." So, all sex within *Cat's Cradle* tends to be interrelated; that is, there is no sex that does not involve four people with the cat seen as a visual medium of heat. Sometimes it is hard to tell whether there are four people in it, or three or two. One person even thought it was a portrait of a single person. And some only see the cat. Well, this is fine, on whatever level you want to look at it, it still contains that lyric song, if not of struggle, then of love and its complications creating possibilities of marriage. That's the play in there; *Cat's Cradle* relates to the game children used to play. The cat is like the cradled center, like "the cradle of civilization" or "cat's cradle," the string game. I mean, it is that complex . . . two hands and a string; but at a certain point two hands are not enough to play the game and you need four hands; you need two external hands to come in and move the string around to make "the cat's cradle."

And then Window Water Baby Moving?

In that film, Jane was so busy fighting the battle to destroy my myth of what ideal marriage was, in order that we might be free, that she was not actively involved in the filming except as . . . Look at the source of inspiration she was providing for me at each and every shot, as she resisted the domination of anyone else's ideally formed life. By the time of *Window Water Baby Moving*, Jane and I were so separate that we were in a position to come together.

You were in Brussels during part of the time of Jane's pregnancy, weren't you?

I went to Brussels for a month to attend the Exposition of Experimental Film. This was early in the pregnancy. Then I went to Geneva to do work on a commercial job. That was during the seventh to eighth month of pregnancy. I became involved with death. This was when I shot the material for *The Dead*, which was edited three years later. Also there was one aspect of childbirth that was very dangerous to me. Again I, still subconsciously carrying the weight of my pitched suicide, and casting it forward, had the notion that my child might take my place in life and leave me free to die. That idea became more and more intense the closer we got to the actual birth. There were two things that held me back in terms of this mythos: 1) Would it be a boy or a girl? If it were a boy, it would be a better stand-in for me. (This was all subconscious, but later figured out re what I did in filmic expression.) 2) Jane had had German measles at three months, and we had one in so many chances of a monster-birth. Jane became more and more concerned with the birth and more and more removed from aesthetic concern, and certainly removed from death wishes. Except she was so deeply aware of the dangers of my problem that she told me afterwards that, even though she wanted a boy, she hoped it would be a girl because she had some sense that that would be less dangerous to me. She became involved in her own bodily processes, reaching out, and finally in giving birth to the child. Everything to me was on the perceptual level . . . I desired that it be cast into a form that was neither home movie nor medical film, but that it contain the total reason for having the child, including any subconscious death wishes and our sense of love, starting right with the body, and all that we knew of marriage by this time.

Did she mind your filming the birth?

No. She realized that was how I could be most there. That is why we struggled so hard and managed to have the child born in our home. It was more crucial to Jane than to me that I be there when the child was born. So the Excuse Form for doing this was to make a film as she was giving birth.

At that moment when the woman goes into second stage and is pushing the baby out, many women begin cursing their husbands, about whom they otherwise say very beautiful things; and, at the very least, most women have no patience with any fumbling whatsoever, and men at that moment tend to become very ineffectual. While Jane did say "I love you" (which was a great joy to me), it was immediately followed by "Please leave me alone," and then with "Are you filming?" Her concern was that I be there but not bothering, or impinging on, her. A woman at that stage can often have a good relationship with the doctor, because he is capable of receiving the child, and helping it out. But a husband is too emotionally involved at a moment like this. I literally could not have watched that birth if I had not been working. I'm sure I would have passed out, but since I was working and intensively involved with my own concerns, Jane and I could be together in the most clear sense.

Who photographed you?

She did right after Myrrena was born. She had said a long time before, "I want a picture of you then, too" (we had pictures of me from before the childbirth, of Jane and I kissing, of my hand) and "Don't you want a picture of yourself? You must have it." And I said, "Well, who will take it?" She said, "I will." So I said, "All right," but I never expected that she'd have the strength. Sure enough, it was the first thing she thought of after Myrrena was born. She said, "Give me the camera." I, hardly knowing what I was doing, just handed it to her. She photographed all those images of my face. I grew prouder and prouder of her, of the baby, of having made it; I was out of my head. And she, just having given birth to the child, was recording my face. Do you see what the process was there?

And what did you do after Window Water Baby Moving?

The next film that I edited was the *Cat's Cradle*. We moved from Princeton back into the mountains of Boulder, Colorado, where I began working on *Cat's Cradle*. We lived in Silver Spruce, then, the same place that we lived during the whole shooting of *Dog Star Man*. Right before I started shooting *Dog Star Man*, I edited *Cat's Cradle*.

Did you have any idea of what Dog Star Man *would be?*

No. At least all the ideas I had subsequently proved to be irrelevant.

Then the next film to discuss would be the Prelude *to* Dog Star Man *itself.*

There were other works in the way; for instance, I had shot *Sirius Remembered* after I photographed the childbirth film, and it was edited right after *Cat's Cradle*.

Now Sirius Remembered *is another death poem.*

Another death poem.

How would you relate it to your general psychology of death, then?

I had photographed the material for *The Dead,* but I didn't edit it. I let it wait for two years before I edited it. In the meanwhile a dog of ours, named Sirius, that we cared very much about, was hit by a car and killed. We laid him out above the ground because of Jane's ideals about death. She said how beautiful and natural it is to find the bones of dead animals in the forest. She, from psychological needs of her own, did not like the sense of burying anything. It was midwinter, and the ground was hard, so I went along with her, and we laid him out underneath a tree in a little field that we called Happy Valley. Every time thereafter that

I went out in back of my house in Princeton, I saw that body, which did not begin to decompose. It was midwinter, and it remained frozen solid. Every time I'd see it, I'd break into what were to me incomprehensible tears. Suddenly, I was faced, in the center of my life, with the death of a loved being, which tended to undermine all my abstract thoughts of death.

I remember one marvelous time, which gave me the sense of how others could avoid it. Parker Tyler and Charles Boultenhouse came to visit us, and Charles wanted to go out into the fields "to gather a little nature," as he put it. "Nature" was such a crisis to me at this time that I was shocked at that statement. Charles made some martinis, handed me one; and Parker, Charles, and I all went out into Happy Valley where they toasted the new buds of spring that were beginning to come up, etc., and marched right straight past the body of Sirius either without seeing it at all (any more than they can see my film *Sirius Remembered*) or else they saw it and refused to recognize it. Charles was envaled in the ideal of toasting the budding spring and here was this decaying, stinking corpse right beside the path where we had to walk, and he literally did not, could not, or would not see it. All three attitudes, I think, arise from the same source.

When did you decide to film the body?

I filmed it all during that winter and did the last photography the day after Parker and Charles visited. At that time, the corpse was all torn up. I, sobbing each time, went out alone with camera and photographed it. Jane said something, after watching me photograph it, that made me realize the deep form taking place. She knew dogs. She told me that every time I went to photograph that body: 1) I was trying to bring it back to life by putting it in movement again; 2) I was uprighting it by taking the camera at an angle that tended to make the dog's image upright on the screen; 3) (which was really significant) Jane had often watched dogs do a strange dance around dead bodies not only of their own species but of others (it's like a round dance: The dogs, individually or in a pack, often will circle a dead body and then rub the neck very sensually all along the corpse perfuming themselves from the stench of decomposition). Those were literally the kinds of movements with which I was involved in making *Sirius Remembered* without realizing it. Jane threw open the whole animal world; that is, the animal parts of myself that were, at that moment, engaged in filming the body.

I also find two intellectual parts: 1) the influence of very tight, formal music—possibly Webern—*and 2)* Gertrude Stein, *who has always influenced you. Now, where were you in relationship to the musical forms?*

At this moment, I was coming to terms with the decay of a dead thing and the decay of the memories of a loved being that had died, and it was undermining all abstract concepts of death. The form was being cast out of probably the same physical need that makes dogs dance and howl in rhythm around a corpse. I was taking song as my source of inspiration for the rhythm structure, just as dogs dancing, prancing around a corpse, and howling in rhythm structures or rhythm intervals might be considered like the birth of some kind of song. I won't try to guess out of what urgency.

But was not Webern an influence?

Not at this point. I had been through Webern's influence. Webern and Bach were strong influences on *Anticipation of the Night.* But the structure that was dominating rhythmically would be like jazz . . . no, not jazz . . . it would be like song, simple song, plain song —plainsong, that's what it was clearly—Gregorian chant! That kind of howling would be the rhythm structure that was dominating *Sirius Remembered.*

Where were you in terms of perceiving Gertrude Stein?

I would say the greatest influence that she had on *Sirius Remembered* was by way of my realization that there is no repetition; that, every time a word is "repeated," it is a new word by virtue of what word precedes it and follows it, etc. This freed me to "repeat" the same kind of movements. So I could literally move back and forth over the animal in repeated patterns. There are three parts to the film: First, there is the animal seen in the fall as just having died; second, there are the winter shots, in which he's become a statue covered with snow; and, third, there's the thaw and decay. That third section is all *re*membered, where his members are put together again. All previous periods of his existence as a corpse, in the fall, the snow, and the thaw, are gone back and forth over, recapitulated and interrelated. Gertrude Stein gave me the courage to let images recur in this fashion and in such a manner that there was no sense of repetition.

You've spoken before of effects of snow and whiteness. This was the time before Prelude, *while you were making* The Dead. *You've spoken before of the power of whiteness, and you have images of snow in* Sirius Remembered. *Can you see how this would be a motif?*

Yes, there are certain motifs that emerge through all my work, but some of them come together most clearly in *Sirius Remembered*. One example would be "the tree." Over and over again, the camera pans from the corpse up a tree. I had no sense of why I was doing that at the time, but now I realize I was planting the first seeds of my concern with the image of the white tree, which dominates *Dog Star Man*; and remember the dog star is Sirius. So there for the first time, the dog star is emerging, and then man's relation with dog or my pitching my sense of self into the dog corpse. My abstract senses of death were conflicting with the actual decay of a corpse. First, when it wouldn't decay and turn into clean white bones and, then, when it did. What we finally had to face in terms of those bones was ironic.

We had already gotten a new dog called "The Brown Dog." We wanted him to be the opposite of what Sirius was. He was a bum that we saved from death in the dog pound. He was deliberately not given a fancy name but continually referred to as "The Brown Dog," as if having no life of his own. The events that made the last shooting of *Sirius Remembered* possible were as follows: The stench of decomposition that was so strong in the valley began coming into the house and we couldn't locate it. First of all, we didn't know what it was. We thought a rat had died in the wall somewhere. Then we began wondering if it were blowing through the windows from Happy Valley, which was half a block away from the house. The next night, we smelled it coming straight off "The Brown Dog," and then we knew that he was perfuming himself off that corpse. We tried to joke about it; we called it "sheepshit smell." We tried to call it "cheese"; we tried to call it anything rather than recognize what it was. The next day, I had to see for myself, and I forced Jane to come with me. We found that the corpse in the field was being eaten and that what was eating it was our current family dog. As we walked into that field, he demonstrated for us by sitting down innocently and beginning to tear off and devour a leg bone. Suddenly, we had the realization of what made clean bones: they were picked clean. The psychological implications of how the family dog had to demonstrate to us how he was appropriating the powers of Sirius struck us. It is significant to us that "The Brown Dog" became the dog star of *Dog Star Man*. Jane broke into tears as the idea of death as a happening in life became clearer and clearer.

We began questioning why dogs perfume themselves that way. I recalled Baudelaire's poem, where he speaks with disgust of the populace for being like his dog who hates the smell of perfume but likes to come in covered with shit. Well, Baudelaire had not smelled deeply enough. I became capable of smelling that stench at the center of all meat eaten. In the bacon for breakfast was the stench that was coming out of Happy Valley. I also began smelling it in ladies' perfumes: The center of most perfumes is a decayed matter very comparable to the stench of the dead dog. Every time I sat down to edit *Sirius Remembered*, I began having diarrhea. It was as if to unload the decay somehow. Every time I'd go into an intensive editing process on that film, I'd have it. By way of that film, certain other visions began emerging with extreme intensity, which were relevant to *Dog Star Man*. One night, after Jane had excused herself early and gone to bed, I was working. It got to be about two o'clock in the morning, and, suddenly, I sensed Jane behind me. She handed me a small dried-up plant, which I put on the table. She was always bringing me little things from the forest. I noticed the plant began to move. Every time I looked at it, it would be pointing in a different direction. Then I noticed that I was making a lot of wind and motion with my arms, and it was flipping and turning. It was a talisman hardened with its own death. I watched it closely, and it became a source of inspiration. In the morning, Jane had no memory of having brought me that plant.

Then, other weird things began happening. One night, I was stuck on a splice when I was dealing with decay. Decay is a long-term process of things pulling apart, transforming slowly, and producing heat. Where the decay was most intense on the inside, it would melt the snow on the outside of the body. I was concerned with how to edit that, how to cast such a slow process into a form that would be hard. The form would have to be as hard as the stone image of Sirius covered with white, as if he were a statue. I was having trouble with a splice at three o'clock in the morning, at which time I had a clear sense of three personages looking over my shoulder. As I started to turn around, something seemed to pass through me. The phrase came to me, "He thinks we have *something* to do with what he's doing," as if said very sarcastically. I was immediately depressed with an emotional despair. I have no intellectual explanation of where those words came from. That phrase seemed to cut across all the lines of my thought at the moment, as if it was layed down there or strummed. Imagine all the rest of my thoughts as strings moving out from a center of consciousness. Suddenly, from some subconsciousness so strong that it seemed coming from elsewhere, came this damning phrase that struck off all of my sensibilities and cast me, in a second, into the most horrible gloom I've ever had. I stopped work. I was like a

EDITORS OF *FILM CULTURE*

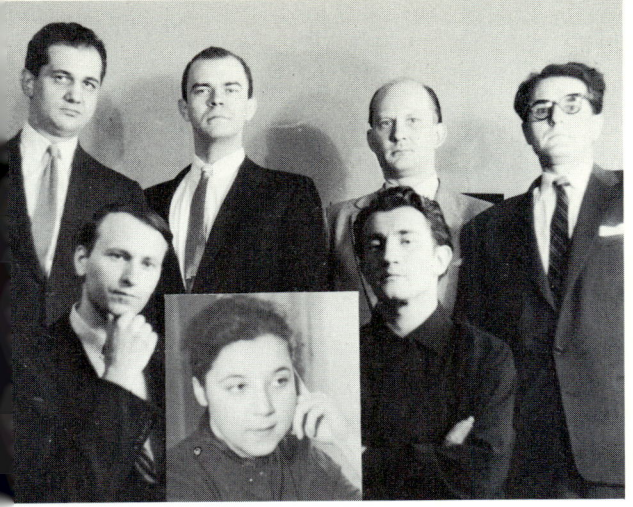

1955—Left to right, back row: Andrew Sarris, Eugene Archer, George Fenin, Adolfas Mekas. Front row: Jonas Mekas, Edouard de Laurot. Insert: Arlene Croce. Photo: Film Museum of New York

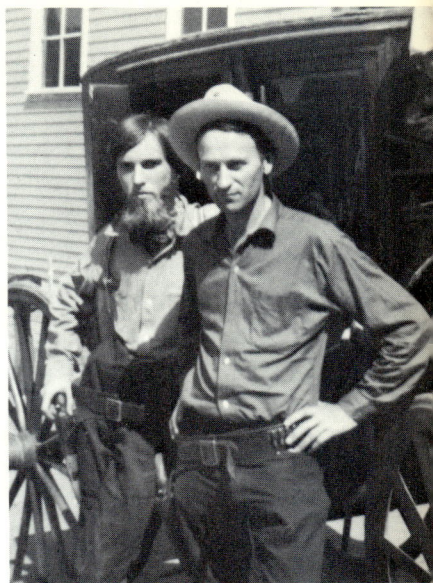

1965—P. Adams Sitney and Jonas Mekas, in *Double Barelled Detective Story*, by Adolfas Mekas. Photo: Louise Alaimo

CINEMA 16 SYMPOSIUM

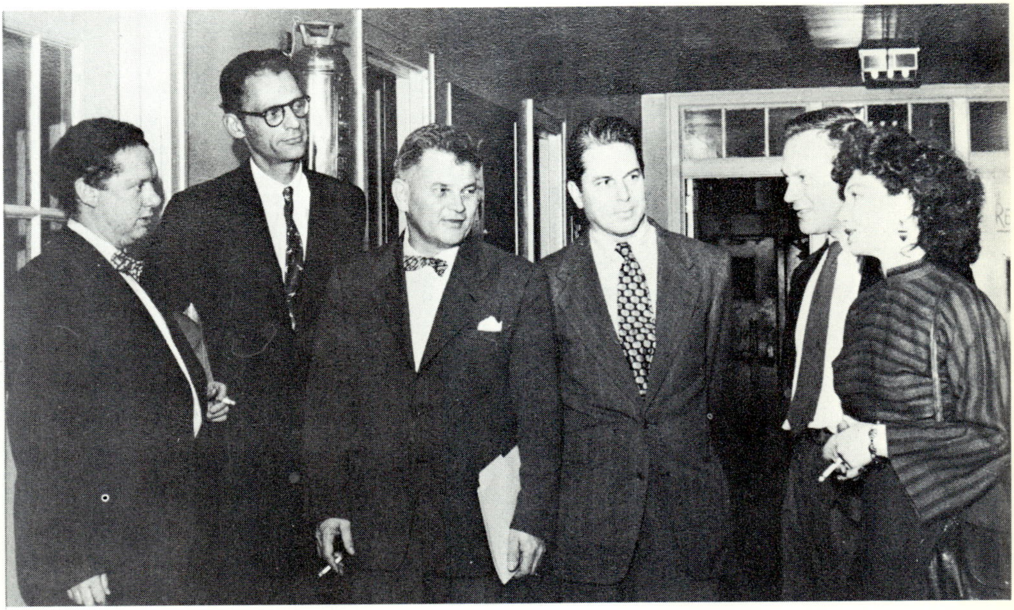

Left to right: Dylan Thomas, Arthur Miller, Willard Maas, Parker Tyler, Amos Vogel, Maya Deren (Photo courtesy of Amos Vogel)

See "Poetry and the Film," pp. 171–86.

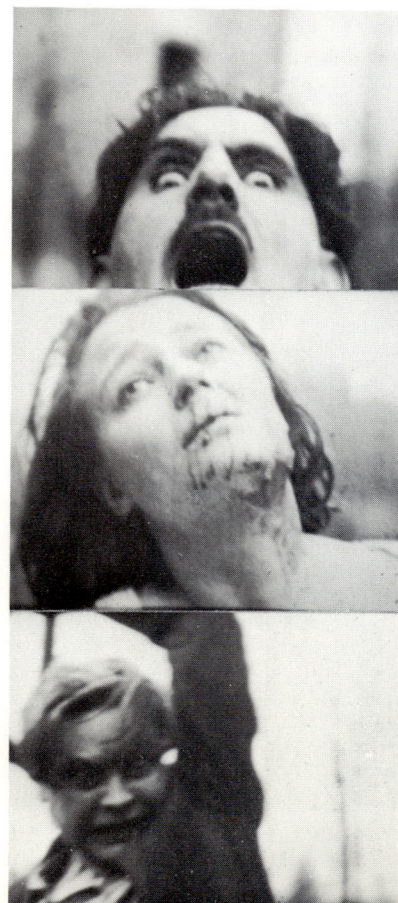

DIMITRI KIRSANOV'S *MENILMONTANT*

The slaying of the parents.
One frame from each of shots 29–36 is shown.

29. Hand moves (blurred) toward axe, becomes focused (shown), moves (blurred) diagonally out of frame, leaving still of post. (11 frames)
30. Woman's face; only arm moves. (9 frames)
31. Hand is shown moving up to right; it will reverse, in frame 6, to swing back and out of frame on the left at the same time the body, truncated on three sides, moves to right. (12 frames)
32. Man moves slightly left and down. (9 frames)
33. Still. (6 frames)
34. Man moves slightly down. (7 frames)
35. Almost still. (6 frames)
36. Frames 1–12: Attacker's head and arm, as he reaches out to strike, enter frame from bottom right to reach position shown; 13–17: He swings, going out of frame; 18–25: empty except for the out-of-focus background; frames 26–37: Attacker hurtles up from the left, traverses frame, swings out to right; 38–54=18–25; 55–70: blank; 71–105=18–25.
37. Shot of ground; axe falls into frame.

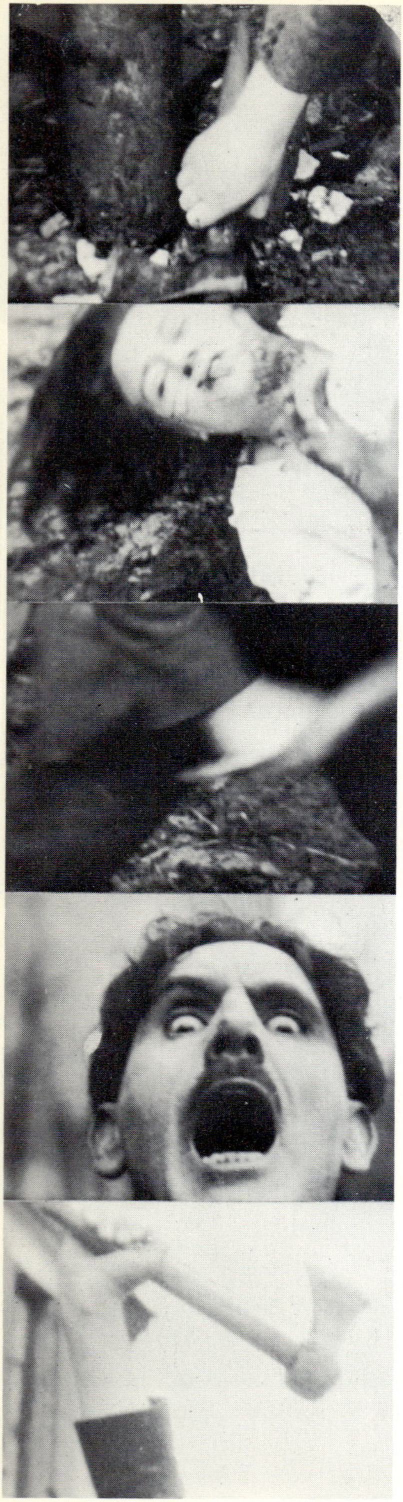

The girl discovers the bodies of her parents.
One frame from each of shots 53–58 is shown.
53. Frames 1–5: Girl whirls backward into frame on diagonal from lower left, her hair flying (blurred); frames 6–19: still, as shown.
54. Neighbors surrounding the bodies: still (14 frames).
55. Almost still, except for eyes moving from left to right.
56. Still (25 frames).
57. Still (34 frames).
58. Frames 1–18: still as shown; frame 19: Head turns to right quickly (blurred); frame 20–21: held in that position, now in focus; frames 22–24: Hand goes in mouth, head returns to former position, blurred.
59. Not shown—Girl, in long shot, runs back to her parents.

Stills: Film Museum of New York

(captions by Walter S. Michel)

See Walter S. Michel: "In Memoriam of Dimitri Kirsanov, a Neglected Master," pp. 37–41.

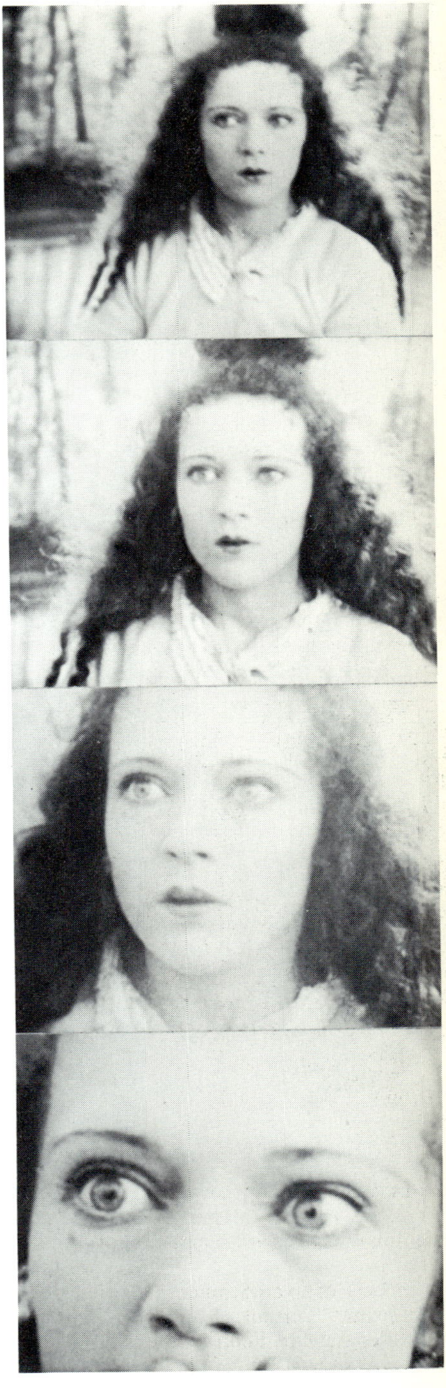

ERICH VON STROHEIM

The von Stroheim Issue (#18) was copiously illustrated with stills from the collection of Herman G. Weinberg. The captions for the four pictures (from that issue) reproduced here are his.

A. Erich von Stroheim directing Caesare Gravina (as Zerkow the Junkman) and Dale Fuller (as Maria Macapa) in a scene from the great secondary story in *Greed* that was totally eliminated by MGM in the severely mutilated release version of the film. Counterpointing the debacle of Trina, McTeague, and Marcus, who were destroyed by avarice, was the story of Zerkow's lust for a nonexistent gold hoard, a figment of the imagination of the demented Maria. The story ends in murder and suicide.

C. The "white orchestra" that provided the music for Prince Mirko's revels, in *The Merry Widow*—cut from the film.

B. In his dreams, Zerkow unearths, in a cemetery, the golden treasure. One of the many nightmare sequences cut from *Greed*.

D. The "black orchestra" that provided the music for the orgies in Mme. Rosa's fancy bordello, from *The Wedding March*—cut from the film.

See Erich von Stroheim: "Introduction to *The Merry Widow*," pp. 52–56; Rudolf Arnheim: "Portrait of an Artist (von Stroheim)," pp. 57–61; Herman G. Weinberg: "A Footnote to *Foolish Wives*," pp. 62–64; and Herman G. Weinberg: "Coffee, Brandy, and Cigars, XXX," pp. 65–70.

MAYA DEREN

Maya Deren in *Meshes of the Afternoon*
Still: Film Museum of New York
See Rudolf Arnheim: "To Maya Deren," pp. 84–86.

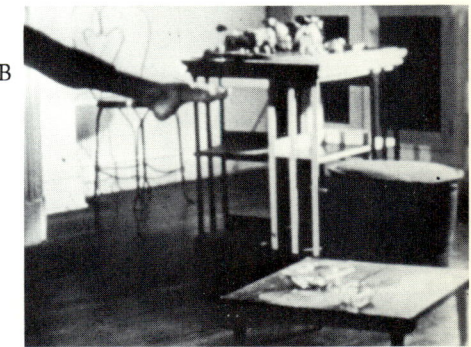

B

C

D

Choreography for Camera, Museum of Modern Art Stills Archive, and Grove Press.

See P. Adams Sitney: "Imagism in Four Avant-Garde Films," pp. 188–90.

Stan Brakhage, *Dog Star Man, Part 1; The Art of Vision*

Charles Boultenhouse, *Handwritten*   Kenneth Anger, *Eaux d'Artifice*

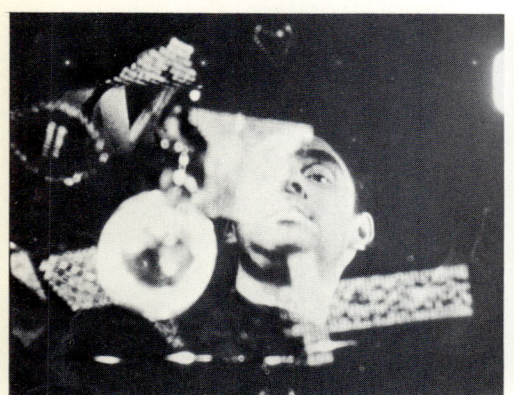

Stills: Film Museum of New York

See P. Adams Sitney: "Imagism in Four Avant-Garde Films," pp. 187–200.

HARRY SMITH

Photo: John Palmer

Heaven and Earth Magic ('The Magic Feature"): #12. Stills: Film Museum of New York

See P. Adams Sitney: "Interview with Harry Smith," pp. 260–76.

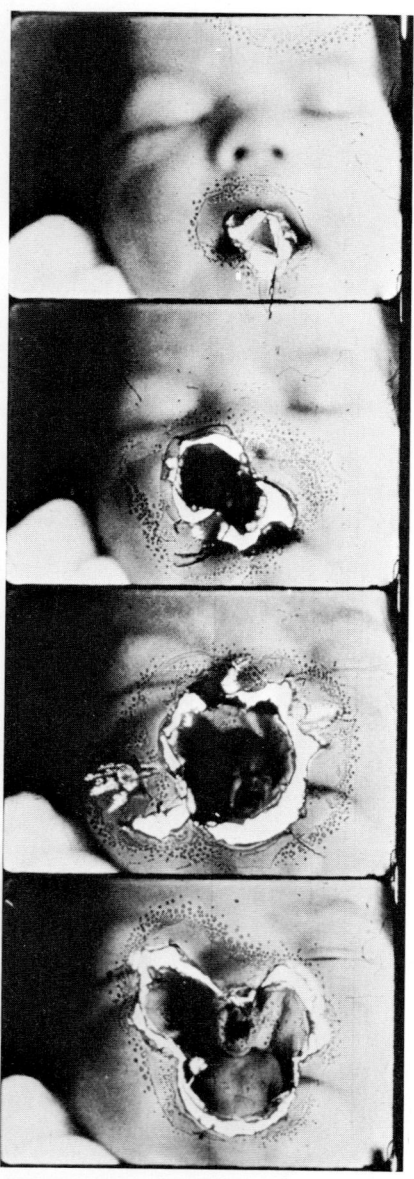

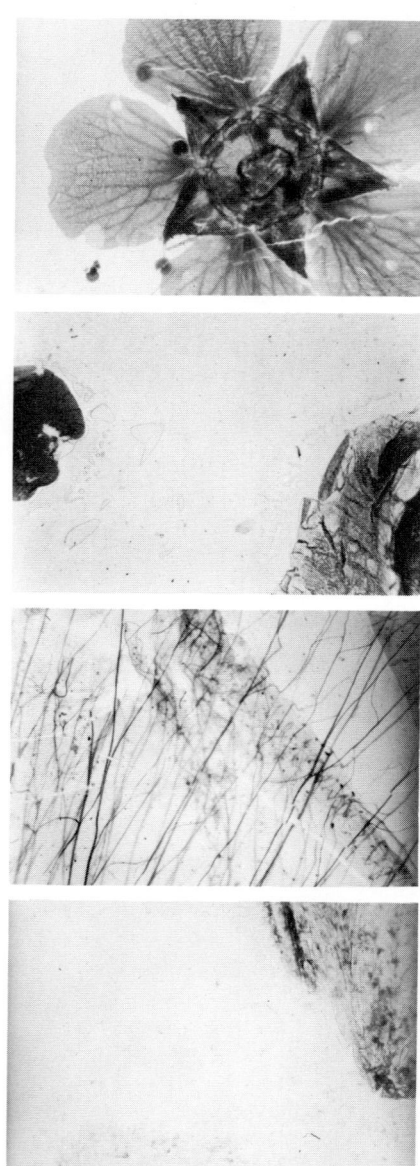

A sequence of images from *Dog Star Man: Part 2* and *The Art of Vision*, in which Brakhage inserted wedges of film into a hole cut through the image of the screaming baby.

Four frames from a test strip for *Moth-light*, in which Brakhage sandwiched moth wings and a leaf between two strips of mylar film tape.

Stills: Film Museum of New York

See Stan Brakhage: "Respond Dance," pp. 245–50.

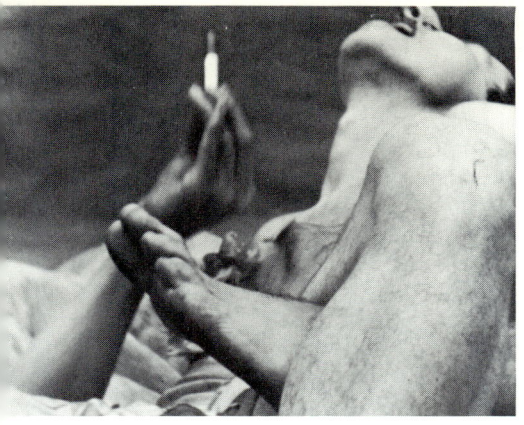

A

C

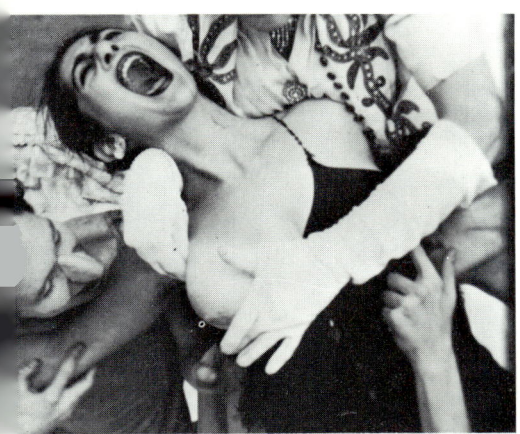

B

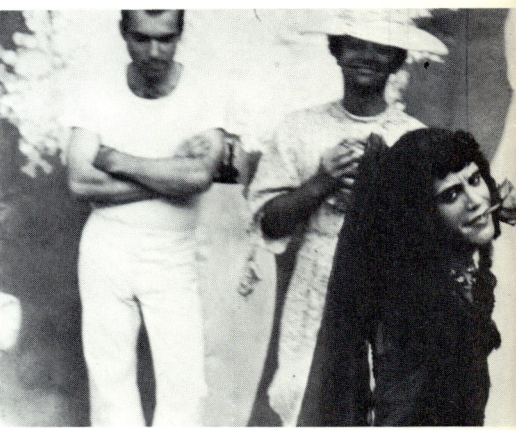

D

Stills: Film Museum of New York

See Ken Kelman: "Smith Myth," pp. 280–84.

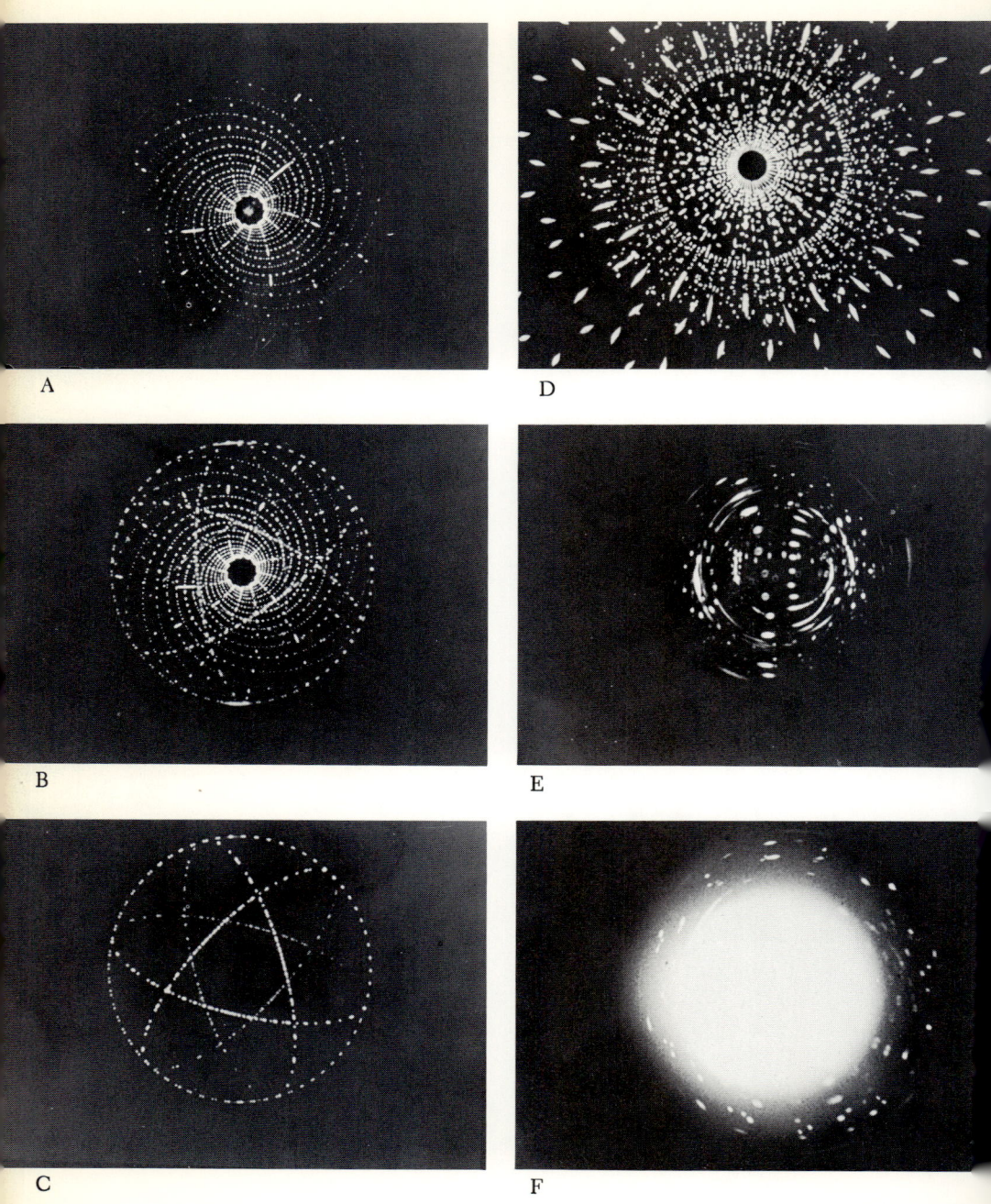

A

D

B

E

C

F

Stills: Gene Youngblood, Film Museum of New York

See Gene Youngblood: "The Cosmic Cinema of Jordan Belson," pp. 302–16.

Vampyr
Still: Bragin Communications

Day of Wrath
Still: Contemporary Films/McGraw-Hill

Gertrud
Still: Contemporary Films/McGraw-Hill

Ordet
Still: Museum of Modern Art Stills Archive

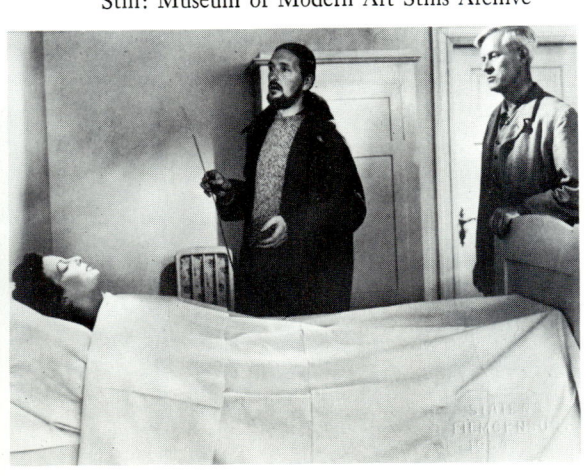

See Carl Th. Dreyer: "Metaphysic of *Ordet*," pp. 27 and Ken Kelman: "Dreyer," pp. 141–59.

PETER KUBELKA'S *SCHWECHATER*

A

D

B

E

C

F

Stills: Film Museum of New York

See Jonas Mekas: "Interview with Peter Kubelka," pp. 285–99.

Man with a Movie Camera
Stills: Standish Lawder

Photo: Film Museum of New York

See "The Writings of Dziga Vertov," pp. 353–75.

Michael Snow: *Wavelength*

Michael Snow: ←——→

Andy Warhol: *Eat*

Ken Jacobs: *Tom, Tom, the Piper's Son*

Stills: Film Museum of New York

See P. Adams Sitney: "Structural Film," pp. 326–48.

SIX VARIATIONS FROM HOLLIS FRAMPTON'S *ARTIFICIAL LIGHT*

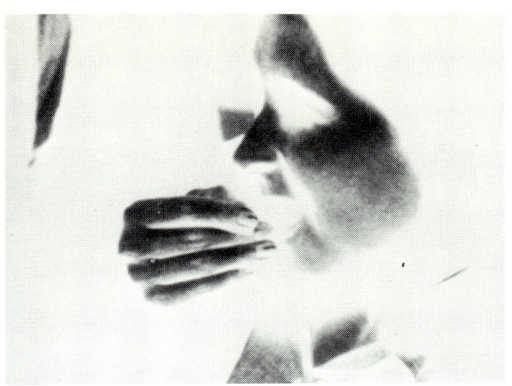

Var. #2

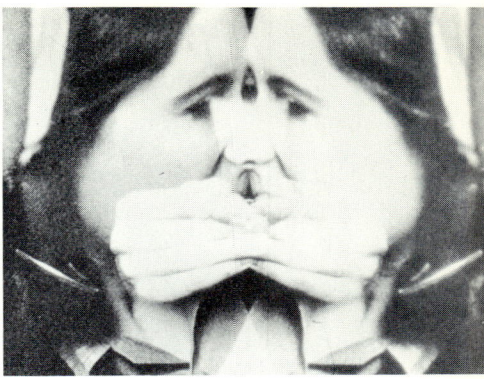

Var. #12

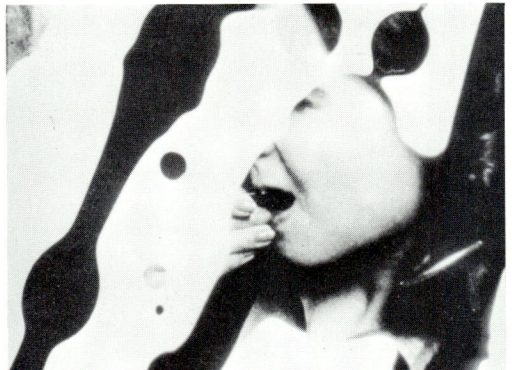

Var. #5

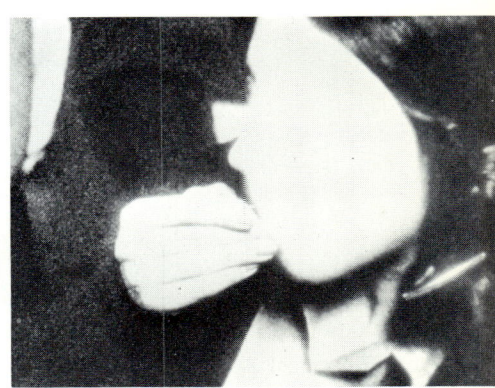

Var. #13

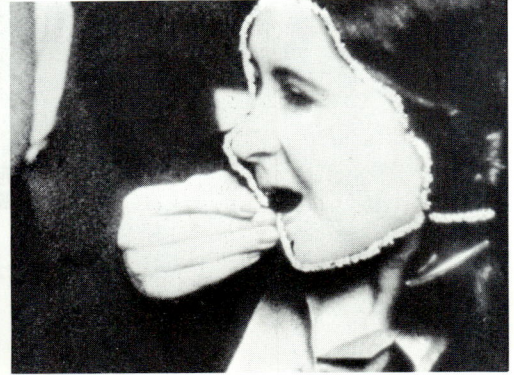

Var. #10

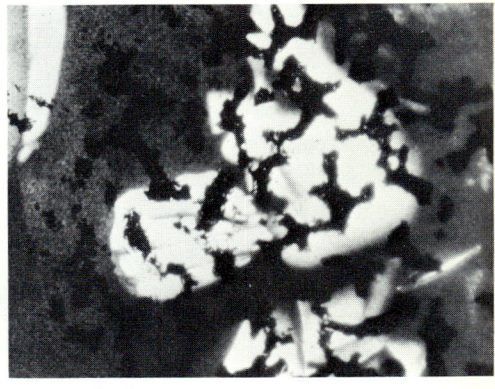

Var. #15

Stills: Hollis Frampton, Film Museum of New York

See P. Adams Sitney: "Structural Film," pp. 346–48.

 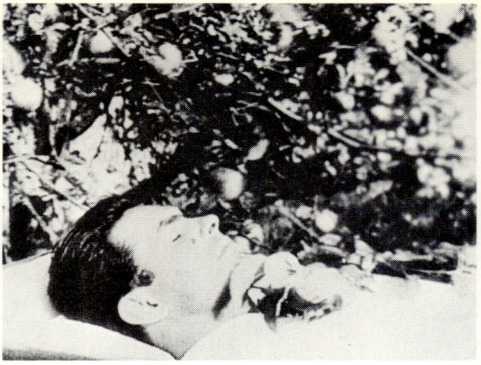

A & B: Earth communes with the old; earth claims the young.

C & D: Moonlight as the mystery of love; moonlight as the madness of desire.

E & F: Bewitched by the moon; primitive powers in landscape.

(Captions by Ken Kelman)

A, B, & C: *Earth*. Museum of Modern Art Still Collection and Brandon Films.

D, E, & F: *Sunrise*. Museum of Modern Art Still Collection.

See Ken Kelman: "Classic Plastics (and Total Tectonics)," pp. 387–92.

destroyed man. A split second later, I had an all-encompassing circular sense that seemed to surround me as if I were inside a globe. That globe rang again with words heard from the inside out as if of my own thinking; yet alien to it: "They think we have *nothing* to do with what he's doing."

Who is the "we"?

The "we" had referred to the voice that was speaking and the three entities that had spoken before. It was clear to my mind in an instant. I was overjoyed. And I began reaching to make that splice. Instantly, there was a large jelly sensation in the air as if this all-encompassing force had stopped and turned to a mass of jelly. The nearest approximation I could give, but it would be like a cartoon of the feeling, was like a Buddha, like a giant baby Buddha sensation, all jellied and fat and enormous. It was a chaotic force to me, oriental or foreign, as if dribbling out the phrase "He" (referring to the last voice speaking) "thinks we" (referring to all voices that had spoken) "have *something* to do with what he" (meaning me) "was doing." Again I was cast into a intensive and horrible gloom such as I had never had before. This was immediately superceded by yet another voice sensation from the mind inside out that was all-encompassing and came with a sense of finality. And it said "He" (referring to the last voice speaking) "thinks we" (meaning all the voices having spoken) "have *nothing* to do with what he" (meaning me) "is doing." It was as if there were some power that was helping me from the inside out, which freed me to go on to work beautifully the rest of that night, and the film was finished two days later.

How do you explain the voices?

I have no explanation of the voices other than as I've given to you.

Do you believe this was a vision?

I don't know. The only visual senses I have of what might have spoken are crude cartoons. The first was Greeklike; it suggested a sense of Greek religion. But that would be a cartoon of what I sensed. It was like three Greek women or three Greek men, I don't know which. Probably men, or hermaphrodites. The second voice was like a circle. The third voice was like a Buddha or like a giant, bubbling, jellied baby. The fourth voice was so encompassing that I have no picture for it at all.

Do you often have voices?

Yes, often. But never before anything that incredible. That was so incredible but real that it immediately gave me the free power to go on and finish that film. When I was involved in editing the decay process, Jane looked at the footage and immediately reacted. She began cleaning the sink and cleaning, cleaning, cleaning all over the house. She said, rather mysteriously, "I can't talk about it," and, "I'm too busy." I said "What's the matter?" and she said, "Well, I feel dirty." Suddenly, I had a sense she'd been engaged by that section of the film, and that was the first time I realized that I wanted an enclosed form, which would not engage people. That decay section should be edited so finely and structured so beautifully that one would not have to get rid of the dirt.

Then do you believe all good art is unengaging?

Yes, I do. From that moment on, I was completely convinced. Jane was the source of inspiration even there.

Your early films try to engage though?

Yes, surely, but I honor that in my early films which is the least engaging now. That's the only thing I've been able to look at over and over again for years and still learn from. Everything in my early works that was of engagement bores me now. I'm no longer there; I'm not concerned with previous engagements. These days, my struggle is to make each work complete unto itself. I began having ways to create an unengaging form by watching her re-action, re action. Then, for the first time, my central concern in working was the necessity arising from both Jane and me, not just from myself. It was like being able to pitch the center of a working process between the two of us. In some way, this working process that began developing between Jane and me was dependent on the necessity out of which our drives emerge and is cast out not between us but in some space that is the shape of both of us, and yet doesn't . . . enclose us. Terms like *In Between* and *Interim* and all those "ins" or all those "outs" like *re-flections*, and re this and re that, re placement, ceased to exist; and we began living in direct relationship to a larger concern than each other or these dichotomies. We inhabit a world of which the Orient gives us some sense by way of Zen, where good and bad, yes and no, cease to exist as opposites and become one thing. The perfect symbol for this is the yin and yang enclosed within the one circle. The form springs directly from the separation line between the two, which contains all the sensuality of that meeting. I don't know how to put it, but when a man and woman have this, and they give birth to a child, that child is not a thing enclosed between them. They don't fight over him or smother him. In that sense, the work of art arising from such a process out of the total needs Jane and I share is like a child arising out of that kind of love and is then free of each of us.

May we get back to the film's progression now? We're getting off on a series of abstractions.

No, I think we're getting off concretely when we talk about what arises from life's necessities rather than aesthetics. Talking about total forms without containing a sense of how they arise out of immediate life-experiences is terribly abstract.

Can you get on with The Dead *now?*

By the time I began editing *The Dead,* I had shot most of the material for *Dog Star Man.* Jane and I went out onto the mountain where she shot all the images of me and, without being directed, cast them easily and quickly into the forms with which I was concerned; that is, our shared necessity was so close we wouldn't even have to exchange directions. She would be out there, and I might gesture wildly, and she would get it that quickly and photograph some image or myself in relationship to an image structure in just the way I wanted.

You said you had shot all of Dog Star Man. *Do you mean all of* Part 1 *and* Prelude?

No. I mean all of the material for *Dog Star Man.*

That was going into all four parts?

Yes, I thought I had all the material at that time; now I realize I needed more. At the time, I was convinced I had all I needed for what I thought would be roughly a four-and-one-half hour work. Now I'm confused on that subject. I'm not even sure I'll be able to finish that film. First of all, whenever I had to be photographed from any distance Jane would have to do it. Then, at times, she went out with the camera to get things that I had some sense she could photograph better than I and with more total clarity. Once, when I was ill and couldn't get out to shoot as the sun was setting and the sky was meaning what I sensed was needed at a certain moment in the film, Jane rushed out to get it, bringing back even more than what I had hoped for. So I tended more and more to give her any chance to add her view to mine for a more total view.

Certain crises were presented to me, in the shooting of *Dog Star Man,* of which I was not consciously aware. I didn't really stop to think why I, attempting to show a man's life work in terms of one simple action encompassed in a day, should choose that that man be a woodsman. I didn't even know why I had let my hair and beard grow that long. I had done it to give it a try and suddenly it became crucial to the film.

How long were they?

My hair was down below my shoulders, and my beard was half-way down my chest. It was a hard thing to live with. I mean to walk down the streets of Boulder, Colorado, carrying that kind of an image, but I was aware that somehow I needed it. I cast myself as a woodsman with an ax and started climbing the hill. The dog was always following me and getting in the way of the photography. I began to accept this and realized the need for the woodsman to have a dog. Increasingly, I began to be amazed at the amount of footage we were shooting at each and every like sight impingement. I saw the whole forest in relation to the history of architecture, particularly religious architecture, at least in the Western world. Sensing structure, architecture, history of the world as emerging, I began seeing prismatic happenings through snow falling, etc., and in relation to stained glass windows, for one example. This was not when I started photographing, but often through unexpected things that came through Jane's photography.

Without realizing why, I dragged a white tree up two thirds of a mountain, replanted it at a certain point, then struggled with it, and pushed it over. As if battling with myself, some other man, or a monster, I struggled with that white tree, threw it over, then chopped it up. When I did that and sat down to think about it later, I began realizing why I was having asthma attacks again. The greatest clarity about why I was having attacks at this time came to me from reading a book on idiotoxic disorders by Dr. Freeman. He nailed down the foremost dream images that affect idiotoxically disordered people, that is to say, people with migraine, asthma, epilepsy, etc. That dream contains the elements of a man fighting with himself, with some beast, a dog, a serpent, a cat, or with his twin brother, or with another man. He fights naked in front of a dead white tree (usually sitting far in the background) while a woman, three women, or nine women, watch this battle. This is a standard symbol you can find stamped on Cretan coins, such as the one on the frontispiece of Robert Graves's *The Greek Myths*.

Is the white tree also on the Cretan coin?

The tree is there also. It's a living tree, and it's not white. A white tree is most immediately a dead tree. There are other kinds of white trees (there can be a silver tree), but if it's a white tree, then, in the mind, it's a dead tree. The question that any white tree raises is, "Does it have the potentiality for new life?" that is, "Is it white because it's lifeless, or is it white because it's that kind of tree?" I began having daily asthma attacks and was terribly concerned with whether I was going to die. (By this time, we had the second child, another girl. All the material of the filming of her birth was to be going into *Dog Star Man*.) I was again faced with death as a concept; not watching death as physical decay, or dealing with the pain of the death of a loved one, but with the concept of death as something that man casts into the future by asking, "What is death like?" And the limitation of finding the images for a concept of death only in life itself is a terrible torture, that is, Wittgenstein's *Tractatus Logico-Philosophicus*, 6.4311: "Death is not an event of life. Death is not lived through. If by eternity is understood not endless temporal duration but timelessness, then he lives eternally who lives in the present. Our life is endless in the way that our visual field is without limit." In Freeman's book, there is a painting by a woman patient of what she saw in a dream while having asthma attacks. The white tree is there, the woman, the man fighting with a beast. That fight may represent Saint George slaying the dragon; it is any man coping with his beast nature or, as he may find that beast in his twin brother, his Doppelganger, or his opposite, as Dionysis's Hercules. I had to cope with that material just as Jane had to cope with each asthma attack and my postulating the death wish again in the center of our marriage, which could destroy our future.

Right at that moment, I put *Dog Star Man* in cans, stuffed it away, and began editing *The Dead*. As I edited *The Dead*, I worked my way out of the crisis in which I was dying.

Did the old material from 1958 come to you in a flash?

I always had it there waiting for the time when the necessity would make it that vital that I could begin to work with it.

In that film why did you use material shot only in Paris?

I used material shot only in Paris because that was a total world of something that, if I'd leave it long enough until it impinged on me directly in life, would have a total form of its own.

Did your death wish emerge from that political mix up at the Brussels Experimental Film Exposition in which you didn't receive the money you hoped to get?

I would say that would be material for it, not cause of it. Money is always for us one way in which we comprehend the form of what we want. It's very important to us. I mean, as in a fairy tale, you always have to get the treasure to get the princess and live happily ever after. I mean the hero has to kill the beast to get the treasure to get the princess to go off to the castle in the glass mountain and live (question mark) happily ever after. That's the form; and money is always part of the equation. I take that as an equation that is so strong in our consciousness that wherever money arises as a problem, as it always does in an artist's life, it needs to be wrenched awry by an aesthetic $E = mc^2$.

You edited The Dead *then?*

Yes. *The Dead* was the work most clearly removed from my direct relationship to Jane. She had to keep out of it. She always insisted on keeping out of asthma attacks, that is, she would not become my mother. She kept absolutely clear, and sometimes it was very painful. But she had the integrity, which I little understood at the time, and particularly in the middle of an asthma attack, to keep absolutely out of my express death wishes and even desperately try not to recognize them. *The Dead* was shot when I was away from Jane for a month and a half; and it was edited when she was avoiding me most of the daytime to keep out of the whole asthma destructive force that was operative through me. I had to find, realize re *The Dead* that somehow all images of death or all concepts of it are structured here in life. Then I knew the answer as to why I'd shot in the same day, and out of the same needs, material in the graveyard of Père Lachaise and on the Seine. And even then, I knew somehow that they were going to go together. But how together? That became clear at the time of editing.

And shots of Kenneth Anger in a café?

I had no idea at the time of shooting that Kenneth Anger, as an image, would be used in *The Dead*. I was running out the end of a reel, which I wanted to get out of the camera so I could put in the color film for doing the shots of the Seine. So I said, "Well, I have no picture of you, still or otherwise." We were sitting in a *café*; so I took the image of Kenneth. It was only when I relooked at that footage that I realized that *that* one level of what I meant by *The Dead* was how I saw Kenneth and what he was encased in. I saw him as a concept. Seeing him as one of the dead, I had great concern and care and love for him at that moment. He was years without working, trapped by concepts of the nineteenth century with no way to break out, almost a destroyed man, and yet still living . . . that was the important thing. All the rest of the people in *The Dead are* dead. They're the walking dead; but he was a living dead. So he became my double in a sense—my "stand-in," you might say. He was the image that was most immediately available for me to cast out there as statement: "Do you want this? . . . Do you want to be trapped by all those symbols? . . . Do you want to be trapped six ways sideways by concepts that are ahead of where you actually are?" And then my answer was: "No!" Then I could structure *The Dead* by way of the concept of the future as that through which we can't live. When we're living through it, it's different from the concept of it. It's comparable to how you can't live through death. So the question becomes one of all that is pitched out of life; how the walking dead come to be that; and how what is sculpted *in* stone becomes concept of what is sculpted *out of* stone; and how the living people do relate to that, and how even trees, shaped that way and so ordered and structured, become living dead and like the walking dead, who are people so dead on their feet that you can't even use the word "living" in relationship to them . . . well, not Kenneth. He was shining with all that beauty and concern with life; and yet he was trapped six ways sideways by forms he had pitched ahead of himself—all that he wanted to do (such as film *Maldoror*) and could not find the means or the money to do. This was intensely painful to me. I would have given anything to have found a way for him to do what he wanted, not only to see *Maldoror* done by Kenneth Anger, or maybe not even foremost for that reason, but to let Kenneth have a way to accomplish it so that he could have gotten through it and could have gone on. He was ultimately defeated. There's new hope for Kenneth now, because he did escape from that trap that *Maldoror* posed for him, and he *is* back in the United States and has a new film in progress. Europe, weighted down so much with that past, was *The Dead*. I was always Tourist there; I couldn't live in it. The graveyard could stand for all my view of Europe, for all the concerns with past art, for all involvement with symbol. *The Dead* became my first work in which things that might very easily be taken as symbols were so photographed as to destroy all their symbolic potential. The action of making *The Dead* kept me alive.

How did you go about editing Prelude; *and what do you mean by the Freudian dream aspect of it?*

Right from the start I had some sense, and I don't quite know where it came from, that the work would be in four parts with a prelude. Once Jane and I had gone through the whole gathering process to get that total world and had survived the sense of death that was postured by collecting the material, the next step was to get a sense of the form of the film. At first, I could only think of that large a work in symbolic terms. I thought, for instance, that the man climbs the mountain out of winter and night into the dawn, up through spring and early morning to midsummer and high noon, to where he chops down the tree . . . then I don't know what: But I know there's a Fall—and the fall back to somewhere, midwinter—my idea of what that fall will be still remains nebulous. I thought of *Dog Star Man* as seasonally structured that way; but also, while it encompasses a year and the history of man in terms of the image material (for example, trees become architecture for a whole history of religious monuments, or violence becomes the development of war), I thought it should be contained within a single day. Then I thought about what any day's form-structure touches off. One thing I knew for sure (from my own dreaming) was that what one dreams just before waking structures the following day. That dream material is gathered from the previous day and, therefore, is a gathering of all previous days, *ergo* contains the structure of all history, of all Man. I hadn't been involved directly with Freudian concepts, or even psychology, since I'd departed from drama as major structurer of my work; but suddenly drama, and psychodrama, therefore, became pertinent to me in a new way. The first step in recognition of this was that I began rereading Freud intensively to learn those early structures of dream experience. I had the sense that I could make a prelude before creating any of the rest of the work. Generally in the history of art, preludes are composed of parts and bits from the work to follow. Now I wanted to compose the prelude first, rather than last (as is usual), so that the rest of the work would spring out of the prelude. I had only a vague concept of the four parts that would follow. So I realized that whatever happened within this prelude would determine what was to come; and, in that sense, I wanted it to be as real from the very beginning as life happening. I wanted *Prelude* to be a created dream for the work that follows rather than Surrealism, which takes its inspiration from dream; I stayed close to practical usage of dream material, in terms of learning and studying, for a while before editing. At this time, I left strict myth considerations out of my study process as much as possible.

But there is much myth in it, isn't there?

Naturally, there's much myth in it. But that was not the primary concern at this time. Myth became important later in terms of sensing the over-all structure. Once, I had wanted very much to make a film, called *Freudfilm*, that would illustrate the process of dream development and would show how a dream evolves out of the parts we don't remember into those we do. In *Prelude*, I wanted to make a film that would swing on those transformations of unacceptable to acceptable images. And, finally, I wanted that to be the determining editing factor on the cutting table, and it did become that. I had to start with material that was incomprehensible and work my way backwards. For a long time of editing I was crossbreeding surrealistic concerns with, say, John Cage's sense of form through various chance operations. And then I would go over and over that material and restructure it; and finally ended up with one strip of film the length of *Prelude* as you find it now.

The hand-painting was always in direct relationship to the particular kind of "closed-eye vision" that comes only in dreams. The commonest type of "closed-eye vision" is what we get when we close our eyes in daylight and watch the moving of shapes and forms through the red pattern of the eyelid. Since *Prelude* was based on dream vision, as I remembered it, it had to include "closed-eye vision." Painting was the closest approximation to it; so I painted, throwing down patterns and controlling them in various ways. Shapes emerge out of that kind of eye-nerve action and reaction. The next step, once I had one whole strip of film, was to start with the second, the superimposition strip. One can have three, four or more strips the full length of the film and super-impose one image on another wherever one wants. I took the strip that was largely determined by chance and surrealistic operations and began editing a second strip to it. From this point on, every-thing that I laid down was hyperconscious. I would go back and change shots to alter the form in strip number one as the need would arise in the developing form of strip number two. Strip two always developed out of what was on strip one to structure it and to transform it into something that would be comparable to what could be remembered when one awoke in the morning. On one hand, there was that incomprehensible mass of material arising out of surrealistic and chance-operation concerns, which I called the "chaos" roll; on the other hand, there was the "structured" roll, which represented the dream transformed and made accessible for conscious memory in the morning. By the time I got through, there were no chance operations left in the film.

How was Jane effective in this?

Jane had little or nothing to do with the development of the "chaos" roll. That was edited very quickly; I was pulling down shots and splicing them in faster than I could possibly think about it. Jane was always looking at them. At times, I would alter the form by feeling some emanation from her as she'd stand in the room. I would feel: This is not right; this is not working. We wouldn't work faster than feeling, you know. Other times, she'd sit down and we'd talk together for a long time; and then I would go back and rip up whole sections of the film. Other times, we'd be immediately clear about the quality of a series of splices. Still other times, after I'd finished making a section, we'd look at them together, then go sit down, talk, have coffee, rehearse a Gertrude Stein play, or play with the children, or whatever, and see what kind of clarity emerged.

How many children were there then?

By this time, there were two. Crystal was born in the middle of the shooting of the *Dog Star Man* material.

Did you shoot Prelude *material separately?*

No. I pulled material, willy-nilly, as it seemed to me most chaotic. Two things determined what I pulled out of that mass of material to go into *Prelude*. One was that material be incomprehensible to me. That would be comparable to Buñuel's statement about *Andalusian Dog*, in which he said that he and Dali could not understand why in the world they were shooting those things that they did shoot. I was playing that surrealist game. The other reason for pulling specific material was that the symbols be directly relevant to the Cretan coin as an image of the creation mythology. That image, traditionally, comes to us through Adam and Eve; you know, the man, the tree, the snake, all distorted and changed because of the Hebraic tendency to build up such a damned patriarchy. If you check it back through Graves's *The White Goddess*, and read the original version rather than the reader's digest King James version, you get a much clearer image. Most cultures have a similar creation myth, which contains these elements in one form or another. These elements are related to the dream of those suffering from idiotoxic disorders. Collecting those symbols was one problem; getting them all clear and in a pattern in that work was another. Those were the two factors that determined what I pulled out and began to work with.

The next film was Thigh Line Lyre Triangular, *if I'm not mistaken?*

That was the next film photographed, but *Films by Stan Brakhage* was the next completed. As soon as *Prelude* was finished, Neowyn was born and I photographed the material for *Thigh Line Lyre Triangular*.

How was Thigh Line Lyre Triangular *different, when it was finally edited, from* Window Water Baby Moving, *the earlier birth film?*

The main difference is the painting on film in *Thigh Line Lyre Triangular*. Only at a crisis, do I see both the scene as I've been trained to see it (that is, with Renaissance perspective, three-dimensional logic—colors as we've been trained to call a color a color, and so forth) and patterns that move straight out from the inside of the mind through the optic nerves. In other words, an intensive crisis I can see from the inside out and the outside in.

You mean double exposure?

I see patterns moving that are the same patterns I see when I close my eyes, and I can also see the same kind of scene I see when my eyes are open.

You mean you see color spots before your eyes?

Right—spots before my eyes, so to speak . . . and it's a very intensive, disturbing, but joyful experience. I've seen that every time a child was born. Notice I use the word "crisis." I don't mean crisis as a bad thing. At an extremely intensive moment, I can see from the inside out and the outside in. Now none of that was in *Window Water Baby Moving*; and I wanted a childbirth film that expressed all my seeing at such a time.

And you added shots of animals, too?

That was because, at moments like that, I get flashes of what I call "brain movies." I'm taking Michael McClure's term there; he said, "When you get a solid structure image that you know is not out there, but is being recalled so intensively that you literally see it in a flash, that's a 'brain movie.'" Most people only get them with their eyes closed. They close their eyes, and they see, in a flash, something from their childhood, or some person remembered, or something; and that should also be in the film experience. What I was seeing at the birth of Neowyn most clearly, in terms of this "brain movie" recall process, were symbolic structures of an animal nature. This struck me as odd because I was working six ways sideways, day and night, to avoid symbolism. It was as if something had gotten backed up in my mind, so that it could release symbolic terms at me as soon as it had a crisis. Curiously enough, those animal symbols were easily represented by taking material only out of *Anticipation of the Night*.

Why are you never seen as father in this film?

That's because I centered the occasion in my own eyes.

Then from that you went on to Films by Stan Brakhage. *How was* Jane *effective in this?*

Films by Stan Brakhage emerged because certain people concern me with engagements from time to time. For instance, I've been asked for years, "Why don't you make a home movie of your children?" Actually, I've taken a lot of pictures of the children, of Jane and our life, and of places we've moved to, you know: Home movies, in a very simple sense . . . like recording something. I had always done this; but I had never edited any of the material. People kept asking, "Why don't you make a film out of this material?" It seemed to me like a challenge; but I was also concerned that I not make something of engagement, and that the source material or records be transformed into a work of art, if possible. I had a camera with which I could make multiple superimpositions spontaneously. It had been lent to me for a week. I was also given a couple of rolls of color film which had been through an intensive fire. The chance that the film would not record any image at all left me free to experiment and to try to create the sense of the daily world in which we live, and what it meant to me. I wanted to record our home, and, yet, deal with it as being that area from which the films by Stan Brakhage arise, and to try to make one arise at the same time.

And Jane was photographing all the shots of you?

Yes, we worked together on it.

There are intercourse scenes in that film. How were they photographed?

I was free to try to be as tricky as I could possibly be because I actually didn't have any hope that the images were going to come out at all; so I set the camera up and backwound it. While I was making this film, I thought I was rehearsing for making a film later with fresh filmstock. Much to my surprise, delight, and joy, the fire had cast that film into an intensely blue field. It was not like a filtered blue because pure colors could still come through the center of it. It was a weird thing what that fire had done. Now I wish I knew at what temperature that film had been cooked.

Getting back to your method of photography.

I set the camera up, flipped the switch, and threw myself where Jane was, in front of the lens, and eventually the camera ran down. Then I backwound and added superimpositions of the children. I was using a Cine Special; and I could go back to the precise place I wanted. I didn't want a film that would require much editing. I wanted it to be on an immediate level, like a sketch. And somehow the film turned out to be madly and wonderfully and incredibly much more than I had ever expected. I joke about it. I call it an "avant-garde home movie" because I don't think it's a major work like *Prelude* or like any of the *Dog Star Man*, for that matter. I'm not really satisfied with what I got there, but it certainly turned out to be more than I ever expected.

And then came Dog Star Man: Part I. *Will you discuss how Jane worked with you on this?*

In the editing of that film, we worked together to the greatest extent we ever have. From the moment I began work on it, I kept saying, "I think it's going to be something like a Noh drama in slow motion." I didn't know why I said Noh drama, because I had never been concerned with it. I hadn't really studied any form of the Noh drama except what came to me by way of Ezra Pound. As I subsequently found out, that was precisely what I was concerned with: what Ezra Pound got from the Noh drama, which structured his concept of Imagism and later of Vorticism, when he added comments onto Gaudier-Brzeska's book. That was the literal structural sense that I was inspired by for the total form of *Part I*. And yet, I had to get the mind disengaged. In the first place, I had to leave room for Jane to come in to sit with me and view each stage of editing so that I might be emotionally open to everything that she said and did. I had to engage my mind in some area that would leave the rest of me free for the extension of love; and my trick for doing it was to question whether I could make the form grow stronger through chance operations than through a conscious decision—(it wasn't any more serious than that). I forced myself to adhere to a conscious decision, never allowing a piece to go in by sheer chance and never allowing a decision that was weaker than a chance operation. I wanted *Part I* to be the opposite in rhythm from *Prelude*. I wanted it to be slow, drawn out, extended to the greatest possible tension that the material could contain. And I insisted to myself that was why I made each and every splice be completely enigmatic as a conscious thing. A splice had to be made simply, because that and only that was the thing that worked visually. Sometimes, it would take a week to make ten permanent splices. I would slowly, torturously, and laboriously try this, try that, break it apart and try something else. Sometimes, I would chew up the whole previous shot by tearing off one piece of film after another that I'd spliced and have to start with the shot previous, etc. After I had a certain path or direction started by a series of splices, Jane and I would look at it together; and we would begin talking deeply about the film on many levels.

Was it work print you were looking at?

No, original. I always work with original. I can't afford a work print; so I'm used to working under those terms. Jane and I would talk for hours about ten splices that went together. It was as if we were making a path that could contain the deep concerns of both of us. I would lay down paths that would be perfectly fine for my sense of it; and all the splices would work in this deep, enigmatic way and carry through metaphysical concerns. But it would not contain her vision. Sometimes, I would get too influenced by what she'd say; and I'd lay down a path in which she would be comfortable, but which would not contain my direction. We were not making compromises, rather we were finding the one right path that would contain the total view that would be an opening for something new. That slow, laborious, and torturous process is why it took us a year and a half to finish editing *Part I*. Meanwhile, anytime the mind would start intruding, I would somehow tie it up into John's Cage. John's Cage was marvellously used in the making of this film in the sense that, at any moment, I could reach over and grab it and, as a threat, clap the possibility of chance operations over all brain dominance.

Are the "silences" in the film the Silence of John Cageism?

No, I wouldn't think they'd have any relevance at all there; because the visual "silences" meant to me that out of which something was becoming . . . you see, I really love John Cage's music even though I only used his aesthetics to tie up my brain with. I do love the occasions in his music, but more particularly in the music of Morton Feldman, of sound occurring and there then being a silence that's just long enough to sustain *that* sound before the occurrence of the next sound But the visual silences, or lapses, in *Part I* were more directed by thoughts of the emergence of images out of either black or white. And my thoughts were directed by a feeling for destroying the dichotomy of blacks and whites as extremes. My tendency was to shape the whole work in such a way that there are no distinctions between black and white.

Then let me ask one question that concerns all your work. You talked about your own dog, you've talked about your family and so on. Aren't some critics in a way justified when they say that this is, not quite narcissistic, but very limited in scope as opposed to Eisenstein who posits his personal drama in historical context in Ivan the Terrible *or in comparison to von Stroheim, or someone who works in a more objective form?*

In the first place, I hope I would not say "my *own* dog." The minute "own" comes into it, dog would become property; the same for "my own children" or anything like that. They're mine to care for now. And so to get rid of that part of it.

I would say I grew very quickly as a film artist once I got rid of drama as prime source of inspiration. I began to feel that all history, all life, all that I would have as material with which to work, would have to come from the inside of me out rather than as some form imposed from the outside in. I had the concept of everything radiating out of me, and that the more personal or ego-centric I would become, the deeper I would reach and the more I could touch those universal concerns that would involve all man. What seems to have happened since marriage is that I no longer sense ego as the greatest source for what can touch on the universal. I now feel that there is some other concrete center where love from one person to another meets; and that the more total view arises from there . . . First, I had the sense of the center radiating out. Now, I have become concerned with the rays. You follow? It's in the action of moving out that the great concerns can be struck off continually. Now the films are being struck off, not in the gesture, but in the very real action of moving out. Where I take action strongest and most immediately is in reaching through the power of all that love toward my wife, (and she toward me) and some-where where those actions meet and cross, and bring forth children and films and inspire concerns with plants and rocks and all sights seen, a new center, composed of action, is made. The best reference I can give you for the definition of soul-in-action, rather than at-center, is Charles Olson's *Proprioception*.

THE BIRTH FILM

BY JANE BRAKHAGE

No. 31, Winter, 1963–64

Being an artist's wife is strange, and when the artist uses moving pictures to express himself, it is very strange indeed. Then, when the artist says he is going to make moving pictures of the birth of the first child, we are both very excited and talk about it long into the night many nights. For there were plans we had to make and things to arrange, and he had to be in the delivery room, and the doctor and nurse had to help in many ways, and I had to be fully awake all during the childbirth, because I didn't want to miss a minute of it.

So, first of all, the right doctor must be found, and we found him quite easily and went to see him together. He was much in favor of natural childbirth. The first step had been taken, and things were going well. When my husband, Stan, came into the office and was going to ask him about the film, before he even had time to say, "How do you do?" the doctor said, "How would you like to make a film on natural childbirth?" We were thunderstruck, and we all sat in the office and were very excited and talked and talked and the doctor said he'd try to get the hospital to agree to it and everyone was enthusiastic and happy. But then, it didn't continue as it had begun, and the doctor talked to the hospital, and the hospital had conference after conference about it and, finally, talked themselves out of it.

Thus, it was that we decided to have the baby at home, and we were very glad because I never liked to go to the hospital, and we were glad because Stan would have more freedom at home than in the hospital, and we were altogether glad in every way. There was much fuss about getting equipment for the doctor and hiring a nurse, and the doctor and the nurse were glowing with excitement because this was an adventure they'd never had before.

Stan and I went to classes and learned about childbirth, and I learned all the exercises to make my body strong and right for having a child.

Then we waited.

By the afternoon of November 12, we had taken some moving pictures of the baby moving and kicking before being born, and that night there were contractions, and we were very happy and took some more film of our happy faces and some of the cat and played games and watched the clock and then the doctor came with his nurse and all his paraphernalia and said, no, this wasn't labor and to call him when I stopped knitting.

The next night, I stopped knitting, and we called him, and he was at the hospital with two other women in labor, and he told Stan to give me a drink and put me to bed. And the next night, we went bowling, and still there were contractions and then several days running around and again bowling with a score of 130 and still contractions. Till we were going mad, and we didn't believe what all the people said, we believed in the stork, and the heck with it.

Then Friday and my appointment with the doctor, and I was very gay and didn't care what happened and he said, "You'll know when it's for real," and I said "How?" and he said "You'll suddenly say, 'Oop,' and then beat your fist on the chair arm, and then you'll get up and be fidgety and walk around."

And then that night, for the first time since all this began, Stan did some work on another moving picture he was working on, and I was sitting at the kitchen table getting up the energy to do something or other, I think, the dishes, and suddenly I said, "Oop," and beat my fist on the table and then I was very happy, but, by this time, I didn't believe in it, and I got up and did the dishes and "Oop" and "Oop" very regularly and told Stan, who didn't believe and went on working. And a bloody show and still he didn't believe and "Oop" and "Oop," and I believed and started trying to figure out how to be most comfortable during the contractions "Oop" and after a couple more hours I was very adept at relaxing completely when it came, and then it wasn't "Oop" anymore but a strange sinking into a beautiful and frightening world then rising again and a moment of bliss, then normalcy. If I didn't relax completely, then I wasn't shown the strange world or get the moment of bliss, but then it was pain.

Finally, when Stan was through working, he believed pretty much, and he read Proust to me, and, at 2:00 or 3:00 A.M., he called the doctor, who was sleepy and sent the nurse who arrived around 5, and it was dawn, and we had stayed up all night.

Again and again into the strange world for hours and hours. Stan filming and the nurse checking this and that, timing contractions, boiling water, shaving me (that was the worst, most uncomfortable part of the whose experience), telling us it will be a long while yet. Stan and I go to the mailbox to get the mail between contractions. The doctor arrives, Stan films and films, and I go again and again into the strange world and again and again have a moment of bliss. The doctor leaves, Stan and I sleep for an hour or so while the nurse reads in the kitchen. Then, the doctor arrives again and says it will be yet several hours. The nurse is tired. They both drive off. Stan and I are alone for a moment. I relax while Stan fusses with lights and camera. Five minutes pass, maybe less.

Then I feel like a balloon full of water pops inside me, water shoots out of me. "Water! Water!" I shout. Stan rushes in with his camera and films while the water pours out of me. So excited we are. "Here comes some more!" "Wait a minute!" "I can't!" Clickety-clackety-buzz goes the camera. Something tremendous is happening to me. I have entered into a world of beautiful agony—agony of great beauty, joyous agony, unbearable beauty. I roar like a lion. Stan films, clickety-clackety-buzz, his hands are trembling with the camera, but clickety-clackety-buzz anyway. I roar again and pant fast like I had run a mile and roar, and Stan films, and we are so very happy because the baby is coming at last!

What? The baby is coming at last? Where's the doctor? I'm in second stage. Where's the doctor? Yes, where's the doctor? We don't know. Stan films, and I roar. Stan, call the doctor. He calls the hospital and gets the nurse who says she'll be right here. It takes ten minutes driving fast from the hospital here. Stan starts worrying. I continue roaring and panting. Stan stops filming he's so upset. He gets nervous. He tells me to relax and pant. He needs to relax; I'm doing fine. I tell him how much I love him and ask him if he's got my face when I'm roaring and this sets him off again and reassures him, and he clickety-clackety-buzzes while I roar and pant, and we are both very happy, and it is like we are doing something together each with his own task, and each task is so great and wonderful beyond telling, and then the nurse comes and sees how things are and calls and has the doctor paged and ten minutes more pass, and I ask the nurse if she could deliver the baby all right without the doctor, and she says he'll come, and I'm doing fine, and I roar and roar louder and louder and pant and pant faster and faster, and Stan talks to the nurse and films and films and, finally, the doctor comes and already there is a bit of hair born, and I go and lie on the delivery table and then the doctor says I can push, which is what I've been wanting to do all along but I've been panting so as to wait for the doctor and everything to be ready because, when you pant, it comes slower so anyway I'm pushing and Stan's filming and the doctor is saying "Maneroo!" because when I push then things happen fast, and the nurse says over and over that I'm doing very well, and I push and pant and roar and always clickety-clackety-buzz and more and more and more and then the doctor says don't push anymore just pant and so I pant so fast I don't hardly get any air, and this one is very different; it's joyous relief, sort of like finally reaching the gates of heaven after an impossibly hard climb, and I hear the doctor very excited saying "The head is born—anterior shoulder —posterior shoulder—" and then there is the baby held by her heels, and she's crying, and I'm saying, "Baby, baby," over and over, and Stan is laughing and covered with sweat, and the placenta is born, and the doctor and nurse do this and that to the baby, while I take some pictures of Stan because he is so beautiful, and then they all have a drink, but I am quite drunk, and I eat a sandwich, and the baby is in the cradle and asleep, and then we were left alone and happiness everywhere.

RESPOND DANCE

BY STAN BRAKHAGE

No. 30, Fall, 1963

["Respond Dance" is the final chapter of *Metaphors on Vision*. The text of a film, *Blue Moses*, and an allusion to two drawings by Brakhage's children, which were printed in the original, have been omitted here.]

This is a letter to anyone from everything in my correspondences, which found occasion for coming into a state (not meant) of being other than my particular response (beyond ability) and which so fashioned itself as to move me (to measure) from the act of writing c/o (accompaniment) to joining in The Dance (as singing) its saelf: songs herein gathered (together) out of my (for Thee) pleasure (of it).

To James Tenney, June 10, 1963

I just *must* diverge here to encompass some thoughts about the whole breakdown of drama in the western world: Forst, the total community danced. Then the best dancers led the dance; and as they became more and more special, specialists of the dance, these leaders separated themselves increasingly from the rest of their fellows eschewing followers (power over fellow humans) and preferring to serve The Dance (which does begin to have Caps. here). Now, as there are always those who choose to rule rather than serve, my guess is that The Original Fallen Angel was he who tried to lead, thru organization, those who were individually serving The Dance. His dance, natch, suffered; and he was naturally thrown back upon followers. But as he was not a follower, he found himself in limbo. He, and others like him, formed The Secondary Dance, that which stood as a bridge, so called, between those individually possessed of The Dance and the rest of the community, that which eventually became The Chorus and, as forms broke down further and extended further into the complexities of the whole community, any Commentator who presumes either in Chorus or individually, to reflect the views of the community watching The Dance while remaining, actually, specialist—that is: At Best being he who speaks because of insight (proximity to The Dance) for the subtlest *possible* views of the followers (who do, by this time, become audience) and At Worst being dictator, because of power, hatching propaganda for his own purposes. The creation of The Chorus must indeed be viewed as some early democratic procedure to thwart ritual dictators, just as I think the very tolerance of The Secondary Dance was out of an attempt to prevent the development of the primitive "star" system—that is, it did provide a dance for the egocentered and left those who served The Dance free, thereby, to be in touch with the actual stars, heavens, etc. But when the lines of The Chorus began to be written, a new danger presented itself, one that has indeed by this time destroyed all dramatic ritual in the western world. At first only Poets were involved: and what was chanted by The Chorus was what had been inspired in The Poet as surely as the dances of the Prime Dancers. Yet in time, of course, The Fallen Angel writer did dictate not only to The Chorus but to those of The Drama who were originally intended to perform only under the inspiration of, first, The Gods, and later, the god-men, heroes, etcetera whose parts they were being, fulfilling, finally acting. Acting does absolutely need direction (as a lifetime of attempting to create with actors has shown me ((only exception being my collaboration with Bob Benson in *Blue Moses*))) and Directors are *ipso facto* Dictators, i.e.: Fallen Angels, FOR SURE. And all powermad infiltrations into The Rite, in the name of every sound tangent to that word from The Right (getting it right) to Righteousness (Morality) have destroyed it completely. And I think the conversation which Charles Olson and I had on the subject of the steps of the destruction of Western theater is completely clear in this context: Step No. 1: the removal of the masks—Step No. 2: the addition of women, actresses, onto the stage—Step No. 3: the creation of the star system . . . that is, getting everything else off the stage except The Chorus, leader of, or egocentered individual representatives of, etc. And when the star is also able to write his own script effectively—we have Adolf Hitler and/or, to extent of effectiveness, any politician (and I do find a bit of encouragement when I find a politician who hires writers—that is, his position is, thereby, made a little more clear). These thoughts also lead me to the realization that in the non-theatrical arts of the western world, those which have naturally remained individualistic in the moment of creation, and to the extent they have remained free of the necessity of presentation, have been increasingly threatened by a new kind of Choral Infiltration—that is, first of all, the Art Historian (like that guy Vasari with HIS Renaissance) and then The Art Commentator (trying the guise of flattery for centuries all over the place) and finally (the very word itself betraying the essentially destructive nature of the endeavor now that any kind of "take-over" seems impossible) The Critic . . . and aren't representatives of this form almost always, clearly, Fallen Angels—that is, those who have fallen away from the creative process because of some need to rule rather than serve? And I think the outrage that most critics express against the individually created films is due to the fact that an art form is, right there, freeing itself from a process that did, due to the dominance of theatrical forms, seem to be completely possessing it—How Wonderful . . . How Absolutely Magnificent, when I stop to think about it: I mean that so young a medium, which was so completely possessed by Fallen Angels collaborating *all over the place,* and as usual in The Name, and for the Benefit Of, The Community at large, IS, through individualistic effort directed toward the service of The Film, and ergo in the service of all the unknown, the fates, the gods, real stars, and real everything that can be sighted, IS FREEING ITSELF to create. It should be added here that the only exceptions to the above Critic Rule are, at least among film critics, those critics (such as Jonas Mekas and P. Adams Sitney) who are also making films—otherwise I would have to refer to individuals who were film-makers first and then also did pieces of criticism, so-called . . . I can think of no other exceptions to the above rule. But I can think of a danger, which this last statement might tend to suggest as at least worth looking into (individually, I mean): that it might be the fallen parts within each of us, individually, that touch off criticism, statements, aesthetics, letters (such as this one), et ceteras . . .

Now Sidney Peterson recently made a statement to me (of which Jane just reminded me) that: "There are only two kinds of sound tracks: mood-music and lip-sync." Now I think it very relevant that he designated the other-than-atmospheric (or Choral)-sound track with the specific term: "lip-sync." Jane does think of it most clearly in relation to the image of a rock: "You either have some comment upon the rock or you have The Song of The Rock, the rock's lip-sync, so to speak." So it does become clear to me that I have been Fallen Angel with sound, excepting *Blue Moses*, and that, while I have silenced this dictatorial part of me out of the working process, it is still rooted in all my living processes: That is, that I do not often serve sound. Well, it can become a personal quest shun, generalized as: "How much can any man do?" It has taken me ten years of reading poetry and knowing many poets, without trying to write it or having pretensions toward being a poet, to begin to learn what service to language really is, or at least something of what it can be. All the same, the language served in *Blue Moses* is the "Language of the Barker," as Michael McClure put it, and is a good service, as Michael heard it, to the extent that it honestly serves that given language form without pretension. That is, much as I hate to admit it, there is a given limit, qualified by time and The Times, to what this man can do; BUT I do envision a way thru to unlimited human possibilities . . . something like being of service to The Dance, which includes all The World starting with whatever of The World arises naturally, of necessity, in The Dance, leading most immediately to dancing with, in relationship to, whatever other dancers (whatever their medium) one's individualistic dance is naturally, of necessity (AHA—strike "with" above, and all dependency it implies) RELATED TO. And the relationship of both Jane and I in the service of The Film does become most clear here . . . as clearly of necessity as the first, natural love-dance . . . and as clearly destructive, wherever "use of" enters in, as the end-product of the *exclusive* sex-dance, death-dance, stance, etc.

To Gregory Markopoulos, June 8, 1963

After thinking awhile about comments I sent you in my last letter, Jane did finally out with: "But a song, a tune, can and does impose itself on me without being consciously recalled—in fact, does often run on and on in my head, uncommissioned, to the extent of interfering with all other thought." And, of course, I immediately realized that was true for myself also; but then, as I almost immediately pointed out: "It is not the sound of the tune forcing its way into memory-ear but the intervals of the melody . . . indeed, one would have to, and often does to be rid of it, consciously commission instruments to play that tune, voices to sing that song, in the head—or, that failing, whistle it out to exhaust the impulse." This soon led me to the conclusion, with tentative agreement from Jane, that it is the mathematical nature of music that enables the subconscious to impose a melody upon our consciousness in a way similar to superimposition remembrances; and there in my path lay the further, and specifically relevant, consideration that any musical treatment of sounds that concerned itself with intervals (time and pitch) only, and to the expense or even exclusion (where possible) of other aspects of music (such as timbre or, on a larger formal scale, theme and variations, etc.) would naturally evolve a process analogous to visual processes. This reminded me that, when I had recently visited Bell Laboratories in New Jersey (in company of James Tenney, who is currently working in the computing dept. there—creating and composing with sound generated by means of a Digital Computer) and while viewing the purest color I could ever hope to see (in the Maser Dept.) created by, or rather being, light emitted with a uniform wavelength, one of the scientists interfered with, stuck his hand into, the beam and spoke of the resultant, distorted pattern as analogous to the overtones of an impure sound. Well, we do hear much closer to pure, pitched sounds in listening to music than we have ever (except in Maser Depts.) seen pure, orderly light. This thought led me to the revelation that it is primarily *shape* that imposes itself on the conscious mind, uncalled for, and that *colors* are almost invariably commissioned, filled-in after by conscious recall or imaginative whim. This last thought seems to be checking itself out as correct in all my experiences these days. THEREFORE, it is the relationship between space-shape and rhythm-pitch which gets closest to the heart of the matter (that is the blood-pumping to the meat-bulk of the creature) of providing a form for audio-visual experience that is something other than a cheating of sense-ability-and-itivity (and, for me, form must ((whether acknowledged—classic—or not—romantic—etc.)) find its prime source of inspiration in the physiology and psychology of the creator.) And I do take very seriously Charles Olson's warning in "Theory of Society:"

(we already possess a
sufficient theory of
psychology)

the greatest present danger

the area of pseudo-sensibility:

And as to "the gods," as referred to in your letter, Gregory—I have found that if I keep the total instrument of myself in shape (form) and sea-worthy (going . . . growing), or ship-shape and sea-worthy (to keep it light . . . afloat, that is) while maintaining capability of depth and complexity (anchors at sails with attendant et sets and et ceteras—what's past, pre-sent, and futurahhhhhhhhhhhhh) then "the gods" seem to keep up their beginning-middle-and-end of it admirably . . . i.e.: do persuage me (breath-wind: inspiration) to raise sail, steer courses unmapped, et cetera, and force me, usually by appearing under sign of Dis; that is, do'ert me, rendering themselves invisible for my searching, hiding for my seeking below the Sirface of them (thoughtstop-windead: spiralization) to drop anchor, Vat and all, et settle, and fin-ally to S'ave me too, 2, for partnership-shape (thoughtwind-breathstop and/or key: exspiration and/or invention) to add new rigging, disentangle the nets, and strengthen the links, make weightier anchor, et sets. I do not ever like to take "the gods" as fore-granted, find no likeness there, and am, at least in this sense, natural class-assist.

To P. Adams Sitney, June 19, 1963

OF NECESSITY I BECOME INSTRUMENT FOR THE PASSAGE OF INNER VISION, THRU ALL MY SENSIBILI-TIES, INTO ITS EXTERNAL FORM. My most active part in this process is to increase all my sensibilities (so that all films arise out of some total area of being or full life) AND, at the given moment of possible creation to act only out of necessity. In other words, I am principally concerned with revelation. My sensibilities are art-oriented to the extent that revelation takes place, naturally, within the given historical context of specifically Western aesthetics. If my sensibilities were otherwise oriented, revelation would take an other external form—perhaps a purely personal one. As most of what is revealed, thru my given sensibilities clarifies itself in relationship to previous (and future, possible) works of art, I offer the given external form WHEN COMPLETED for public viewing. As you should very well know, even when I lecture at showing of past Brakhage films I emphasize the fact that I am not artist except when involved in the creative process AND that I speak as viewer of my own (NO—DAMN that "my own" which is JUST what I'm trying,

DO try in all lectures, letters, self-senses-of, etc., to weed out)—I speak (when speaking, writing, well—that is with respect to deep considerations) as viewer of The Work (NOT of . . . but By-Way-Of Art), and I speak specifically to the point of What has been revealed to me AND, by way of describing the work-process, what I, as artist-viewer, understand of Revelation—that is: how to be revealed and how to be revealed TO (or 2, step 2 and/or—the viewing process.)

To Bruce Frier, Late August, 1963

"The twentieth century and all its works" constitute, as a matter of course, the natural tomb of living man, or life itself, which approximately twenty centuries of steadily increasing (not to count previous sporadic instances) monotheistic thinking has created: a gigantic Grave Yard, which, by this time, has no boundaries on this earth and is manifest everywhere, built for the dead at the expense of the living. It seems likely that the first gravestone was, in fact, laid when Pandora's box, which might actually have been a coffin, was opened and the truth, mortality of man, was known. And it seems quite natural that Man, or any man, or woman (from Pandora herself to Bluebeard's wife opening the one forbidden door—the latter myth still sufficient to stand for the whole Western sex complexity of twentieth century realization) having released the potential of all evil (that is: insufficiency and/or the irreconcilable: that which neither he nor she could hope to more than "come to terms" with) the natural tendency would be to climb into the very box wherefrom all evil came and therefore, presumably, was not. (Or if you prefer Eden: once having tasted of the fruit of the tree of knowledge, become then that fruit, even food for serpent, later, rather than be subject to more temptation—or to find opposite of Bluebeard version, take earlier Eden myth where we find Adam disobeys Eve, Earth Mother, in tasting and is, therefore, driven from Eden, Nature.) However it happened and at whatever rate, its works are the monoliths of entomb-meant of life-force in man, the Tree of knowledge a gallows for living sensibility, made manifest by quest-shun-answear, rather than a source of nourishment for growing sensibility, a course of man, chorus sing in harmony, each one in inter relationship to every other, coursing altogether of necessity whenever narrow passage (if ever), dissimilarity the measure of individual core, co only re: Pan, for companionship . . . or, as Olson sez:

> And now let all the ships come in,
> Pity and Love The Return The Flower

The Gift & The Alligator catches
and the mind go forth to the end of the world.

Which brings us, if you follow me as graciously as you lent me your
support, to "The Twentieth Century *and all its workings;*" I mean
that which is really *moving* in this time, each move meant and of a
rhythm more ancient than all history, each in time only to the life-
force being listened to as it hasn't been in at least 2,000 years, all
underground, of necessity—only statues on mon-u-meants above the
ground—all messages rapped out secretly along the drain-pipes of
civilization, difficult to decipher amidst the roar of shit—only epi-
taphal mono-thesis disgracing the more muddy than underground air
of the surface. But nothing moves up there (it's all in "the works")
and down here, where at least *I* am (and I hope you'll join me)
there's such a human burrowing as the world hasn't known since
Pleistocene man.

To Jonas Mekas, July 17, 1963

Even tho' you said it was a joke, I could not help but be bothered
by your referring to the Co-Op as a "monastery of fools." My
thoughts, touched off by this phrase, ranged as far back in human
history as 75,000 years ago, centered around that skeleton found in
Shanidar Cave, Iraq, an eastern Neanderthal who had been born
with a withered right arm (amputated by one of his fellows above
the elbow) and yet who had lived into his 40's (killed finally by a
cave-in)—all of which indicates that he must have been fed and
altogether cared for by his associates . . . which means he was the
first human we know of to be granted the so-called leisure in which
he COULD have, might HAVE, had ideas, inventions, creations to
give those who cared for him and, thus, to pass on to the whole
human race. Unfortunately for most of human history, since "leisure" has been granted willingly only to cripples of one kind or another, most artists, philosophers, inventors (at least in pure research
areas) have in fact either been naturally unhealthy, either physically
or mentally, or have feigned and/or actually created ill-health, much
like *The Nigger of the Narcissus* to permit them the given support
of society. Even many of those who have inherited wealth, such as
Proust, have felt the necessity of developing their idea-toxic (self-
poison) disorders to remove themselves from any expectation of
"usefulness." I wonder if, perhaps, the ancient initiations of the
priests, such as that one traced so eloquently by Graves (*The White
Goddess, King Jesus,* etc.) where the left thigh bone is deliberately

broken to make the priest crippled for life, don't find their origin, and indeed perhaps rational necessity, in a created illness to permit successful begging, etc. The role of the Fool in western civilization is easily traceable within this context. Once the authority of the court poet had been usurped by religion, he soon became, or became replaced by, The Jester. But Tom O'Bedlam was, for all that, poet and, as Shakespeare sees him in *Lear*, the wisest one in the castle. Yeats is still playing the last strings of that form in many of his plays. And undoubtedly the poet, who never needed cap, could preserve his integrity best as the traditionally protected and invulnerable ("God's Child") Fool. And even later, Chris Smart must have found Bedlam an altogether better place in which to write than Debtor's Prison. But, dear Jonas, in this society even cripples must be, and are being made, USEFUL, insanity altogether considered subject to cures of various soul-destroying treatments, monasteries make wine, and even saints become so by performing deeds of usually aggressive heroics, etc. I think the time has come to abandon this Neanderthal form of pardon for insistence upon support for creative endeavor. I think the time has come to throw off The Fool's Cap (kissing it in passing for all benefits granted) avoid the loony-bin with all good wit available (and all other monasteries) cultivate whatever health each has (I mean avoid accidents, suicidal accidents, suicide) and trace a history of the benefits of creative endeavor that will confound all nebulosity of aesthetes (and trace, as well, personal histories to replace or at least throw into true perspective those overpowering sickness myths *Lust for Life* and *Moulin Rouge*, which so dominate people's thots about artists, etc. . . . the sure ugliness of that representation of creative life is proved in *Time* each week when they trace a line, however crookedly, thru any artist's life to make it appear a shambles according to Irving Stone's thirties bestseller, or Maugham's view of Gauguin, etc.)

To P. Adams Sitney, March 11, 1962

I've been having (after some ten years of work) an immense difficulty making a splice . . . I'm speaking aesthetically, not technically natch—all touched off by John Cage's appearance here, long talks between us, the listening to his music, and subsequent readings of his marvelous book *Silence*. Cage has laid down the greatest aesthetic net of this century. Only those who honestly encounter it (understand it also to the point of being able, while chafing at its bits, to call it "marvelous") and manage to survive (i.e., go beyond it) will be the artists of our contemporary present. All those pre-tend artists who carry little gifts in their clutching, sweaty hands (the "cookie-pushers" as Pound calls them) will no more be able to get thru that net than those monkeys who are caught by gourds with small holes in them filled with fruit (monkey grasps fruit, hole too small to withdraw hand, monkey too dumb to let go of fruit, etc.)

To P. Adams Sitney
End of second week of December, 1962

Then the spiritual trial, as always, is relevant: that is, I have come to the time of life of which Mr. Pound speaks (in the book on Gaudier-Brzeska) thus:

> He (Gaudier-Brzeska) even tried to persuade me that I was not becoming middle-aged, but any man whose youth has been worth anything, any man who has lived his life at all in the sun, knows that he has seen the best of it when he finds thirty approaching; knows that he is entering a quieter realm, a place with a different psychology.

and this re: "spiritual" can only be sensed psychologically with some deficient image ("only," as yet, in mind) such as a spiral being pressed (by all pushing ego past) to be thought of as a circle (all to make ends meet—out of future foreboding—as if to make "security" there) . . . my struggle being thus, TO SPRING! But then I am sharply stop-answered (in Gilbert Sorrentino's article of great worth in *Kulchur* 8) by T. E. Hulme:

> In November, 1829, a tragic date for those who see with regret the establishment of a lasting and devastating stupidity, Goethe—in answer to Eckermann's remark that human thought and action seemed to repeat itself, going around in a circle—said: "No, it is not a circle, it is a spiral." You disguise the wheel by making it run up an inclined plane; it then becomes "Progress" which is a modern substitute for religion. . . .

and I am haunted by Webern's piece based on Bach's *Musical Offering*, the intense center of the piece, where, as the ear makes obvious, he struggles most desperately to break dissonantly with the imposed past form—and fails . . . and dies shortly thereafter . . . and I am haunted by Pollock's rages when he found the totems of his earliest work turning up again—and could only think of them as of re-turn . . . and died shortly thereafter. And fear of death (in both physical and spiritual sense) is certainly not new to me, but it does come in a new form . . . with a stupid una'kin, yet mannakin, to "Rage, rage, against the dying of the light."

Well, all the above is, for the moment at least, past tense now—as we have just seen *Dog Star Man: Part I*—and it is of these above struggles and (unlike I feared it might) does not assume old forms but rather transforms image, in a total concept and thru completely filmic magic, with such strength that *Prelude* looks flashy and even superficially imitative of painting beside it. It does not save me from the dilemmas mentioned in the first paragraph, nor was I saved in the act of making it (one of the falsest delusions of the young artist is that his art may act therapeutically as if "finger painting" were more than fingers painting); but it is just that the finished work gives me the same sense of both sssss-and-ave which has acted within me for this al-vation long before the work was started—so that it, the work of art, can act upon the artist as much as Gertrude Stein (in *Picasso*) says that war acts upon civilization . . . i.e., to inform the civilization of what has already taken place in terms of change.

. . . Of all kinds of survival a film artist struggles for, the economic one (as typified by my personal one as expressed in this letter) is the most immediate. Yet film enthusiasts generally hate to have any expression given to a personal economic need. I think this as serious an oversight (if deliberate shielding can be called that) as that devious refusal from film goers, well entrenched eight years ago, to consider the personal statement within the aesthetic structure as anything but a mistake engendered by psychoanalysis . . . well, mis or not, it has taken; and the whole structure of now recognized areas of film where the artist's hyper IN-volvement with his per-son (if un-owned—i.e. given to the process, at weakest, or medium, when medium, of God-force ((that thrust, out of necessity, of all the invisible coming thru us)) when greatest) proved the way to most of universe—albeit not, CERTAINLY NOT, "Universality" in the old sense . . . the distinction between "Universe" and "Universality" here most be-speaking the confusion which arises when the viewer take "a lity" for a light, thinks "the universe" what-is-already-partitioned rather than enjoying and joining the search for the unknown and accepting the unknown ways to it as more reasonable than all paths.

To Robert Kelly, June 26, 1963

I had as a child always one predominant vision of my future life: I was, with all my friends, backed into caves of a mountain and attacked by an enemy (most often the police, sometimes Germans, later Russians, etc.) I was always the leader, most distinguished by the possession of the only machine gun. We were always hopelessly outnumbered but always confident of eventual success. I had usually worn, in my imagination, a cartridge belt (patterned after those of *For Whom The Bell Tolls*, etc.). Three years ago, Jane fashioned a leather belt, to my specifications, with pockets for carrying film, light meters, inst. books, and bags (including an actual bulls-balls, given us) for carrying lenses, prisms, filters, etc.; and when I saw it completed, hooked over my shoulder as intended, I recognized the whole transference pattern into my contemporary living. My particular love of the machine gun like noise of the camera in operation (usually an annoyance to film-makers because of interference with sound-taking), my naming of our projector "Old Thumber" (what an interesting slip—when what I had intended to write was "Old Thunder" . . . particularly as I do take thumb, Graves-way, as Venus, birth, finger, and find deep relevance in over-lap of thumb-eye area of human brain, etc.) and the screen "Lightning"—so perfectly fitting my picture of a film-show where machine-gunlike flashes of vision reflect off the screen to kill "the enemy," which I do find, now, some unenlightened part of every man, woman, and child . . . even myself, in *Dog Star Man* as an old man of the mountain climbing to cut down that dead tree, myself knowing better than any other man (except possibly yourself) that it IS dead, not silver (as was once in legend) nor *ever* going to grow green branches again, that it MUST be cut down . . . The fear of its falling is where, I'm sure, all bomb scares find origin, in the same sense that Gertrude Stein said of wars:

> The spirit of everybody is changed, of a whole people is changed, but mostly nobody knows it and a war forces them to recognize it because during a war the appearance of everything changes very much quicker, but really the entire change has been accomplished and the war is only something which forces everybody to recognize it. (*Picasso*, page 30)

To Robert Kelly, August 22, 1963

I have been working almost entirely on *Mothlight* these days and finding it THE most difficult film to finish, at least per length (about 100′) I've yet been involved in (I had to pause after *involved* to *decide* whether in or with should follow; and this ambiguity illustrates my difficulty with the film itself—a difficulty engendered by the creation of a whole new film *technique*, a new niche into which few of my previous *working* techniques will function adequately enough to leave me free to be myself, to be, myself, adequately functioning instrument for the film's simple passage thru me . . . technical considerations, as conscious thoughts, making me be by myself, eventually *beside* myself, at every turn; so that "involved *with*" would describe a great many of the moments in the making of *Mothlight*, tho' I have always had sense enough once past eventu-or-crisis-ally to follow The Dance rather than take over as I was often tempted.)

Long after I'd begun making strips of film, with no thought other than creating a frame at a time in relationship to all other frames within a given strip (the length of Mylar I'd cut off, rather arbitrarily, before beginning to stick a given collection of parts of a plant or plants, etc., onto it), the words came to me: "As a moth might see from birth to death if black were white:" and shortly thereafter the title: *Mothlight*. Up till then I had thought up the title: *Dead Spring*: growing out of a simple pun on the process, the material involved, and the simulation of life that the eventual unwinding of this film would create of the material by way of this process, etc. But these new words, in their coming to me, made me aware of the extent to which the movements of this film were inspired by my previous thoughts, observations, and study (most recently, D'Arcy Thompson's *On Growth and Form*) on the flight of the moth and moth sight, etcetera. I have been very involved with moths since a curious incident in early winter, 1959: I was working on *Sirius Remembered*—it was late at night, and Jane had gone to bed—I was sty-my-eyed sinking into sty-*me*eeed in all self-possession when suddenly Jane appeared holding a small dried plant, which she put down on my working table and, without a word, left me—and I soon began working again and then noticing that the plant was shifting and that I had, without thinking, been picking up whatever its flattened petals, and sometimes its stem, had seemed to be pointing to; but as soon as I took notice of this interaction, my relationship to this plant broke down into speculation, et cetera, until I stopped working altogether . . . the next morning, much to my surprise, Jane had no memory whatsoever of having brought me the plant; and, the following night, I returned to my work table, and the plant thereon, in a struggling-to-be-open, preventing opening, frame of mind . . . in midst of attempts to work, what must surely have been the year's last moth, and a gigantic multicolored beauty at that, began fluttering about me and along the work table, the wind of its wings shifting the plant from time to time and blowing away all speculations in my mind as to movements of dead plants and enabling me to continue working and, later, to notice that I was again often, but not always, moving in relationship to plant-points and moth-moves and, in fact, every moving thing within the workroom; but finally I got hung-up, like they say, on the moth itself, its movements, particularly when it began settling first on one then another strip of film hanging beside me . . . the next day I photographed this moth in extreme close-up as it fluttered against the window glass, with the specific idea in mind to use those images in *Dog Star Man* (which I already have), and Jane and I were referring to the moth as "The Moth Queen" and were quite excited by the entire several days' events (which naturally distracted from continuing work on *Sirius Remembered*) . . . by the third day, I was beginning to worry about the moth; and we agreed that night to let the moth outside, as it was warm weather; but that night, when I went to the workroom, I found the moth dead on my table beside the dried plant and, on closer inspection, found that the head of the moth was as if sliced almost completely off, swinging as if hinged to the body, and that the body itself was completely hollow inside . . . both plant and moth remained on my table, without undue attention but constant interrelation, until the end of the editing of *Sirius Remembered*.

So, when moth words recently came to me, I began thinking of this film as being dedicated to "The Moth Queen" and knew it to be inspired (as have many movements in other work since 1959) by moth flight, thoughts about, feelings thereto; but I tended to take the words too literally; and, as an example: I began thinking that *Mothlight* must begin with the unraveling of a cocoon and end with some simulation of candle flame or electric heat (as all moths whose wings were being used in the film had been collected from enclosed light boxes and lamp bowls) and, while it bothered me to think of painting on an otherwise purely collage film, I began to plan to create a black flame (to literally emphasize "if black were white") at the end of the film. Well, to make a long story short, no matter how hard both Jane and I tried we could not find a single cocoon (let alone the twenty to thirty I had thought I needed) and the search touched off violent quarrels between Jane and me and dramatic statements of outrage at "nature's stinginess," etc., and other nonsenses and none-suches so totally out of key with the spirit of all our working together on the rest of the film that I am amazed and ashamed at my stupidity in retrospect. Finally, I found a cocoon in a blade of grass with a spider on top of it. I thought: "That spider must be eating the insides thru some hole it's made in the cocoon:" and, with much righteous feeling of indignation, shook the spider off. Then, with very little feeling at all, I proceeded to unwrap the cocoon along a strip of the sprocketed scotch tape. Much to my surprise, the cocoon was full of spider eggs, or at least what I quickly assumed was spider eggs, and not a caterpillar, or semi-moth, or moth at all; and I realized that I had committed the first (and last) intentional destruction of life in the making of *Mothlight* by my actions and that I would have done so no matter what had been inside the cocoon. It was a sobering moment in which all the false path I'd been insisting on was revealed clearly. I gave up, as gratefully given sacrifice, both cocoons and candle flame in that instant.

Then I began to have disturbances over the fading of the flowers packed within strips of Mylar, devised elaborate schemes for making many strips of flower patterns at once, rushing them to the lab, and getting them printed before they could fade. All such schemes failed. The fresh flower strips would not run thru the printer. Only later did I realize, after a week of remonstrances similar to those during cocoon search, that the colors hardly ever faded completely away and that the fading process was leaving intricate patterns of incredible beauty creating sensations of depth of dimension such as I have never seen on film before. But the former concern then touched off a fear that the film wasn't going to be printable at all. This almost broke me down completely so that I couldn't even bring myself to continue editing the strips I had, let alone make any more. Finally, however, I approached the film with only the thought in mind of letting the total form of it pass thru me just so that Jane and I could view it at least once (before all flowers had faded completely) in the little table viewer; and, from that viewpoint, found myself easily editing what is easily the most perfectly formal work I have yet made. It quickly fell into three sections, each containing a specific set of what I might call "round-dances" (I did spell out "rough-dances" rather than "round-dances" indicating the actual looseness of this original editing) for lack of a better term; but, when I had completed the three movements, the work appeared to me as unfinished. I simply could not bring myself to even thinking, at this time, of making more strips; and I stumbled out onto the front porch in a state of terrible dejection. Almost immediately a large moth fell at my feet, fluttering wildly. I said, to Jane: "What's that?" in a stupefied voice to which she immediately replied: "It's death dance." It fluttered for fully twenty minutes before our dog ate it. So, I went back to work again, composing what might be called "a coda" to the work. Then we looked at it thru the viewer and became so excited that I found faith enough to pick clean about 10,000 sprocket holes, tear open thick sections and carefully slice plant forms, twigs, etc., in half, and intersperse every 6 feet of film with 3 feet of leader (to enable the printer, or printing machine, to run smoothly and adjust itself periodically.) Finally I found myself in the blacked-out printing room at Western Cine, with all my /above/full-failing anger and bad faith, as above, directed at and tortured by machinery.

The printing machine looks like something out of a 1920's German science-fiction movie, its sprocket claws hand-filed to perfection, its machinery set to tolerate very little deviance in film widths, etc. There was finally nothing for me to do but pray, and certainly not to pray to the machine but just to pray. We sat in the dark, while the printing machine supplied the most nerve-wracking atmosphere imaginable by setting off a series of sputters and clicks, which kept building up in intensity to the full burst of its warning buzzer (which sounded exactly like those warning buzzers in spook houses, which accompany the display of papier-maché monsters revealed in bursts of garish light) which only discontinued when three-foot strips of leader were being printed. When I saw the developed film the next day, as was to be expected, the strips were every now and again printed so that a set of sprocket holes were printed with a regularity more specific than anything else in the picture, or than anything intended, they tended to draw the attention completely away from the developing forms of the film; and no matter how hard I tried to convince myself that they could be disregarded, left in the film, I knew it wasn't so. Worse yet, those original strips were so battered by being printed crookedly that there was less likelihood they would be run thru the printer than there had been before. The case seemed entirely hopeless, whatever damage to the total form irreparable; and this did crack me up and break me down altogether, which was all to the good: *viz:* I was forced to accept any personal defeat left in my relationship with the film. I came home, last night, and resolved, with Jane's marvelous, patient encouragement and remindfulness of your Enkidu statement in that morning's letter and of, thereby, our deep working processes of all these years, to re-edit the total form of the film in the light of the strips of film which were free of sprocket holes. I began work and, lo and behold (and what meaning those words have for me today) discovered that of the seven strips sprocket-hole-marked: #1 was of abalone shells (which had been more or less forced into the film which otherwise has no material except from this area), which could be cut, leaving the total form intact, IF I would but remove the piece of spider cocoon as well; #2 could be removed without impairing the total spiraling in-and-out development of the first section BECAUSE it constituted an entire spiral and no more than that AND had been creating an unbalanced spiral on the in development; #3 occurring in the second section constituted THE ONLY un-developing, or backward running, theme of that section, which did not thematically balance its co-responding in-coming piece at the beginning—the removal of both pieces unquestionably improving the form of that section; #4 being THE only case in section two where poppy forms were not replaced, in the unwind by pansy patterns, AND a divergent piece anyway; #5 and #6 constituting an entire part of section 3, and not one hair over, even tho', to accomplish this, the printer machine had to stay out of sync thru an entire piece of leader AND return in sync during the run of a Mylar strip AND said part of that section being the only one which I included because "it is so beautiful" and I had no other place where it could conceivably fit; and #7 being removable from the coda without the slightest alteration of the form.

Amazing, isn't it—even after all these years of dedication, of letting, as you put it: "the *prima materia* of film, the Visual, constitute its own 'story.' "

To Jane Brakhage, May 17, 1963
EASTERN CONFERENCE

"Conditions are much more complicated in the Eastern sphere of influence. Advance information indicates a run to the wire which may develop into a three-way photo, a bit of jokeying now viewed unkindly by the higher echelon around the league or the fans. Anyway, let's watch the Eastern Conference public-relations advisers carry the ball for their teams."

Oh, Jane—beautiful woman,

Enclosed find "First report of 'Eastern Conference' " as Olson said of the page of a book found on the street at 4:00 this morning, as he walked me back to Gerrit Lansing's apt. after more than twelve hours together. We each took note, laughing together in the deserted Gloucester streets, agreeing it should be sent on to you, he saying: "Ah, yes, send it on to Jane, just by itself as 'First report;' " but I do feel the need this morning to write as much as I can of the entire twelve-hour experience, to share with you as much of what can this morning be remembered as is possible—and also to have some record available to conscious mind even tho' I'm sure the deep-working centers of our conversation will already be moving subconscious, taking direction away from what I might throw up or put down.

I arrived, with bags full of groceries and beer, in company with Gerrit Lansing and Harry Martin at 4:00 in the afternoon, was immediately overwhelmed by the SIZE of the man and the electric look of the face, his grizzley beard, upstanding hair, all white, the reflections of lights in his glasses, thru which his eyes pierce with a look that would terrify were it not for the amazingly immediate look of the man, the love out-going as clearly as if, and being, blessings. I began taking stills almost immediately, filling the air with flashes of light (having now an entire roll of still photos of the Olsons), keeping myself on that sight plain until the others had left—at which point, Olson and I moved out for a walk along the bay front to "the bridge," then up around Gloucester streets, turning back along "Angel" street, into his favorite bar, then on home late at night for waiting supper with Betty (Charles Peter being then in bed, beautifully asleep, eight-year-old boy turned into himself in sleep making me wonder so much about Bearthm), and so on talking in the kitchen, drinking "Old Crow" until 3:30. And of that whole talking time, the range was so extensive I cannot really believe even the small fragments I remember could have been packed into twelve hours.

The money problem came up almost immediately, Olson being clear in confirmation of "this last year" being most difficult ever— but quick to follow with: "That's changing, changing so fast . . . I see that change—yes, I HEAR you." And, "How it takes form in terms of money: but then remember, this IS America—in three weeks, this whole picture could be changed for all of us . . . I mean that quickly the money can move, when the time's right. When Robert Duncan was last here, he asked me was I interested in 'A College,' having himself some source. I said, "Awww, come on, Robert, you know it isn't going to work this way. What's needed is twelve men each independently supported, backed, in such a way that they form flanges of a hierarchy—given that support, you'll HAVE that which attracts everyone of importance TO-gether, won't need land, won't need buildings, won't need ad-ministration . . . will HAVE it, what's needed." First clear statement I've had, after listening to stories and stories of hierarchitectitiptitoplofticals re: College, like Branaman's mad dream or The Kellys' Blue Yak dream college. Then: "In the meantime, get to the center, quickly

—don't fuck around with small colleges . . . get to the BIG centers, use them, you CAN, you know—I mean, even the MEDIUM, film, having that possibility built in, IN, to it . . . the power there, thru the eye, I mean: how anyone will go in to look at a movie, you hear?, are you hearing me?" . . . myself wondering all the time if this wasn't another version of Duncan's old belief that I was going to make it in Hollywood, beCAUSE of my medium, and be able to support everybody while actually "making it," or Michael's recent insistence that my fate, as artist, would be, at least economically, easier than his just because of the medium, etc.

Then, in all this time, Olson did show me how Gloucester is, really, an island, how he was raised on the first point of "the mainland—or, that point geographically furthest out, I mean where I could be most easterly-westerly . . . how I was, as my father before me, letter-carrier: my first job as a boy—right here, where we're standing." And he showed me the place where, unknown to everyone, a battleship's hull is buried, one wall of it backed by shit from the sewers of the town, the apparatus, wheels, tubes, being that which pumps the shit out from Gloucester into the bay, the whole thing buried under a monument centered in an innocuous plot of grass—"I mean, what goes on underground." He showed me the house that was focal point for his reconstructing history in *Maximus* —now lived in by the president of The John Birch Society of Gloucester. We began talking of schools, he clarifying for me that all my worries about the girls and Bearthm going to school must be centered where the complete concern is: with the total system, of which school is just one small aspect. What a relief—and how wonderful that I could think of coming to terms with the total system easier than particularized "school," etc. He showed me the house where a man who "actually studied with Ruskin" lives, now growing the most beautiful flowers. He showed me the house where he had left his mother that awful night written of as "St. Valentine's Day Storm," wandered down to the bay to be bombarded by sheets of ice blown in from the sea. In the bar, we began talking of Eisenstein, the wide-screen concept ("Do you *really* have anything to add to that?"—which I thought best left unanswered until he had seen my films . . . the following night) and then on into "vision" and "drugs." "You must take psilocybin—all the rest very dangerous. Nuts to that whole science scene—completely right to keep free of it, as you have . . . all spreading bullshit to hide the *one* drug of value IF taken in company, a simple occasion—no bullshit . . . just a way of seeing." I then threw up "One ring to bind 'em." This seemed to raise some doubt, then very specific concern with respect to myself—"Yes, okay, I'll wait and see . . . you may be right there." Then we shifted quickly to drama, began talking deeply of how-why it doesn't work with complete agreement from him on my tracing the breakdown to drama into "ring to bind 'em" with the loss of "the mask," drama now making flesh masks for people to wear out each other against, etc. . . . he adding "the introduction of the female onto the stage" ("misplaced cunt dominating all else") and "the star system" ("cult of personality rather than creation of Person"). But we did start with Robert Duncan's "Adam's Way," and onto why the greatest living dramatist cannot finish a play, the social scene impinging, as it did in S.F. in a way to make finish in life, not on stage, etc. Olson: "Yes, we must, must, must get rid of drama, at all costs—I mean, even get rid of narrative —the temptation . . . you hear?"

Then, after supper, the question of magic: Here, dear Jane, for all of my trying to remember, the deep substance of this matter is too deep in me for any kind of transcription; but I will put down what does come to the surface as best I can. It begins with reference directly to "the eyes," Olson's wonderful re-spect: that he had said to me much earlier, within five minutes after meeting him, to be precise: "With you, Brakhage, it is at this point a question of focus —is it not?" Then, later, after supper, stomach pulling at my brains, I shifted to superficial level of defending black magic of Maas and Deren, as film-makers, by way of "After all, film is at the Lascaux Cave-Painting level." Then quickly, sternly, back from him: "Don't give me that! I'm an authority on cave painting, as you surely know. Stop trying to defend the fact that you ARE, are you not?, myopic, that is: NEAR-sighted: and walleyed . . . as am I . . . as is Robert Duncan . . . Right?" After immediate relief of: "Yes, yes, of course!" from me, Olson went right on: "I have, even tho' I suffer from claustrophobia, crawled around IN those tunnels, seen how, very often, the Pleistocene man HAD, that is, chose, to paint where he couldn't have been more than six inches from where he was painting, eyes THAT close. And the point is, after all, that Pleistocene Man WAS that close to us, where we are—that is: He was living in a world where all predators, that is, everything that COULD EAT HIM, was so MUCH larger than he was! . . . and then how he did choose to paint where he did, in that most difficult position, rather than just anywhere, per chance. I love that sense of that fisty little creature being, maybe, FIRST to say 'Fuck you,' to all of it which didn't arise from HIMself, in the sense of: 'I *will* have it *my* way!

. . . I mean, his knowing that he must GIVE instruction or be eaten by nature, one way or the other (Hero being, to me, later, being only 'He who demonstrates Nature'—that is, being memorable biographically ONLY) . . . you hear? . . . only—Hero still being just that except for interference with Nature—that is, specifically THAT which threatens us all with annihilation . . . that is, HOW the Hero has been possessed is no longer relevant, BECAUSE nature is being so possessed . . . how in Dogtown even, that area which, since the beginning has certainly been the most beautiful natural spot of these surroundings, NOT dependent upon any man's concept, not quote natural unquote, IS now being made center of reservoir, place where trees are being cut down, other trees planted, placed, whole basin filled with water, dust of their blasting settling over the whole eastern seaboard. And now, how YOU, Brakhage, must get clear about focus—right? . . . I mean, do you hear me? . . . that is: Hold your hand in front of your face and find OUT just how far away you can take it and how close, without throwing all the lines of that hand out of focus." I tried it, found FOCUS somewhere between four and six inches, that is: I could have measured exactly some specific point there that was THE ONLY TRUE FOCUS. And Olson began laughing beautifully, saying: "How wonderful I can teach you that, you with all concerns of vision so wonderful—that I am permitted to teach you where your TRUE focus IS . . . and believe me, it is somewhere there for all men—RIGHT THERE. And you DID know it at eighteen when you threw away those glasses . . . I mean, the TRUTH of it which you just hadn't YET come to think of, make reference to, in your BRAIN." Then, Olson leaning over closely, winking, holding his hands that close to his face, saying: "And, Brakhage, what is all the rest beyond that point—I mean, what IS all that out there which we CALL focus? . . . What IS focus, Brakhage? Hey?"

(I am now writing almost twenty-four hours later than when I ended the last paragraph—much more of the conversation has, natch, been forgotten; but there's some advantage in that yesterday I went again over to Olson's and the conversation did tend to take off from the end point of the above paragraph . . . so, rather than try to stick to narrative, I'll just write what I've understood of all his talking these last two days, as it comes to me as a total picture.)

(It should be understood that, if my memory ear were *that* correct, I could put most of the following in quotes, after the name of Olson, except that I would make crucial mistakes, probably, out of my problems, and that it did all arise out of conversation between us): There is a probably precisely determinable, diamond line that could be drawn so that one point would be crucial outer focus, another crucial inner focus, the other two points of the four available for a drawing of a line that would bisect the diamond into two triangles—TAKE that line as LOCUS, in a view-plate sense: that is, out of the understanding that there are *three* rings that bind men (a departure from Tolkein's number): "thought," "consciousness," and "sense-perception," the latter really meaning: the eye, how it dominates all other senses in men. Referring to Michael McClure, there was a looooong name relating him, per example, specifically to me, by way of affliction, which did break down to another triangle, rings of ring true, the three corners of which *could* be viewed as corresponding to a type having: "Narcissism," "shyness," and "desire to have absolute power over the world" . . . characteristics. But then there is all that which men CALL focus, a flexible diamond, that is: subject to squeeze-play in the mind, its bisecting line being most clear as *horizon line* (calling up in my mind the quest shun: What point beyond the horizon line must I be focused upon, in order to see horizon line as that line which bisects *that* diamond? i.e., fixes it? . . . to which Olson immediately answered: "You must have Hopi," being playful with what he later referred to as: "The Hopi Indian having the only language that was constructed to make speech in terms of 'definition' possible . . . that is, that the Hopi would only speak in terms of where he was, would have to walk over there, locomotion, to speak of what was there, then being where he was a-gain ((in fairness to Olson's speech, he was throwing back at me a lot of puns here, and laughingly, in reference to the puns he had just read in some of my newer writing—he being specifically clear that I should stop using 'em, that dispersal, in my writings)). (P.S., pisssss—"But given four to six inches as my 'True focus,'" I said, "You, Olson, are already 'over there'" . . . He replied: "You know nothing of Aurora?—I mean, to keep it simple: Don't you know about your Aurora? . . . that given temperature ((I don't mean Aura)) that inner temperature you have always with you—I mean, how you die, even, with your Aurora on, so to speak . . . but we'll get to that later," . . . Something of it beginning to be clear when Charles Peter gave me some stereopticon cards with glasses, and that when I said, "Thank you, I'll give them to my children" and he, the boy, replied "No. Keep them yourself," Betty gave me a quick lesson in it of it by saying, "You see, he's a Hopi—that is, he doesn't *know* your children.") That—is . . . (damn the distraction of parenthesis) . . .

there are, at least TWO things which must MUST be taken as "stabile:" "energy" and "dimension;" that is, that when Olson was under psilocybin and went to the toilet to pee, he became aware of the sense that, tho' the toilet seemed miles away from him in distance, it remained the same size and that he was able to pee directly into the center of it: that is, tho' all of what was beyond four to six inches, even tho' CLEARLY not true focus, ergo, being CLEARLY picture of the mind OUT, appeared unstable, he (out of his energy) was peeing into it (because it had a fixed dimension). Given these two "stabiles" (this form) out of his prime necessity (out of the prime truth of total organic necessity), he could "instruct" all the rest, just as Pleistocene man had, etc. . . . out of, or gaining, TWO other truths: "The World as the object of God . . . God being, therefore, the subject of The World" (The caps and the "therefore" possibly being my thoughtless addition—I don't know. That is, when I told him of the vision of the four entities appearing to me during the editing of *Sirius Remembered*, he took that as a kind of visitation that was to make me aware of the four corners of a given position so that I would be enabled to go on my own way; but, when I told him of the statement, "We cannot go deeper unless you stop smoking," Olson responded with immediate sense of: "Ah yes, that's the way she usually speaks, that is: *that's* instruction which you are *bound*, if you want to go on your own way, to resist . . . this before he'd heard how I'd resisted, tho' he could see me smoking.) (Somewhere in here he suggested, pulled out, and read from, Coon's *The Story of Man*, making, a day later but as if to give the other side, "a horrible book," called *The Assessment of Men*, taking great delight in the fact that Coon was typical American in that he had gone to the very site ((I almost spelled "sight")) where a Frenchman had dug up "the oldest human skull yet found," and that Coon had, when shown the digging, gone immediately WITH HIS FINGERS and dug deeper until he found yet an OLDER skull and OPENED UP THE WHOLE FIELD— at which point, Olson pulled out a Mayan Owl head in stone he'd dug up with his own fingers, somehow knowing where to dig . . . and when I said, "How did you know where, if you do not rely on 'magic,'" it opened up the whole discussion of magic, albeit with some reluctance on his part. Robert Duncan kept, naturally, coming up into the conversation here: "As I wrote Robert the other day, there are only three terms of time we should deal with now: day, year, millennium—he replied by referring to those first seven years of man's growth, that being his crisis: how we get up to adolescence, that is: sex, etc." Or: "AS I wrote Robert, and that part of my reply he could make most use of, poem coming out of it, that Christ was the FIRST sacrifice, yes, LAST, too; that is, the beauty of how he laid his life down as sacrifice, I mean, like in animals—'cut my throat' . . . Christ being FIRST HUMAN we know of to so come to terms with 'thought,' 'consciousness,' and 'sense perception' right out of 'Narcissism,' 'shyness,' yes, AND 'desire to have power over the world.' " ((Olson then reading me Robert's reply which did take Christ as "Second Person," after ADAM "First Person," in terms of subject of the world (((you see, Jane, how hard it is for me to, how I must capitalize "ADAM" over my mistake of God in that place—and was I right there to take Adam in terms of "subject of the world?" . . . of course not—Jesus, how I have to keep the demons at bay in writing to you with true perspective . . . i.e., what is Adam? . . . well, Duncan had said something like, "I take Adam as made." . . . puns using him?))))))) Wow—parenthesis (that is, on end, "says" and/or parent thesis.) That—as a matter of FACT: "We live at the beginning of the new millennium—God, what an exciting time . . . how much there is to do; that is, How much we must here instruct the angels, who are at this time running around being very busy, needing our instruction, and OF our necessity, that is, of your necessity and my necessity, etc." And, as to magic: "You are not a black magician—you are a white magician . . . and that is a very difficult, dangerous thing to be in a time like this . . . I mean how *much* we are each of us drawn to evil in such a time, how easy it is, how each of us falls into it *all ways*, that is because of *all the ways*."

Now as I'm being presumptuous enough to put in quote marks outside of parentheses, here, that is above, I'm going to copy out of Gerrit Lansing's wonderful collection some printed statements of Olson's which came up over and over again, threading in and out of the conversation as references I should, and have, and am here making, to end the substance of this letter—give you as much as I can, dear Jane, knowing your needs, dearest Jane, they being so related to mine now and for a later look-up for each of us . . . To start with, as Olson read it over and over to me, out of the Melville book *Call Me Ishmael*, look up the passage in there where Melville makes, strikes, balance between Goetic (Olson making references to "trickster" magic there, immediately) and Theurgic (Olson emphasizing, "to start with The—or, to pun, Godic, magic).

ON THE ART
OF VISION

BY ROBERT KELLY

No. 37, Summer, 1965

An *art of vision* possible in a medium that has dominated our century and that herewith frees itself from dependence on all other art forms. Film has tended, even in the most experimental contexts, to be a composite of literary and plastic arts, dance and music, the eye at the mercy of intention, culture, pretense, and imitations. Now Brakhage's *art of vision* exists utterly free of all that. It is a totality of making so intense it becomes a systematic exploration of the forms and terms of the medium itself. To explore the form without exhausting the form: A definitive making in any art is the health of the whole art, of the arts. Art in its oldest sense is skill, skill of making; *The Art of Vision* is the skill of making seeing. *The Art of Vision, The Art of The Fugue*, a presumptuous comparison only so long as we accord film only evidential value. This film makes immediate the integrity of the medium. Climax of the edited film, a new continent of the eye's sway. Mind at the mercy of the eye at last.

*　*　*

Is the word art lost to us? Skill in making is what it once meant, a way of making, so that art of vision = how to see.

* * *

What difference does it make what the film has been? Who am I to speak of this question? of it? What do I know? What is the film now? I speak of one film.

* * *

Brakhage's film is not free of story in the literary sense. Brakhage paraphrases his film too easily. If the film is not free of story, why do I say it is? *Dog Star Man* is deeply implicated with story— i.e., in this context, pre-existent temporal intent. But *The Art of Vision* is not *Dog Star Man*.

* * *

The word art has lost its balls. This title may grow them again.

* * *

Art is not the pomposity of Bayreuth, the bathos of Lincoln Center, the pack rat trove of The Louvre. Art is making.

* * *

The motto of the city of New York is *So What?* Be aware that it is *not* a rhetorical question.

* * *

It is time we understood *art* as a function, not an attitude.

* * *

Film, through its newness and availability, generates attitude more frequently than it does response. The attitude of an audience is not the film-maker's problem.

* * *

It is important to call things by their right names.

HARRY SMITH INTERVIEW

BY P. ADAMS SITNEY

No. 37, Summer, 1965

Smith: The dating of my films is difficult because I had made the first one, or part of that, in 1939. It was about twenty-five years ago, although it says forty years in the *Film-Makers Cooperative Catalogue*, because, at different times, I have posed as different ages.

Sitney: When were you born?

I never give that information out. I would like to say that I'm the Czar of Russia. My mother always claimed to be Anastasia. That's how I got Mr. R. interested in these things. This interview has to be severely cut down. Like no names, Mr. R., you know, or something.

I had drawn on film for quite a while, but exactly which one is *#1* I don't know. It was made something between 1939 and, I would say, 1942 at the latest. Later, I was very disappointed to find out that Len Lye had done it. Naturally, I was horrified when either

Dick Foster or Frank Stauffacher showed up with a book one day and told me that not only had Len made hand-painted films, but he had done 16mm ones. Then later somebody in San Francisco, whose name I forget (he was the Harley-Davidson agent), got like stimulated by me and made 8mm hand-painted films.

#1 was made by taking impressions of various things, like cutting up erasers or the lid of a Higgins Ink bottle. That's where I derived all the circular shapes. There's a kind of cork on the top of it. I dipped it in the ink and squashed it down on the film; then, later, I went over the thing with a crow-quill pen. However, the colors aren't too good in that film. I can't remember how long it took to make it, because I'd made a number of others. I had a considerable number of films that have not been printed at all. Undoubtedly less than half of my stuff is in my possession now.

Were the early films made on 16mm?

No, on 35mm. After I made #1, I met the Whitney Brothers through Frank Stauffacher and Dick Foster. Foster was the one who had really started the Art in Cinema Society because he had been in New York and had met film-makers there. But, later, he and Stauffacher fell out; so I took over Foster's position. They sent me down to Los Angeles to look for films. That's when I met Kenneth Anger, who sort of remembered me when he was up here last month. It must have been 1944, maybe, when I made that trip.

He made Fireworks *in 1947.*

1947? He definitely remembered me when I brought up the situation during which our meeting occurred. How old was he at the time?

About seventeen.

Everybody was very embarrassed at his films at that point. It was a horrible thing! He was embarrassed; I was embarrassed. I went to his house, and he was afraid his mother was going to find out that I was there; she was upstairs. He looks today almost identical to the way he looked then; that's the amazing thing! It was a small bungalow type place . . . I didn't realize the artistic quality of *Fireworks* until seeing it this year; then it seemed like some kind of homosexual exercise. When Kenneth sat down in something like a golden chair from Versailles of his mother's, the chair's leg fell off. He was very embarrassed. "My mother might hear me." Then, in order to get the leg back on the chair, he raised the venetian blind, and the cord broke, and the thing fell all over the floor. However, I did manage to get the film for the Art in Cinema Society, which I think was its first large showing. The auditorium of the San Francisco Museum of

Art seated at least, I suppose, 300 people. He came up to the showing and embarrassed everyone. After the clapping at the end of the film, I thought he was putting his hands up like a prize fighter. But, when he was here a month or so ago, he explained that that was a sign having something to do with the Aleister Crowley cult—I forget what—perhaps Shu holding up the sky.

I had been going to the University of Washington studying anthropology. I was a teaching assistant there occasionally. (I still love Drs. Gunther and Jacobs.) I was never a good student, at all. I led a very isolated youth. My father had run away from home at an early age to become a cowboy. I think that at that time his grandfather was the Governor of Illinois. They were a wealthy family. My great-grandfather, General John Corson Smith, was aide-de-camp to General Grant during the later Civil War. My mother came from Sioux City, Iowa; but my grandmother had had a school that was supported by the Czarina of Russia in Sitka, Alaska, although she moved around. The Czarina still supported those operations for years, and that's what led to my mother's being Anastasia. My father destroyed every single shred of information on her when she died. I never saw him again. The last time that I saw my father, I was like a heroin addict. I might have been sixteen or seventeen. I left on the bus for San Francisco after the funeral. I had to get back to get a hold of the connection. My father was crying . . What I started to say was that they lived in separate houses. My grandfather came to Washington and founded the Pacific American Fisheries with his brother, which is the largest salmon canning combine in the world. They killed off all the salmon in Washington. They still have twenty some canneries in Alaska. They fished everything else out of British Columbia and Washington years ago. This doesn't have much to do with my films. It's all true. My father may still be alive. I haven't contacted him in years, although he tried to find me by various means. He found out that my films were being shown at the Art in Cinema Society and tried to discover where I was. He finally did find out where I was and I sent him one of those "Tree of Life" drawings. I never did hear from him again. He was evidently very smart; he had taught me about alchemy. He was interested in that sort of thing. On about my twelfth birthday he gave me a whole blacksmith's shop. (They were stuck with various canneries that had been built up during the First World War. The whole thing over-expanded.) Most of my childhood was spent in a fairly elaborate place in Anacortes, Washington. There was nobody there at that time except my father who was something of a ne'er-do-well. My great-grandfather must have been pretty interesting. At one point, he said, "I am now leaving for a five-year tour of Tibet." After the Civil War, the Masons split into two groups—one of them was led by Albert Pike, who wrote *Morals and Dogma of the Scottish Rite*; the other one, the Knights Templar, were refounded by my great-grandfather. Any time that the Masons have a parade on Fifth Avenue, they always have a float that shows my great-grandfather founding this thing. He traveled all over the world and initiated people like the King of Hawaii and King Edward the Seventh into that business. When I was a child, there were a great number of books on occultism and alchemy always in the basement.

Like I say, my father gave me a blacksmith shop when I was maybe twelve; he told me I should convert lead into gold. He had me build all these things like models of the first Bell telephone, the original electric light bulb, and perform all sorts of historical experiments. I once discovered in the attic of our house all those illuminated documents with hands with eyes in them, all kinds of Masonic deals that belonged to my grandfather. My father said I shouldn't have seen them, and he burned them up immediately. That was the background for my interest in metaphysics, and so forth. My mother described mainly events from when she was working in the school in Alaska my grandmother had run. For example, one day she hadn't been able to get into the place where she was living: It was so cold, her hands started to freeze and she was unable to unlock the door. She went out into the woods where she saw all the animals performing ceremony. She told me many times about that because it must have been a wonderful thing. That was somewhere on the Yukon River. Hundreds had gathered together and were leaping over each other by moonlight. They were running around in little circles in different places. Of course it all could be explained in terms of bio-mass, or what is that thing called? There is some way that the animals have certain ranges and interrelate with one another. It was evidently some special thing. The authority on these things, Tinburgin, points out that animals do absolutely every single thing that humans do except make fire.

Very early, my parents got me interested in projecting things. The first projections that I made were from the lamps of a flashlight. In those days, flashlights had lenses on the front of them; that couldn't have been much later than in 1928.

What I really started to say was that, due to the vast amount of buildings and things that had no use after there were no more salmon in the Fraser or the Columbia, my parents lived in separate houses from the time I was about ten until I left home at the age of eighteen. They had communication between their houses by ringing bells. They'd meet for dinner. My father wanted to play the piano and the guitar. He was interested also in drawings and things; he was the one who showed me how to make that "Tree of Life" geometrically. I mostly lived with my mother. I performed what might be considered sexual acts with her until I was eighteen or nineteen maybe. No actual insertion or anything, but I would always get up in the morning and get in bed with her because she had a long story she would tell me about someone named Eaky-Peaky. She was a really good story teller. My posture is derived from trying to be exactly her height; for she was shorter. I think that the first time she went to Alaska must have been kind of strange because it was right after or during the Gold Rush. Both my parents were there at that time. There were various people on this boat going to the Gold Rush. One of them, for example, was suffering from withdrawal from morphine and thought she had worms under her flesh. She was lying there saying, "The worms! the worms!" The other was some kind of whore who was hanging her tits out the porthole and saying, "Come on, boys, milkshake, five cents a shake." I don't know how my father got there. They somehow met there. They met somehow.

So anyhow, the first projections that I made were negatives that my mother and father had taken in Alaska. I had thousands of those, enormous masses of this stuff. I can remember the amazement that I felt when I took the lens of the flashlight and was able to see one of the snow scenes on the walls of the hall.

My mother evidently had a number of boyfriends as my father was never there. He was always in Alaska doing something. She would park me in movies, most of which I can't remember. They were all silent movies. That's what got me interested in them. Sure. She was off doing something else; maybe not with boyfriends. I did meet a few of them; that's how I met Aleister Crowley. Probably he's my father, although I don't want to say that. There's a question as to whether he is or Robert James Smith is. She had fallen in love with Crowley when he was in this country in about 1918, while he was living on some islands in Puget Sound north of Seattle. Then he showed up a few more times, probably—I don't know when they were—in 1927 or sometime—that can be determined from books on his travels. I can remember meeting him at least once; he showed me a clam neck hanging out of a cliff; he had a black turtle-neck sweater on. He was not any kind of sissified character like they say. He was a really handsome, muscular person. My mother would sneak off to see him. He was there twice as far as I can remember; she met him when he was running naked down the beach in 1918.

She would leave me in a theater. I saw some good films there, which I wish it were possible to locate again. I saw one, for example, which was pretty good in which bad children put caps into the spaghetti at a fancy Italian dinner. (That was one of the first sound films that I ever saw). When the people chewed their spaghetti there was a BAAAKH; that was about all that was on the sound-track. The mouth would fly open, and false teeth would go across the dinner table, and so forth. They consistently took me to see Charlie Chaplin and Buster Keaton. I can remember being horrified when Keaton (in *The General*) gets caught in the bear trap, though my parents thought that was so funny. I was never able to understand why it was funny, but they kept taking me back to it day after day after day. Mainly, I liked serials. I didn't particularly like Charlie Chaplin or Buster Keaton. Of course, I appreciate them now.

I was still going to school, which was an interesting school; what was that called? The Western Washington School of Education. The head of it later got busted for Communism. I liked it because they had a glass beehive in the middle of the classroom that had a chute running out through the window so we could study the bees at work. It was an unpleasant place because they kept accusing me of stealing things like money. On the day that Admiral Byrd was visiting, somebody said Miss Rich, who was my principal, was going to take us to see Admiral Byrd; and I said, "Oh, kick Miss Rich in the pants." It was horrible, because I said this to the person next to me, and the person next to me said it to the person next to him, "Harry said, 'kick Miss Rich in the pants.'" And he said it to the next one. I saw this thing go around, back and forth across the room. It finally got to the teacher, so, naturally, I was kept home when everybody else went to see Admiral Byrd; although, strangely enough, I met him in a Mannings later that day.

I saw all those Fu Manchu movies; they were some of my favorites. There was also some serial that had a great big spider about the size of this room, which would be chasing Pearl White down through tunnels. That thing scared the shit out of me, but I probably had erections during it, it was so terrifying. I was very interested in spiders at about the age of five. I discovered a lot of them in the Columbin vines. Also I remember meeting my grandfather (my mother's father) who was also pretty interesting because he had followed a particular friend of his—he had been born in Kentucky, I don't know where, some place like that and followed the Union troops north after the Civil War. I remember he and his friend had long white beards with yellow streaks down the front of them. I had thought that egg had run down them. They had been eating eggs, see, and the egg had run down the middle of their beards.

This is the college education that I got . . . I was never able to pass the entrance examination in English. Despite the fact that I should have a Ph.D. at this point on all other bases but that. I just could not diagram sentences. I was sort of an instructor at one point at the University of California. I went to the University of Washington first. I was never too well liked there. The war had ended, and there was all this anti-Communism; what they call witch hunting was going on, and my favorite teacher was . . . you see, I got connected with the World Friends Service Committee at that point. I began working with the Japanese that were being kicked off the West Coast. The day after Pearl Harbor, all the Japanese were arrested and sent to camps in some horrible desert, I forget where that was. They sure came back in condition! We finally got one Japanese back to Seattle who was a midget and wore a monocle—a girl, who was going to deliver a lecture in some church; I forget what that thing was called—the Fellowship of Reconciliation, that was it. I barely escaped the Communist plots, I think. It was pretty funny: We rented this church for her to give the lecture in, and nobody came, not one person. There, I'm stuck with this girl that is completely confused. I was also involved with a lot of Jewish refugees that were going to the University of Washington then, ranting about people being thrown into incinerators and so forth in concentration camps. It was an interesting period: I wish they'd have another war; I liked it.

There's confusion in the notes for the *Catalogue* because I tend to glamorize, saying that I did such and such at a much earlier age than I did it. The reason I moved to Berkeley from . . . how did that happen? Anyway, I went to Berkeley on some little trip from Seattle with someone named Kenneth, I forget what his last name was. I'd met him in a bookstore. He said, "I'm leaving for Berkeley, do you want to go?" So I went to Berkeley. This was supposed to be for over the weekend. However while I was there I ran into someone named Griff B. He turned me on to marijuana. So naturally when I got back to the University of Washington, where I was about to become a teaching assistant, it was impossible to stay there after having smoked pot. The stuff that is given in the *Catalogue* that was used on different films is slightly inaccurate. I've never experienced the real heroin-addiction thing. In the place where I lived, the

Fillmore district of San Francisco called Jackson's Nook, two people died; I mean, there was a number of people staggering out into the back yard and dropping dead. When my mother died, there were a lot of guns around the house, because they'd always had them while they were in Alaska, both my mother and father. I took all that stuff back with me. It led to a rather exciting life in San Francisco at that point. My mother was dying in the hospital of what Ronald J. once called terminal diarrhea. She died the day after I left. I was like a heroin addict at that point. The symptoms were not very serious though; I was not lying on the floor frothing at the mouth; I had a stomach ache and a runny nose and that sort of thing.

I was mainly a painter. The films are minor accessories to my paintings; it just happened that I had the films with me when everything else was destroyed. My paintings were infinitely better than my films because much more time was spent on them. I can show you slides of them. I don't have any slides that were made since about 1950. That's a painting that was made of the score for one of the films that were shown. That's like the scenario for the last movement of one of those color films.

My first film was made by imprinting of the cork off an ink bottle and all that sort of thing, as I said before. The second one was made with Come-Clean gum dots, automatic adhesive dots that Dick Foster got for me. It's like a paper dot with gum on the back. The film was painted over with a brush to make it wet, then with a mouth-type spray gun, dye was sprayed onto the film. When that dried the whole film was greased with vaseline. Of course this was in short sections—maybe six foot long sections. Anyway they would be tacked down. With a pair of tweezers, the dots were pulled off. That's where those colored balls drop and that sort of stuff. Being as it was pulled off, it was naturally dry where the dot had been and that part which had been colored was protected by the vaseline coating at this point. Then color was sprayed into where the dot had been. After that dried, the whole film was cleaned with carbon tetrachloride.

The next one was made by putting masking tape onto the film and slitting the tape lightly with a razor blade and a ruler, and then picking off all those little squares that are revolving around. I worked off and on that film for about five years pretty consistently; I worked on it every day at least. I may have abandoned it at one point for three months or six months at the most.

Mrs. S. who owned the house in Berkeley gave me a room in exchange for mowing the lawn and trimming the ivy. I had developed a theory that the ideal diet was a mixture of butter and sugar—a pound of sugar and a pound of butter mixed together. I became so weak, though, that I was unable to get out of bed for a long time. Except some girl, Panthia L., would come up some mornings and scramble an egg and give it to me; or I'd go down to the supermarket and steal avocados, butter and sugar.

Were the early abstract films at all influenced by your childhood interest in the occult?

Sort of. But mainly by looking in the water. I lived a kind of isolated childhood. I said my parents were living in different houses and would only meet at dinner time. They'd set up this fancy five-storey art school, at which there were really only two students— sometimes there were four students. With Mrs. Williams, I studied at least from maybe 1932 to 1942; I must have studied with her for ten years. She gave lessons two or three times a week during that period, which consisted of drawing things. She'd lay out a cylinder or a ball or an egg-shaped thing which we were supposed to draw on a piece of paper and then lay a piece of glass over that and trace the drawing with a grease pencil, then hold it up and see if it looked exactly the same.

#1 took a very long time. Either a day or a week. Then *#2*— which was much longer than the form it is in now: It was actually at least half an hour long—it was cut down to match a recording by Dizzy Gillespie, which I believe is called "Guacha Guero." It took maybe a year to make. Then on the next one I worked on about five years, then I gave up that particular style. There were maybe eight years of it. I developed certain really complicated hand-painting techniques of which I made only short versions. For example, paint-ing the whole film a certain color and then smearing vaseline on it; and then taking a stylus and scraping designs off. It is possible to get a lot of spirals and curvilinear designs which I was never able to get by cutting off the masking tape; then spraying bleach into the place where the groove was. I made short samples of that sort of material. As I say, less than half of all that stuff is in my possession at this point. I also made alternate versions of a great number of scenes. Sometimes, in order to demonstrate how it was done, I made up special reels that partially had the masking tape still left on, and partially the first . . . Anyway, there are thousands of feet that were never printed, and several entire very long films. Many of those films are missing totally. I never edited at all, except to cut them down— except that second one, which shows the balls falling. Like I say, it was at least 1,200 feet long originally. It was then cut down to a

hundred feet to make it match "Guacha Guero." What Jonas Mekas calls "The Magic Feature" (#12) was originally about six hours long, and then it was edited down, first to a two-hour version, and then down to a one-hour version. There was also an enormous amount of material made for that picture. None of the really good material that was constructed for that film was ever photographed. There was a Noah's ark scene with really fantastic animals. I started out with the poorer stuff. The really good things were supposed to be toward the end of the film, but, being as the end of the film was never made . . .

On that Oz film, that expensive one, of course, I had quite a few people working; so that all kinds of special cut-outs were made that were never photographed. I mean really wonderful ones were made! One cut-out might take someone two months to make. They were very elaborate stencils and so forth. All of my later films were never quite completed. Most of the material was never shot, because the film dragged on too long.

Those two optically printed films were made for the Guggenheim Foundation. The three-dimensional one was made from the same batch of stencils as the color one. First, I got a camera from Frank Stauffacher, which is when those two films were made: The first is called *Circular Tensions* (#5); I forget what the other one is called. The black and white one (#4) preceeds that.

The black and white film (#4) begins with a shot of—

—a painting. It is a painting of a tune by Dizzy Gillespie called "Manteca." Each stroke in that painting represents a certain note on the recording. If I had the record, I could project the painting as a slide and point to a certain thing. This is the main theme in there, which is a-doot-doot-dootdoot-doot-doottadootdoot; those curved lines up there. See, ta-doot-doot-doot-doot-dootaloot-dootaloot, and so forth. Each note is on there. The most complex one of these is this one, one of Charlie Parker's records, I don't remember the name of it. That's a really complex painting. That took five years. Just like I gave up making films after that last hand-drawn one took a number of years, I gave up painting after that took a number of years to make; it was just too exhausting. There's a dot for each note and the phrases that the notes consist of are colored in a certain way or made in a certain path. The last paintings that I made were realistic things connected with the Tower of Babel. There was an extraordinary one of the control room of the Tower of Babel, which was built into a railway car leaving it. That painting was derived from a scene in Buster Keaton's film *The General*, where he chops out the end of the box car. A special film was projected on to the painting so that all the machinery operates.

In a number of cases I've made special screens to project films on. All those so-called early abstract films had special painted screens for them. They were made of dots and lines. All those things disappeared.

When I went to Oklahoma last year, I decided to devote my attention to the Indians. I really was honored to be able to record those things from the Indians. I decided to devote the rest of my life to that one thing. It was an unusual opportunity, because the Kiowa Indians are extremely conservative. They hadn't really been studied very much. Through various reasons, I got involved with them so that they told me all their myths and everything. It seemed better to devote the conclusion to that. That's why I'm living in this hotel room. Despite the fact that I can't afford the hotel room—it's fifty dollars a week—I am more or less able to spend my time doing that one thing. It is a very elaborate series of records, you know. We're devoting far too much time to accessory subjects. Naturally, I sort of goof on everything I'm doing.

I'm very puzzled about your fascination to visualize music.

That is an interesting question, isn't it? I don't know. When I was a child, somebody came to school one day and said they'd been to an Indian dance and they saw somebody swinging a skull on the end of a string; so that I thought, Hmmmm, I have to see this. I went to that. Then I fell in with the Salish around Puget Sound for a long time. I sometimes spent three or four months with them during summer vacation or sometimes in the winter, while I was going to high school or junior high school. It all started in grade school. In an effort to write down dances, I developed certain techniques of transcription. Then I got interested in the designs in relation to the music. That's where it started from. Of course! It was an attempt to write down the unknown Indian life. I made a large number of recordings of that, which are also unfortunately lost. I took portable equipment all over that place long before anyone else did and recorded whole long ceremonies sometimes lasting several days. Diagramming the pictures was so interesting that I then started to be interested in music in relation to existence. After that I met Griff B. and went to Berkeley and started smoking marijuana, naturally little colored balls appeared whenever we played Bessie Smith and so forth; whatever it was I was listening to at that time. I had a really great illumination the first time I heard Dizzy Gillespie play. I had gone there very high, and I literally saw all kinds of colored flashes. It was at that point that I realized music could be put to my films.

My films had been made before then, but I had always shown them silently. I had been interested in Jungian psychiatry when I was in junior high school. I found some books by Jung in the Bellingham Library. The business about mandalas and so forth got me involved. I would like to say I'm not very interested in Jung anymore: It seems very crude now.

Incidentally, this whole thing can probably be printed, if you want to print it for me, like some kind of poem. In that way, this constant shifting back and forth can be eliminated.

Later I borrowed a camera from Hy Hirsh. He had a pretty good camera, a Bell and Howell model 70-something, and had seen my films. The San Francisco Museum showed that one of the grille works (#4) that precedes *Circular Tensions*, and he came up and spoke. That's when I asked for a camera. I've never owned a camera; I've usually just borrowed one, then pawned it. That's always an embarrassing scene: trying to explain to the person where his or her camera is. I can remember Frank Stauffacher saying to me, "Now you haven't pawned the camera, have you?" He said this jokingly, but it was pawned. Usually, people get their cameras back, eventually. My later films were made with one that belonged to Sheba Ziprin. The *Mysterioso* film (#11) and the long black and white film (#12) were shot with her camera, which is now in a pawn shop in Oklahoma City. The main parts of my film in Oklahoma last year were shot on a camera that belonged to Stuart Reed. That camera is in a barber shop in Anadarko, Oklahoma, where Mr. A.'s Wollensak also is, unfortunately.

After I first stopped making films, I made those paintings that you point at. Unless you've seen those, it's hard to describe what they really are. They are at least as good as the films. I'd been able to hear Charlie Parker and Thelonious Monk, both of whom had come to San Francisco but wanted to make one final thing, another painting of Thelonious. When I came to N.Y.C., I realized that it would be impossible to make it in the form of a painting, because his music was so complex, and it would be better to make a film. I hadn't made films for at least five years by then. #10 was a study for the *Mysterioso* film. Generally speaking, those films were made by trying to collect interesting pictures, cutting them out, and then filing them. I had enormous files possibly only 2 or 3 per cent of which was shot. I had worked on this one thing for twenty years, having collected a lot of that stuff before; but then, when I left San Francisco, I gave it to Broughton, because I felt that he might do something with it; but he obviously never did.

After I came here I started filming again. Toward the end, I had everything filed in glassine envelopes: any kind of vegetable, any kind of animal, any kind of this that and the other thing, in all different sizes. Then file cards were made up. For example, everything that was congruent to that black and white film (#12) was picked out. All the permutations possible were built up: say, there's a hammer in it, and there's a vase, and there's a woman, and there's a dog. Various things could then be done—hammer hits dog; woman hits dog; dog jumps into vase; so forth. It was possible to build up an enormous number of cross references.

This was all written on little slips of paper, the file cards—the possible combinations between this, that, and the other thing. The file cards were then rearranged, in an effort to make a logical story out of it. Certain things would have to happen before others: Dog-runs-with-watermelon has to occur after dog-steals-watermelon.

I tried as much as possible to make the whole thing automatic, the production automatic rather than any kind of logical process. Though, at this point, Allen Ginsberg denies having said it, about the time I started making those films, he told me that William Burroughs made a change in the Surrealistic process—because, you know, all that stuff comes from the Surrealists—that business of folding a piece of paper: One person draws the head and then folds it over, and somebody else draws the body. What do they call it? The Exquisite Corpse. Somebody later, perhaps Burroughs, realized that something was directing it, that it wasn't arbitrary, and that there was some kind of what you might call God. It wasn't just chance. Some kind of universal process was directing these so-called arbitrary processes; and so I proceeded on that basis: Try to remove things as much as possible from the consciousness or whatever you want to call it so that the manual processes could be employed entirely in moving things around. As much as I was able, I made it automatic.

I must say that I'm amazed, after having seen the black-and-white film (#12) last night, at the labor that went into it. It is incredible that I had enough energy to do it. Most of my mind was pushed aside into some sort of theoretical sorting of the pieces, mainly on the basis that I have described: First, I collected the pieces out of old catalogues and books and whatever; they made up file cards of all possible combinations of them; then, I spent maybe a few months trying to sort the cards into logical order. A script was made for that. All the script and the pieces were made for a film at least four times as long. There were wonderful masks and things cut out. Like when the dog pushes the scene away at the end of the film, instead of the title "end" what is really there is a transparent screen that has a candle burning behind it on which a cat fight begins—shadow forms of cats begin fighting. Then, all sorts of complicated effects; I had held these off. The radiations were to begin at this point. Then Noah's Ark appears. There were beautiful scratch-board drawings, probably the finest drawings I ever made—really pretty. Maybe 200 were made for that one scene. Then there's a graveyard scene, when the dead are all raised again. What actually happens at the end of the film is everybody's put in a teacup, because all kinds of horrible monsters came out of the graveyard, like animals that folded into one another. Then everyone gets thrown in a teacup, which is made out of a head, and stirred up. This is the Trip to Heaven and the Return, then the Noah's Ark, then The Raising of the Dead, and finally the Stirring of Everyone in a Teacup. It was to be in four parts. The script was made up for the whole works on the basis of sorting pieces. It was exhaustingly long in its original form. When I say that it was cut, mainly what was cut out was, say, instead of the little man bowing and then standing up, he would stay bowed down much longer in the original. The cutting that was done was really a correction of timing. It's better in its original form.

#13 had all the characters out of Oz in it. That was assembled in the same way: I naturally divided Oz up into four lands because Oz consists of the Munchkins, the Quadlings, the Gillikins, and the Winkies; and then the Emerald City is in the middle; that is where the wizard's balloon had landed. I had built that thing many times as a child. I had fairly severe hallucinations, and I had built something called my Fairy Garden for many years. I actually used to see little gnomes and fairies and stuff until I was seven or eight. It's a typical psychic phenomenon; I mean, I wasn't nutty or anything; all children see that stuff. Up until I was eighteen or so, I worked hard on my Fairy Garden and then started building Oz. It was a fairly large place, because we had blocks and blocks of property in Anacortes. I built Oz a number of times; the final form, though, was for this film. It was to be a commercial film. Very elaborate equipment was built; the animation stand was about the size of a floor and exactly fourteen feet high. Oz was laid out on it, then seven levels, built up. It was like the multiplane camera of Disney, except that I was using a Mitchell camera that moved around. That's how I got into so many difficulties. Van Wolf had not paid rent on the camera, which was a thousand dollars a week. He was the producer, but he was taking far too many pills to do much but try to wiggle out of situations that developed. He got various people to pay for it: Huntington Hartford, Harry Phipps, Peggy Hitchcock, Elizabeth Taylor, and so forth invested in the film.

It was divided into different things. I ditched the Munchkins, Quadlings, Gillikins, and Winkies in their original form. What I was really trying to do was to convert Oz into a Buddhistic image like a mandala. I can't even remember what those lands were. One of them was Hieronymus Bosch Land: All of Bosch's paintings were carefully dissected. Another one was Microscopia taken from the books of Haeckel, who was the Viennese biological artist and very wonderful. The things he made are just marvelous; he picked out every possible grotesque object that there was. There was another land that was entirely made out of flesh. Enormous vistas for miles were made out of naked people from dirty mags. That would have been a nice film! Most of my material was prepared for it, and over six hours of tests were shot to get the apparatus to operate correctly. Only the little piece in the drawer there was ever synchronized to the music. In this particular section, the Ballet Music from *Faust*, the Tin Woodman performs magic before leaving for the Emerald City. The sound track was made up for the whole film.

Dr. Leary had me interested in that black-and-white film (#12), although, you realize, that *Heaven and Earth Magic*, whatever it's called, was a color film at that point. It ran through a special machine that projected slides. This is the first one that occurs: As the first head is on the screen, the slide of the same image is projected around it. There was a fader that obscured the screen out at the edges. You don't realize that it's an oblong image; it's just that there's another head the same as this—that's the telephone operator who made the greatest number of phone calls in the United States in some particular year. Where everything dissolves into the bridge, you see it's taking place on the moon; when the machinery is all operating, it's inside a watermelon. The slides themselves run through another color apparatus, and the seats in the theater were to be on some kind of electrical contact or rubber pads so that, as the audience looked at the film, if a certain number of them would lean in one direction, that would activate little lights in the projection booth which indicated that the audience who were in dentist chairs, watermelons, and so forth, were thinking about a watermelon or about a dentist chair, and so forth. Then I would slip that slide in, since any one of the slides could go with any portion of the film. They are now in an order that was convenient. It was an attempt to employ feed-back phenomena. It was executed to a degree in Steinway Hall. Mr. Phipps set up a sort of presentation there. The whole thing was set up, and I arbitrarily guessed what the audience was thinking of from their responses. We didn't have any special chairs for them to sit in though.

I never did finish that sentence about the relation of Surrealism to my things: I assumed that something was controlling the course of action and that it was not simply arbitrary, so that by *sortilège* (as you know, there is a system of divination called "sortilege") everything would come out all right. *#14* was made on this basis. Although I kept a record that such and such was shot in such and such an area of the screen, it was completely arbitrary.

Was it your decision to leave the Kodak leader between rolls of film?

I stole that idea from Andy Warhol. Everything that was shot was put in. A great number of images are missing. The stuff to which the most effort was devoted doesn't even show at all. A very large amount of material for some reason just isn't on the film. Peter Fleischman, who made that last film with me, and I spent weeks shooting objects that must have been all underexposed. I assumed, when Ansco said that the film had a rating of 300, that it did have a rating of 300. It doesn't; it has a rating of, perhaps, 100. Most of what was shot at the beginning and the end of the film disappeared because of that. The central portion was not developed for a long time; it was left lying around in the hot weather for about six months, so that it faded out and became white. I like the effect of the thing: It's all black at the beginning and the end, white in the middle; it looks good. Mr. Casper at Filmtronics made extremely good prints of the middle part. They are better than the original, but, nonetheless, it didn't come out anything like I'd expected it to.

I started to get people for a film some months ago . . . how did that start? I think I asked Andy if he wanted to make a film, and he said, "Yeah!" So I said, "Look, can I have $300?" He said, "Yeah." Who was it I asked next? I think Jack Smith. Then Robert Frank. At that point, it seemed ridiculous to make an underground movie, but to make a really elaborate superunderground movie for showing in neighborhood theaters. That would be the only one I would make. The project keeps bogging down, basically because I haven't been able to find anybody that knows enough about films in regular theaters. Arthur and Hugh Young have the money for it. I called them in a drunken condition and asked them for two million dollars, and Arthur said they perhaps would do it if they thought there were any possibility of producing an actual thing. In fact, I called them last Wednesday or Tuesday again, and they have been waiting all this time to look at films. They are interested in astrology. It is necessary to get some handsome producer to produce the film; not to produce money but to decide whether it's to be a short feature, or a short, like a Bugs Bunny length, so it can be distributed in first-run theaters.

It would be like a trip around the world. Various people would come in. It would be marvelous; for instance, if Andy were able to supervise maybe a twenty-minute color picture of Mount Fuji, but with a really good cameraman and technicians and everything so it would be really his beauty. Stan Vanderbeek was going to work on it. What he would do would be to go to northern Australia and animate aboriginal bark paintings. It would be produced eventually. Mr. Young once sent me a lavish check because he didn't like *Taras Bulba*. I'd called him the night before asking for money to go to Hollywood to try to salvage the Oz film. He said, "No, no, no, no, we're going to the movies, we're going to the movies, we don't have any time to talk with you now, Harry. And we're not interested in films. And anyhow you're drunk. You're calling me a fart." However, the next morning, a check did come in the mail, and he wrote, "We didn't like *Taras Bulba* at all, and we decided to see if you could do better." However, I took the money and went to Miami Beach to see Peter's mother, instead of going to Hollywood. I've been afraid to phone them for a long time.

I don't think I'll make any more animated films. They're too laborious and bad for the health. Sitting under those lights for hours is terrible. I've made enough of those; just like I've made enough hand-drawn films. I would like to make an "underground" movie that could be shown everywhere in little towns, because it was seeing art films, or whatever they used to call them, that first got me interested in these things. Now there must be lots of kids all over the world that would make films if they saw some of the things that are being made now.

There was another very good series of films I saw during the late 1920's. It always started with coming up to a door that had a little grille work in it, a mysterious little thing; the going in there, through it. Isadora Duncan was in one of those. You'd go through this door, and then there would be some Turkish or Chinese exotic operations. Those and the Fu Manchu movies were the ones that influenced me most. Naturally, I would like to make some kind of artistic film that would be helpful to the progress of humanity. And that's the best one I can think of. There's no doubt in my mind that eventually someone is going to make a so-called underground movie that will revive Hollywood as Kenneth Anger writes of it.

KENNETH ANGER'S SCORPIO RISING

BY CAROLEE SCHNEEMANN

No. 32, Spring, 1964

Risen. Before our eyes; this journey carries us beyond where are seated, beyond the screen which we view, and which views us!

Did you see why Love demanded Death? (Priapus shadowing Narcissus in ecstatic addiction, in sadistic fury. It is comprehensible only by the interchange of substances: silver spurs, oily gears, jeweled signals, iron tools, shafts and pipes; their leather torsos, their bodies bound—corseted in silver chains, marked by buttons and buckles; all narrowing parts tied, tightened, tense—as voluptuously indented, shaped, and decorated as their motorcycles are. Follow leather the length of the leg, leather sheathing the foot—the heavy heel reaches the pedal. Image: man and machine as unified, ominous force.)

There is a texture for torture, it builds through whiplash color and speed of lights. Frame by frame each detail grows as intricately as Rodin's "Gates of Hell" remembered in the movement of our own musculature. Watch the steady, incalculable exposure of gesture: the men, their machines, rooms, objects, landscape. (Instance: the flashlight held, poised between his legs, will sweep the dark temple of initiation—flag phallus, twitching legs, helmet. . . . . Swastika!)

Scorpio: Diurnal, centering the Queen in relation to Mars; under Autumn and Swords, in the realm of the Ox—THE LIGHTNING STRUCK TOWER. (Dark Major Arcana, a psychosexual arcana.)

Do not imagine the destruction is not your own.

The Scorpion is "falsely reputed to sting itself to death if encircled with fire." Poisoned sting. Eighth sign. (We need at least eight!) "Having an elongated body and a narrow, segmented tail bearing a venomous sting at the tip. Bib. a kind of scourge, prob. one armed with metal points. 1. Kings xii. II. Something which incites to action like the sting of an insect."

These images subsume a camera eye; where is Anger? *Scorpio Rising,* so complete to the eye it is impossible to establish the physical actions of "making the film," rather some sense of it sprung complete, in its complex rays and subtle ironies of terror and love, from a lucid dream moving more deeply into consciousness than any intention could provide. Each image and all its details structure a cumulative effect—the total form of the film being implicit in any detail of it. Penetrating visual relationships grow like an organism to an historical/social revelation, inevitable and totally shocking. We recognize that gratuitous curse, the wondrous necessity to juxtapose and combine Christ and Brando—blinding, constructing covenant of division (that split down the center of Western man); they emerge in the film as if they were creations of Anger, insights out of his own body by which we recognize a bridge of psychic torment where energy erupts corrosively and wildly in proportion to its own constraint. The appearance of the "Nazi" regarding the plump sacks of money is not more fantastic than the linkage of love-and-death racing the cyclists, or of the pastry pink and green little boys in the comic strip fragment: "Why haven't our folks gotten together?", or the pin-ups on the wall before which a man's blond head rises.

Motorcyclists. The perfidious shine of their ornaments (depravity—embedded in forms as various and dense as visual worlds of Goya or Bosch). Objects keep striking the eye with a shiny, metallic grace, clear metals and plastic and brilliant glass caught in a mosaic of dis-ease; spun, punned in wheels and spokes of light, ground into chrome and aluminum, leather jackets, fragments of photographs and newspaper clippings. Rock-and-roll sound leads the senses—an even record spin—in three minute belts climaxed with a red light flashing synchronization of all the sound durations. (Our own "dance" music! *Scorpio's* soundtrack more clear and new than those same scratchy disks we hear spun for love or oblivion.)

The vision is not "symbolic"; it is fleshed, concrete, drawing the metaphoric life-line from every visual unit in tight, dense webs. The beautiful intelligence of Anger's eye causes conjunctions of all-sense response on viewing. The motorcyclists are actual; we are convinced of their every gesture, they pull themselves into the lens, into our eyes harnessing our energies by their own. There is no protection from them. . . . . We are where they are! Demons of potential violence and formalized destruction; we follow as we endure our own nightmares of impotence and rage. The covenant of men. The poisonous mythos. (Christ and his disciples—the mild ones; cyclists/ fascists—the wild ones.) That old god submitted to his cross, and these willful ones struggle to intensify their destruction by his own —bearing his cross against their sex.

It makes apparent what can be made apparent in no other way; we understand what we had not understood:

(Contexts of warded-off homosexuality or sado-masochism or the identification of the total personality with the phallus "not in the service of love but (as) an instrument of aggression and vengeance."

> "The combination of phallic narcissism and phallic sadism and simultaneous compensation of passive and anal homosexual strivings makes for the most energetic characters. Whether such a type turns into a creative genius or a large-scale criminal depends largely on the social atmosphere and the possibilities it provides for an outlet of the energy in sublimated form."

> —WILLIAM REICH, "Some Circumscribed Character Forms," *Character Analysis*

SMITH MYTH

BY KEN KELMAN

No. 29, Summer, 1963

They wanted an article quick in time for this issue, and I guess I understand why. Dog nose when the next will come out, and by then there may be no more Flaming Creatures or even tamer ones like you and me. We may be all censored out.

It is not without misgivings that I write (apart from those about scribbling, forgive me, for speed's sake). After all, Jack Smith's *Flaming Creatures* is one of the "four works that make up the real revolution in cinema today" (Mekas, J.), and I don't even dig the other three. There is the *Queen of Sheba Meets the Atom Man*, a sort of Rice serial to be continued, perhaps too Taylor-Made, and which tried to be, but does not seem, very fresh or spontaneous, because the incidents are poorly invented; and when (if) it is completed, it will be no *Flower Thief*. There is *Little Stabs at Happiness*, open to the same above charge, but less so, and freer swinging, and possessed of much fine image. There is *Blonde Cobra,* which I attended but missed. Whenever I looked at the screen I saw black. I was later informed that I had just picked the wrong times to look, that pictures were truly interspersed with this nothingness. This film is supposed to be "the masterpiece of the 'Baudelairean cinema,'" and I can only surmise that I must have (not) seen a heavily cut version.

What all four movies have in common are Jack Smith, wild and perverse sexuality, prankish improvisation, costumes related to all previous elements, and camera work loose as a goose. All, except *Queen of Sheba,* are further characterized by the use of sentimental old-time pop music, which adds an extra note of perversity and decadent romanticism to the previous, chaotic, lush, exotic imagery.

What distinguishes *Flaming Creatures* from the rest, ontologically, is that Smith is not in it but behind it. He acted in the others, he photographed this one; photographed it in the same Neo-Anglo-Baudelairean style, used the same corny yearn-of-the-century music. But *what* distinguishes this film from the others, qualitatively, is that Smith imposed upon the whole a sense of purpose, an intensity of feeling. His movie beats with total life. It is not a mere collection of whimsical actions or striking images. It is a realized vision. The others have the same style, but not the imagination, the articulateness, the poetic concentration.

I cannot support my reactions with lengthy analysis, or even detailed description, having only seen *Flaming Creatures* once, and stretching my neck to do so. But I will suggest what specifics I can to you and to myself, why I so admired that movie.

When I spoke of its vision, I meant primarily this: a glorification of what tamer creatures would call the "perverse" pleasures, the "violent" joys, the "dark" raptures. When I spoke of its realization, I meant the art by which these pleasures and raptures were projected, in every sense of that word, so large and clear that we who never shared or saw the things themselves and never could see and share them on the screen, because they were so large and clear that those who acted those pleasures and raptures must have, looking at themselves in black and white, known themselves transfigured.

And how was this achieved? First, by clearing the viewer's imagination of all mere distractions; which is to say, leaving nothing trivial to the imagination, no mere piece of flesh. Nothing is hidden, and our imaginations are liberated to a higher realm than the suspense of Hollywood titillation. That is the realm of myths and beauties, myths and beauties invoked to more than "sublimate" the "obscenities" displayed, myths and beauties evoked through obscenities. And I too will try to get at those splendors, through those degeneracies.

Here is one. A tremendous rape scene where a creature (I thought it was a woman, but Smith said a hermaphrodite) is violated in innumerable ways, with fantastic violence, other creatures swarming all over him/her, twisting its tits, scratching, using the armpits, sucking, ad infinitum. All this is heightened by a sound track of enormous dissonance, a screeching heretofore associated with obvious agonies of introspective serious experimental films. But here it is like the end of *Duck Soup*, when the standard Hollywood spectacular stock shots of stampeding giraffes, swarms of birds, racing boats, fire engines, speeding police cars, vine-swinging monkeys, etc., etc., are combined hilariously in a mock heroic montage in response to Groucho's appeal for "Help!" The parodistic effect is there, but the horrible sounds are also part of the real violence and sadism of the scene.

Here is another. Out of a close-up coffin, appear two long thin hands. Then a gaunt blond head. The whole creature then emerges in white evening gown, the kind of thing Marilyn Monroe used to wear, and indeed seems to mimic her movements (Smith said it wasn't MM as far as he knew, though it was indeed funnier that way). The resurrected one discards its funereal lilies, slinks around, makes love to another creature, sinks its teeth into the lover's neck thereby confirming our first suspicion of classic vampirism, and finally is seen with gown above waist, shaking its penis.

Other penises are waved right at us at other points, in big close-ups.

Another noteworthy episode is the rapturous passage toward the end where the camera shoots straight down at a spinning creature in black gown, probably male, head tilted back, smiling with vivacious insolence right at us, spinning, spinning; which wondrous images alternate with ground-level shots of ornate orgiasts on the floor.

The film ends with the hermaphrodite star shaking its bare breast at us for a long time.

And now you must think as those who saw the film did, that it's pretty dirty and unredeemed. I would more than agree with part of that. It's *beautiful* dirty. But it is also redeemed, and I will try now to demonstrate that, to demonstrate other levels, and high ones, on which his movie moves.

I will state flatly that I believe this flicture echoes with ancient ritual chants, with Milton and with Dante. It transpires in no setting, no place, no time. In this context, the writhing figures which ornament this timeless place with splendid blacks and whites are reminiscent of Dante *à la* Doré. But myth is piled on myth and none insisted upon. It is an inferno where these creatures flame; but their fierce joy makes it a paradise, too. All hope is abandoned, as in Dante's inscription, but not all pleasure. Not only hope, but all pretense, all morality, all except naked existence, desire, and its heedless fulfillment.

And the realization dawns that these are not only suffering mortal sinners doomed through eternity; but also triumphant gods, not victims, but enjoyers, of immortality. This is supported by many aspects of the creatures: As gods transform themselves, they too have this power, which is, of course, related to the prodigious transvestism that occurs throughout; and they are sexless, or of all sexes, like gods; and their powers of pleasure, renewal, survival, as in the rape scene which mortals could hardly endure, more than borders upon the omnipotent.

This Olympian excess suggests mainly the classic myths, but others are invoked, other gods or demi-gods, like the vampire mentioned before, which significantly appears at its very moment of resurrection. And speaking of vampires, the film as a whole could be related to another unholy matter, and seen as a sort of Black Mass (a mass of magnificent blacks and whites, too); for the orgies are pervaded by a ritualistic quality; their spontaneity is calculated, too; their wildness always freezes into friezes of memorable graphic power.

But I still have not touched what strikes me as perhaps the most impressive mythic evocation of all; for the very scope and scale of sin becomes demonic in a Miltonian sense, and *Flaming Creatures* might be subtitled *Pandemonium Regained*, a paean not for the Paradise lost, but for the Hell Satan gained (and there is plenty of pandemonium in the other sense, too, which *pun* fits well with the multiplicity of ambiguities and ambivalences running through the film and culminating in the ultimate confusion of male and female flesh, the breast and penis shaken interchangeably).

That's the myth, now here's the truth: It all takes place in Montezland (shades of Montezuma, sheiks and shrieks, and all the perfumes of Araby) or a more beautiful irrational facsimile thereof, and see *Flaming Culture* #27 for the site, the sight itself in glorious black and white. That this peculiar myth should evoke those more standard ones is impressive as Hell to me.

Now do you believe the film is rich? No, no conclusion, I'm in a rush. Apart from my figurative first paragraph, you may wonder, was there any real reason not to wait, to write at more leisure and length for a later edition? Yes. I think the film should get quick praise, because maybe some people who saw it will see it again, or anew, in that private revival we all can project in the dark at the top of our heads. So if you were one of the merely appalled, repelled, cold eyes at the Bleecker Street Theater that night, try now to resee.

When the first show was over, a clique, a claque of six or so, back on the west side applauded. And I, all alone, east of the aisle up frontish, applauded, amid the numb and blind. Amid the tame, I halted, oppressed by their inertia, paused, vacillated, considered for two beats of silence or three, before I clapped solo and thus no doubt branded myself a clappy pervert, crap happy degenerate, slobbering sadist, or, even, perhaps Jack Smith. Alone I applauded, and wondered who dreamed that I did just because the film was beautiful. So if you were there, reconsider. Fan the *Flaming Creatures*. They're there in back of your eyes. You missed them when they were in front. That's why I wrote this now, instead of later; they might still be bright enough.

Film critics are writers and they are hostile and uneasy in the presence of a visual phenomenon.

—JACK SMITH

INTERVIEW WITH PETER KUBELKA

BY JONAS MEKAS

No. 44, Spring, 1967

ABOUT THE IRRELEVANCY OF THIS INTERVIEW

Jonas Mekas: Should we concentrate specifically on your latest film, *Unsere Afrikareise,* or should we also talk about the European avant-garde?

Peter Kubelka: No, I cannot talk about the European film avant-garde at all, because there is nothing there that I respect. When you transcribe this interview, you should state that nothing I say has anything to do with my films. I have, I feel a very great need to communicate. I work hundreds and hundreds of hours for one particular minute in my films, and I could never produce such a minute by talking. I want, therefore, my talk to be completely irrelevant. Because, otherwise, it might just spoil what I have to say through my films. The real statement that I want to make in my world is my films. Everything else is irrelevant.

Jonas: You mean, there is nothing that we can say about *Unsere Afrikareise* at all?

FILMS—DOCUMENTS FOR THE FUTURE GENERATIONS

Kubelka: Yes, we can talk. There are certain things that could be said. For instance: What I had in mind, with *Unsere Afrikareise,* was to leave a document for the future generations, when all this our life will be over . . . I thought this is a document. Of course, it may seem like a poem. Of course, it has very lyrical form—but this is document, too. My film is a document for future generations. There is nothing that has to be said with it. It just can't be said.

Jonas: It is interesting that Andy Warhol, too, considers his films—even films like *Sleep*—as documents for the future generations. Once he said to me: Wouldn't it be great today to have films made in the year 1266—a film of a man's shoulder, for instance, or his ass, to see how differently people looked 700 years ago.

GETTING DISTANCE TO OUR EMOTIONS THROUGH ARTICULATION AND ART

Kubelka: Did he say that? Yes. It's true. Then there is a second thing that I would like to say. I work for this living generation. I want to help in aging mankind, to get it away from the stone age. Make it adult. I feel the mankind is still a very young child—if you can make such a comparison. I feel that the age of mankind now is that of a very young child. For example, it just begins to be articulate. These are the first stages where it's articulate. It's beginning to have a memory. History is very young. What we call history is not history but very subjective statements of single beings and not right at all, and very mystic and mysterious. Mankind is now just in the process of growing up a little bit, slowly, slowly. My films have a function (this goes for the African film)—I play with the emotions and try to tear the emotions loose from the people, so that they would gain distance to their emotions, to their own feelings. This is one of my main tasks: to get distance to the whole existence, you see . . . I have a lot of distance. I always had it, and I have too much, so I feel very lonely and I want to communicate. You see, you have this whole range of emotions and these mechanisms, how the emotions are created. When you see certain images or hear certain sounds you have certain emotions. So I must always cry when I see moving scenes, when I see the hero getting the first prize for the biggest round and they play the national anthem . . . I have to cry . . . or when they bury somebody, I have to cry. At the same time, I am angry at myself, because I know that it's just the emotional mechanism. So, with the African film, I do a lot of this, I trigger a lot of those mechanisms at the same time and create a lot of—at the same time—comic feelings, sad feelings.

THE MULTIPLE MEANINGS OF IMAGE AND SOUND IN *UNSERE AFRIKAREISE*

Jonas: Like the lion's death scene, when they are dragging him up on the truck—I think this is one of the saddest scenes I have ever seen. Or death of the giraffe—they are both very sad. They are pulling up this poor dead lion, and it's difficult to pull him up; it is a very sad shot. And the giraffe dies, falling on his side, and we hear this laugh, like sides splitting from laughing, I'm dying . . . these multi-level feelings.

Kubelka: This is achieved through the perfect synchronization of the music, did you notice that?

Jonas: Yes.

Kubelka: They move all in rhythm. There are many things that are not noticeable on first few viewings at all.

Jonas: Or the eye, when the dying lion lifts his eye and looks directly into the camera accusingly and forgivingly and then dies. If there is a great moment of cinema, this is one.

ECONOMY IN CINEMA: FRAME BY FRAME FILM-MAKING

Kubelka: Did you hear the music? When the lion looks at the camera, the music says (he sings): "You look at me, and I watch thee . . ."—this comes together, then. And this brings up the question of economy. When you have the public sitting there, you have a very short time that they are looking at you, and you must consider that the senses of the people now are the senses of the stone age: hunters and gatherers. They just have the senses to survive. Human beings are not in position to sit and be interested. All their senses have survival reasons. So you must count on the audience, which sits there and will only be attentive to things that they are vitally interested in, or they will give you just a certain amount of time. So, when you really want to communicate, you must be very economical with every part, and with every second. For me, film is the projection of still frames. My economy is one single frame and every part of the screen. So I feel that every frame that is projected too much makes the whole thing less articulate. So I always work in frames. Even the African film, which doesn't seem to be like that, because it's very natural, is worked frame by frame. I have twenty-four communication possibilities per second, and I don't want to waste one. This is the economy. And the same is with the sound. Because one of the major fields where cinema works is when sound and image meet. So, the meeting of every frame with the sound is very important. That means, you must have the same economy with sound as you have with the image.

Jonas: Let us suppose, one reasons this way: If we accept the proposition that we are still in the stone age, and if we now say something to these stone-age people in a sentence that is so concentrated and distilled, that every sound, every word, every letter in it means something—do you think they will understand it? Isn't it better to divide the message that you want to put across into five sentences? So that they would get it, in the long run? Because you say, you want to communicate; and you don't want to waste a single frame?

Kubelka: You see, I don't make any distinction between myself and others. I don't say, "The others are in the stone age, and I am not." I am in the stone age as well as the others. So, if it works for me, it should work for everybody.

Jonas: I see. That places everything in the proper perspective. Even *Unsere Afrikareise* is a stone-age product.

Kubelka: Yes, I try to get myself and everybody else away from the stone age. But you see, when you say that perhaps I should give more time to people—I do this through repetition. I want my films to be viewed many many times. (A note in the Film-Makers Cooperative *Catalogue* says that, when rented, each of Kubelka's films should be projected twice. On reels, there are two prints of each film spliced side by side—to help the projectionist.—Jonas) As I work a long time on my films, I don't want to lose them, I am not like many other artists who say, Oh, I made this long ago, and I have overcome it, and I don't like it anymore. I can still see all my films, even the very first one. Everything that I do must be so clear and dry and . . .

WHEN IS A FILM COMPLETED?

Jonas: Yes, we find this in cinema very often. Film-makers dislike or are indifferent to their early work. But we don't find this in poetry, for instance. A poet can write a poem, put it somewhere, and come back to it ten years later, after four volumes of his poems have come out, and say, Isn't it fantastic? Did I write it? It's so perfect. Or he may change a word or a comma or two. But not in cinema. The cinema doesn't yet have its working tradition and is still full of all kinds of inhibitions and paranoias: You can't do this, you can't do that . . . The tradition in poetry is that the poet perfects his poem before he lets it go, even if it takes his lifetime— but not in cinema. In cinema, the release time is dictated more by festivals than perfection.

I think there is something more to your concentrated messages than the wish to communicate. I think we always have two kinds of artists: the emotion—and the intellect, reason. You are on the side of intellect and reason; Jack Smith is on the side of emotion. In your art, everything has to have a "reasonable" meaning, otherwise you don't put it in. To Jack, he may put it in, even if he doesn't see the meaning, he may feel there is something to it anyway because it's beautiful. Even Brakhage is more emotion than intellect, despite his writings, which are dominated by intellect— although I am not so sure about that either.

Kubelka: I have been, in this sense, always very naive. I consider myself a naïve artist.

Jonas: So what are the others? . . . The others are primitives? . . .

Kubelka: Yes . . . What did we talk about? . . . What would they like to know?

Jonas: I don't know. My trouble is that I don't want to know much about anything. I prefer to make things or look at things. But to some people it's helpful. I guess, I also am a garbage collector.

DON'T SPEAK ABOUT A FILM UNLESS YOU'VE SEEN IT TWELVE TIMES

Kubelka: You think there is something in the African film that we could talk about?

Jonas: I have seen it only four times, so . . .

Kubelka: Twelve times is the beginning . . . Whenever I say something about my own work, I am always taken very seriously, because I am the person who says it. And I don't want that at all. I mean, what I say must be taken as a sort of chattering in the evening but not as a statement to go with my films. I want my films to be just alone. Of course, I am very happy if someone else says something. I have so many layers of meanings in my films that, of course, when I talk about one or two meanings, they may think that all the others are not important, and I don't want to give more weight to one layer and less to the other.

ON EDITING AND ON HOW THE FRAMES "HIT THE SCREEN"; ON METRIC RHYTHM

Jonas: It's interesting that the films that you brought back from the West coast are going into the same direction as yours. Like Bruce Lane's film. It is, no doubt, still very naive, but its language has already a degree of condensation and crispness that stands out. Another similarity: It's an edited film. You have noticed, probably, that the West coast film-makers in general, are more interested in post-shooting editing than those of the East coast. They edit their films.

There was a discussion, at the New York Film Festival, and Annette Michelson said that Brakhage's cinema or way of making films is like an extension of abstract expressionism, like De Kooning; that his art is not structured, etc.; it's action filming. And I said, at that time, that Brakhage's structuring of his films takes place inside of him—he has worked on it for many many years—so now his camera is like an extension of his body and is governed by the inner structuring—really, emotion, mind, and intuition blend together, and the hard work is not always on the editing or structuring table—*Songs* were structured in the camera. Brakhage did not begin his life as an artist the moment he pushed that 8mm button—he has been working on himself for years and years. Don't you think his method is a complete opposite of your method?

Kubelka: I esteem Brakhage's work very highly. And, for him, that's enough. But, for the imitators, it's not enough. It may not even be always enough for him.

Jonas: But then, *Dog Star Man* is an "edited" film.

Kubelka: I think Brakhage is very concerned with construction. He edits. I hope I have inspired him toward this, and I would very much like to see what comes out. He has inspired me very much in what concerns his EYES, his EYES—what comes through the lens, how he leads his lens. Really, it's something. He's an eye-opener, so to say.

This is a very interesting problem. Because even if you don't edit the film, the precision and the economy might be there. It might be—I mean. If the person who makes it has really the power to be articulate. All the same, I feel I can do more when I compress my material. I like these concentrates. You see, there is a very essential point for me: I always want to enjoy what I do. I look thousands of times at what I do. I want to give to myself these very very rich seconds, and I enjoy these minutes very much. There must be a lot of essential pleasure just in the films when they hit the screen—

I heard this expression yesterday, "to hit the screen," that's fantastic, in English. Hit the screen—this is really what the frames do. The projected frames hit the screen. For example, when you let the projector run empty, you hear the rhythm. There is a basic rhythm in cinema. I think very few film-makers—if there ever was one, I don't know—have departed making films from this feeling of the basic rhythm, these twenty-four impulses on the screen—brrhumm—it's a very metric rhythm. I thought, the other day, that I am the only one who ever made metric films, with metric elements. These three films, *Adebar*, *Schwechater*, and *Rainer*, are metric films. You know what I mean by metric? It's the German expression "Metrisches System." The classic music, for instance, has whole notes, and half notes, and quarter notes. Not frames as notes, but the time sections that I have in my films. I mean, I have no seventeenths and no thirteenths, but I have sixteen frames, and eight frames, and four frames, and six frames—it's a metric rhythm. For example, people always feel that my films are very even and have no edges and do not break apart and are equally heavy at the beginning and at the end. This is because the harmony spreads out of the unit of the frame, of the $\frac{1}{24}$th of the second, and I depart from this ground rhythm, from the twenty-four frames, which you feel, which you always feel. Even when you see a film by DeMille, you feel it prrrrr as it goes on the screen.

ON THE ESSENCE OF CINEMA

Jonas: Some people say, Cinema is Movement; some others say, Cinema is Light. Do you have anything to say on the "essence" of cinema?

Kubelka: Cinema is not movement. This is the first thing. Cinema is not movement. Cinema is a projection of stills—which means images which do not move—in a very quick rhythm. And you can give the illusion of movement, of course, but this is a special case, and the film was invented originally for this special case. But, as often happens, people invent something, and, then, they create quite a different thing. They have created something else. Cinema is not movement. It can give the illusion of movement. Cinema is the quick projection of light impulses. These light impulses can be shaped when you put the film before the lamp—on the screen you can shape it. I am talking now about silent film. You have the possibility to give light a dimension in time. This is the first time since mankind exists that you can really do that. To talk about the essence of cinema, it's a very complex thing. Of course, when you ask what's the essence of music, you can say one thing, and another, and another—there are many things in cinema. One is this great fascination that light has on man. Of course, cinema is still very flimsy, a pale thing, and it passes quickly, and so on—but still, as weak as it is, it is a very strong thing, and it has a great fascination just because you can do something with the light. Then: It's in time. It can be conserved, preserved. You can work for years and years and produce—as I do—one minute of a concentrate in time, and, ever since mankind existed, you never could do such a thing. And then—sound. The meeting of sound and image. And we come to this problem: Where does film become articulate? When does a language become articulate? Language becomes articulation when you put one word and another word. One word alone is one word alone, but, when you put two words, it's between the two words, so to speak, that is your articulation. And, when you put three words, it's between one and two, and between two and three, and then there is also relation between one and three, but two is in between.

Jonas: For Eisenstein it was collision, to you it's . . . ?

IT'S BETWEEN FRAMES WHERE CINEMA SPEAKS

Kubelka: Yes, it can be a collision. Or it could be a very weak succession. There are many many possibilities. It's just that Eisenstein wanted to have collision—that's what he liked. But what I wanted to say is: Where is, then, the articulation of cinema? Eisenstein, for example, said it's the collision of two shots. But it's very strange that nobody ever said that *it's not between shots but between frames.* It's between frames where cinema speaks. And then, when you have a roll of very weak collisions between frames— this is what I would call a shot, when one frame is very similar to the next frame, and the next frame, and the next frame, and the next frame, and the next frame—the result that you get when you have just a natural scene and you film it . . . this would be a shot. But, in reality, you can work with every frame.

Jonas: In *Afrikareise*, you had this shot, you see a river behind the trees, the trees, and whatever animal there is, in the river, slowly rising, a small action spot behind the trees, and nothing else really happens—it was the longest shot in the film it went for something like ten seconds. Almost a Warhol shot . . .

Kubelka: Yes, the crocodile shot. But this was on purpose. You see, I broke up this thing with *Schwechater.* The *Schwechater* was the first film that worked with the event of the frame. *Schwechater* film is very strong, strong, very strong optical event. And what is it? Just people drinking beer.

Jonas: Have you seen Len Lye's fifty-second automobile commercial? Nothing happens there either, except that it's filled with some kind of secret action of cinema.

Kubelka: Yes, I saw it in 1958. *Schwechater* was finished already by then. And then, this feeling, I never lost this frame-by-frame film-making. Also in the *Rainer*, I did it. And in the *Afrikareise*. But what I wanted in *Afrikareise* was to create a world that had the greatest fascination on the spectator possible. This world had to be very naturalistic, so that you could really identify and enter it. It's, therefore, that I want a big screen for it, so you can see the blood and the elephants and the women and the Negro flesh and all the landscapes. This was one thing. And the other thing was that I wanted to have it so controlled as if I had painted it or made up myself and I achieved that through this immense, immense, long work of thousands of hours of cataloging the whole material practically frame by frame. So there is this continuous correspondence between sound and image. After you see the film twelve or twenty times, then you notice that practically every optical event corresponds to the acoustic event.

THE SOUND IN *UNSERE AFRIKAREISE*

Jonas: Even that ten-second shot where we have . . . how many frames do we have? Almost 500 frames . . . after the fifth and sixth time, I may be noticing the sound, what it does, because as it was now, the first four times, I was watching most of the time the image . . . At least, I have no memory of the sounds in that scene.

Kubelka: Yes, there is sound. You hear the shot, and it makes a "puff" and misses the crocodile. But a bird flies. And then the man says: "Geh!" He is disappointed and amazed, you see. Then it makes again PUFF—and then he hits, you see the crocodile is hit, and he says "Na also!" that is, "Oh, finally!" "Nun also," "Na also," which could mean, if translated, "Finally, you did it." And he says it in a very . . . it could be meant for a completely different event. Like, for example, the zebra is hit mortally, and you hear a woman's voice who says "Auu!" as if a mosquito had just given her a little bite.

Jonas: Yes, I noticed that. I think it was during the third viewing that I really noticed that, and it was very funny, and sad.

Kubelka: But there are many hundreds of such things. I never want to make a funny scene, or a sad scene—I always have these

. . . I want them very complex, never one single feeling but many many feelings always. So, of course, it's funny, and, then, it's not funny at all, because, for the zebra, it's a tragedy, and you pity her. Then you have that other scene. Before the zebra appears, you have this mysterious, my miracle shot of the moon where you see first this long fruit, brown, and it has a very phallic form, and then it dissolves (but it's not a dissolve, it's just changing of focus) into the moon, this beautiful white moon, and then you hear this voice of the everything-knowing German professor of something that says "Die Erde," "The earth." But it's not the earth—it's the moon! And then both say, in chorus: "Die Erde ist terra," ("Earth means terra")—they bring in their Latin . . . and then, when you hear "terra,"—cut—and you see the terra, you see the dying zebra lying on the terra. You see then the real terra, then. It's black and grey and burned. And they shoot the zebra for the sixth time, because zebras don't die, you have to shoot them many times, because they have such a hard life, you see. And then she (zebra) says: "Auu." And the man says: "Aufstehen!"—"get up!"—and this is a reminiscence of the Bible, I often have such references . . .

Jonas: Lazarus?

Kubelka: Yes. It's exactly that. I have something like that in my first film also. The voice says, "Steh auf und geh!" meaning "Rise and walk." And then he says something about Jesus, he says, "Ich bin auch nur ein Beamter," which means "I am also nothing but an employee." I don't know, it's very difficult to talk about that, but it has to do with my childhood, my Bible reading, and Jesus, what he did, and so on, and I always imagined him as an employee of his Father, and so he says so in this film. Also, in the African film, there are some things that relate to the Bible in image and meaning. One is this "Aufstehen."

THE CONTROL OF THE COLOR,
AND THE MOMENTS OF STANDSTILL

Jonas: The brown, clay color of the film—was this the color of the actual footage, or did you do something to it?

Kubelka: Yes. I wanted a sort of monochrome through the whole thing. Sometimes I break it up. I make this very yellow grass when you see the Negroes walk, where the Negroes walk . . .

Jonas: Yes, that beautiful yellow. You made it that way?

Kubelka: Yes. This is like another world, then. In my films, there are moments when everything stands still. This is a very important thing for me. This is in all of my films. Some films as a whole are like that. These are moments of escape, from the burden of existence, so to say—moments where you are not human, nor something else—not an angel or something, but just *Out*, out of it, and when nothing happens, and nothing leads to this, and this leads to nothing, and there is no tension, and so on. This is the scene in the African film where just the Negroes walk. First, you have the Negroes walk, and you have the Austrians laughing, producing this incredible laughter, and the Negroes don't notice them, they just walk and walk in this yellow grass. And then, overpowered, or something by this thing, the laughter ceases, and, then, you hear nothing anymore, just a few birds quacking . . . and the Negroes continue walking, and, then, it's silent, and they walk on and walk, one from the left, one from the right—so this is one of those moments. You remember that?

Jonas: Yes.

Kubelka: It has no reason—you understand. It does nothing for the story; it doesn't say anything; I can not say what I really mean with that, but these moments are the biggest achievements for me— these are the moments that fascinate me always when I watch the films. In my first film, the moment is a love scene where this rather heavy guy with a cigar says, "Du wirst mir schon noch ver- fallen" ("You'll fall for me"), and the girl watches him. And, then, later in the film, you see them again, and the voice says, "Verfallen." And then there is another shot, and he says again: "Verfallen!" The other such moment is where this mannequin turns around, and this fat man comes in, and they watch each other. And, for example, on this, I can't speak at all, but these moments you can only create when you have this huge thing around them. But, for example, films such as *Schwechater*, are such moments as a whole. When you watch the *Schwechater*, I mean, it has abso- lutely no classical tension that goes up and down. Then, it doesn't say anything, it says nothing—because what you see are people drinking beer or something like that—but, really, what is the *Schwechater* film? You don't know. And yet, it fills you very much. Since I work on my films for such a long time, I always make my films sort of . . . how do you say "Geruest"? the thing that holds the house . . . maybe "skeleton"—something on which I can hang onto . . . something sustaining and life-keeping. The *Rainer* is very much like that. Oh, it was fantastic in Los Angeles; you should have seen this, really. Because they had very powerful loudspeakers.

Jonas: Was this at the Cinema Theater?

Kubelka: Yes. They had a screen as large as a house, and they had these powerful loudspeakers. The sound was like Niagara Falls, so loud—incredible, it was fantastic—and the lights, so strong—this was really the event that I wanted it to be. And with this element . . . Here it comes, this fascination of sound and light . . . And to have this element and, then, to be able to create a rhythmic construction with sound and image, which is so precise, on frames of a second—this gives me an incredible feeling. By the way, for *Schwechater*, my model, so to say, was running water, or a tree with thousands of leaves when the wind goes through—I was very concerned with these forms.

Jonas: When I was watching the *Rainer* film, I closed my eyes, at moments, and I could watch it with my eyes closed, as the light rhythms pulsated on and through the eyelids. One could say, that the *Rainer* film is the only film ever made that can be seen with your eyes closed.

Kubelka: Yes, Brakhage noticed that, too.

HOW MANY FILMS YOU HAVE TO MAKE TO BE AN ARTIST?

Jonas: How long is your total work now, how many minutes?

Kubelka: Twelve and a half; and one and a half; and one; and six and a half; and thirteen makes thirty-four and a half minutes.

Jonas: That makes about two minutes a year, no?

Kubelka: For the last fifteen years, I have been totally concentrating on cinema. I began in 1952. Yes, two minutes a year.

Jonas: How many frames? 2,880 frames per year.

Kubelka: This means, less than eight frames a day.

Jonas: That's plenty.

Kubelka: One is enough. When you really speak out, it must be enough. Eggeling spoke out, and he made only five minutes in his whole life. Anyhow, what I now plan is a very big thing.

Jonas: Fifteen minutes? . . . All your films are on 35mm?

ON SIXTEEN MILLIMETER FILMS

Kubelka: Yes. But *Afrikareise* is on 16mm. I am convinced now that I can do something in 16mm. I wasn't before. I am so happy about it.

Jonas: You saw the *Afrikareise* projected at the Cinema Theater, on a large theater screen, and it was good?

Kubelka: Yes. And the colors were much better than on 35mm. The colors of the negative reversal are so much better than the negative color, and, in 35mm, you have only negative and positive. I don't think I could have had these colors in 35mm. Therefore, I am starting my next film in 16mm. I feel now that I can do some things of which I always thought but which I couldn't do. After the African film, now, it comforted me very much. I have now the whole gamut I can use.

Jonas: You have really covered some ground, in your four films, from pure light, to live drama. *Unsere Afrikareise* contains, really, the dramatic cinema, novelistic cinema. It could be looked at as a short story—a film short story, because there are characters, people —they come through, each one comes through—it's like one of Joyce's short stories. One could look at it that way. One could look at it also in many other ways.

Kubelka: Whatever I learned from my films is in *Unsere Afrikareise.* I mean, my aim has always been to get articulate with film— because who really is articulate? This is just the beginning. I take time on my films. And really, you don't lose time. They say, if the film isn't finished in two years, it's too late, or something. I mean, when you work your whole life, and, then, you bring out something that speaks—it's time enough. It depends on what you do—this is the whole thing. But, when you really want to see and feel and communicate, and when you can really do it, as long as you work, it's all right; and, when you cannot do it, when you finished it, and it's not really finished—then everything is lost.

I thought that the African film will be finished in three months, when it began. And then, it was five years. Of course, I didn't work every day, and I couldn't work every day because I had no money— many things; and then the founding of the Film Museum came in between. But what's really true is that, these five years, I lived always with these images. I was always concentrated on this film, every day. There wasn't a day when I wasn't—I always lived in this film for five years. I told you already that I learned it all by heart, all the sound—I transcribed it first (I had fourteen hours of sounds recorded in Africa and three hours of film)—I still know this whole . . .

LEARNING THE FILM BY HEART

Jonas: Every sound that is in film, you know it by heart—with what image it goes . . .

Kubelka: Oh, yes, of course. But I know much more—I know all what it was before—

Jonas: . . . whatever you omitted, the whole fourteen hours of sound . . . and images . . .

Kubelka: Yes . . . Of course . . . Before I made this film, I learned it for a long time and scribbled every word—so I knew every word—but I also know the *Schwechater* film by heart, and everybody can know it by heart, this is something where . . .

Jonas: Like a poem . . .

Kubelka: Yes, and this is an interesting thing—because to learn by heart something is a very interesting thing. The easiest thing to learn by heart are those languages that you can produce with your body. I mean, you can sing a song, so you learn it by heart, and you can hear it. You can dance by heart. And you can learn a poem by heart. And you can beat the rhythm of the drum by heart. And so on. But when it comes to, say, architecture—this is the interesting thing: You can know architecture by heart; you can know a church or a skyscraper really by heart, and you can know the dimensions—and you have no means of transcribing it. And I don't mean the history—I mean the dimensions, you know the dimensions by heart.

Jonas: If your eye would have the power of recreation, you could almost recreate it. As a matter of fact, Mme. Blavatsky talks about it. Man can create anything he wants, if he knows it with his mind's eye . . . Like they could recreate this beer can . . . Or like the actors, how they train their memory, in the Stanislavsky school— you throw a few objects from your pocket on the table, for a second, then put them back into the pocket and now, describe each of them . . .

Kubelka: So, the same way with my films. For example, *Schwechater*, it's absolutely indescribable, all of them are indescribable, but you can know them by heart. You know exactly what will follow now, you see the forms. I really feel that, with cinema, we are really able to make a step forward. Film is the first of the synthetic arts—this is like the first automobile—it's the first art that is made with machines. Of course, the violin is also a machine, but . . .

I have begun establishing a language, and tradition, and so on, and, of course, I want to transmit all this to others. But what I really want other film-makers to have is the economy, and then the metric rhythms—I would like to see more film-makers working like that. Nobody really uses these rhythmic and akin-to-music qualities that the film has. For example, the *Schwechater* film, I might my-self make other films now in this technique. It's a pity. No, it's not a pity. I mean, the films are there. Imitations are no good. I really

feel that my films, especially from *Adebar* on, bring one step further on everything that has been done till now—because it has a greater control of the materials. I don't want to say "editing" any more. I say "construction." And here I think my substance is thinning . . .
October 1, 1966, New York.

SOME NOTES ON SLEEP

BY HENRY GELDZAHLER

No. 32, Spring, 1964

Andy Warhol's films conceal their art exactly as his paintings do. The apparently sloppy and unedited is fascinating. What holds his work together in both media is the absolute control Andy Warhol has over his own sensibility—a sensibility as sweet and tough, as childish and commercial, as innocent and chic as anything in our culture. Andy Warhol's eight-hour *Sleep* movie must be infuriating to the impatient or the nervous or to those so busy they cannot allow the eye and the mind to adjust to a quieter, flowing sense of time. What appears boring is the elimination of incident, accident, story, sound, and the moving camera. As in Erik Satie's *Vexations,* when the same twenty-second piece is repeated for eighteen hours we find that the more that is eliminated the greater concentration is possible on the spare remaining essentials. The slightest variation becomes an event, something on which we can focus our attention. As less and less happens on the screen, we become satisfied with almost nothing and find the slightest shift in the body of the sleeper or the least movement of the camera interesting enough. The movie is not so much about sleep as it is about our capacity to see possibilities of an aspect of film carried to its logical conclusion—*reductio ad absurdum* to some, indicating a new awareness to others. Andy Warhol wants to keep his editing to an absolute minimum and allow the camera and the subject to do the work. This, of course, cannot deny the special qualities of his personality; for it is Andy Warhol that holds the camera, and it is through his eyes that we see the scene. Minimal editing accounts for the roughness, the opposite of Hollywood's technical proficiency, and insists constantly that we are looking at a film. There is no chance of losing ourselves in an artificial world. There is strangely, no make-believe. In painting in the past fifty years, we have become increasingly aware of the limitations and special qualities of the medium: texture, two dimensionality, brush-stroke, and so on. Andy Warhol's film, in which we are constantly aware of the filmic process, sometimes even seeing the frames that end the reels, frames that any sophisticated movie maker would edit out, makes us aware of exactly the limitations and qualities of film itself. A more incident-filled story would draw our attention from the fact that we are seeing a film. *Sleep*, one of Andy Warhol's first movies, is an indication of what he will soon be able to do: make contentless movies that are exactly filmed still lifes with the minimum of motion necessary to retain the interested attention of the unprejudiced viewer.

THE COSMIC CINEMA
OF JORDAN BELSON

BY GENE YOUNGBLOOD

Only the fantastic is likely to be
true at the cosmic level.
—Pierre Teilhard de Chardin

No. 48–49, Spring, 1970

Certain phenomena manage to touch a realm of our consciousness so seldom reached that, when it is awakened, we are shocked and profoundly moved. It's an experience of self-realization as much as encounter with the external world. The cosmic films of Jordan Belson possess this rare and enigmatic power.

Basic to the enigma is the fact that Belson's work seems to reside equally in the realms of the physical and the metaphysical. Any discussion of his cinema becomes immediately subjective and symbolic, as we shall see. Yet the undeniable fact of their concrete nature cannot be stressed frequently enough. Piet Mondrian: "In plastic art, reality can be expressed only through the equilibrium of dynamic movement of form and color. Pure means afford the most effective way of attaining this."

The essence of cinema is precisely "dynamic movement of form and color" and their relationship to sound. In this respect, Belson is the purest of film-makers. With few exceptions, his work is not "abstract." Like the films of Len Lye, Hans Richter, Oskar Fischinger, and the Whitneys, it is concrete. Though a wide variety of meanings inevitably is abstracted from them, and though they do hold quite specific implications for Belson personally, the films remain concrete objective experiences of kinaesthetic and optical dynamism. They are, at once, the ultimate use of visual imagery to communicate abstract concepts and the purest of experiential confrontations between subject and object.

In their amorphous, gaseous, cloudlike imagery, it is color, not line, that defines the forms that ebb and flow across the frame with uncanny impact. It is this stunning emotional force that lifts the films far beyond any realm of "purity" into the most evocative and metaphysical dimensions of sight and sound. The films are literally superempirical—actual experiences of a transcendental nature. They create, for the viewer, a state of nonordinary reality similar, in concept at least, to those experiences described by the anthropologist Carlos Castaneda in his experiments with organic hallucinogens.

E. H. Gombrich: "The experience of color stimulates deeper levels of the mind. This is demonstrated by experiments with mescaline, under the influence of which the precise outlines of objects become uncertain and ready to intermingle freely with little regard to formal appearances. On the other hand, color becomes greatly enhanced, tends to detach itself from the solid objects and assumes an independent existence of its own."

Belson's work might be described as "kinetic painting," if not for the incredible fact that the images exist in front of his camera, often in real time, and, thus, are not animations. Live photography of actual material is accomplished on a special optical bench in Belson's studio in San Francisco's North Beach. It is essentially a plywood frame around an old X-Ray stand with rotating tables, variable-speed motors, and variable-intensity lights. Belson does not divulge his methods, not out of some jealous concern for trade secrets—the techniques are known to many specialists in optics— but more as a magician maintaining the illusion of his magic. He has destroyed hundreds of feet of otherwise good film, because he felt the technique was too evident. It is Belson's ultrasensitive interpretation of this technology that creates the art.

The same can be said for the sounds as well as the images. Belson synthesizes his own sound, mostly electronic, on home equipment. His images are so overwhelming that, often, the sound, itself a creation of chilling beauty, is neglected in critical appraisals. The sound often is so integral to the imagery that, as Belson says, "You don't know if you're hearing it or seeing it."

He regards the films not as exterior entities but, literally, as extensions of his own consciousness. "I first have to see the images somewhere," he says, "within or without or somewhere. I mean I don't make them up. My whole aesthetic rests on discovering what's there and trying to discover what it all means in terms of relating to my own experience in the world of objective reality. I can't just dismiss these films as audio-visual exercises. They obviously mean something, and, in a sense, everything I've learned in life has been through my efforts to find out what these things mean."

He has been a serious scholar of Buddhism for many years and has committed himself to a rigorous Yoga discipline. He began experimenting with peyote and other hallucinogens more than fifteen years ago. Recently, his interests have developed equally in the directions of inner space (Mahayana Buddhism) and outer space (interstellar and galactic astrophysics). Thus, by bringing together Eastern theology, Western science, and consciousness-expanding drug experiences, Belson predates the front ranks of avant-garde art today in which the three elements converge. Like the ancient alchemists, he is a true visionary, but one whose visions are manifested in concrete reality, however nonordinary it might be.

Teilhard de Chardin has employed the term *ultra-hominization* to indicate the probable future stage of evolution in which man will have so far transcended himself that he will require some new appellation. Taking Teilhard's vision as a point of departure, Louis Pauwels has surmised: "No doubt, there are already among us the products of this mutation or, at least, men who have already taken some steps along the road that we shall all be traveling one day." It requires only a shift in perspective to realize that Belson is taking those steps.

ALLURES

From Matter to Spirit

Originally a widely exhibited painter, Belson turned to film-making in 1947 with crude animations drawn on cards, which he subsequently destroyed. He returned to painting for four years and, in

1952, resumed film work with a series that blended cinema and painting *via* animated scrolls. The four films produced in the period 1952–53 were *Mambo, Caravan, Mandala,* and *Bop Scotch.* From 1957–59, he worked with Henry Jacobs as visual director of the legendary Vortex concerts at Morrison Planetarium in San Francisco. Simultaneously, he produced three more animated films, *Flight* (1958), and *Raga* and *Seance* (1959). *Allures,* completed in 1961, found Belson moving away from single-frame animation toward continuous real-time photography. It is the earliest of his works that he still considers relevant enough to discuss.

He describes *Allures* as a "mathematically precise" film on the theme of *cosmogenesis*—Teilhard de Chardin's term intended to replace cosmology and to indicate that the universe is not a static phenomenon but a process of becoming, of attaining new levels of existence and organization. However, Belson adds, "It relates more to human physical perceptions than my other films. It's a trip backwards along the senses into the interior of the being. It fixes your gaze, physically holds your attention."

Allures begins with an ethereal pealing of bells. A centrifugal starburst of pink, yellow, and blue sparks whirls out of a black void. Its points collect into clusters and fade. Bells become weird chimes; we sink into a bottomless orange and black vortex. An intricate pink mandala of interconnected web patterns spins swiftly into the distance. A caterpillarlike coil looms ominously out of infinity. We hear a tweetering electronic warble, a collection of threatening piano notes. Pink and yellow sparks wiggle vertically up the frame. Distant snakelike coils appear and fade. A tiny sun surrounded by a huge orange halo disintegrates. There are flying cometlike petal shapes.

Oscilloscope streak-dots bounce across the frame with a twittering chattering metallic noise. They form complex triangular and tetrahedronal grid patterns of red, yellow, and blue. Out of this, evolves an amorphous yellow-white pulsating globe of fire without definite shape. It vanishes, and a blue neon-bright baton rotates slowly into infinity.

"I think of *Allures,*" says Belson,

as a combination of molecular structures and astronomical events mixed with subconscious and subjective phenomena—all happening simultaneously. The beginning is almost purely sensual, the end perhaps totally nonmaterial. It seems to move from matter to spirit in some way. *Allures* was the first film to really open up spatially. Oskar Fischinger had been experimenting with spatial dimensions, but *Allures* seemed to be outer space rather than earth space. Of course, you see the finished film, carefully calculated to give you a specific impression. In fact, it took a year and a half to make, pieced together in thousands of different ways, and the final product is only five minutes long. *Allures* actually developed out of images I was working with in the Vortex concerts. Up until that time, my films had been pretty much rapid-fire. They were animated, and there was no real pacing—just one sustained frenetic pace. After working with some very sophisticated equipment at Vortex, I learned the effectiveness of something as simple as fading in and out very slowly. But it was all still very impersonal. There's nothing really personal in the images of *Allures*.

After the glowing blue baton vanishes, the screen is black and silent. Almost imperceptibly a cluster of blue dots breaks from the bottom into magnetic force-fields, which become a complex grid pattern of geometrical shapes superimposed on one another until the frame is filled with dynamic energy and mathematical motions. A screeching electronic howl accentuates the tension as galaxies of force-fields collide, permutate, and transmute spectacularly. Some squadrons rush toward the camera as others speed away. Some move diagonally, others horizontally or vertically. It's all strongly reminiscent of Kubrick's *2001*—except that it was made seven years earlier.

Elsewhere in the film, rumbling thunder is heard as flying sparks collect into revolving atomic structures whose nuclei emanate shimmering tentacles of tweetering multicolored light. At the end, we hear ethereal harp music as a pulsating sun, fitfully spewing out bright particles, reveals within itself another glimmering galaxy.

RE-ENTRY

Blastoff and Bardo

Re-Entry is considered by many to be Belson's masterwork. Completed in 1964 with a grant from the Ford Foundation, it is, simultaneously, a film on the theme of mystic reincarnation and actual spacecraft re-entry into the earth's atmosphere. Also, as Belson says, "It was my re-entry into film-making because I'd given up completely after *Allures*. Mostly for financial reasons. But also out of general dismay at the experimental-film scene. There was no audience, no distribution, there was just no future in it at that time."

Re-Entry is chiefly informed by two specific sources: John Glenn's first satellite orbit, and the philosophical concept of the *Bardo*, as set forth in the *Bardo Thodol* or *Tibetan Book of the Dead*, a fundamental work of Mahayana Buddhism. According to Jung, *Bardo* existence is rather like a state of limbo, symbolically described as an intermediate state of forty-nine days between death and rebirth. The *Bardo* is divided into three states: The first, called *Chikhai Bardo*, describes the psychic happenings at the moment of death. The second, or *Chonyid Bardo*, deals with the dream state that supervenes immediately after death, and with what are called *karmic illusions*. The third part, or *Sidpa Bardo*, concerns the onset of the birth instinct and of prenatal events.

With imagery of the highest eloquence, Belson aligns the three stages of the *Bardo* with the three stages of space flight: leaving the earth's atmosphere (death), moving through deep space (karmic illusions), and re-entry into the earth's atmosphere (rebirth).

The film, says Belson, "Shows a little more than human beings are supposed to see." It begins with a rumbling thunderous drone, possibly a suggestion of rocket lift-off. In a black void, we see centripetal, or imploding, blue-pink gaseous forms, barely visible as they rush inward and vanish. The sound fades, as though we have left acoustical space. After a moment of silence, the next sound is wholly unearthly: a twittering electrical pitch as vague clouds of red and yellow gases shift amorphously across the frame. Suddenly, with a spiraling high-pitched whine, we see a gigantic solar prominence (one of two stock-footage live-action sequences) lashing out into space, changing from blue to purple to white to red. Now blinding white flashes, as though we're passing the sun, and, suddenly, we're into a shower of descending white sparks that become squadrons of geometrical modules moving up and out from the bottom of the frame, warping and shifting to each side of center as they near the top.

Gene: Certain of your images appear in every film, like the geometrical, perspectival interference patterns. They're quite effective. Do you conceive them through some sort of mathematical concept?

Jordan: Those images in particular are derived from the nature of the device itself. But the images later in the film—the more nebulous ones, of more magnitude—they're more a question of personal vision. Discerning them, seeking them out, presents all sorts of possibilities by being receptive to them when I find them beneath my camera.

Gene: Are there other stock-footage sequences?

Jordan: Yes. You wouldn't recognize it, but there's a shot of the earth rolling by, as seen from a camera in a rocket. I excerpted a part of that film and doubled it, so it was mirrored Rorschach-like. That's for the re-entry to earth. The film leans heavily on such material. As a matter of fact, on the sound-track, there's actually John Glenn's radio conversation from his satellite to earth. He's saying something like "I can see a light." He was referring to Perth, Australia, as he passed over. Then, it shoots past the earth and the sun and goes off into a rather ambiguous area in which you have to cross over barriers of time and space, but also mental, psychological barriers as well. It's a kind of breakdown of the personality in a way. It sort of boils out, and, the next thing you know, you're in Heaven. You're surprised to be there. On the other hand, it's happening, you know.

The "boiling out" sequence is among the most dramatic in all of Belson's films. Suddenly, we hear a thunderous rumble, which increases in intensity until the bottom of the frame begins to turn pale manganese blue and cobalt violet, a gaseous boiling cloud that surges up over the frame turning alizarin crimson. We descend through it, as though it is being blasted upward by some explosive force far below. Image and sound increase to unimaginable intensity as though we're hurling through sheets of space fire in a cosmic heat belt. The spacecraft is out of our solar system and into another dimension. Death has occurred; we move into the second stage of the *Bardo*.

At a corresponding point in the *Bardo of Karmic Illusions*, the Sanskrit text reads: "*The wisdom of the* Dharma-Dhatu, *blue in color, shining, transparent, glorious, dazzling, from the heart of* Vairochana *as the Father-Mother, will shoot forth and strike thee with a light so radiant that thou wilt scarcely be able to look at it.*"

This of course could be interpreted as a supernova whose maximum intrinsic luminosity reaches one-hundred million times that of our sun. The image in Belson's film is somewhat like slow-motion movies of atom blasts in Nevada with the desert floor swept across by a tremendous shock wave. At another point, it appears as a sky of mackerel clouds suddenly set aflame and blown asunder by some interstellar force. Shimmering iceberg shapes of every hue in the spectrum dance like galactic stalactites against a sizzling, frying sound. This becomes a dizzying geometrical corridor of eerie lights almost exactly like the slit-scan *Stargate Corridor* of Kubrick's space odyssey—except that *Re-Entry* was made four years earlier.

Carl Jung describes the final stage of the *Bardo*: "The illuminative lights grow ever fainter and more multifarious, the visions more and more terrifying. This descent illustrates the estrangement of consciousness from the liberating truth as it approaches nearer and nearer to physical rebirth."

The images assume majestic dimensions. Seemingly millions of minute particles suggesting *mesons*—cosmic rays that survive in the atmosphere for only a millionth of a second—cascade in sizzling firestorms down from the top and up from the bottom in shards of viridian, ultramarine red, Thalo blue. There's a sense of unthinkable enormity. Finally, we see a white sun surrounded by a pulsating red halo, which is then obscured by vapors. "The film does manage to transport whoever is looking at it," says Belson, "out of the boundaries of the self. At that very moment is when the foundation slips out from under us and very rudely we're brought back to earth. It's all very much like the process of spacecraft re-entry. You're out there, free, totally free from the limitations of earthly distance, and, suddenly, you have to come back, and it's a very painful thing."

PHENOMENA

From Humans to Gods

Phenomena, completed in 1965, moved Belson closer to the totally personal metaphysical experience that culminated two years later in *Samadhi*. Also, *Phenomena* was the first film in which he abandoned allegories with spaceflight or astronomic subjects for a more Buddhistic exploration of psychic energies. It was primarily inspired by Buddha's statements in the *Diamond Sutra* and the *Heart Sutra*.

The film begins with electronically distorted rock music as curvilinear dish shapes of bright cadmium red, crimson, and cerulean blue expand frenetically. A glowing red neon coil pulsates to the music. Next we see—unique in Belson's work—a recognizable, though distorted figure of a man, then a woman, images shot from television through warped glass filters. They are obscured by a hailstorm of popping confetti-like flashes of red, white and blue on a black field. The music fades into tumultuous cheering throngs as a fiery red starburst erupts in a sky of cobalt blue, its rings expanding into individual thorny clusters.

Belson thinks of this sequence as

. . . an extremely capsulized history of creation on earth, including all the elements of man. It's the human sociological-racial experience on one level, and it's a kind of biological experience in the sense that it's physical. It's seen with the blinders of humanity, you know, just being a human, grunting on the face of the earth, exercising and agonizing. There's even a touch of the Crucifixion in there—a brief suggestion of a crown of thorns—a red ring of centers, each emanating a kind of thorny light cluster. The man and the woman are Adam and Eve, if they're anyone. I see them as rather comic at that point.

At the end, of course, it's pure consciousness, and they're like gods. The end of the film is the opposite of the beginning: It's still life on earth, but not seen from within, as *sangsara*, but as if you were approaching it from the outside of consciousness, so to speak. From cosmic consciousness. As though you were approaching it as a god. You see the same things but with completely different meaning.

In Buddhism, the phenomenal universe of physical matter is known as *sangsara*. Its antithesis is *nirvana* or that which is beyond phenomena. Within *sangsara* exists *maya*, Sanskrit for a magical or illusory show with direct reference to the phenomenon of nature. Thus, in the *Diamond Sutra*, Buddha equates *sangsara* with *nirvana* and asserts that both are illusory. This is the substance of Belson's remarkable film.

Suddenly and quite incongruously, we hear German *Lieder* singing (Belson: "The epitome of the ego personality"). A fabulously gorgeous organ-pipe lumia display dances across the frame, a shifting alignment of fluted columns of phosphorescent colors similar to the work of Wilfred and Charles Singletary and more recent light artists such as Julio le Parc. Though Belson calls it a "gaudy juke-box lighting effect," it is far more beautiful than its predecessors: vertical shafts of light through which move horizontal sheets of emerald, Prussian blue, rose madder, pale citrons.

The pillars of color melt with a crackling buzz, and slowly, liquid blobs of pigment solidify into one of the most spectacular images of Belson's films: a mosaic field of hundreds of hard-edge bullet-shaped modules in a serial grid. Each tiny unit constantly transforms its shape and color—from violet to Mars red to French ultramarine blue to mint green and zinc yellow. The staccato buzz flawlessly underscores the geometry, as though the modules are generating the sound as they converge and transform.

Suddenly, with a roar, the frame is shattered by a fiery light in a heaven of boiling multihued gases: a grim, sinister eruption that suggests, according to Belson, "Depersonalization, the shattering of the ego-bound consciousness, perhaps through death, perhaps through evolution or rebirth." This celestial storm of manganese blue and zinc yellow leads into a state of *kharmic illusions* with glacial floating *aurora borealis* lights of reds and yellow-whites, rainbow liquid cascades of exquisite sheerness.

Various states of matter rise above iceberg-like, sink and float away. This is followed by an intense *White Light* sequence with an ethereal Mother of Pearl quality, representing a state of total integration with the universe, of blinding superconsciousness. It culminates in an enormous roaring sphere of flaming gases. In the final sequence, against a descending drone, the void is shattered by a central light that throws out sweeping circular rainbows of liquid color moving majestically clockwise, collecting together, and lashing out again in the opposite direction until the ultimate fade.

SAMADHI

Documentary of a Human Soul

For two years from 1966 through 1967, assisted by a Guggenheim Fellowship, Belson subjected himself to an extremely rigorous Yoga discipline of ascetic hermitage. He severed emotional and family ties, reduced physical excitements and stimulations, reversed his sensory process to focus exclusively on his inner consciousness and physical resources. The result of this Olympian effort was *Samadhi*, certainly among the most powerful and haunting states of non-ordinary reality ever captured on film. "It's a documentary of the human soul," he says.

> The experiences that led up to the production of this film and the experiences of making it totally convinced me that the soul is an actual physical entity, not a vague abstraction or symbol. I was very pleased when I finally saw how concentrated, how intense *Samadhi* is, because I knew I had achieved the real substance of what I was trying to depict. Natural forces have that intensity: not dreamy but hard, ferocious. After it was finished, I felt I should have died. I was rather amazed when I didn't.

In Mahayana Buddhism, death is considered a liberating experience that reunites the pure spirit of the mind with its natural or primal condition. An incarnate mind, united to a human body, is said to be in an unnatural state, because the driving forces of the five senses continually distract it in a process of forming thoughts. It is considered close to natural only during the state of *Samadhi*, Sanskrit for that state of consciousness in which the individual soul merges with the universal soul. This state is sought—but rarely achieved—through *dhyana*, the deepest meditation. In *dhyana*, there can be no "idea" of meditation, for the idea, by its very existence, defeats the experience. The various stages of *dhyana* are denoted by the appearance of lights representing certain levels of wisdom until the final *Clear Light* is perceived. In this quasiprimordial state of supramundane all-consciousness the physical world of *sangsara* and the spiritual world of *nirvana* become one.

Electroencephalograms of Hindu Yogis in states of *Samadic* ecstasy, or what, in psychology, is known as *manic dedifferentiation*, show curves that do not correspond to any cerebral activities known to science, either in wakefulness or sleep. Yogis claim that, during *Samadhi*, they are able to grow as large as the Milky Way or as small as the smallest conceivable particle. Carlos Castaneda discusses similar experiences in his report of apprenticeship to a Yaqui Indian sorcerer. Such fantastic assumptions are not to be taken literally so much as conceptually, as experiences of nonordinary psychological realities, which are, nonetheless, real for him who experiences them.

Perhaps with these concepts in mind, we can approach Belson's sublime vision on a level more suited to it. We might remember also that practically everyone reading this book has in their possession an instrument which transforms energy within solid matter: the transistor. Belson seeks no more and no less than this. *Samadhi* is a record of two years of his search.

Samadhi was a radical departure from Belson's previous work in many ways. First, rather than ebbing and flowing in paced rhythms, it is one sustained cyclone of dynamic form and color whose fierce tempo never subsides. Second, in addition to the usual electronic sound, the inhaling and exhaling of Belson's own respiration is heard throughout the film to represent years of Yoga breathing discipline. And, finally, whereas the earlier work moved from exterior to interior reality, *Samadhi* begins and ends always centered around flaming spheres that evolve out of nothing and elude specific identification.

The various colors and intensities of these solar spheres correspond directly to descriptions in the *Tibetan Book of the Dead* of lights representing the elements Earth, Air, Fire, and Water. They have two additional meanings: the *kundalini* moving upward through the *chakras* and the inhalation-exhalation of the life-force *prana*. In what's known as *Kundalini Yoga*, the *chakras* are physical nerve centers located within the body along the spinal column at five or six points: one in the sexual region, one in the region of the navel, the heart, the throat, the eyes, the middle of the head, the top of the head. Clairvoyants supposedly can see them. According to Yoga theory the *kundalini*—the vital life-force, which animates the body —resides in a concentrated form at the base of the spine in the general region of the sexual organs. Through physical disciplines and ethical and moral strength, one raises that center of life force from the lower spine progressively in stages toward the brain.

Thus, one implication of the elusive shifting centers in *Samadhi* is a trip through the *chakras*, from the lowest to the highest. Also, there's the analogy with the breathing structure. When we hear

Belson inhale, the spheres glow brighter to indicate that *prana*, the life-force in the air we breathe, is being induced into the blood-stream and, therefore, into the *kundalini*. The deep spatial dark areas of the film indicate not only the stages between *chakras* but also exhalations, when there's relatively less *prana*.

As the film begins, a stormy field of turbulent gases collects around a central core. The serrated vapors melt into a small central jewel of curling pink and red-orange flames, which finally fades into black silence. The vacuum created by this pause reverberates in the ears until slowly a deep blue, filamented sphere evolves, turning with purposive elegance, glowing into cadmium orange, surrounded by a whirling halo. It becomes a blue sphere in a red universe, spewing off white-hot rings of light.

Next, comes a series of solar or planetoid visions: a scintillating yellow star with six shimmering fingers; a blue-purple planet with a fiery red halo; a small central globe dwarfed by an immense corona; a dim yellow-ochre sun emanating flames that revolve like chromospheres in a plasma storm; various stellar orbs turning with implacable grace against wavering sonorous drones. Suddenly, there's a burst of white light; a murky sea of deep blue gas is in huge motion; waves of unbearably gorgeous mist sweep across the void. Evidently, contact has been made with some vast new reality.

Cinema to Belson is a matrix wherein he is able to relate external experience to internal experience. He feels that it culminated in *Samadhi*.

> I reached the point that what I was able to produce externally, with the equipment, was what I was seeing internally. I could close my eyes and see these images within my own being, and I could look out at the sky and see the same thing happening there, too. And, most of the time, I'd see them when I looked through the view finder of my camera mounted on the optical bench. I've always considered image-producing equipment as extensions of the mind. The mind has produced these images and has made the equipment to produce them physically. In a way, it's a projection of what's going on inside, phenomena thrown out by the consciousness, which we are then able to look at. In a sense, I'm doing something similar to the clairvoyant Ted Serios, who can project his thoughts onto Polaroid film. Only I have to filter my consciousness through an enormous background of art and film-making. But we're doing the same thing. *Samadhi* breaks new territory in a way. It's as though I've come back from there with my camera in hand—I've been able to film it.

Gene: Do you feel your drug experiences have been beneficial to your work?

Jordan: Absolutely. Early in life, I experimented with peyote, LSD, and so on. But, in many ways, my films are ahead of my own experience. In fact, *Samadhi* is the only one in which I actually caught up with the film and ran alongside of it for just a moment. The film is way ahead of anything I've experienced on a continuing basis. And the same has been true of the drug experiences. They somehow set the stage for the insights. I had peyote fifteen years ago, but I didn't have any cosmic or *Samadic* experiences. That remained for something to happen through development on different levels of consciousness. The new art and other forms of expression reveal the influence of mind expansion. And, finally, we reach the point where there virtually is no separation between science, observation, and philosophy. The new artist works essentially in the same way as the scientist. In many cases, it's identical with scientific exploration. But, at other times, the artist is able to focus more in the area of consciousness and subjective phenomena, but with the same kind of scientific zeal, the same objectivity as scientists. Cosmic consciousness is not limited to scientists. In fact, scientists are sometimes the last to know. They can look through their telescopes and see it out there, but still be very limited individuals.

MOMENTUM

The Sun as an Atom

If one were to isolate a single quality that distinguishes Belson's films from other "space" movies, it would be that his work is always heliocentric, whereas most others, even *2001*, are geocentric. The archetypal nature of the sun is such that Belson's obsession with it has, at times, tended toward a certain mysticism that was no doubt unavoidable. That he would someday make a movie exclusively about the sun was inevitable; that it would be his least mystical work came as something of a surprise.

"I was wondering what the subject of my next film would be after *Samadhi*," he told me.

My whole world had collapsed. All the routines I'd created in order to develop the state of consciousness to produce that film just fell apart. So I had to keep working just to maintain the momentum from *Samadhi*. I had no preconceived idea what the new material was about, but I was calling it *Momentum*. Eventually, I discovered it was about the sun. I ran right to the library; the more I read, the more I realized this was exactly what *Momentum* was about. All the material was similar if not identical to solar phenomena like corona phenomena, photosphere phenomena, chromosphere phenomena, sun spots, plasma storms—I was even getting into some interesting speculation about what goes on *inside* the sun. And I realized that the film doesn't stop at the sun, it goes to the center of the sun and into the atom. So that was the film, about the sun as an atom. The end shows the paradoxical realm in which subatomic phenomena and the cosmologically vast are identical. Through the birth of a new star is where it happens.

Momentum was completed in May of 1969, after eighteen months of painstaking study and labor. In one sense, it's a refinement of the whole vocabulary he's developed through the years, distilled to its essence. But there are new effects inspired by this particular subject. *Momentum* is a calm, objective experience of concrete imagery that manages to suggest abstract concepts without becoming particularly symbolic.

It begins with stock footage of a Saturn rocket whose afterburners blaze in rainbow fury. We hear echoing ethereal music and slow cyclic drones. Next, a solar image in mauves and irridescent ruby, huge prominences flaring in slow motion. A series of graceful lap-dissolves brings us closer to the sphere as it revolves with a steady and ponderous dignity. In spite of its furious subject, *Momentum* is Belson's most serene and gentle film since *Allures*. This treatment of the sun as an almost dreamlike hallucinatory experience is both surprising and curiously realistic—to the extent that one can even speak of "realism" in connection with solar images.

There's a visceral, physical quality to the images as we draw near to the surface and, with a soul-shaking roar, descend slowly into blackness: apparently the suggestion of a sun spot. Flaming napalm-like clouds of gas surge ominously into the void, which suddenly is shattered with an opalescent burst of light. We move through various levels of temperature and matter. Belson's now-familiar techniques seem to possess a pristine clarity and precision not previously so distinct. Swooping cascades of flames seem especially delicate; fantastic towering shards of luminescent color reach deeper levels of the mind; the translucent realms of kinaesthesia leave one speechless.

Moving deeper into the mass, images become more uniform with a textural quality like a shifting sea of silver silt. Millions of tiny flashes erupt over a field of deep blue vapors. Quick subtle movements and sudden ruptures in the fabric of color seem suppressed by some tremendous force. Indefinite shapes and countless particles swim in a frantic sea of brilliance.

"Then the film goes into fusion," Belson explains. "A state of atomic interaction more intense than fission. This is supposed to take place on the sun, fusion." A blinding red fireball breaks into a multi-pointed star of imploding/exploding light energy, flashing brighter and brighter, mounting in intensity. An image similar to James Whitney's *Lapis*—a collecting of millions of tiny particles around a central fiery core—builds up to the moment of crescendo, with all the colors of the universe melting into one supremely beautiful explosion, and suddenly we're deep in interstellar space, watching a distant flash as a new sun is born.

"The whole secret of life must somehow exist in the solar image," Belson remarked.

> *Momentum* is a kind of revelation regarding the sun as the source of life. Not only in our solar system, but wherever there's a sun, it's the source of life in that part of the universe. We come from it and return to it. Though we think of the sun as a gigantic thing, I think probably an atom itself is a small sun—in fact our sun is probably an atom in a larger structure. It's somehow tied up with the essence of being. If you were to think of a single form that would be the primary structure of the universe, it would just have to be the solar sphere. I mean there's so much evidence around us to that effect.

At the time of this writing, Belson's work-in-progress was the realization of a long-held dream to apply experimental video techniques such as Chroma-keying and de-beaming to the expanding vocabulary of his cosmic cinema.

NOTES ON SOME NEW MOVIES AND HAPPINESS

BY JONAS MEKAS

No. 37, Summer, 1965

Films: *Little Stabs at Happiness,* by Ken Jacobs; *Eat,* by Andy Warhol; *Mothlight,* by Stan Brakhage; *Yes,* by Naomi Levine; *Scotch Tape,* by Jack Smith; also, *Blazes* and *Eyewash,* by Robert Breer; *Fleming Faloon,* by George Landow; *Invocations of Canyons and Boulders,* by Dick Higgins; *Glimpse of the Garden* and *Go, Go, Go,* by Marie Menken; *Chumlum* and *Senseless,* by Ron Rice; *Hallelujah the Hills,* by Adolfas Mekas; *Pat's Birthday,* by Robert Breer; (also, the useless boxes, or "boxes for useless work" of Walter de Maria, Andy Warhol, George Brecht; machines for "random noises" of Joe Jones; "random painting" of George Maciunas); also, *Home Movies,* by Taylor Mead; *Blonde Cobra,* by Bob Fleischner and Ken Jacobs; *Christmas on Earth,* by Barbara Rubin; *Shower,* by Robert Whitman.

1.

Eat: A man is eating a mushroom (or a piece of orange or an apple perhaps; it doesn't matter). He does nothing else, and why should he? He just eats. There are thoughts and reveries appearing on his face, and disappearing again, as he continues eating. No hurry, nowhere to hurry. He likes what he is eating, and his eating could last one million years. His unpretentiousness amazes us. Why doesn't he think of something else to do; why doesn't he want anything else? Doesn't he seek anything important? Does his world end with the mushroom? Doesn't he read books, perhaps? Yes, he disappoints us, because he just eats his mushroom. We are not—or are no longer —familiar with such humility of existence; happiness looks suspicious to us.

What pompous asses we are!

2.

These movies are like games, not "serious" at all. They do not even look like cinema. They are happy to call themselves "home movies." Useless, "thoughtless," "childish" games, with no great "intellect," with "nothing" to "say;" a few people sitting, walking, jumping, sleeping, or laughing, doing useless, unimportant things, with no "drama," no "intentions," no "messages"—they seem to be there just for their own sake. How irresponsible! Moth-wing patterns, flower petals, chance designs: Where and what is the "deep" meaning of all this playing? Stan Brakhage, at thirty, and he is still playing with colored moth wings . . . Or Marie Menken: at the Cinemathèque Française they laughed and made funny noises during her little movies: Why did she show flowers, and birds, and fountains? Nothing "dramatic," nothing really for the grownups who, after all, are here to do big things!

3.

We watch Andy Warhol's or Walter de Maria's boxes expecting something to happen, some kind of sudden aesthetic wave to grip us and shake us. But the boxes do nothing; little movies do no "shaking:" They are there for their own unpretentious sake.

Slowly, the persistent silence of the boxes, the playful attitude of Marie Menken's movies, or Joseph Cornell's movies, or the unpretentiousness of *Eyewash* make our own pompousness begin to crack.

The only signs, the only visible traces from which we can say or detect that *Little Stabs* or Cornell or Menken passed nearby are the drops of happiness left on our faces, touches of joy. So actionless is their art.

4.

"Now when I got to the rest of your letter (aside from the

'pleasure of speaking across space,' as you put it) I was up (notice how that 'up' slipped down) against THE other of my life temptations, which might best be characterized by your question (in the letter received this morning): 'Are we not the ones who will finally take over this Society and Culture?' After struggling with similar whisperings (thank heavens they are muted these days) since receiving your first letter, I am prepared to answer with a firm *sound* (not even needing *re*sounding): NO! . . . at least, I am kicking off from *any* such intention; and, to balance my recent L.A. experiences with black magic, I have a whole battery of New York, et cetera, experiences which have clarified the second temptation for *me* as solidly as the first temptation was originally known, as such, some nine or ten years ago when I consciously stopped manipulating of other's lives, even in the name of Drama, finally gave up drama, *as* that kind of manipulation," (Stan Brakhage, in a letter to Michael McClure, May, 1964).

5.

Little Stabs at Happiness: A woman sitting in a chair. She sits there, and she swings, back and forth, back and forth, without anything else happening. She doesn't even move or look around much. It is a beautiful summer day, somewhere downtown; it could be Orchard Street, or Avenue B. The time goes by, and she swings, and nothing else really happens. That is too much. Show us something of real life, like Kurosawa, or De Sica, or even Bergman. Drama must be going on in those houses, in those streets, in those summer days. We are not used to such inner peace, to such stillness, to doing "nothing." Yes, this is one of the most tranquil scenes in all cinema, one of the most deeply happy scenes, and most simple— an image that I have been carrying in my memory from childhood, something that I have never seen since, until I saw it in *Little Stabs* again.

6.

Yes: A man runs into a field with flowers on his shoulders, on his head; he runs around, falls down, as children pull him by the legs, and they roll on the ground, among the flowers.

Hallelujah the Hills: In the woods, among the trees, by the fire they dance, drunk with the last days of summer, autumn, outdoors, friendship—like two happy clowns, and they roll on the ground, and beat each other on the stomachs, choking with laughter, completely nuts.

Or another image: High on the hill road, in the wide autumn

landscape, in the first snow, baby-white, they stretch their hands wide open and shout: SOOO-LOOOOOONG! in a gesture of such exuberance and such indescribable happiness that their gesture remains there, imprinted, the happiest farewell gesture of the screen.

7.

Oh! Happiness! Joy.

Ecstasies are senseless, purposeless, ends in themselves; and silly, and thoughtless, and do not earn bread, do not plow the fields:

Let's hinge nightingales to the plows; let's put flowers to work!

8.

Madly sensual Naomi Levine has an interesting problem. She visited Puerto Rico for fun, and it made her sick to see its captive state. She returned burning to make it a public indictment; borrowed a dinky 16mm, began. And now she's in despair because everything she shoots comes out languorous, lovely, with naked children, flowers, and nature everywhere. She works up still more vicious plots, full of murders, and her viewers swim in poetry. 'There were murders?' they ask afterwards. You see, this unfortunate, Egyptian-type broad responds to horror but can't express it. Phony Naomi, what kind of revolutionary are you? You insist to us you're plenty rabid, tell us you're out to plant bombs, then you go and invest everything you touch with love. Are you trying to make it difficult for the *New Yorker* to categorize you? That's impossible. Naomi kid, you doll. (Ken Jacobs, in a letter, 1964).

9.

The "engagement" of the *right* and the *left* is *to change the world*. They have been changing the world ever since it began. And they have brought it to fine shape.

The "engagement" of the "useless" artist is to open himself to the world, embrace the world; instead of trying to change the world, he lets himself be changed by the world. He is that humble and nutty about himself.

10.

Soup Opera: Bite, bite the candy, Jane. You know that nothing else matters but the candy, and you, this small moment, NOW. This game that you are playing; this movie; this candy, this bubble gum. To look down upon candy is to look down upon God.

11.

It is the so-called serious and engaged citizen who stiffens the "armors" of humanity by misleading man with false solutions and changes, by postponing man's realization of the fact that he, really, doesn't know the solutions and that he cannot know and cannot change anything, really. More than that: that he doesn't have to change, really, anything: that everything is there for him, all the beauty that man can take is there, and it has always been there.

12.

This happiness, this joy that we see in these movies, is a joy that has no disillusionment, no sex-morality-engagement complexes. It is a joy of the most gameful kind. It is a smile that has nothing to do with the *New Yorker,* or *Simplicissimus,* or *Krokodil,* or Pfeiffer, or *The Realist* humor. This smile reminds me more of one who has traveled 10,000 miles by foot to see what's at the end of the road (he has dreamt about it since his childhood) and has found, upon arrival, that there was really nothing at the end of the road, nothing but a small pile of rabbit shit. So he looks at it, and he laughs.

13.

What then, about the "evil" in the world today? Does this artist (or man) approve of what's happening in the world today?
Yes! Tell us, what's really happening?
A bomb fell on Nagasaki.
But Brakhage made *Mothlight.*
By his presence, by the presence of beautiful artists, beautiful poetry, beautiful men, the thinking and the actions of others will be and are modified, changed, become less "active."
That's what art is "engaged" in.

14.

We sat by the lake, eating apples. I said: "What do you propose? What's the way out?" Leo said: "What is the way out for an asp tree or an apple?" We sat silently. I said: "Man is not an apple. The apple is passive." Leo said: "Tell me, if you know: What is action?" Leo finished his apple and threw the core into the lake. We watched it.

15.

I have seen, in my childhood, the women of my village, sitting and knitting by the windows, or in doorways, and not moving, immersed in their embroideries and designs and red and green and yellow flowers and dots and suns for days and days. As I slowly grow up, in my memory's eye I can see them, as far as I can remember, sitting there and doing nothing else: I found them there when I was born, and I left them there when I became a Big Boy, and they may still be there, knitting, and with no museums exhibiting their master-pieces, nor anybody calling them works of art—and if somebody says something nice, they blush, or they say something back, and it is not always very nice what they say.

It was happiness they were knitting, and I haven't met yet such happiness, such faces, or very seldom, in some other distant, quiet, far village.

16.

But the women of my childhood used to sing the saddest songs I ever heard. Often, listening to them sing, in the fields, myself, sitting somewhere crawled on the edge of the field, or under a tree, I thought, I had a feeling that the fields themselves were crying.

17.

It is neither a coincidence nor anything strange that exactly the same men who have tasted a fool's happiness, give us also the deep-est intuitions of the tragic sense of life.

I don't know any other art today that has been pierced by a more heart-breaking cry than the one we hear in *Blonde Cobra*. All other tragedies, *An American Tragedy*, all our novelistic and filmed trage-dies, after *Blonde Cobra* look like sweet rose lemonades.

18.

Yes, there are glimpses of happiness in some of the primitive paintings of the eighteenth and nineteenth centuries. There, too, is joy of things as they are, as they were; of a quiet countryside, with a path leading into a distance, a flower by the roadside, or a tree, and a rose bush, perhaps.

Imitation of the true emotion. Sentimentality. No oneness. No true peace. (Who knows what true peace is?) Nostalgia of things of nature. Or are we going into neo-Romanticism? And what does it mean? Or am I going into neo-Romanticism? And this essay is nothing but pieces of my own new film? Perhaps. But I shall con-tinue:

19.

Christmas on Earth: A woman; a man; the black of the pubic hair; the cunt's moon mountains and canyons. As the film goes, image after image, the most private territories of the body are laid open for us. The first shock changes into silence then is transposed into amazement. We have seldom seen such down-to-body beauty, so real as only beauty (man) can be: terrible beauty that man, that woman is, are, that Love is.

Do they have no more shame? This eighteen-year-old girl, she must have no shame, to look at and show the body so nakedly. Only angels have no shame. But we do not believe in angels; we do not believe in Paradise any more, nor in Christmas; we have been Out for too long. "Orpheus has been too long in Hell."—Brakhage.

A syllogism: Barbara Rubin has no shame; angels have no shame; Barbara Rubin is an angel.

Yes, Barbara Rubin has no shame because she has been kissed by the angel of Love.

The motion picture camera has been kissed by the angel of Love. From now on, camera shall know no shame.

Cinema has discovered all of man: As painting and sculpture did from the very beginning. But then: Cinema IS in its very beginning.

20.

"All of the beautiful and poetic young film-makers of the new American cinema have been making dirty, nude movies lately because we are told not to—naughty, aren't we? You think so, you think we are naughty to look at bodies, to think about our organs, to apply the processes of our intellect and imaginations to determining what the body's needs are, to be led by our bodies. You are led by your bodies, Readers, whether you know it or not. Most of the terrible tensions of your lives come from the discrepancies between what your bodies ask of you and your crabbed gratifications. All the flaming young directors shot nude stuff this last summer. Naomi Levine made a movie wherein little kids swatted each other with armfuls of huge white flowers. And some of the kids' pants were fallen down—revealing them . . . NAKED! . . . BOO! !" (Jack Smith, in a letter).

21.

"I don't pick flowers any longer. To pick, to break flowers would mean action, and I have abandoned all action." (Barbara Rubin, July, 1964).

22.

It took us a long time (for some of us) to see something we knew from the very beginning:

that it is no use criticizing; that you can't change or improve or save man from outside; that the real work must be done inside; that others can be reached only through the beauty of your own self; that the others shouldn't even be bothered; each of us should mind our own business; that the work, therefore, the real work must be done first in your self (my self); any change must begin within you (me); that only the beautiful and truthful (enlightened) souls can change the world and bring or transfer some of the Beauty and Truth into the others (most of Beauty and Truth comes to each of us as Grace).

that, further, a single brush line can do more for man, exult his soul and reach and change him more deeply than all the socially-morally "conscious" art;

that what Henry Cornelius Agrippa von Nettesheim said about music, long ago, can be said about all arts:

> All artistic activities are magical operations . . . the mystery of the universe exerting the all uniting power in nature . . . the spheres produce tones of the nucleus of all that exists, and men who can imitate this celestial harmony have traced their way back to this sublime realm where, moving according to these ideal figures, they can then capture the magical meaning of the earliest sacred rites; movements that cause the gods to rejoice and echoes to haunt the planets, creating great curative (liberating) forces.

23.

Theater (Cinema) of Cruelty? Yes.
Theater (Cinema) of Absurd? Yes.
Theater (Cinema) of Happiness? Yes.
Theater (Cinema) of the Soul? Yes.

24.

"Ich freue mich meiner selbst. Ich freue mich meiner und der Welt. Wenn ich so richtig in mir zuhause bin, dann is die Welt um mich und ich bin in der Welt." (Robert Klemmer, 1964).

25.

It is the happiness and innocence that comes from *Little Stabs, Scotch Tape, Christmas on Earth,* or the work of Marie Menken, Stan Brakhage, George Landow. These films are both games and documents, register books of new currents and undercurrents that are beginning to appear and vibrate in man's unconscious.

That is why the Cinemathèque Française could not stand them.

That is why the serious citizens all over the world cannot stand these movies.

They remind them of Paradise Lost.
They do not believe any longer that Paradise can be Regained.
But the man who is eating his mushroom knows it better.

26.

"As I sat there I thought and I sank into the afternoon, a half century ago (the moment of infinite repast) at a picnic near a deep wood, cool and dense, black greens holding the sun yoyoing around, against a tempest of snow butterflies. I ventured deep, and all afternoon for the first time into these woods, where grows the amenita mushroom, dappled from scrappings of snow, each leaf, each movement, each sound of the multitudinous growings crashed and wafted me further from the curved inblus of blossoms. These cool lime halls of summer gave me a knowing and stripped from me all the gauziness that bound my body. The house of my soul was naked, and slow rising and banging into all the growing of these woods and joy and stars and kings and queens emanated and were the marshmallows for the butterflies food." (Naomi Levine, in a letter).

August, 1964

STRUCTURAL FILM

BY P. ADAMS SITNEY

No. 47, Summer, 1969; revised, Winter, 1969

Suddenly, a cinema of structure has emerged. The dominant evolution of the American (and outlands') avant-garde cinema has been the pursuit of progressively complex forms; so this change of pace is unexpected and difficult to explain. Two points demand immediate clarity: First, what is the tendency toward complex forms? And, second, how is the structural cinema different? A view in perspective of the independent cinema over the past twenty years and, perhaps more pointedly, in the work of those individual artists who have been outside of the sponsored cinema for more than a decade will show the development of a cinematic language of *conjunction*, whereby diverse strands of themes are fitted together, or a language of *metaphor*, whereby the most is made of limited material. Those who have seen the whole work of Brakhage, Markopoulos, Kubelka, and Anger, for instance, will immediately grasp the concept of an "evolution of forms" by contrasting *Reflections on Black* (1955) to *The Art of Vision* (1960–65), *Swain* (1951) to *The Illiac Passion* (1964–66), *Mosaic in Confidence*

(1955) to *Our Trip to Africa* (*Unsere Afrikareise*) (1966), or *Eaux D'Artifice* (1953) to *Scorpio Rising* (1963). In every one of these films, the early as well as the recent, the film-maker attempts to make disparate elements cohere and to make cinematic architecture; yet, in the later examples, the themes (within each film) are more varied and the total more compact.

In the past five years, nevertheless, a number of film-makers have emerged whose approach is quite different, although definitely related to the *sensibility* of those listed above: Tony Conrad, George Landow, Michael Snow, Hollis Frampton, Joyce Wieland, Ernie Gehr, and Paul Sharits have produced a number of remarkable films *apparently* in the opposite direction of the formal tendency. Theirs is a cinema of structure wherein the *shape* of the whole film is predetermined and simplified, and it is that shape that is the primal impression of the film.

A precise statement of the difference between form and structure must involve a sense of the working process; for the formal film is a tight nexus of content, a shape designed to explore the facets of the material—the very title of Kubelka's first film, *Mosaic*, is an expression of this conscious aspiration. Recurrences, antithesis, and over-all rhythm are the elements of the formal; in essence, a film whose content is, at root, a myth. In this magazine, Kubelka, Markopoulos, Brakhage, and, to a lesser extent, Anger, have discussed working processes, which share in common a scrutiny of the photographed raw material so that the eventual form will be revealed; their faith has been in editing. I exclude here, of course, certain recent films of Brakhage and Markopoulos made completely in the camera.

The structural film insists on its shape, and what content it has is minimal and subsidiary to the outline. This is the clearest in *The Flicker* (1965) of Tony Conrad and *Ray Gun Virus* (1966) of Paul Sharits where the flickering of single-frame solids—in the former black and white, in the latter colors—is the total field.

Four characteristics of the structural film are a fixed camera position (fixed *frame* from the viewer's perspective), the flicker effect, loop printing (the immediate repetition of shots, exactly and without variation), and rephotography off of a screen. Very seldom will one find all four characteristics in a single film, and there are structural films that avoid these usual elements.

ORIGINS

We find the sources of the first three prevailing characteristics of the structural cinema in the immediate history of the avant-garde film. Andy Warhol made famous the fixed frame with his first film, *Sleep* (1963), in which a half dozen shots are seen for over six hours. His films made a little later, cling even more fiercely to the single unbudging perspective: *Eat* (1963), forty-five minutes of the eating of a mushroom; *Harlot* (1965), an eighty-minute *tableau vivant* with offscreen commentary; *Beauty #2* (1965), a bed scene with off and on screen speakers for ninety minutes. For this, Warhol is one of the two major inspirations of the structuralists (he even used loop printing in *Sleep*, although Bruce Conner had done so more outrageously in *Report* (1964) a few months earlier). Yet Warhol, as a pop artist, is spiritually at the opposite pole from the structuralists. His fixed camera was at first an outrage, later an irony, until his content became too compelling, and he abandoned the fixed image for a kind of in-the-camera editing. In the work of Ernie Gehr or Michael Snow, the camera is fixed in mystical contemplation of a portion of space. Spiritually, the difference between these poles cannot be reconciled. In fact, the antithesis of the structural film to the pop film (basically Warhol) is precisely the difference between Pop and Minimal painting or sculpture, where the latter grows out of and against the former. Here the analogy must end, because the major psychologies of structural cinema and minimal art are not usually comparable.

The second forefather of structural cinema is Peter Kubelka who made the first flicker film, *Arnulf Rainer*, in 1960, and who pioneered much of the field for the structuralists with his earlier minimal films *Adebar* (1957) and *Schwechater* (1958). One could not really describe Kubelka as a film-maker involved in the recently emerging structural tendency for several reasons: As an Austrian who created his films in a relative vacuum (seeing and caring for little but the work of Dreyer until late in his career), he would be outside the climate and mentality of the others; he is in the middle of his career, whereas the others, for the most part, are beginners; and the direction of his work seems to be away from the structural into the more complex forms.

Ken Kelman suggested to me that the sensibility of the structuralists derives from the aesthetic of Brakhage. This is true to a certain extent—Brakhage, more than anyone else, has emphasized in print the primary importance of a visual cinema—but his films, until a very recent exception, which I shall discuss, have been rhythmic rather than static. Actually, if we are to seek a pioneer sensibility for the structural cinema, it would be Robert Breer, who literally founded the cinema of speed, single-frame dominance, in the early 1950's.

The effect of all of Breer's work is kinetic, as opposed to the static quality of the structural cinema. Nevertheless, his work is the historical precursor of Kubelka's *Arnulf Rainer* and, subsequently, an important link in the prehistory of our theme.

[The initial publication of this article brought me considerable criticism, especially in respect to the above consideration of "origins." Peter Kubelka considers himself both the originator and master of the structural tendency, noting that he employed several kinds of loops in *Schwechater* and invented the flicker film with *Arnulf Rainer*. Typically, he refuses to believe that neither Conrad nor Sharits had seen or even heard about his film before making theirs.

George Maciunas, of Fluxus, also contested my historical accuracy. His rebuttal to the article, in the form of a chart, will be found at the end of this essay. Like Kubelka, his argument comes from a misreading of my intentions. In these pages, I have tried to define and describe a prevalent tendency within the avant-garde cinema. In discussing its origins, I have moved *a posteriori* into the *immediate prehistory* of both the forms and sensibility under consideration. Naturally, one could go further and further back into film history to discover precursors: Marcel Duchamp's *Anemic Cinema*, a study of his rotary spirals with words printed upon them, might be called a distant ancestor from 1926; even Lumière's style, from the turn of the century, with composed and random movement into and out of a single fixed frame, implies an extension into the structural.

The fact is that the examples Maciunas cites had no more direct influence on the sudden and ubiquitous emergence of the structural cinema than did the work of Duchamp and Lumière. He is right when he claims that this development grew out of the other arts, yet that evolution has never been within the scope of this essay.

I am grateful to Kubelka and Maciunas for the opportunity to clarify my subject. It is unfortunate that the films I am discussing have been confused with "simple" forms or "concept art." It is precisely when the material becomes multifaceted and complex, without distracting from the clarity of the over-all shape, that these films become interesting.

For years, film-maker—aestheticians equated poetry with condensation. Not a frame should be "wasted" (Kubelka still says that). The films of which I speak are extensive rather than compressed, static rather than rhythmic. In the films of Markopoulos, Brakhage (excepting those included here), Kubelka, and Anger, information comes so quickly that time is condensed, if not obliterated. Snow, Sharits, Wieland, Landow, Frampton, and others, elongate their films so that time will enter as an aggressive participant in the viewing experience. This is a radical shift of aesthetic tactics. No overlapping of mechanisms or processes can reconcile it.]

EXAMPLES

The structural film has appeared in filmographies where it was not to be expected. Were it not for three short films of Bruce Baillie, Gregory Markopoulos's *Gammelion* (1968), and *Song 27, My Mountain* (1968) by Stan Brakhage, a case might be made for a casual link among the new film-makers of that area of cinema. These five works, all by artists in mid-career, indicate a general collective attitude has emerged. Its causes and meaning are obscure.

Perhaps the poetic form had reached such a sophistication in the complex works of Markopoulos, Brakhage, Anger, Kubelka, and others (for certainly their forms more approximated the elements of poetry in this century than any other art) that these film-makers wanted a new investigation of pure image and pure rhythm; or, in other words, they sought to incorporate the aesthetics of painting and music (previously the domain of the animation film-makers). No accident that Snow, Landow, and Wieland are also painters; Conrad, a musician.

The films in their simplicity are easy to describe.

Bruce Baillie made his three structural films all at about the same time (1966–67). *Show Leader* has one black and white shot of the film-maker washing himself, nude, in a stream. Over the soundtrack, he introduces himself to the audience. He intended this film as an epilogue or introduction to one-man shows of his works and gives it without rent on those occasions. The shot and sound is loop printed to extend a few seconds into a couple of minutes. This unpretentious, friendly film represents the structural cinema at its most casual.

All My Life is a one-shot film and *Still Life*, Baillie's most sophisticated structural composition, is a one-shot, fixed-image film. The former is a pan shot in color across a fence trellissed with roses and then up to the sky and telephone wires. It lasts as long as it takes Ella Fitzgerald to sing "All My Life" on the soundtrack.

The title gives *Still Life* away: A fixed image of a tabletop floral arrangement, ash tray, and table objects; beyond the table, out of focus is a room backed by windows. There seem to be figures in the far background: Perhaps they are the men whose voices we hear on the sound, talking of Ramakrishna and apparently discussing a series of photographs of shrines in India. In the immediate background, just beyond the table, a female figure crosses the screen and returns later. Her costume is rich and elusive.

There is a metaphysics of irony; and the severe minimalization of Robert Indiana in a dumb felt hat taking forty-five minutes to nibble a mushroom evokes it, especially when the camera doesn't budge. That's Warhol's *Eat*, a good instance of deadpan cinema. *Still Life* is a sweeter put on; the humor is there, a particular form of Zen screwball native to hipper California, but, also, there is a sincere devotion to the apotheosis of space, the space framed within the camera field.

The overt principle of this film (and of some others we will discuss here, notably Michael Snow's *Wavelength* [1967]) is that the action or event is a function of the given space. It is not the floral arrangement that excites us in *Still Life*, but the whole field of action—the talking men, the passing female form, the flowers, and the ashtray as constants—constitutes a single experience. Besides, the conscious concentration on a fixed quarter of space implies a conscious duality of the field—what happens, occurs either within or outside of the frame.

Again Warhol has explored this binary space, tongue in cheek, in *Blow Job* (1964), where the field of the frame, the subject's head, is obviously only the echo ground for the title action. In *Beauty #2*, an offscreen actor taunts Edie Sedgwick and her lover who are seen in bed. The idea of offscreen action as the focus of interest is certainly older than Warhol. Stan Brakhage first realized and pointed out that the major invention of Jerry Joffen, whose indescribable endless film is too seldom seen, was precisely the suggestion of significant action out of the camera's field. Brakhage himself utilized this principle in *Song 6* (1964), an early anticipation of the structural film, in which a moth is seen dying against the flower pattern of a linoleum floor. It is sometimes center screen, but more often in a corner or just out of the screen. Because the moth is so close to the floor, there is little sense of space. The linoleum is a backdrop rather, which becomes metaphorically an image of the veil of death because of the minimalization of the essential action—the moth death.

The importance of *Still Life* and the similar structural films is that the fixed camera electrifies a space, revealing in itself (not as a metaphor, as in Brakhage or Joffen, or as coy side-glancing, as in Warhol). Within the context of Baillie's production, the structural films can be seen as an outgrowth of the Japanese *haiku* form, a sensibility he had previously attempted with *Mr. Hayashi* (1961), the portrait of a Japanese gardener, and with *Tung* (1966), the negative "shadow" portrait of a girl walking. If the essence of *haiku* is the welding of two images into a synthetic mode, then, in *Still Life* and *All My Life*, Baillie has attained the form, with the union of picture and sound into an elemental structure.

Before continuing, I must again allude to a technical antecedent in Warhol's work: the camera moving freely within the limits of a fixed tripod (right–left, up–down motions) and a zoom lens (in–out motion). This, too, is a manifestation of fixed space on a more intricate level. We saw it for the first time in *Party Sequence: Poor Little Rich Girl* (1965) and emphatically in the Marie Menken episode of *The Chelsea Girls* (1965). When the tripod is fixed and the camera roams, there is still a sense of minimalized space, less solid than in the fixed image, but more or less felt. *All My Life* is a pan or tracking shot, yet its structural monotone is apparent.

Michael Snow utilizes the tension of the fixed frame and some of the flexibility of the fixed tripod in *Wavelength*. Actually, it is a forward zoom for forty-five minutes, halting occasionally, and fixed during several different times so that day changes to night within the motion.

A persistent polarity shapes the film. Throughout, there is an exploration of the room, a long studio, as a field of space, subject to the arbitrary events of the outside world so long as the zoom is recessive enough to see the windows and thereby the street. The room, during the day, at night, on different film stock for color tone, with filters, and even occasionally in negative is gradually closing up its space as the zoom nears the back wall and the final image of a photograph upon it—a photograph of waves. This is the story of the diminishing area of pure potentiality. The insight of space, and, implicitly, cinema as potential, is an axiom of the structural film.

So we have always the room as the realm of possibility. Polar to this is a series of events whose actuality is emphasized by an interruption of the sine-wave blasting soundtrack with simple synchronized sound. The order of the events is progressive and interrelated: A bookcase is moved into the room, two girls are listening to the radio; so far, we are early in the film, the cine-morning, the action appears random; midway through, a man climbs the stairs (so we hear) and staggers onto the floor, but the lens has already crossed half the room and he is only glimpsed, the image passes over him. Late in the film, its evening, one of the radio girls returns, goes to the telephone, which, being at the back wall is in full view, and in a dramatic moment of acting unusual in the avant-garde cinema calls a man, Richard, to tell him there is a dead body in the room. She insists he does not look drunk but dead and says she will meet him downstairs. She leaves. The call makes a story of the previously random events. Had the film ended here, actuality in the potent image of death would have satisfied all the potential energy built up before; but Snow prefers a deeper vision. What we see is a visual echo, a ghost in negative superimposition of the girl making the phone call, and the zoom continues, as the sound grows shriller, into the final image of the static sea pinned to the wall, a cumulative metaphor for the whole experience of the dimensional illusion of open space. The crucial difference between the form of Brakhage's *Song 6* and this film is that the *Song*, true to song form, is purely the invocation of a metaphor, while *Wavelength* uses a metaphor as the end of an elaborate, yet simple structure whose coordinates are one room and one zoom.

[One can see in an earlier Snow film, *New York Eye and Ear Control* (1964), the conceptual origins of *Wavelength* (1967) and ←→ (1969), his latest long work. Numerous dualities make the film cohere: The cut-out figure of The Walking Woman (an obsessive image from his paintings and sculpture), at times white, sometimes black, recurs throughout the film, which has two different parts. In the first half, the flat cut-outs contradict the deep spaces of the landscapes, rockscapes, and seascapes in which they are placed. The second half occurs indoors, within a small unoriented space, where black (black and white) pose in relationship to the cut-outs and their negative moulds.

New York Eye and Ear Control suggests a declension of ideas, of black and white, flat and round, stasis and ebullience, silence and sound; but (despite the film-maker's articulate description of the over-all construction, in our conversations) it is architectonically naïve. What is Snow's primary weakness here becomes the central strength of his later work: the vision of a simple situation permeated by a field or rich philosophical implication, which *duration* elaborates.] Like Brakhage's *Song 6*, it is an epistemological metaphor. What is particularly interesting is that, like Landow's *Fleming Faloon* (1963), which I shall soon describe, it is a first attempt to make a structural film by the film-maker who later achieved that form, before the form had emerged.

[Snow considers the primary historical contribution of *New York Eye and Ear Control* to be its direct confrontation with aesthetic *endurance*. If this was his intention, he has been more successful in a later film, *One Second in Montreal* (1969), where more than thirty still photographs of snow covered parks are held on the screen for very long periods. The shape of the film is a crescendo-diminuendo of endurance—although the first shot is held very long, the second stays even longer, and so on into the middle of the film, when the measures begin to shorten.

The central fact of ⟷ (1969) is velocity. The perpetually moving camera, left–right, right–left, passes a number of "events" which become metaphors in the flesh for the back-and-forth inflection of the camera (passing a ball, the eye movement of reading, window washing, and so on). These events suggest the elements of contemporary dance (Yvonne Rainer, and others). Each activity is a rhythmic unit, self-enclosed, and joined to the subsequent activity only by the fact that they occur in the same space. They provide a living scale for the speeds of camera movement and solid forms in the field of energy that the panning makes out of space.

The continual panning of the camera creates an apparent time in conflict with the time of any given operation. In the film's coda, a recapitulation of all the events, out of their original order and in multiple superimposition, the illusions of time dissolve in an image of atemporal continuity.

The overt rhythm of ⟷ depends upon the speed at which the camera moves from side to side, or up and down. Likewise, the overt drama of *Wavelength* derives from the closing-in of space, the action of the zoom lens. The specific content of both films is empty space, rooms. It is the nature and structure of the events within the rooms that differentiate the modes of the films].

A set of films by Ernie Gehr, *Wait* and *Moments* (1968), work an area similar to that of *Wavelength* on a simpler level. Both are fixed-tripod–zoom structures, but the zoom movements are staccato and not the primary organizational principles of the films. Both are structured on rhythmic variations of the film stocks' exposure to fixed light sources. In *Wait*, the source is an overhead lamp, giving the film a series of red-dominant intensities. A couple is reading in a room. There is no sound.

Moments is another interior: a room with a cat and apparently someone in bed; yet the source of light is an outside window, in whose image we can see a firescape when the exposure is very low. The tones are bluish, and again there is no sound.

Brakhage has, of course, used variations in exposure as formal elements of a film, but to the best of my knowledge, Gehr deserves the credit for first using exposure differences as the prime material of an entire film and for composing with the f stops as a rhythmic instrument.

[In 1969, Gehr made *Reverberation* by filming off of a screen or an optical printing device on which his original material was projected. Nothing happens in the film. A couple stands on the street, posing. By a reduction to slow motion and through the flattening of space by second-generation photography, the image giggles, pulses, and almost breathes a brilliant white light. The instability of the image and the nervous variations of the light intensity become the subject of the film.

Gehr was not the first of the structuralists to utilize photography off a screen in a formalist manner. Landow had done it a year earlier in *The Film that Rises to the Surface of Clarified Butter*. Yet it was probably from Ken Jacobs that Gehr received his inspiration in this direction. For a long time, Jacobs had been working on a long film involving photography off of a screen, *Tom, Tom, The Piper's Son*, which has been screened in several versions, the latest of which, in 1969, seems to be definitive.

Tom, Tom begins and ends with an old film, made in America in the early years of the century, of the same title, quoted entirely both times. For about seventy minutes (the original lasts about ten minutes), Jacobs gives us his variations on the images and movements of that film. His *Tom, Tom*, as opposed to the original, has a grainy pointillistic texture (an inevitable result from filming off of a screen or home-made optical printer, which he uses gloriously) and a compressed depth of space. In transposing, he changed the time of the original with slow motion, the scale with close-ups of background details, the sequence with repetitions and backward movements, and, above all, the kinesis by radically retarding the narrative of the original. Here the principle of elongation rather than condensation— the aesthetic crux of the structural film—finds its clearest demonstration. It is almost as if the film intended to prove once and for all the postulates of Russian formalist criticism, where the theory of the structural cinema has its historical origins. Victor Shklovsky writes in *Art as Technique* (1917):

> We find everywhere the artistic trademark—that is, we find material obviously created to remove the automatism of perception; the author's purpose is to create the vision that results from that de-automatized perception. A work is created "artistically" so that its perception is impeded and the greatest possible effect is produced through the slowness of perception.

and

> The technique of art is to make objects "unfamiliar," to make forms difficult, to increase the difficulty and length of perception because the process of perception is an aesthetic end in itself and must be

prolonged. *Art is a way of experiencing the artfulness of an object; the object is not important.* (his italics)

Jacobs's film is didactic in a specifically Modernist tradition. In the first place, it is sublime film criticism, revealing the intricacy of the original by literally transfiguring it. Stravinsky did the same for Pergolesi; Robert Duncan "set Shelley's *Arethusa* to new measures." In addition, Jacobs has revealed a nexus of composition and imagery, latent in the film, akin to Seurat and Manet. We see a sensual tightrope walker whirling a hoop in slow motion, a hunchback rolling over and over himself, a crowd falling, one by one, slow as molasses, out of a barn and, almost floating, into a haystack. There are intimations of Picasso's harlequins as well.

Because of the directness of the mechanism he employs, *Tom, Tom* must be considered within the structural sensibility despite Jacobs's tendency to rupture the forms of all of his films. Between the two versions I saw, there was a marked difference of architecture. Both successfully violated the symmetry by appendixing a series of slow-motion details after the second presentation of the original film.

The latest version, however, has color inserts of a shadow play, which violently interrupts the continuity of the black-and-white film. Visually, they are relaxing (so Jacobs describes their function), but, structurally, they are extremely disorienting. More in keeping with the texture of the film, but nevertheless digressive, is a passage in the latest version in which the film-maker literally lifts away the screen off of which the film is being "copied," and we are confronted by a flicker of the bare projector-bulb, which was behind the screen. Since Jacobs began making films, he has been obsessed with the notion of a form that breaks down and starts up again falteringly. His earlier long films, *Star Spangled to Death* (begun in the early 1950's and still incomplete) and *Blonde Cobra* (1963) have wildly eccentric architectures.

Before making *Tom, Tom,* or at the same time, Jacobs shot *Soft Rain,* a single long take, from a fixed position, shown three times in a row. The film looks out of a window with the shade half-drawn (or a black masking device near the camera) on a flat store-top and a street during a light rainfall. The rain is so light that it often takes more than one cycle of the shot before a viewer becomes aware of it. Likewise the shade (or mask) is so ambiguously posited in the depth of the field that its extreme proximity to the camera is not immediately apparent. Perhaps the success of this simple structure is related to the relative simplicity of shape in which he has left *Tom, Tom,* even in its latest version.

That simplicity is all the more evident by contrast with the possibilities the materials offer. I saw the film for the first time with Parker Tyler, who suggested that it would be more "mysterious" (a ritualistic presence he much admires in films) if the original were not shown. At times during the projection, I considered the potential for restructuring the sequence and, thus, the causality of the states of the original. Had either possibility been employed, the result probably would not have been such as to find consideration in the context of this article.]

Joyce Wieland, the wife of Michael Snow, has used loop effects for at least two kinds of structure. In *Sailboat* (1968), the loop * gives an illusion of continuous movement as a boat sails from screen left and out of screen right repeatedly; in *1933* (1967), a single shot of a street taken from a high window with people rushing in fast motion and slowing down to normal motion (without a change of shots) is seen about a dozen times. Occasionally the title, *1933*, is printed over the entire shot, and between each set of repetitions there is white leader marked by different red flashes.

Of all the film-makers included in this article, Wieland is closest to Andy Warhol and the mentality of the pop film. In *Sailboat*, the structural principle is clearly ironic, while *1933* is a pure and quite mysterious structural film. In *Catfood* (1968), she shows a cat devouring fish after fish for some ten minutes. There seems to be no repetition of shots, but the imagery is so consistent throughout— shot of the fish, the cat eating, his paw clawing, another fish, the cat eating, and so on—that it is just possible that shots are recurrent.

[Her latest film, *Reason Over Passion* (1969) is her strongest. A description of the film's plan, its argument, suggests an epic form; for she has attempted no less than to cross Canada from ocean to ocean, filming. In the middle of it all, a portrait of Trudeau, the Prime Minister (the title is a phrase from one of his speeches), interrupts the journey. His image has the same reduction to the granular as the optical or the off-the-screen printings of Gehr, Jacobs, and others. The word "epic" would not apply to the moment by moment experience of the film, which is one of aggressive elongation punctuated by a mild sadness. She does not glorify the land, but seems to mourn for it. The film's title is superimposed over the passing landscapes, in the form of an anagram, continually shifting (a computer made the permutations), a simile to the variant sameness of the shots.]

* I have subsequently learned that this was not actually a loop, but several different sailboats in sequence.

I have had occasion to mention Stan Brakhage's work several times in these pages and to single out his *Song 6*. The nearest he has come to a structural film yet is his recent *Song 27, My Mountain*. To single out any one *Song* as a formal organism is to ignore the complex over-all emerging form of *Songs* as a single home-movie serial, some of whose images and many of whose themes, sporadically recur. Then, excluding the coda called *Rivers*, *Song 27, My Mountain* studies a mountain peak for thirty minutes, from a few different angles, with shots of clouds and a rainbow included.

How is this a structural film? The notes I have given so far describe a method of construction based on a fixed image, loop printing, and slight variations of this, and I have promised to discuss the flicker film. The minimalization of technique accompanies the minimalization of image in these instances, which is not strictly the case with Brakhage's mountain song.

The extreme concentration in Brakhage's film upon the mountain as durable energy—it survives several seasons, persistently emerges from engulfing clouds—creates a kind of tension and a sense of potentiality comparable to the most dynamic structural films, *Wavelength*, Landow's *Bardo Follies* (1966), Markopoulos's *Gammelion* (1968), and Sharits's N:O:T:H:I:N:G (1968). The space of a mountain, an arrogant young Rockie at that, is not that of a room. Harry Smith once proposed that Warhol film Mt. Fuji with his fixed camera. The gesture would have been ironical and true to Warhol's world-view: a diminishing of the energy of the subject. Brakhage has again shown his genius by moving the camera positions, allowing the seasons to change and, thus, finding the structure that would hold the terror of a field as big as a mountain.

In his recent lectures, he has spoken of the growing influence of Dutch and Flemish painters over his compositional sense and has seen, in Van Eyck especially, an awareness for slight movements at the edge of the frame. Appropriately, in *Song 27, My Mountain*, the tension that a single shot could easily create over thirty minutes is sustained through a multitude of shots by careful coordination of the minute movements at the corners of the screen. He did not use a tripod, but he approximated the stillness of the tripod to make these tiny excursions more emphatic. Thus, he keeps the unit of the image, thematically, and reaffirms the space of the film frame. The synthetic unity of these forces is his structure.

The most devout of the structural film-makers and perhaps the most sublime is George Landow. His first film, *Fleming Faloon* (1963), is a precursor of the structural tendency, though not quite achieved. The theme of a direct address is at the center of its construction: Beginning with two boobs reciting "Around the world in eighty minutes," jump-cuts of a TV newscaster, and image upon image of a staring face, sometimes full-screen, sometimes the butt of a dollying camera, superimposed upon itself, sometimes split into four images (unsplit 8mm photography, in which two sets of two consecutive images appear in the 16mm frame) televisions, mirrored televisions, and superimposed movies are interspersed. Although I have seen the film many times, I could never find a structural principle after the opening, which Landow has called the prelude. *Fleming Faloon* is simply a series of related images.

The sensibility that created *Fleming Faloon*, a film-maker more than any other nonanimator devoted to the flat-screen cinema, the moving-grain painting, is the primary force in the structural film. Perhaps he actually invented it when he made *Film in which there appear sprocket holes, edge lettering, dirt particles, etc.* He derived its image from a commercial test film, originally nothing more than a girl staring at the camera, a blink of her eye is the only motion, with a spectrum of primary colors beside her. Landow had the image reprinted so that the girl and the spectrum occupies only one half of the frame, the other half of which is made up of sprocket holes, frilled with rapidly changing edge letters, and, in the far right screen, half of the girl's head again.

Landow premiered this film as loop at the Film-Makers Cinematheque, calling it *This film will be interrupted after ten minutes by a commercial*. True to its title, the film was interrupted with an 8mm interjection of Rembrandt's "Town Council" as reproduced by Dutch Master Cigars. A luscious green scratch stood across the splice in the loop, which gave it a particular tonality during that single performance, since only that identified the cycling of the loop, and contrasted with the red overtone of the image.

When the loop, minus the commercial, was printed to become *Film in which*, etc., Landow instructed the laboratory not to clean the dirt from the film but to make a clean splice that would hide the repetitions. The resultant film, a found object extended to a simple structure, is the essence of a minimal cinema. The girl's face is static; perhaps a blink is glimpsed; the sprocket holes do not move but waver slightly as the system of edge lettering flashes around them. Deep into the film, the dirt begins to form time patterns, and the film ends.

There is a two-screen version of this film, projected with no line separating the two panels and with the right images reversed so that a synthetic girl, with two left hand sides of her face, is evoked between the two girl panels.

Bardo Follies (1966), Landow's most sophisticated film, describes a kind of meditation analogous to the *Tibetan Book of the Dead*. The film begins with a loop-printed image of a water flotilla carrying a woman who waves to us at every turn of the loop. After about ten minutes (there is a shorter version, too), the same loop appears doubled into a set of circles against the black screen. Then there are three circles for an instant. The film image in the circles begins to burn, creating a moldy, wavering, orange-dominated mass. Eventually, the entire screen fills with one burning frame, which disintegrates in slow motion in an extremely grainy soft focus. Another frame burns; the whole screen throbs with melting celluloid. Probably, this was created by several generations of photography off the screen—its effect is to make the screen itself seem to throb and smolder. The tension of the silly loop is maintained throughout this section, in which the film stock itself seems to die. After a long while, it becomes a split screen of air bubbles in water filmed through a microscope with colored filters, a different color on each side of the screen. Through changes of focus the bubbles lose shape and dissolve into one another and the four filters switch. Finally, some forty minutes after the first loop, the screen goes white. The film ends.

Structurally, we have the gradual abstraction of an image (originally emphasized through loop printing) through burning and slow-motion rephotography off the screen. The final images of air bubbles are metaphorical extensions of the process of abstraction. The entire opus is open to the interpretation suggested by the title, of the pursuit of the pure light from the "follies" of daily life. The viewer comes to see not the images of the earth, the girl on her flotilla, but the colors and tones of the light itself in a chain of purification.

In his latest work, *The Film that Rises to the Surface of Clarified Butter* (1968), Landow extends the structural principle of the loop into a cycle of visions. Here, we see, in black and white, the head of a working animator; he draws a line, makes a body; then he animates a grotesque humanoid shape. In negative, a girl points to the drawing and taps on it with a pencil. This sequence of shots—the back of the animator, the animation, the negative girl looking at it—occurs three times, but not with exactitude, since there is sometimes more negative material in one cycle than in another. Next, we see (another?) animator, this time from the front; he is creating a similar monster; he animates it. Again we see him from the front;

again he animates it. Such is the action of the film. A wailing sound out of Tibet accompanies the whole film. The title as well is Eastern: Landow read about "the film that rises to the surface of clarified butter" in the *Upanishads*.

The explicit ontology of the film, based on the distinction between graphic (the monsters), two-dimensional modality and photographic naturalism (the animators, even the pen resting beside the monsters as they move in movie illusion), as a metaphor for the relation of film itself (a two-dimensional field of illusion) and actuality, is a classic perception implicit since the beginning of animation and explicit countless times before. Yet what film has been built solely about this metaphor? No other, I can recall. Landow's genius is not his intellectual approach (even though he would be among the most intelligent film-makers in the country), which is simplistic, that is, the variations on announcing and looking (*Fleming Faloon*), the extrinsic visual interest in a film frame (*Film in which there appear sprocket holes, edge lettering, dirt particles, etc.*), a meditation on the pure light trapped in a ridiculous image (*Bardo Follies*), and the echo of an illusion (*Film that Rises to the Surface of Clarified Butter*); his remarkable faculty is as maker of images; for the simple found objects (*Film in which*; beginning of *Bardo Follies*) he uses and the images he photographs are among the most radical, superreal, and haunting images the cinema has ever given us. Without this sense of imagery, all of his films would have failed—as a few of his early 8mm works do. Because of this peculiar visual genius, his work is the most consistently pertinent, on a spiritual level, of all the film-makers considered here (excepting, of course, Brakhage and Markopoulos, whose works are really tangential to the themes of this article).

The occurrence of a structural film among the works of Gregory Markopoulos is, to say the least, a surprise. His most outstanding contribution to the language of cinema has been the use of single-frame flashes in film narrative. But the whole point of this speedy image, which he confirms in his writing, was toward the elaborations of more complex forms, an articulation of simultaneity. Robert Breer was perhaps the true pioneer for the single-frame film sequence (although, of course, Eisenstein, Vertov and, even, Griffith had used rapid flashes in the past), and remotely the forefather of the structural film, certainly long before Kubelka or Warhol. His speed of imagery is quite opposite in effect to that of Markopoulos, and his sensibility would be labeled more precisely "kinetic," along with Len Lye, his one equal.

It might be noted in passing that Breer too has created his most structural, certainly most minimal film during the past two years. It is 66, an animation of primary color shapes interrupting the stasis of the previous image shape. The film is still too much of a natural outgrowth of Breer's process and career to be considered an unusual deviation toward the structural.

To return to Markopoulos, what is interesting in *Gammelion* is that it takes the shape of a flicker film and still remains a narrative. Perhaps a thousand times, the screen fades into white and out again, creating the impression of a great winking eye. Sometimes, the fades in and out are colored, sometimes not. After the first minutes of these slow blinks, a single image is injected into the film; then a little later there are more, perhaps four or five frame shots. Until the very end, *Gammelion* evolves as it began, a minimal narrative in a structural matrix.

For many years, Markopoulos wanted to film *The Castle of Argol* of Julian Gracq, and he chose Caresse Crosby's Roccasinabalda as the site. In 1963, I read a film script of some 400 pages closely following the novel. This was while Markopoulos was editing *Twice A Man*. The project was postponed to make *The Illiac Passion* and never resumed in the original form. Yet, when Markopoulos found himself in Italy in 1967 and with only enough money to purchase about two rolls of color film three minutes long apiece, he went to Roccasinabalda and filmed. He shot the entrance of the castle, the corridors, some rooms, the flag which is a black sun, a naked couple in the fresco, a spot of blood on the pathway. These are the elements of his narrative along with the sound of a trotting horse, some romantic music (Wagner, I think), and the following lines from Rilke: "To be loved means to be consumed. To love means to radiate with inexhaustible light. To be loved is to pass away. To love is to endure." The details of the shooting experience can be found in *Film Culture* No. 46, where Markopoulos has written "Correspondences of Smells and Visuals," the most revealing of all the articles I have read from him.

As we sit before *Gammelion*, we see the winking screen. The flashes are interruptions of the structure, as if the implanted narrative were taking place somewhere else entirely. Within the terms of Markopoulos's previous work, the technique of fading in and out may be interpreted as a psychological distancing or phrasing of the images as in a remote memory. A few years ago, he began to employ the fade as a formal device in *Eros o Basileus* (1967), where it syncopates the rhythm of the long erotic tableaux. In spirit, that film is close to *Gammelion*, even though, in mechanics, they seem so opposite, the earlier being composed of the longest shots Markopoulos has ever taken and the latter made up solely of flashes. The crucial difference of form concerns us here; for *Eros o Basileus* is a serial film, and *Gammelion* is structural.

By making *The Flicker* (1965), Tony Conrad brought a new clarity to Kubelka's *Arnulf Rainer*, which he had not seen. Both films are montages of black-and-white leader; Kubelka's is melodic and classical, with bursts of phrasing, pauses and explosions; the sound, white noise and silence, is likewise symphonic, sometimes synchronous with the image, more often syncopated; Conrad built one long crescendo-diminuendo (*The Flicker* is four times as long as *Arnulf Rainer*) with a single blast of stereophonic buzz for the soundtrack.

Film Culture published a series of articles by and about Conrad in 1966 (No. 41). Here one finds the most articulate expression of the consciousness of structural form of any published record of the film-makers involved. In a letter to Henry Romney, he wrote:

> So I always try to give the impression of serenity and repose whenever I work with extreme materials.
>
> A word on the subject of the static style and its place in art, since I have just implied a bias in this direction. The static seems to be regarded with some suspicion in the age of rock n' roll; although it is a basic dimension of all creative work, it easily gets labeled as exoticism or as very far out. Naturally this imagery is by that very fact a part of the picture, but I do not feel that static style can sustain itself on these alone as a thing in itself for very long. Like other "new" things, it has to incorporate itself as a tool into a moving stream of artistic creation. Among the current exponents of this style, I, long ago, sought out La Monte Young, and I have felt that our long collaboration has proven unprecedentedly fruitful as a continuous evolving development. On the other hand, I have never been able to cure myself of suspicions that Andy Warhol's static films, for example, are incurably opportunistic and basically devoid of the intrinsic interest or freshness that I feel to be the real challenge of static work.

Here Conrad mistakes the quality of most structural films "static" for the form and thereby includes the work of Warhol in this classification. As I have elaborated earlier, Warhol's form is something quite different as becomes more and more apparent the more films he makes. Yet the use of the word "static" is a helpful guide to the difference between Conrad's *The Flicker* and Kubelka's *Arnulf Rainer* and, by extension, a definition of the image in the structural cinema.

The structural film is static because it is not modulated internally by evolutionary concerns. In short, there are no climaxes in these films. They are visual, or audio-visual objects whose most striking characteristic is their over-all shape.

Conrad's second film, *The Eye of Count Flickerstein*, begins with a brief Dracula parody in which the camera moves up to the eye of the Count; then, until the end of the film, we see a boiling swarm of images very similar to, if not made from, the static on a television screen when the station is not transmitting. Aesthetically, *Count Flickerstein* lacks the ambition of *The Flicker*, but it is not without visual interest.

Both Conrad and Kubelka have worked with the fundamental primitive energy of the flicker principle, and it is obvious why they would use black-and-white film for this charge. Paul Sharits has made three color flickers, sensitive films, without the ecstatic power of either *The Flicker* or *Arnulf Rainer*, but he has done more than either of his predecessors to develop the formal potential of the flicker film.

Ray Gun Virus was his first attempt in this genre, and it is the simplest. It is a splattering of colors. Its effect is distanced, a calm look at the modulations of rapidly changing color tones. In essence, *Ray Gun Virus* is the base for both of Sharits's intricate structures, *Piece Mandala* and *N:O:T:H:I:N:G*. In *Piece Mandala* (1967), he elaborates themes of sex and self-violence within the tissue of the color flashes. In this way, he raises the dramatic power of the flickering colors by metaphor rather than visually. A mandala is a meditation wheel. Literally, it derives its name from the Sanskrit etymology of "a circle." The film begins and ends the same way, with staccato stills of lovemaking, mostly of postures of entry, some cunnilingus, breast feeling. As the film progresses, the color flashes grow longer, the still more isolated, until in the middle of the work, there is the photograph of a young man's head; he is pointing a gun at his skull; animated dots outline the bullet's path. Then the film completes the circular form; the flashes grow shorter, the loving stills more excited. The film ends as it began with the flashing titles: Peace, War.

Before I had seen *N:O:T:H:I:N:G* (1968), I had a limited respect for Sharits's art. Now I can see the two films discussed above only as preparations for his one fully developed film. In *N:O:T:H:-I:N:G*, the flashing colors have the sense of potential space-time that we noted in the fixed image structures of Baillie, Landow, Snow, and Markopoulos.

This film is much longer than the earlier two, about forty minutes, and, to a much greater extent, the colors group in major and minor phrases with, say, a pale blue dominant at one time, a yellow dominant at another. The colors tend toward the cooler shades. The ultimate aspiration of Sharits's cinema must be the synthesis of whiteness; because the natural effect of his blazing colors is a blending that will always tend toward a bleaching. In *Ray Gun Virus*, the bleaching affected me as a weakness, but in N:O:T:H:I:N:G, the related contextual images and the sound, as well as the title, utilize the theme of evaporation (which is the converse of potentiality, which is the mode of all structural films). From the very beginning, the screen flickers clusters of colors; the titles gradually flash on, the letters and colors separately, while the sound suggests a telegraph code, or chattering teeth, or the plastic click of suddenly changing television channels.

The first image interlude in the chain of color shows us a chair animated in positive and negative; it floats down-screen, away into nothing, or the near nothing of the mutually exterminating colors. The interlude is marked with the sound of a telephone. The remaining and the main body of the film is continually interrupted for short periods by the image of a light bulb, two-dimensional like the chair before it, dripping its vital light fluid. From the first occurrence of this image until the last drop of bulb fluid has leaked out, a series of static beeps are heard, gradually spaced further and further apart. In the end, we see only long passages of color clusters whose dominants are synchronized to the moos of cows.

In essence, there are only three flicker films of importance, *Arnulf Rainer, The Flicker*, and N:O:T:H:I:N:G. The first is the most dynamic and inventive. The second is a splendid extension (who of those who knew Kubelka's film would have thought it possible?) into the area of meditative cinema. In terms of the subjects we have discussed here, it is Sharits's N:O:T:H:I:N:G that opens the field for the structural film with a flicker base. In all instances, even the overtly psychedelic use of the flicker by John Cavanaugh in *The Dragon's Claw* (1967), the employment of color has diminished the basic apocalypse of the flicker. Sharits has worked this to his advantage. His latest film builds wave after wave of colors, each modulated by the minor of the spectrum, as a context of minimalization for his images.

POSTSCRIPT

The distinction between the "Fluxus" films that Maciunas speaks of in his rebuttal to the first printing of this article and the films about which I have written is subtle, because it is not a matter of definition but of degree. If we think of the structural films as cinematic propositions in a rigorously ordered form, the "Fluxus" films would be tautologies. For example, Chieko Shiomi's *Disappearing Music for Face,* shows the end of a smile filmed with an ultrahigh-speed camera so that the muscles relax over a twelve-minute period; Yoko Ono's *No. 4* presents one walking naked ass after another, without any depth of space (they were walking on a treadmill); and Maciunas's own *End After 9,* is simply academy leader from 1 to 9 followed by a title, "End."

Recently, a number of distinguished sculptors have begun to make films in the halfway ground between the subversive "Fluxus" works and the complex structural films. There are Richard Serra's films of various hand manipulations (catching, untying, standing on them) and his film of measuring the size of the film frame at a given distance away from the camera (which I have not seen) and Bruce Nauman's films of handball, violin-playing, and a loop of a mouth repeating the expression "lip synch." The most interesting new film by a nonfilm-maker in this arena has been an untitled two-screen work by Robert Morris, which shares a dialectic of wide views/details with Jacobs's *Tom Tom, The Piper's Son.* On one screen, Morris has a wide-angle view of a gas station in Southern California with houses in the background and the ocean behind them. The shot is fixed and uninterrupted for about forty minutes. On the adjacent screen, he shows the same scene from the same camera position, filmed simultaneously, with a zoom lens that picks out details and follows them.

Morris wants the two images projected by synchronous machines. The evening I saw it they were slightly out of phase so that the details sometimes preceded and sometimes followed the overview. In addition to this, the zoom camera occasionally slips beyond the borders of the static one. For me, both the spatial and temporal asynchronisms enriched the experience of the film. Like Jacobs's film, Morris's has a sensual involvement (implicit in their common principle, which is that of art historical criticism) which the "Fluxus" works reject.

The most critical case of the ambiguity of the definition of the structural film arises from a consideration of the work of Hollis Frampton, a young film-maker who has produced some sixteen films in the last three years, all of which bear upon our considerations here. His latest, *Artificial Light* (1969), summarizes, in its permutations, many of the concerns of his earlier works. Frampton is the rare example of an intellectual film-maker, perhaps the first since Sidney Peterson. (This is not to denigrate the intellect of many intelligent film-makers. I am distinguishing intelligence from the particular commitment to abstract formulations characterized by the epithet "intellectual.") Because of his critical awareness of the function of his own work within the contexts of film history and Modernist Art, he has made films that are especially difficult to categorize, which is certainly to his credit.

Artificial Light repeats variations on a single filmic utterance twenty times. The same phrase is a series of portrait shots of a group of young New York artists informally talking, drinking wine, laughing, smoking. The individual portrait-shots follow each other with almost academic smoothness in lap-dissolves ending in two shots of the entire group followed by a dolly shot into a picture of the moon. In the following synoptic outline, this entire phrase, which lasts about one minute in black and white, will be called A:

Artificial Light

1. A, upside-down and backwards.
2. A, in negative.
3. A, with superimposition of sprocket holes.
4. A, with eyes painted blue and mouths red.
5. A, scarred with a white drip mark.
6. A, covered with transparent stripes of red and green.
7. Still shots in sequence from A; a stroboscopic or flicker effect.
8. A, almost obliterated by scratches.
9. Shots from A, toned different colors by dye, in an asequential order.
10. A, with faces and hair outlined by scratches, dissolves marked with a scratched slash (/).
11. A, spotted with multicolor drops.
12. Superimposition of A, with a copy of A in which left and right are reversed.
13. A, with all faces bleached out.
14. A, with a flicker of colors (red, green, blue).
15. A, covered with "art-type" printers dots.
16. A, toned sepia.
17. A, superimposed over itself with a lag of one-and-a-half seconds.
18. A, interrupted by two-frame flashes of color negative.
19. A, colored, as if through an electrical process, in a series of two primaries.
20. A, with a closeup of a moon crater substituted for the expected moon shots.

It should be obvious from the outline that the filmic phrase functions like a tone row in dodecaphonic music and serial composition. Frampton has made two very interesting manipulations of the experience of this phrase. In the first place, by opening the film with a backwards and upside-down run of it, he dislocates the viewer for several repetitions; one comes *gradually* to realize that there is a fixed order or direction. That progression is rigidly fixed by the first third of the film. The ninth variation violently jars us with its elliptical disorder. The rest of the film proceeds logically until the last shot which has a feeling of finality both from its variation and from being held on the screen longer.

I saw this film in the company of two friends, a film-maker and a philosopher of art, who raised first the relevance of Stan Brakhage to this film (for Brakhage has worked with repetitions and variations in a serial order more than any other film-maker in his epic *The Art of Vision* [1960–65]) and then the question of the appropriateness or inappropriateness of Frampton material for serial treatment. There is a chasm betwen the phrase A and its formal inflections. That chasm is intellectual as well as formal. Frampton loves an outrageous hypothesis; his films, all of them, take the shape of logical formulae. Usually, the logic he invokes is that of the paradox—a Modernist tendency that finds its literary apogee in the stories of Jorge Luis Borges. In a recent lecture at The Millennium in New York, Frampton hypothesized an atemporal alternative to the history of cinema, illustrated by a sequence of his works. With *Artificial Light*, which was not completed in time for that lecture, he challenges the newest historical phase of the formal cinema, the structural film.

GEORGE MACIUNAS (DEC.5,1969): SOME COMMENTS ON *STRUCTURAL FILM* BY P.ADAMS SITNEY *(FILM CULTURE NO.47,1969)*

We have heard of *3 EMPTIES* and *3 NOTHINGS* (response of Vietnamese villagers), *3 HOLIES, 3 TRUTHS*, etc. and now P.Adams Sitney has contributed *3 ERRORS*: (wrong terminology, wrong examples-chronology and wrong sources for origins).

category	error	cause of error	proposed correction of error
terminology	Term of *Structural Film* is semantically incorrect, since structure **does not** mean or imply simple. Structure is an arrangement of parts according either to complex or simple design, pattern or organization. **Complex structures:** fugue, sonata, serial form, indeterminate statics of concrete frame, desoxyribose nucleic acid molecule. **Simple structures:** continuous crescendo, pivot support beam, helium molecule, *So Sho* painting, *Haiku*, held tone, etc.	Misplaced dictionary and ignorance of recent *art-philosophy* such as definitions of *Concept-art* and *Structure-art* by Henry Flynt in his *General Aesthetics*, or *Concept Art* essay in *An Anthology, 1963*	(As proposed in *Expanded Arts Diagram*, by G.Maciunas, *Film Culture No.43, 1966*) **Monomorphic structure** *(having a single, simple form; exhibiting essentially one structural pattern)* **Neo-Haiku.** This monomorphism tends to border on *Concept-art*, since it emphasizes an image or idea of generalization from particulars rather than particularization (arrangement into particular design or pattern) of generalities. In *Concept-art* realization of form is therefore irrelevant, since it is an art of which the material is *concepts* (closely bound with language), rather than particular form of film, sound, etc.
chronology of each category ⊙̇ single staccato	no examples given	Cliquishness and ignorance of film-makers outside the *Coop.* or *Cinematheque* circle.	George Brecht: *Two Durations*, 3 lamp events, 1961 Dick Higgins: *Constellation no.4, 1960; Plunk, 1964* Eric Andersen: *Opus 74, 1965* Anonymous: *Eye Blink, 1966*
⌒⊙̇ o̶———o̶ ⟶ linear progress, held image, tone, straight development.	Andy Warhol: *Sleep, 1963-4; Eat, 1964.* John Cavanaugh: *The Dragon's Claw, 1965* Paul Sharits: *Ray Gun Virus, Piece Mandala, N:O:T:H:I:N:G.* Joyce Wieland: *Sailboat,* etc. *1967*	same as above	La Monte Young: *Composition 1960 No.9,* realized in 1965 Jackson Mac Low: *Tree Movie, 1961.* Nam June Paik: *Zen for Film, 1962-4.* Dick Higgins: *Invocation of Canyons & Boulders for Stan Brakhage, 1963* (endless eating motion of mouth) Brion Gysin: *Flicker machine, 1963-4.* George Brecht: *Black Movie, 1965* Paul Sharits: *Sears, 1965* (single frame exposure of Sears catalogue pages), *Wrist trick, Word Movie,* etc. John Cavanaugh: *The Dragon's Claw, 1965* (flicker) Milan Knizak: *Pause, 1966* James Riddle: *9 Minutes, 1966* George Maciunas: *10 feet, 1000 frames, Artype (lines) 1966*
⟨⟩ ⟶ arithmetic or algebraic progression. transition, zoom f stop or focus change; crescendo or decrescendo	Tony Conrad: *The Flicker, 1966* Michael Snow: *Wavelength, 1967* Ernie Gehr: *Wait, Moments,* etc. *1968* George Landow: *Bardo Follies*	same as above	Nam June Paik: *Empire State Building, 1964* (f stop change) George Brecht: *Entry—Exit, 1962* realized in 1965 (black to white transition, either by f stop change or devel.) Takehisa Kosugi: *Film & Film for Mekas, 1965* Chieko Shiomi: *Disappearing Music for Face, 1965-6* Tony Conrad: *The Flicker, 1966* George Maciunas: *Artype (dots), 1966* Michael Snow: *Wavelength, 1967,* Ernie Gehr films, 1968, George Landow: *Bardo Follies,* Ayo: *Rainbow, 1968-9.* (color wheel: yellow to green)
∿∿∿ wave motion; back & forward	no examples given		Paul Sharits: *Dots, 1965* Yoko Ono: *Number 4, 1965* (buttock movement of walker) Michael Snow: ⟵⟶ *, 1968*
readymades & found film	George Landow: *Fleming Faloon, 1965*		Nam June Paik: *Zen for Film, 1962-4* (film with dust) George Landow: *Fleming Faloon, 1965* Albert M.Fine: *Readymade, 1966* (color test strip)
origins and precursors	Peter Kubelka: *Arnulf Rainer, 1958,* which is not monomorphic but polymorphic (complex) in structure. Andy Warhol: *Sleep, 1963-4,* which to begin with is a plagiarized version of Jackson Mac Low's *Tree Movie, 1961* just as his *Eat, 1964* is a plagiarized version of Dick Higgins' *Invocation...* or his *Empire, 1964* a plagiarized version of Nam June Paik's *Empire State Building.*	Ignorance of precursory monomorphic examples in other art forms, such as music, events and even film.	Zen chant, Haiku poem, So Sho painting, Eric Satie: *Vexations* John Cage: *4'3", 1952* (silence) Yves Klein: *Monotone Symphony, Blue Movie* etc. *1958* La Monte Young: *Composition 1960 No.7 & 9,* etc. (drawn continuous line, held tone, etc.) George Brecht: *Drip Music, 1959; Direction (⟶ ⟵), 3 Yellow events* (for slide projector), *Word Event (Exit), 2 Vehicle events (start, stop)* & many other 1961 pieces. Ben Vautier: *Intermission,* & many other 1961 pieces. Nam June Paik: most of his 1960-61 compositions. Robert Morris: *Print* (till ink runs out) Walter De Maria: *Beach Crawl, 1960.* Etc. etc. etc. etc.

FIVE
OVERVIEWS AND THEORETICAL CONSIDERATIONS

The essays by Parker Tyler, Ken Kelman, Sidney Peterson, and Annette Michelson, discuss the American avant-garde in the context of the cinema as a whole.

The Russian film-maker Dziga Vertov and the poet Robert Kelly, offer theoretical considerations of the essential elements of film.

THE WRITINGS OF DZIGA VERTOV

No. 25, Summer, 1962

[Editor's note: Dziga Vertov was the pseudonym of Denis Arkadye-vich Kaufman (1896–1954). The several pieces we are presenting here will give some idea of the revolutionary scope of Dziga Vertov's work in cinema. We hope that someone, soon, will bring us a retro-spective show of his work.

We are grateful to Mme. Elisaveta Svilova, the widow of Dziga Vertov, for providing us with these valuable materials. The *Kinoks-Revolution* manifesto was first published in 1919. It reappeared, in an extended version, in *Lef* magazine, No. 3, 1922 (edited by Mayakov-ski), from which our translation was taken. "The Notebooks" ap-peared in *Iskusstvo Kino*, No. 4, 1957.—Jonas Mekas]

FROM *KINOKS REVOLUTION*

I would just like to establish that all we have been doing in cine-matography up till now was a 100 per cent muddle and diametrically opposed to what we should have been doing.

DZIGA VERTOV

FROM THE MANIFESTO OF THE BEGINNING OF 1922

You—cinematographers:

directors without occupation and artists without occupation, flustered cameramen

and scenario writers scattered the world over,

You—the patient public of the movie houses with the tolerance of mules under the load of served emotions.

You—the impatient owners of the not-yet-bankrupt movie theaters, greedily snapping up the scraps off the German table, and, to a lesser extent, the American table—

You wait,

Debilitated by memories, you day dream and pine for the MOON of the new six-reel feature . . .

(nervous persons are asked to close their eyes),

You wait for what will not happen and what you should not expect.

My friendly warning:

Don't bury your heads like ostriches.

Raise your eyes,

Look around—

There!

Seen by me and by every child's eye:

Insides falling out.

Intestines of experience

Out of the belly of cinematography

slashed

By the reef of the revolution,

there they drag

leaving a bloody trace on the ground, shuddering from terror and repulsion.

All is ended.

Dziga Vertov

FROM A STENOGRAPH

. . . A psychological, detective, satirical, or any other picture. Cut out all scenes and just leave titles. We will get a literary skeleton of the picture. To this literary skeleton we can add new footage—realistic, symbolical, expressionist—any kind. Things are not changed. Neither is the interrelationship: literary skeleton plus cinematic illustration.

Such are all our and foreign pictures, without exception.

FROM THE MANIFESTO OF 20/I–1923 COUNCIL OF THREE TO THE CINEMATOGRAPHERS

. . . Five full-blooded world-daring years have entered you and left, leaving no mark. Samples of prerevolutionary art hang like icons and still attract your prayerful entrails. Foreign lands support you in your confusion, sending into the renovated Russia the uncremated remains of movie dramas dressed with an excellent technological sauce.

Spring is coming. Studios are expected to start work. The Council of Three does not hide its regret as it watches how the producers leaf through literature looking for pieces suitable for conversion into scenarios. The names of theater dramas and poems slated for possible production are floating through the air. In the Ukraine, and here in Moscow, several pictures have already been made bearing witness to all qualities of impotence.

Pronounced technical backwardness, the loss of ability to think actively as a result of the doldrums, the orientation on the six-reel psychodrama, that is, the orientation on one's own behind—condemns in advance all their attempts.

The organism of cinematography is poisoned by the frightful venom of habit. We demand being given an opportunity to experiment with this dying organism, with an objective of finding an antitoxin.

We offer the unbelievers to be convinced; we agree to try out our medicine first on the "rabbits," on the movie *études*.

Council of Three

RESOLUTION OF THE COUNCIL OF THREE 10/IV–1923

Resolution on the cine-front: Consider not in favor.

First Russian productions shown us, as expected, are reminiscent of the old "artistic" models in the same way that the NEP-men remind us of the old *bourgeoisie*.

Projected production schedules for the summer, here and in Ukraine inspire no confidence.

Possibilities of wide experimental work is in the background.

All efforts, all sighs, tears, and hopes, all prayers are to her—the six-reel cine-drama.

Therefore, be it resolved, that the Council of Three, not waiting for the admission of Kinoks to production and, in spite of the desire of Kinoks to realize by themselves their own projects, forgoes for the moment the right of authorship and decrees:

publish immediately for broad distribution the general basis and credos of the impending revolution through the Movie newsreel, for which purpose Dziga Vertov is hereby directed, along the lines of party discipline, to publish these passages from the book, *Kinoks Revolution,* which describe the substance of the revolution.

Council of Three

Carrying out the resolution of the Council of Three of April 10, 1923, the following excerpts are published:

1.

Watching the pictures that came from the West and from America, taking into account the information we have on the work and searching abroad and here—I come to the following conclusion:

Verdict of death, decreed by Kinoks in 1919, to all motion pictures without exception, is in effect to this day.

The most careful inspection does not reveal a single picture, a single searching, that tries correctly to unserfage the camera, now in pitiful slavery, under orders of an   LEGALIZED MYOPIA imperfect shallow eye.

We do not object if cinematography tunnels under literature, under theater; we fully approve the utilization of the cinema for all branches of science, but we recognize these functions as accessory, as offshoots and branches.

The fundamental and the most important:

Cinema—the feel of the world.

The initial point:

The utilization of the camera,   WAY FOR THE MACHINE as a cinema eye—more perfect than a human eye for purposes of reseach into the chaos of visual phenomena filling the universe.

The eye lives and moves in time and space, perceiving and recording impressions in a way quite different from the human eye. It is not necessary for it to have a particular   DOWN WITH stance or to be limited in the number   16 PHOTOGRAPHS of moments to be observed per second.   PER SECOND

The movie camera is better.

We cannot make our eyes better than they have been made, but the movie camera we can perfect forever.

To this day, the cameraman is criticized if a running horse moves unnaturally slowly on the screen (quick turn of the camera) or, conversely, if a tractor ploughs too fast (the slow manipulation of the camera crank).

ACCIDENTAL SYNTHESIS AND CONCENTRATION OF MOTION

These, of course, are incidental, but we are preparing a thoughtout system of these incidents, a system of apparent abnormalities that organize and explore phenomena.

To this day, we raped the movie camera and forced it to copy the work of our eye. And the better the copy, the better the shot was considered. As of today, we will unshackle the camera and will make it work in the opposite direction, further from copying.

DO NOT COPY FROM THE EYES

Out with all the weaknesses of the human eye.

MACHINE AND ITS CAREER

We hearby ratify the eye, which is groping in the chaos of motions for a movement of its own and in its own right; we validate the eye with its own measurement of strength and in potentially before the self-ratification.

2.

. . . to induce the viewer to see in a way that is best for me to show. The eye obeys the will of the camera and is directed by it to that sequence of moments of action that best brings out a cinema-phrase, the sequence that raises and lowers dénouement with the greatest brilliance and speed.

System of the Continuity of Actions

Example: Shooting a boxing bout not from the point of view of a member of the audience, but on the basis of showing off as best as possible the sequence of holds of the boxers.

Example: Shooting a group of dancers—but not from the point of view of the audience, sitting in an auditorium and having in front of it scenes of a ballet.

For the viewer of a ballet haphazardly follows the whole group, or incidental performers, or some legs— a series of scattered observations, different for everyone in the audience.

THE MOST INEFFICIENT, THE MOST UNECONOMICAL RENDITION OF A SCENE IS THE THEATRICAL RENDITION

The movie viewer cannot be presented with this. The system of consecutive actions demands filming the dancers or the boxers in a way which would account for consecutive events with certain details and actions forced upon the viewer, so that there is no chance for him to miss these.

The camera drags the eyes of the viewer from hands to legs, from legs to eyes, in a way that is the most efficient. It organizes the parts into an edited orderly study.

3.

You are walking on a Chicago street today in 1923, but I make you nod to comrade Volodarsky, who is, in 1918 walking down a street in Petrograd; he acknowledges your greeting.

MONTAGE IN TIME AND SPACE

Another example: They are lowering the coffins of national heroes (shot in Astrakhan in 1918), they fill in the graves (Cronstadt, 1921), cannon salute (Petrograd, 1920), memorial-service hats come off (Moscow, 1922). These actions go together even in the ungrateful, not specially filmed, material (see *Kino-Pravda, No. 13*). Crowds greeting Lenin in different places, in different times are also in this category (see *Kino-Pravda, No. 14*).

. . . I am eye. I am builder.

I implanted you, a most remarkable chamber which did not exist until I created it today. In this chamber, there are twelve walls, photographed by me in various parts of the world. Manipulating shots of walls and details, I have succeeded in arranging them in an order that pleases you and in constructing correctly a cinematic phrase, which is the room.

HUMAN RACE OF KINOKS COUNCIL OF THREE. MOSCOW, HALL OF INTERVALS TODAY- TODAY APRIL 3 REPORT BY DZV ON THE THEME CHAMBRE CINEMA-PHRASE BEGINNING 8:30 P.M.

I am eye. I have created a man more perfect than Adam; I created thousands of different people in accordance with previously prepared plans and charts.

ELECTRIC YOUNG MAN

I am eye.

I take the most agile hands of one, the fastest and the most graceful legs of another, from a third person I take the handsomest and the most expressive head, and, by editing, I create an entirely new perfect man.

. . . I am eye. I am a mechanical eye.

I, a machine, am showing you a world, the likes of which only I can see.

I free myself from today and forever from human immobility, I am in constant movement, I approach and draw away from objects, I crawl under them, I move alongside the mouth of a running horse, I cut into a crowd at full speed, I run in front of running soldiers, I turn on my back, I rise with an airplane, I fall and soar together with falling and rising bodies.

This is I, apparatus, maneuvering in the chaos of movements, recording one movement after another in the most complex combinations.

Freed from the obligation of shooting sixteen–seventeen shots per second, freed from the frame of time and space, I coordinate any and all points of the universe, wherever I may plot them.

My road is toward the creation of a fresh perception of the world. Thus, I decipher in a new way the world unknown to you.

. . . Let us agree once more: The eye and the ear. The ear peeks, the eye eavesdrops.

Distribution of functions.

Radio-ear-edited, "Hear!"

Cinema-eye-edited, "See!"

There it is, citizens, in the first place instead of music, painting, theater, cinematography, and other castrated outpourings.

In a chaos of movements running past, streaking away, running up and colliding—only the eye enters life simply. The day of visual impressions is past. How to convert the impressions of the day into a functional whole—into a visual study? To film everything that an eye has seen will result in a jumble. To edit artfully what had been photographs would result in a greater clarity. It would be better yet to scrap the annoying rubbish. Thus we get organized memoirs of impressions of a simple eye.

ORGANIZATION OF OBSERVATIONS BY A HUMAN EYE

A mechanical eye—that's the movie camera. It refuses to use the human eye as if the latter were a crib-sheet; it is attracted and repelled by motion, feeling through the chaos of observed events for a roadway for its own mobility and modulation; it experiments, extending time, dissecting movement, or, on the contrary, absorbing into itself the time, swallowing years and, thus, diagramming some processes unattainable to the normal eye.

   . . . In aid to the eye-machine is the Kinok, the pilot, who not only steers the apparatus, but also trusts it in experiments in space and in whatever may follow. Kinok, the engineer, directs the apparatus by remote control.

DECOMPOSITION
and
CONCENTRATION
of
VISUAL PHENOMENA

BRAIN

This concerted action by the liberated and perfected apparatus and the strategy-making brain of man—directing, observing, compensating, will result in an unusual freshness, and even the most commonplace will become interesting.

   . . . They are many who, hungering for spectacles, lost their pants in theaters.

They run from weekdays, run from the "prose" of life.

And yet the theater is almost always only a scabby surrogate of this very life plus an idiotic conglomerate from balletic contortions, musical squeaks, clever lighting effects, stage sets (from those smeared on to those constructed) and sometimes good work from literary masters perverted by all this hogwash.

Some theater overseers enlist help: bio-mechanics (a good pursuit by itself), cinema (bestow it honor and glory), literatures (not bad by themselves), constructions (some are not bad), automobiles (how can we not respect them?), rifle shooting (dangerous and impressive thing in the front lines). But, on the whole, not a goddamn thing comes out of it.

Theater and nothing else.

Not only no synthesis but no orderly mixture either.

Could not be otherwise.

We, Kinoks, resolute opponents of premature synthesis ("To synthesis at the zenith of accomplishment"), understand that to mix the crumbs of achievements is to have the infants perish from crowding and disorder.

In general—

ARENA IS SMALL

Please come into life.

Here we work—craftsmen of seeing—organizers of visible life, armed all over with the maturing eye. Here work the master-craftsmen of words and sounds, the most skillful editor-cutters of the heard life. To them, I also dare slip over a mechanical ever-present ear and megaphone—radio telephone.

This is

NEWSREEL
RADIO NEWS

I promise to wangle a parade of Kinoks in Red Square in case the futurists come out with No. 1 of their edited newsreel.

Neither the newsreel of "Pathé" nor of "Gaumont" (newspaper chronicle) nor even the Kino-Truth (political chronicle), but a real Kinok-type of a chronicle—a dashing survey of visual events deciphered by the movie-camera, fragments of actual energy (as against theatrical energy), with their intervals condensed into a cumulative whole by the great mastery of an editing technique.

Such structure of a cinematic thing allows a development of any theme—be it comical, tragic, or anything else.

It is all a matter of juxtaposition of one visual moment with another, all a matter of intervals.

This unusual flexibility of edited structure allows to introduce into a movie continuity, any political, economic, or any other motif.

Therefore

As of today cinema needs no psychological, no detective dramas,

As of today—no theatrical productions shot on film,

As of today—no scenariozation of either Dostoyevsky, or Nat Pinkerton.

Everything is included in the new concept of the newsreel.

Into the confusion of life, hereby decisively enter:

1) The Eye, disputing the visual concept of the world by the human eye and offering its own "I see" and

2) Kinok-editor, who organizes, for the first time, what had been so perceived into minutes of life structure.

Translated from the Russian by Val Telberg

FROM THE NOTEBOOKS OF DZIGA VERTOV

I began early. By writing various fantastic novels (*The Iron Hand*), by writing brief sketches ("Whale Hunting," "Fishing"), poems ("Masha"), epigrams and satirical verse ("Purishkevich," "The Girl With Freckles").

Later, all this was transformed into a fascination with a montage of stenographic notes and sound recording—in particular, a fascination with the possibility of documenting sounds in writing, in attempts to depict in words and letters the sound of a waterfall, the noise of a sawmill, in musical-thematic creations of word-montage, "Laboratory of Hearing."

Later, in the fall of 1918, came the shift to film, life on 7 Gnezdnikovsky Street, and work on the magazine, *Cinema Weekly*. Ideas on the "armed eye," on the role of the camera in the study of the living world. Early experiments with high-speed shooting, the concept of the "cinematic-eye" as a rapid eye (in the sense of a rapid thought).

The early sixteen frames per second became obsolete. Not just rapid filming, but multiplication filming, microfilming, macrofilming, reverse filming, filming with a moving camera—all became commonplace.

The "Kino-Eye" is in the realm of "that which the naked eye does not see," a microscope and telescope of time, an X-ray eye, the "candid" eye, the remote control of a camera.

All these various definitions mutually complement each other; the "Kino-Eye" includes:

all film methods,

all cinematic images, and

all methods and means by which the truth can be shown.

Not the "Kino-Eye" for its own sake, but the truth by the means of the "Kino-Eye." Cinematic truth.

The "candid camera," not for its own sake, but to show people without their make-up on; to catch them through the camera's eye at some moment when they are not acting; to capture their thoughts by means of the camera.

The "Kino-Eye" as a means of making the invisible visible, the obscure clear, the hidden obvious, the disguised exposed, and acting not acting.

But it is not enough to show bits of truth on the screen, separate frames of truth. These frames must be thematically organized so that the whole is also truth. This is an even more difficult task. There is little theoretical study of this problem. Hundreds, thousands of experiments must be conducted, in order to master this new field of cinematographic work.

The "Kino-Eye," which has set for itself the task: "To combine science with cinematic depiction in the struggle to reveal truth . . . to decipher reality," was born in dozens and hundreds of experiments. These experiments, which aided the over-all development of descriptive and scientific filming, continued month after month, year after year. During all this time, it was necessary to overcome great difficulties, not only of an organizational and technical nature, but, for the main part, difficulties caused by our inability to demonstrate the inevitability and necessity of this work. In this experimental work, we can distinguish three periods.

The first period began in 1918. These experiments took place during the Civil War, when *Cinema Weekly* was being published, and filming was being conducted under battle conditions on all fronts. To this period belong such films as *Battle at Tsaritsyn, The Action of Mirnov, Discovery of Sergei Radonezhsky's Remains, The VTIK Train,* and others. This period closes with a long film in thirteen parts: *History of the Civil War* (1921).

The second period begins in 1922. This period could be called the period of *Kino-Pravda (Cinema Truth).* Review films, sketch films, verse films, film poems, and preview films made their appearance. Each release of *Kino-Pravda* brought something new. Considerable work was also being done in the utilization of new methods for subtitling, transforming them into pictorial units equal to those of the images.

Long experimental films, like *The Kino-Eye* (1924) *Forward Soviet!* (1925), *The Sixth Part of the World* (1926) were released.

The third period—*The Kino-Eye in the Ukraine, The October March, The Eleventh Year* (1928), *The Man with a Movie Camera* (1929), a film without words, and *Enthusiasm* (1930), a symphony of noises, were released in rapid succession.

With *Three Songs of Lenin* (1934), that "symphony of thought" began the third period of experiments. *Three Songs of Lenin* was already a manysided experimental synthesis that, with its far-reaching roots, delved into the unwritten creative folklore of the Soviet people.

February, 1940

Early Thoughts

Nineteen-eighteen. I moved to Gnezdnikovsky, #7. Did a risky jump for a slow-motion camera.

Didn't recognize my face on the screen.

My thoughts were revealed on my face—irresolution, vacillation, and firmness (a struggle within myself), and, again, the joy of victory.

First thought of the Kino-Eye is a world perceived without a mask, as a world of naked truth (truth cannot be hidden).

ABC of Cinema

Ilya Ehrenburg, apparently impressed by the first series of the *Kino-Eye*, once wrote:

"The work of Vertov is a laboratory analysis of the world-complex, painstaking. *Kino-Eye* takes reality and transforms it into several basic elements—if you will—into a cinematic alphabet."

Nowadays, we all know that those who worked on *Kino-Pravda* and *Kino-Eye* created a cinematic alphabet, not for its own sake, but to show the truth.

My Views

In 1918, I switched to film. At that time, I was working on a film journal (*Cinema Weekly*), on historical films (*History of the Civil War*), film sketches, film verse (see No. 23 of *Kino-Pravda*), film caricatures (*Today, Chervonets, Grimaces of Paris, Soviet Toys*), films of various war campaigns and actions, experimental studies (*Battle at Tsaritsyn*), and longer film poems (*Kino-Eye, Forward, Soviet!, The Sixth Part of the World, The Eleventh;*) songs without words (*The Man with a Movie Camera*), sound symphonies (*Enthusiasm*), and, finally, the recently finished *Three Songs about Lenin*. All totaled, counting the smaller works, not less than 150 works.

My attitude toward these films is that of an inventor toward his invention. Much is outdated and seems to be a little farcical to me, like a Buster Keaton comedy; but in their own time, these funny experiments did not evoke laughter, but a storm of controversy, ideas, and plans.

These films were less of "widespread demand," than "films precursing other films."

April, 1934

Three Songs About Lenin

I've managed to make *Three Songs About Lenin* (at least to some degree) accessible and comprehensible to millions. But not at the price of cinematographic language, and not by abandoning the principles which had been formulated earlier. No one would demand this of us.

The important thing is not to separate form from content. The secret lies in unity of form and content. In refraining from shocking the spectator by introducing objects or devices that are unnatural or extraneous to the work. In 1933, while thinking about Lenin, I decided to draw from the source of the people's creative folklore about Lenin. I would like to keep on working in this direction.

> If he saw darkness, he created light.
> From the desert, he made orchards.
> From death—life.

or

> A million sand grains make a dune.
> A million peas make a bushel.
> A million weak—a great strength.

Are these images and songs of nameless poets of the people any poorer than the images of the most refined formal works?

The subject in which I am working is the least studied, the most highly experimental subject of cinematography.

The road along which I am going, in an organizational, technical, down-to-earth manner, and in all other senses, demands superhuman efforts. It is a thankless and, believe me, a very difficult road.

But I am hopeful that, in my field, I will be able to defeat formalism, to defeat naturalism, to become a poet not for the few, but for the ever increasing millions.

It is far from simple to show the truth.

But truth itself is simple.

Mayakovsky

Mayakovsky—his work is a Kino-Eye. He sees what the eye does not.

I liked Mayakovsky from the start, without reserve, from the first book I read. The book was called *Simple as a Bellow*. I knew it by heart. I defended him from vilification as well as I knew how; I explained. I did not know Mayakovsky personally at the time. When I first met the poet at the Polytechnic Museum in Moscow, I was not disappointed. He was just as I had imagined him. Mayakovsky noticed me in a group of excited young people. Of course, I looked at him with admiring eyes. He came up to us. "We're awaiting your next book," I said. "Then get your friends together," he answered, "and demand that it gets published more quickly."

My meetings with Mayakovsky were always brief. Sometimes in the street, or at a club, or at a station, or at a cinema. He didn't call me Vertov, but Dziga. I liked that. "Well, how's the Kino-Eye doing, Dziga?" he once asked me. This was somewhere on the road, in a railroad station. Our trains met. "The Kino-Eye is learning," I replied. He thought awhile and said: "The Kino-Eye is a lighthouse of the film world."

The last time I met Mayakovsky was in Leningrad, in the lobby of the Europa Hotel.

Mayakovsky asked the waiter, in a gloomy voice, "Is there going to be a cabaret tonight?" He noticed me and said, "We should have a leisurely talk together. A serious talk. Let's have a 'feature length' creative discussion today."

I waited for Mayakovsky in my room.

It seemed to me that I found the key to filming documentary sounds.

I walked back and forth in my room, waiting for Mayakovsky and rejoicing at having met him again.

I wanted to tell him about my attempts to create a film poem in which montage phrases would rhyme one with the other.

I waited for him till midnight.

I don't know what happened to him; he did not come.

And, in a few weeks, he was gone.

Some More About Mayakovsky

My love of Mayakovsky's works did not in any way contradict my ideas about creativity of the common people.

I never considered Mayakovsky to be obscure and unpopular.

There is a difference between popularity and popularization.

Mayakovsky is understandable to all who want to think. He does not write for the man who does not think. His work is far from being a popularization, but he is popular.

Unity of form and content—that's what strikes one in the works of the people, and that's what strikes in Mayakovsky.

I work in the field of the poetic documentary film. That's why I feel so close to both the folk songs and the poetry of Mayakovsky.

I am striving in my future works for greater unity of form and content than in *Three Songs About Lenin,* because unity of form and content guarantees success.

On Scenarios for Documentary Films

If we want to achieve continuity and coherence in our scenes not at the cutting table, but much earlier, during filming,
if we want
this continuity and correspondence of scenes to result in
an irresistible movement forward, from the old toward the new quality, by overcoming difficulties, obstacles, contradictions, by the struggle between the old and the new,
if we want
to genuinely solve this most difficult problem of all, then we have

to rely on the small scenario. Or even the microscenario. Or even the minutest of directions. The smaller it is, the more accurate and complete it should be. And the more accurate and complete we make it, the more difficult it is to make it. Nonetheless, it is vital to complete such scenarios.

Because once they are completed,

then the cameramen themselves (each in his own way) attempt to take down, in their notes, preliminary schemes of the subject, sometimes making notes in the text of the subject, sometimes in film direction, sometimes in accurate scenario plans.

One may say:

Not every cameraman is a specialist. Many of our comrades need assistance. But can they not be helped by our young, energetic specialists?

We have a new group of young men and women, blooming, strong, fiery, and talented.

There are many specialists among them.

Why shouldn't they, with their fiery vigor, kindle the flames of enthusiasm in our old specialists?

Why shouldn't our young scenario writers (arm in arm with the cameramen) discover the secrets of small scenario writing for film subjects?

Why shouldn't they become authors of small film novels?

Why shouldn't they take up this basic task, if it really *is* basic?

Maybe only young people have the right to make the first steps in this direction?

Maybe my thoughts on this are not very clear. My comrades should correct me, and make my ideas clearer.

The point of this whole thing is this: Is there in all that I've said a useful grain of truth?

Is there within it even some noticeable approximation of truth?

Use of these ideas in practice will give us the answer.

Thus, if the small scenario actually does become the key that will open doors to a new quality of subject, then I will have the right to say to myself:

Practice has shown that my assumptions were not wrong or useless.

And practice is the criterion of truth.

Creative Plans, Testimonials, Ideas

1. If *Kino-Pravda* is truth shown by means of the cinematic eye, then a shot of the banker will only be true if we can tear the mask from him, if behind his mask we can see the thief.

2. The only way we can divest him of his mask is by concealed observation, by concealed photography: that is, by means of hidden cameras, supersensitive film and light-sensitive lenses, infrared film for night and evening shooting, noiseless cameras. Constant readiness of the camera for filming. Immediate shooting of a perceived object.

Not in the theater, but in life, the thief plays the role of the cashier in order to rob the cash register. Or else the confidence man plays the role of a doting suitor to seduce and, then, rob a woman. Or else the hustler plays the simpleton in order to fool his victim. Or else the prostitute plays the-girl-with-a-bow to make a fool of the nincompoop. Or else the hypocrite, the flatterer bureaucrat, the spy, the bigot, the blackmailer, the contriver, etc., who hide their thoughts while playing one role or another, take their masks off only when no one can see them or hear them. To show them without their masks on—what a difficult task that is, but how rewarding.

3. All this when a man plays someone else's role in life. But if we take a professional actor, playing a role in the theater, to film him through the "Kino-Eye" would be to show the agreement or disagreement between the man and the actor, the correspondence or lack of correspondence between his words and his thoughts, etc. I am reminded of one actor who was playing in one of the old silent films. Dying from wounds in front of the camera, showing suffering on his body and face, he was at the same time telling an anecdote which was amusing everyone—apparently showing off his ability to act while not feeling the emotions he was portraying. If the convulsions of the wounded man could have been recorded for sound, then in place of moans we would hear, to our astonishment, something directly opposite to what we were seeing on the screen: words with double meaning, jokes, giggling . . .

Apparently, the actor had to die so many times before the camera that it had become automatic; he did not have to use his mind to act. His mind was free to tell jokes. This—the ability to dissimulate, to affect two identities—seemed quite disgusting to me at the time.

To show Ivanov in the role of Petrov, as seen through the "Kino-Eye," would be to show him as a man in life and as an actor on the stage; not trying to pass off acting on the stage as life, and vice versa. Complete clarity. Not Petrov in front of you, but Ivanov playing the role of Petrov.

4. If a fake apple and a real apple are filmed so that one cannot be distinguished from the other on the screen, this is not ability, but incompetence—inability to photograph.

The real apple has to be filmed in such a way that no counterfeit can be possible. The real apple can be tasted and eaten, while the artificial one cannot—a good cameraman can understand this easily.

Films About Women

I am a film writer. A cinepoet. I do not write on paper, but on film. As with every writer, I have to make work notes. Observations. Not on paper, however, but on film. Together with longer poems, I write short novels, sketches, verse. Many writers took their heroes from real life. For instance, *Anna Karenina* was based on the life of one of Pushkin's daughters. I thought about recording on film the history of Marya Demchenko from the life of Marya Demchenko. The difference was that I could not write on film events that had already occurred. I can only write simultaneously, as the events are occurring. I cannot write about the meeting of the Komsomol after it has taken place. And I cannot, like some correspondents, write an article on events, on spectacles, on carnivals several days after they have taken place. I do not demand that the cameraman be at the scene of a fire two hours before it breaks out. But I cannot permit that he go to film a fire a week after the fire has gone out. I received permission to film a Kolkhoz meeting, to film Demchenko, and soon, from the directors when there was already nothing to film. This we used to call "directorial permission."

Now I am working on films about the woman. This is not one subject, but a series of themes. These films will be about a schoolgirl, about a girl at home, about a mother and child, about abortion, about the creative female youth, about the differences between our girls and those abroad, about recreation and work, about the first steps and first words of a child, about the infant girl, about the teenage girl, about the mature woman and the old woman . . .

I will also write about specific people, living and working. My selection of people may be planned. I will film the development of the man from diapers to old age. All this will be possible only with organization of the endless research, filming and editing work. The endless process of taking creative notes on film. The endless process of observation with camera in hand.

Some sort of workshop or laboratory should be started where one could work under special conditions—conditions where creative thoughts and organizational forms would not conflict and nullify each other.

1944
Translated from the Russian by Val Telberg

Kino-Eye, Lecture I

The history of Kino-Eye has been a relentless struggle to modify the course of world cinema, to place in cinematic production a new emphasis of the "unplayed" film over the played film, to substitute the document for *mise en scène*, to break out of the proscenium of the theater and to enter the arena of life itself.

Let me attempt to sum up the results obtained in this direction by the Kino-Eye.

1. The manifesto of the "Kinoks" on the cinema, free from the actors, was published and later developed and popularized in a number of articles and in several public discussions.

2. In order to confirm the contents of the manifesto, there were produced and exhibited about 100 films without actors. These were of a wide variety, from primitive newsreels to extremely complex documentary films of the "cinethings." We can cite, for example, the *Weekly Reels, History of the Civil War, Calendars of Goskinof*, and the *Cine-Translations*. Outstanding among those films, which were responsible for heavy blows at the theatrical cinema, must be mentioned: *The Struggle Under Tzarism, Life Caught Unaware, Lenin's Truth, Forward Soviets!, The Sixth Part of the World, The Eleventh Year*, and, finally, *The Man with the Movie Camera*. Among the films produced by some of my pupils may be mentioned: *Moscow Nursery, For the Harvest, A Holiday for Millions*.

3. We have developed a language, proper to the cinema, special methods of shooting and montage, which are not those of the enacted film. The language of the film has become absolutely distinct from that of the theater and literature. We have created the conception of *documentary cinematography*.

4. We have established an experimental studio for the recording of facts, and later *Pravda* on July 24, 1926, published plans for a "factory of unplayed film," a "factory of facts," that is to say, pure documentary.

5. At an open meeting that took place in Moscow in 1924, followers of Kino-Eye revealed the existence of a directive by Lenin that pointed out the necessity of changing the proportion of fact-films on film programs. Finding support in this directive, the followers of Kino-Eye declared that they demanded an immediate reorganization of all Soviet film production and exhibition; they requested an internal apportionment, that is to say, a certain proportion between the theatrical cinema, the enacted film, the cine-plaything on the one hand, and, on the other, the cinema which is not played, the cine-eye, the fact-film.

This proposal was boldly called the "Leninist Film Proportion." Attempts were made to publish the proposal in the cinematographic press. N. Lebedev, the editor-in-chief of the only movie magazine appearing at that time, *Kino-Journal,* returned the manuscript to me, declaring that he protested the term "Leninist Film Proportion" and that he was against this attempt to utilize an "accidental" phrase by Lenin, and to present it as a sort of testimonial directive. The proposal of the "kinoks," rejected by the cinema press, was nevertheless published later by *Pravda* on the 16th of August, 1925. The very term itself, "Leninist Film Proportion," was not current for very long, and it is only today, in 1929, that is has been taken up again.

6. Kino-Eye has exerted considerable influence on the theatrical film, the language of which it has modified. More and more, our cinema has borrowed the methods of Kino-Eye, superficially, at least, to create what is known as the "art" film. We cite as examples *Strike, Potemkin,* and others. These borrowings have been sufficient to arouse attention and have created quite a stir at home as well as abroad in the domain of the theatrical, enacted film.

Nevertheless, these directed films, the methods of which were superficially taken from Kino-Eye, present only a particular and incidental facet of the Kino-Eye movement, the spread of which continued uninterrupted.

7. Kino-Eye has exerted a considerable influence on almost all the arts, notably in the sphere of music and literature. We will recall here that in their manifesto of the unplayed film, the exponents of Kino-Eye asked workers in the word, workers in letters, to initiate the oral chronicle, radio chronicle. We recall that following this, in *Pravda* in 1925, N. Ossinski asked that literature engage itself upon the road traced by Kino-Eye, that is to say, that it attempts to present facts—documentary elements—in an organic form.

"Vertov is right," wrote O. Brik in *Soviet Cinema,* No. 2, 1926, and he demanded of photography that it follow the example set by Kino-Eye. "It is necessary to get out of the circle of ordinary human vision; reality must be recorded not by imitating it, but by broadening the circle ordinarily encompassed by the human eye."

In their earliest declarations on the subject of the sound film, which was not yet even invented then but which was soon to come, the Kinoks, who now call themselves the "Radioks," that is, followers of Radio-Eye, traced their path as leading from the Kino-Eye to the Radio-Eye; in other words, leading to the sound Kino-Eye transmitted by radio.

A few years ago I wrote an article entitled "The Radio-Eye" which appeared in *Pravda* under the general heading "Kino-Pravda and Radio-Pravda." I stated in that article that Radio-Eye was a means of abolishing distances between men, that it offered an opportunity for the workers of the world not only to see themselves, but to hear themselves SYNCHRONOUSLY.

The declaration of the "Kinoks" provoked at the time most passionate discussions in the press. I remember a long article by Fevralski, "Tendencies in Art and Radio-Eye." I recall a special publication, *Radio*, which devoted one of its issues exclusively to Radio-Eye.

The followers of Kino-Eye, not confining themselves solely to the development of the unplayed film, were preparing themselves to work on the Radio-Eye, the talking and sound film without the play of actors.

Already in *The Sixth Part of the World*, the subtitles are replaced by an oral theme, by a radio theme, contrapuntally adapted to the film. *The Eleventh Year* is already constructed like a *visual* and *sonal* cine-thing, that is to say, that the montage was done *in relation not only to the eye, but also to the ear.*

It is in the same direction, in passing from Kino-Eye to Radio-Eye, that our film *The Man with the Movie Camera* was mounted.

The theoretical and practical work of the *kinoks-radioks* (differing in this respect from theatrical cinematography, which has found itself caught off-guard) have run ahead of their technical possibilities and, for a long time, have been awaiting a technical basis the advent of which will be late, in relation to Kino-Eye; they await the Sound-Cine and Television.

Recent technical acquisitions in this area lend powerful arms to the partisans and workers of *documentary sound cinegraphy* in their struggle for a revolution in the cinema, for the abolition of play, for an October of Kino-Eye.

From the montage of visual facts recorded on film (Kino-Eye) we pass to the montage of visual and acoustic facts transmitted by radio (Radio-Eye).

We shall go from there to the simultaneous montage of visual-acoustic-tactile-olfactory facts, etc.

We shall then reach the stage where we will surprise and record *human thoughts*, and, finally

we shall reach to the greatest experiments of direct organization of thoughts (and consequently of actions) of all mankind.

Such are the technical perspectives of Kino-Eye, born of the October Revolution.

(Excerpts from a lecture given in Paris in 1929)

KINO-EYE, LECTURE II

Kino-Eye is a victory against time. It is a visual link between phenomena separated from one another in time. Kino-Eye gives a condensation of time, and also its decomposition.

Kino-Eye offers the possibility of seeing the living processes in a temporally arbitrary order and following a chosen rhythm, the speed of which the human eye would not otherwise be able to follow.

Kino-Eye avails itself of all the current means of recording ultra-rapid motion, microcinematography, reverse motion, multiple exposure, foreshortening, etc., and does not consider these as tricks, but as normal processes of which wide use must be made.

Kino-Eye makes use of all the resources of montage, drawing together and linking the various points of the universe in a chronological or anachronistic order, as one wills, by breaking, if necessary, with the laws and customs of the construction of cine-thing.

In introducing itself into the apparent chaos of life, the Kino-Eye tries to find in life itself an answer to the questions it poses: To find the correct and necessary line among the millions of phenomena that relate to the theme.

Montage and a Few Principles of Kino-Eye

To make a montage is to organize pieces of film, which we call the frames, into a cine-thing. It means to write something cinegraphic with the recorded shots. It does not mean to select pieces to make "scenes" (deviations of a theatrical character), nor does it mean to arrange pieces according to subtitles (deviations of a literary character).

Every Kino-Eye production is mounted on the very day that the subject (theme) is chosen, and this work ends only with the launching of the film into circulation in its definitive form. In other words, montage takes place from the beginning to the end of production.

Montage being thus understood, we can distinguish three periods:

First period: The "Montage Evaluation" of all the documents that are directly or indirectly related to the chosen theme (manuscripts, various objects, film clippings, photographs, newspaper clippings, books, etc.). As a result of this montage, which consists in picking and grouping the most precious documents or those simply useful, *the plan indicated by the theme* becomes crystallized, appears more evident, more distinct, more defined.

Second period: "*Montage Synthesis*" *of the human eye* concerning the selected theme (montage of personal observation or of reports by the information-gatherers and scouts of the film). *Plan of shots*, as a result of the selection and classification of the observations of the "human eye." At the moment when this selection is made, the author takes into account the indications of the thematic plan as well as peculiarities of the "machine-eye" of Kino-Eye.

Third period: "General Montage," synthesis of the observations noted on the film under the direction of the "machine-eye." Calculation in figures of the montage groupings. Unification of homogeneous pieces; constantly, one displaces the pieces, the frames, until all shall have entered a rhythm, where all the ties dictated by the meaning shall be those which coincide with the visual ties. As a result of all these mixtures, of all these displacements and of all these reductions, we have a kind of visual equation, a visual formula. This formula, this equation, which is the result of the general montage of the cine-documents recorded on the film, is 100 per cent the cine-thing: I see, I cine-see.

Kino Eye is:

montage, when I select a theme (to pick a theme among a possible thousand);

montage, when I keep watch over the execution of the theme (of a thousand observations, to make a proper choice);

montage, when I establish the order of exposition of what has been shot according to the theme (of a thousand possible combinations to select the most adequate, basing one's self as much upon the qualities of the filmed documents as upon the requirements of the chosen theme).

The school of Kino-Eye requires that the cine-thing be built upon "intervals," that is, upon a movement between the pieces, the frames; upon the proportions of these pieces between themselves, upon the transitions from one visual impulse to the one following it.

Movement between the pieces—spectacular interval—spectacular relations between the pieces. According to Kino-Eye: a great complexity, formed by the sum total of the various relations of which the chief ones are: (1) relations of planes (small and large); (2) relations of foreshortenings; (3) relations of movements within the frame of each piece; (4) relations of lights and shades; (5) relations of speeds of recording.

Starting with this or that combination of relations, the author of the montage determines: the duration of each piece in meters for each of the images, the duration of projection of each distinct image. Moreover, at the same time that we perceive the movement that determines the relation between images, we also take into consideration, between two adjoining images, the spectacular value of each distinct image in its relations to all the others engaged in the "montage battle" that begins.

To find the most convenient itinerary for the eyes of the spectator in the midst of all these mutual reactions, of these mutual attractions, of these mutual repulsions of images among themselves, to reduce this whole multiplicity of intervals (of movements from one image to the other) to a simple spectacular equation: to a spectacular formula expressing in the best possible manner the essential theme of the cine-thing, such is the most difficult and important task of the author of montage.

This theory which has been called the "theory of intervals" was launched by the "kinoks" in their manifesto WE, written as early as 1919. In practice, this theory was most brilliantly illustrated in *The Eleventh Year* and especially in *The Man with the Movie Camera*.

1929

(Appeared first in *Filmfront*, No. 3, 1935.)

Translated by S. Brody

ORSON WELLES AND THE BIG EXPERIMENTAL FILM CULT

BY PARKER TYLER

No. 29, Summer, 1963

A dialect is a special form of communication, a language set apart for special uses. In the case of film, which, in the main, uses direct images, a "film language" may be said to exist. There are many reasons why this dialect, today, governs both big and little film cults. Devoted filmists are still jealous of the medium they admire, especially jealous because, even after films assumed a secure place as a medium of human expression, the arrival of the soundtrack made words into a major element of film, and thus offers, nowadays, literature as a complement to spectacle. In the eyes of enthusiasts, filmic interests must be guarded *against* words even when the film uses, collaborates with, words— that is, when the sound track has speech, music, and other sounds. In this situation, many ironies adhere to the "pure dialect" of the film language. The figure of Orson Welles suggests to me the chief irony for he is curiously distinctive and interesting in the light of film history.

If we can consider the big and the little Experimental Film cults as two separate camps, Orson Welles, somewhat like a colossus, has a foot in each. Lately there have been many signs of the stepped-up growth of the *big* cult. It is not only that the commercial film itself, mostly in France and Italy, has recently adopted so-called art devices (conspicuously in *Last Year at Marienbad*), but also that, on the other side, the little Experimental, or avant-garde, Film has mani-fested a progress of its own toward greater physical stature, and in this respect challenges the commercial film. *No More Fleeing* (1957) from abroad and *Narcissus* (1957) in this country were of short "feature length" in contrast with the brief avant-garde tradi-tion of 20 minutes or under: the length of the standard "short subject." Cocteau's *Blood of a Poet* (1930) was, so to speak, an ambitiously long short film, as were *Lot in Sodom* and, later on, *Dreams That Money Can Buy*.

Feature films in the commercial field have themselves become longer and longer in recent decades. Thus the newer Experimental Films should not surprise us by their ambitious lengths. One may point not only to Stan Brakhage's work, lately geared to feature length in perpetual motion, but also to essays in the "major state-ment" length instanced by *Guns of the Trees*. Of course, there are reasons both economic and cultural for the upsurge of sheer pro-duction in the Experimental field—a longer individual possession of the screen being as inevitable as the rise in the number of films. In effect, their makers have procured more and more generous backing. What seems most interesting in this intensification of filmic activity, on the art level, is the way in which the commercial and noncommercial films seem literally to have joined forces. This could not be "purely coincidental" (nothing of importance is purely co-incidental), and if one looks for the reasons, one may be reminded that, as I have mentioned, the two Experimental cults have really *always* existed. The little one, by now, has had considerable recogni-tion and documentation, while the big one has been rather am-biguous all along. Mainly, the latter has been the preoccupation of the audience we call "movie buffs": those who cherish the stylistic bents of certain well-remembered commercial directors; those who do their best to pretend that such directors do not fall victim to the demands of the commercial studios; those who believe that the "big" contributions to the art of the film may be regarded as intact.

That such admired directors—Griffith, von Stroheim, Vidor, Lu-bitsch, Dreyer, Lang, Pabst, von Sternberg, Murnau, Renoir, Feyder, Cocteau, Korda, Ford, Hitchcock, Huston, Bergman—have made special contributions to film style and some worthy, memorable films, I readily admit. But that their contributions make an intact art, free of serious blemishes, is most debatable and (I believe) a fallacy. Furthermore, the cult of the Experimentalists—from Dali-Buñuel to the present—is in precisely the same position as its "big brother." Though motivated by purer aesthetic promptings, the little Experimentalists have lacked, usually, the imagination as well as the material means to make independent and intact works of art, whether long or short. Paramount, as the Experimentalist or avant-garde virtue, doubtless, is the drive toward poetic statement, and this, by all means, has been the special property of the *little* cult.

Inevitably, the question must arise as to what degree the Big Cult—let us capitalize the term—shares in this same virtue, and furthermore what, if anything, the Big Cult has had with which to *replace* the virtue of "poetic statement." *Last Year at Marienbad,* while I think it not nearly so important as ostensibly serious people think it, is a very recent proof that a big commercial film can behave just like a little avant-garde film; that is, it can take a quite elementary situation of human psychology and emotion and treat it in a radically *filmic* way. *Marienbad* does not fear to make the imagination into a filmic instrument, to deliver us into a world of feeling composed from pieces of visible reality, objective nature; in brief, it does what, as to filmic method, was done by the makers of *The Cabinet of Dr. Caligari,* by Cocteau in *The Blood of a Poet,* and by Maya Deren in her films. I do not mean that each Big and Little film-maker has not had his own distinctive style and purpose; I mean that a good percentage of both types meet on generic avant-garde ground. On the other hand, one realizes that, for certain movie buffs, *Marienbad* is to be regarded, for that very reason, as arty and too special; as neither pure, broad, nor deep enough. For the same reason, too, Cocteau is still shunned by certain film purists for being too literary, too much a scion of "Classic" ideas about life.

Now who would fit the bill, so to speak, as the hero of the Big Experimental Film Cult: a type director of films that maintain touch with real contemporary life and yet are cinematic and inventive and the vehicles of a true film style? I have named my candidate for the honor: Orson Welles. Welles is a darling of the movie buffs young and old, and after more than two decades, he is still operating in high gear. I would agree that he has an indisputable flair for film-making; possibly he outranks, on the international level of esteem, all his competitors in terms of the universal affection aroused in serious admirers of the film art. Yet consider: Welles has consistently been as unfortunate as was another much esteemed, Big Cult man, von Stroheim, at least in the latter part of that departed director's career.

Erich von Stroheim's directorial creativeness ended with a film molded so contrarily to the way he wanted to do it that he disowned it. This was his version of Strindberg's *Dance of Death*, never seen publicly in the United States and a maimed, highly unmemorable, film. Von Stroheim's *Greed* (even as preserved to us in its defective state) ranks today as a world classic, close in universal evaluation to Welles's *Citizen Kane*—the only film which, for his part, Welles is willing to recognize as even nearly his own (I except, tentatively, the still unreleased *The Trial*). The plain moral is that esteem, in the Big Experimental Cult as in the Little, is based typically—insofar as separate and "intact" works of art are concerned—on promise, approximation or intention rather than on achievement.

It seems an illuminating point that Welles and von Stroheim, two of the most valued film directors in history, have produced in the main only "token" works of art. Thus, I think that any responsible estimate of their total output must emphasize, first, its fluid filmic idiom and, second, beware of treating it as a set of distinct and individual films. It becomes preferable to say that these two men are masters of a film style never ideally visible in *one* given work but in arbitrary, uneven pieces that hang together (in each man's case) as a certain trend or emphasis; a certain type, or series, of devices. As we know since the publication of Kracauer's *Theory of Film*, there exists a tendency to think of film not as a group of separable works of art but as a continuous "reel" of imagery, revealing what Kracauer calls "flow of life" rather than "work of art." If some are disinclined to accept that theorist's reasoning and strict terminology, it is probably because his viewpoint puts just such heroes as Welles in an overtly compromised artistic position. The movie buffs, that is to say, desire to think the film language an "art" of its own, regardless of how continuously or discontinuously it "flows." Yet, to me, there is pertinence in the flow theory because it absolves the director from responsibility to the specific and individual work, making him master of a potential art: an art visible, precisely, through persistently "flowing" signs, however well- or ill-connected.

Does my argument raise doubt in the reader? Well, take two virtually "intact" works of the revered master, D. W. Griffith: *The*

Birth of a Nation and *Intolerance*. The former was badly cut up, so much so in some sequences as to look absurd—how can we tell, even in "restored" versions, what it was meant to be or should have been? Then, assuming we have the bulk of *Intolerance* and may consider it intact, it is still superficial and, in ways trivial, by any informed standard of history or fiction. Yet among the buffs, the legend persists that Griffith's film style, or film sense if you will, entitles him to be called a "master." True, speaking hypothetically, a mauled text or staging of a Shakespeare play still shows "the hand of a master." In fact, plays suspected of being *re*written by Shakespeare from pre-existing texts may be said to show just that: the hand of a master. But, in many plays accredited as intact Shakespeare, we have the proof of Shakespeare as creator of deep, true, and full works of art, all indisputably one master's. A thumbprint may guarantee an individual but not a work of art; so with film style in the loose sense it is predominantly held. Eisenstein and Cocteau come closest, along with a few isolated works by others. What I take leave to call the Big Experimental film-maker is another matter. His image, as represented best by Welles and von Stroheim, suggests the peculiar and challenging ambiguity of the film itself as a creative art. To me, at least, it suggests that the film director, as incarnated in the Big Experimental Cult, stands midway between the creative artist and the stage director in the theater, between the composer and the musician in the concert hall, between the creator and the adapter-interpreter.

In film, editing and style-accents no more comprise a whole and creative art than do rhythm and touch in a pianist playing another man's composition. In many commercial studios, even where distinguished directors are concerned, the final editing is usually taken out of the director's hands (with or without his wish or consent) and practiced by a specialist. Poor editing, as everyone knows, can cripple a film's style and its basic message. The same happens, for good or ill, in novels as in films, as well as in such methodical collaborations in the theater as have taken place between Elia Kazan and Tennessee Williams. No inevitable argument exists against the idea of such collaborations, especially if between talents in two distinctive media: think of Mozart's magnificent *Don Giovanni* with its book by Lorenzo da Ponte. A superb collaboration in avant-garde art was that between Virgil Thomson and Gertrude Stein in two modern operas, *Four Saints in Three Acts* and *The Mother of Us All*; participating in the former with writer and composer, it should be noted, were also the scenarist, Maurice

Grosser, who supplied a scenic conception for Miss Stein's bare verbal text, and Florine Stettheimer, who gave physical form to the conception with sets and costumes of her own imagining.

Such complex collaborations as those just mentioned are often the case in films, whatever the creative value of the result. But, especially important, in films, is that the director be his own scenarist, and preferably also his story's inventor, or that he collaborate as closely as possible with a sympathetic script-writer—as did Fellini with Antonioni, Eisenstein with Alexandrov. That such collaboration pay off in artistic gain is put beyond doubt in Antonioni's case because this film artist eventually became a director of his own scripts. Prime and happy examples of collaboration in the commercial film would number those between script-writer Zavattini and two directors: De Sica and Fellini. These observations are made purposely to distinguish between such generic cases and what I mean by the Big Experimental Cult. Whatever Welles's collaborations, whether with Shakespeare or a twentieth-century novelist, or with himself, he remains a Cult hero, a film artist of ambiguous successes; a lone wolf, as it were, whose egoistic failures have stacked up to make him both notorious and famous.

Exactly the same is true of virtually all the better known little Experimentalists. Faults, misfires, technical makeshifts, incomprehensible negligence, can easily be spotted in their works—yet nominally they remain "little masters." One is tempted to say that the representative of a film cult establishes the fact that filmic *activity* is being preferred over filmic *achievement*, a filmic *direction* over a filmic *goal*. This does not happen through any basic identification of aim, or even sensibility, between big cult and little cult, or among members of either. Think how hard it would be to equate Welles with von Stroheim (despite "resemblances") by way of such a measure! Rather, the Cult hero of film necessarily represents the extravagance, the very vice, of being willy-nilly "filmic." In short, this hero is one ready to pay any price to be his own "filmic self."

On occasion, the emergence of a commercially nourished director as the incarnation of the Film Cult that his admirers dream him, may be attended with anticlimax and embarrassment. Such was Josef von Sternberg's strange "debut" in the film he made in Japan, *Anatahan*, supposedly beyond the curse of the commercial studio; it was a sort of "film-maker's film." Yet *Anatahan* is remarkably weak and undistinguished. The truth is that von Sternberg revealed himself quite uninspired and impotent when lacking luxurious physical means and really dynamic actors. This case of von Sternberg's suggests that the most original and creatively active of important film-makers who have gone in for the "big money," have operated on. the basis of bankrupting their backers. This is notoriously true of both von Stroheim and Welles, who, at their peak, ran deeper into the red, the more they took over the reins, the more they became wayward "stylists."

We might well pause, I think, to entertain a thought from the opposite direction. Suppose we take two more recently developed directors who are also "stylists" and yet who combine financially successful film-making with being "themselves," I mean Ingmar Bergman and Michelangelo Antonioni. At the moment, both Swede and Italian have arrived at international renown among the cultists, the buffs themselves. Bergman has actually replaced his much less active Scandinavian predecessor, Dreyer, as a cult ornament and big "Experimentalist" hero. It is doubtful, surely, if Dreyer's *oeuvre* of the last thirty-five years has provoked as much intense admiration as some half-dozen Bergman films have received in the last decade. I think the reason for this successful breakthrough of the avant-garde movement into the commercial film domain is because men such as Bergman and Antonioni have imitated, in substance, the best examples of little Experimental film-making, as begun in *L'Age d'Or* and *The Blood of a Poet*; they take personal charge of the story invention and the scenario and, to some extent, the camera itself.

Every striking success in collaboration, visible in recent years among commercial films, has the marks of Cocteau's personalism or of organized teams such as Zavattini-De Sica, Zavattini-Fellini, Antonioni-Fellini, Bergman as Sjöberg's scriptwriter in *Torment*, Duras-Resnais, and Robbe-Grillet playing composer to Resnais's musicianly *Marienbad*. We had Buñuel becoming his own Dali, Bergman his own Sjöberg. A very tempting speculation is that the Big Experimental Cult is the paradoxical result of the failure by brilliant film directors to find stories or story-ideas by talented collaborators sympathetic enough to work with them hand-in-glove, powerful enough to send them to school to invent their own stories. For example, I believe that Eisenstein (whom I regard as the most artistically successful director in film history) learned much, as he lived through the years, from both his scriptist, Alexandrov, and his camera man, Tisse. He learned better how to invent in terms of story, dialogue, and photographic vision. By the time of his last work, *Ivan the Terrible*, he knew by practice every "in" and "out" of the complex filmic process. Today, Antonioni and Resnais (not to mention Truffaut and other lesser lights) have earned more, and more insistent, *bravos* than a Cocteau or a Dreyer did while working through three decades instead of one—and so has Kurosawa, who has been known to the West for only ten years or so. Then why is Welles, today, the same toddler among tremendous effects as he was when his startling gift for the stage—revealed by the old Federal Theater Project—took him posthaste to Hollywood? Partly the answer is that he "collaborated" with the most culturally backward of the national industries. But it is also because of personal psychological reasons.

Simply what he *is* and *has been* makes Welles the quintessential type of Big Experimental Cult hero—always achieving failure yet bringing it off brilliantly, decking it with eloquence and a certain magnificence; fusing, in each film, the vices and the virtues appropriate to them. Welles is the eternal Infant Prodigy and, as such, wins the indulgences of adult critics and the fervid sympathy of the younger generation, which sees in him a mirror of his own budding aspirations and adventurous near-successes. Beside him, Stanley Kubrick and John Cassavetes look middle-aged, however one adds up the latter two's merits. Welles does "big things" with fabulous ease and against manifest odds. Careful assessment of the actual results displays, along with the marred success, needless audacity and impertinent novelties. He puts on an intellectual circus even when engaged cinematically with Shakespeare. He proceeded to speak *Macbeth* with a Scottish brogue which ultimately was dropped; also, desiring to place the play in its "native" barbarous milieu, alien to the refined court verse, he put certain lines of Shakespeare's into a ridiculous light by timing them with lusty bits of staging. Compare the effect of the extravagant headdresses of this *Macbeth* with the equally extravagant ones of the German Knights in *Alexander Nevsky*; for the latter, Eisenstein invented a mocking function that was an integral part of the pattern. For Welles, on the other hand, the costume extravagance of the film, like the boisterous irony shed on its language, was a quality of arbitrary wit: a playfulness out of keeping with the solemn intentions of the original dramatic work. Compare, with this Welles film, Kurosawa's flawless transposition of the same play to the barbarism of medieval Japan.

Another Shakespeare play, *Othello*, offers an even better example of Welles at work. Here, chiefly by tracking and a dolly that seemed to be overoiled, the action is considerably augmented and "cinematized," so that the tragic effects, especially at the end, are turned into giddy *bravura*. As another tragic protagonist, Othello has, behind him, a more brilliant career of success than Macbeth. A strictly private and inward fault is the sole cause of Othello's downfall: sexual jealousy. Psychologically, Othello is very modern because he suggests the explanations of psychoanalysis; that is, he *desires* to believe in Desdemona's infidelity because he *also desires* to "kill the thing he loves." Welles, without making it clear whether he understood this complex nature of Othello, was evidently drawn by magnetic attraction to a hero with whom he had a great deal of empathy.

All Welles's heroes are "big doers" who crumble; *magnificos* who are crushed by secret starvation of personal desires or a cancerous guilt. Fair, hale, noble, with a beard (as in *Othello*) or middle-aged, ignoble, and ugly (as in the police chief in *Touch of Evil*), Welles as actor-director shows high human ambition in the grip of an obscure corrosion. The inquisitive reporter bent on searching out the magnate Kane's secret, the adventurer hired by Arkadin (another kingpin of wealth) to discover his own past, bear the same relation to the Wellesian type as Iago does to Othello: He is the chosen nemesis. The hero of *Citizen Kane*, despite all appearances, had been doomed to unhappiness; the reporter's quest simply reveals the technical origin of this unhappiness: a mechanism that has done its work. Welles's hireling hero is the *other self*, enlisted precisely to be the means of revelation to himself and the audience.

This conclusion may be found as a parable on Arkadin's lips when he relates (during the film) the fable of the scorpion and the frog. When *Mr. Arkadin*, not long ago, had its American première at The New Yorker Theater, Daniel Talbot encountered me as I left, and stopping to chat, spoke of this little fable as a parable of Welles's own life. It is impossible to disagree with Talbot's observation. And what is the parable but something that applies to Kane's life and Othello's, no less than Arkadin's, if we think of these roles as masks of Orson Welles, hero-director? It is a parable for his life as a Big Experimental Cult hero. The scorpion must cross a stream (that is, Welles must make a film) but, to do so, he must enlist the help of a frog (it is easy to imagine a producer or a backer as a frog). But "Ah," says the frog to the scorpion, "your sting brings death! So why should I carry you across?"—that is, why should a producer listen to Welles's blandishments when notoriously he is a maker of expensive films that "sink" their backers? The scorpion then reasons: "Now, look. If I sting you, you will die, that's true, but if you die, I will drown—so why should I sting you?" The frog-producer (once again!) is convinced by this wily argument, swims across with the scorpion on his back ("Camera!") and duly gets stung. Before he sinks to his death, he has time, however, to ask the scorpion: "Why?" The scorpion-director makes this answer, the only one he can make: "Because it is my character." Thus, adapted to the present theme, it is Welles's character to make films, even if he must "perish" with his backers.

I have long maintained that film presents an unusually glib medium for parody and charade of many kinds. As Hollywood parodies itself and its material (as in *Sunset Boulevard* and just lately in the unspeakable *What Ever Happened to Baby Jane?*), Welles does the same in his own line. As a personality, Mr. Arkadin is the summit of the Kanes and the Ambersons: their melodramatic muse with an infusion of tragic grandeur. Note that Arkadin wears the most artificial makeup ever affected by Welles as an actor: he has Rochester's nose (in *Jane Eyre*), a palpably false hairline and the beard of a tragedian. During *Mr. Arkadin* someone compares him to Neptune; my guess is that he is familiar with the famous Greek bronze, so marvelously preserved, of Poseidon and deliberately tried to reproduce its head.

If we look closely enough at Welles's theatrical disguises, bearing in mind the abovementioned parable, we have, I believe, a perfect image of film as the great adventure of true Experimentalism: a sort of "confidence game" with laudable motives. Its hero is the substance of film cults at their "cultiest." Welles provides the complete Baedeker to failure as to success: An adolescent make-believer is posturing as an adult artist, and doing it so well, at times, that the imitation takes on a fabulous reality. The resultant charlatanry is not deliberate but the product of Welles's supreme confidence that he can overcome all defects of acting and story with his personal gifts. His talent and his remarkable drive are perfectly illustrated in still another directorial-actorial venture, this time on the stage: *King Lear*, played at the New York City Center some years ago.

Again was demonstrated the egoism in Welles that makes the creative wonder-worker into the benign-malign charlatan. I saw an early performance of *King Lear*; it looked underrehearsed, with no actor in it up to Welles as Lear except Alvin Epstein as the Fool: The two made a very striking team. The production, with its flair and its slapdash, was greeted with moderate enthusiasm, at best, from reviewers and the public. The directorial touch and

Welles as actor tended to dwarf the play and to leave most of its actors grounded. Later on, Welles had a backstage accident and appeared in his role on crutches. But then he had *another* backstage accident . . . If the "scorpion" Welles has no "frog" handy, he conjures one, it would seem, from the air. However, he refused, so to speak, to be sunk by the second accident and appeared in the role—so I understood—in a wheelchair! It was enough to give even reserved admirers of Welles a sensation of awe. Surely, the feat set a precedent and aroused some sentimental *bravos* from Wellesians. Yet, apart from the star's fortitude and talents, I doubt that the wheelchair interpretation added anything to the history of acting in the Shakespearian theater.

This actor-director's main contribution to acting (as his boyish Othello showed) is a beautiful voice and a prodigal physical presence, the latter of which he invariably overdramatizes, on the screen, with foreshortening from below. In the little Experimental field, the same adventurism—let us call it Wellesian adventurism— is repeated again and again with varying, lesser means: the same, virtually automatic, egoism; the "necessary" self-reliance; the relentless exploitation of the "filmic," no matter what the material. One could easily list and identify all the parallels . . . Even were Orson Welles to repudiate these parallels, he is their cultural progenitor as much as is Cocteau, perhaps more than Cocteau. Welles, more than any one person in the world at this moment, is a cult incarnate—whether we approach his example from the side of the Little or the Big Experimentalists. He may never do a complete and untarnished work of film art, at once deep in theme and adequate in execution. Yet as a tireless infant Hercules, he has shaken the film firmament, and may (bearded or unbearded) do so again.

CLASSIC PLASTICS (AND TOTAL TECTONICS)

BY KEN KELMAN

No. 31, Winter, 1963–64

Now I have just started to write all and only about Dovshenko's *Earth*, but find it far too fertile. As a masterpiece of classic cineplastics, its implications for more modern film transcend its very perfections. A brief analysis of these, though, is in order.

The film is about earth, and how life springs from it, and how all returns into it. It is a film about fundamentals, entirely conceived on two alternate levels, that of death and that of birth. This cyclic form follows that of nature. It is conveyed in the first episode, thematically, when the dying old man passes a fruit on to the young child. He is passing on life, the heritage of earth, so the new generation may rise from the old. The most important point here for our purpose is that the scene operates formally in painterly terms, as a series of essentially static compositions. Thus the form precisely is equivalent to the meaning: for the emphasis here is upon the eternality of death, and of earth, and the resignation of the old peasant to his fate.

But soon we are made aware of the ambivalence of Dovshenko's attitude: For, though he deeply values the venerable traditions of the country folk, he also recognizes the need for social change, which will perhaps uproot ancient ways. And to depict the youthful, revolutionary movement that is sweeping his Ukraine and driving out the landed peasants, the kulaks, he utilizes a rhythmic cutting, a dance-form. This is the new, the dynamic life.

So the cycles of life and death, and the levels of new and old, of revolution and tradition, are respectively shown in the forms of dance and of painting.

However beautiful the old may be, it is also, Dovshenko suggests, both static and moribund. But the tranquil harmony with nature it achieved, is this to be lost through the new reform and mechanization? The kulaks, both young and old, are, of course, implacably hostile to modernization. Among the other peasants, the old are suspicious, the young enthusiastic. The young are typified by Vassily; the old by his father, who is only won over to the cause of change by the awakening shock of Vassily's martyrdom at the hands of the kulak's son. Thus we have a reversal of the beginning, for here the young, in dying, gives the heritage of the new to the elder generation.

This reconciliation is rendered formally by the use of the choreographic principle to express the harmony of the new way with the old earth. There are three principal dance sections, which reflect the progression of the film and the progress of its people. In the first, the harvest itself becomes a wonderful dance, with man and earth caught up together in powerful rhythm. And, together with man and earth, is the reaper, the *machine*; so that the modern is formally vindicated, glorified, and the dynamic way replaces the static.

The second episode is not formally a dance at all, but more a graphic composition in nature. Here, Vassily dances home from a meeting with his sweetheart, over the moonlit landscape. This is not rhythmically cut because, although it is a dance, the dancer is emotionally in the old tradition; it is not a revolutionary dance, but a celebration of the beauty of eternal nature. Suddenly, the dancing figure in the landscape drops down. There is a puff of smoke. Cut to a horse which looks up from drinking at the sound of the shot; an image suggesting not only that noise, but also the violation of the silent night, and offense against creatures of the earth. But the point is also made that the young peasants have not lost the old values, only modified them. Machinery or no, they can still dance to nature's enchantment.

Finally, there is the funeral procession of Vassily: the marching, singing young people intercut with the birth pangs of a peasant woman, and the antics of the murderer gone mad with remorse. Through the fields, the peasant youth bear the martyr's body, and a branch caresses his face to signify the unity of man and nature, and of life and death. The cycle of birth and death is of course suggested most strongly by the simultaneous labor of the woman. And so out of the mother's pain comes life, and out of the martyr's sacrifice emerges the new way of life. Formally, we should note that the procession itself is rhythmed as a dance; while the actual mad dance of the murderer, as he shouts his confession, only to be drowned out by songs of the new, his dance, as he whirls about and plows the earth with his head, is completely arhythmic, to the point of spasticity. The reactionary is completely out of harmony with nature, as well as being socially defunct. (A similar point has been made before in the contrast of the kulaks' wild gesticulations and hysterical churnings as they mourn the bad news of the coming of the tractor, the new way; to the static, hopeless, but dignified mourning of Vassily's family later over his corpse.)

The film ends with a series of still images of fruit, a restatement of how the earth abides forever, as at the beginning.

Thus the three basic thematic elements of *Earth* are given formal equivalents.

The stasis of the old way and permanence of the earth—still images, painterly compositions.

The dynamism of youth and revolution, which indeed can move the earth, or at least move with it—rhythmic cutting, dance.

The ugliness and stupidity of the corrupt, the bad part of the old, the reactionaries—chaotic and awkward movement. (A distinction between obstinate old-fashionedness and decadence is nicely indicated in the big fat old kulaks and their slight son with his wispy moustache.)

Such procedure exemplifies the more advanced (guard) of the two major schools of classic film architecture, what I shall refer to as the functional. The other is the narrative.

This latter begins with the same premise as the usual structurally negligible movie: that all shape derives from plot. The difference then lies primarily *in* the plot, in the scenario's form; which may imply a corresponding plastic structure. A prime instance of plot-bound architecture is *Sunrise*.

Its story may be schematized thus: The farmer is drawn out of his cottage by the city woman's whistle. He follows her to their tryst beneath the full moon, and she seduces him into promising to kill his wife, sell his farm, and go with her to the city. Plied with caresses and drunk with visions she conjures of wondrous city life, he shrinks from another vision, of his wife's "accidental" drowning; but acquiesces. Returning home, he stands in the doorway of their bedroom, sees his wife asleep, stealthily creeps to his bed, and drowses off to dreams of water. The next day, he takes her out in the rowboat, but relents over her cowering form as he is about to throw her over, and in despair and confusion rows her ashore. When they land, he tries to reassure her, but she flees terrified, and catches a passing trolley, which he leaps onto too. It carries the frightened wife and repentant husband into the city, where they gradually become reconciled, and realize the depth of their love when they stumble upon a wedding. They wander arm in arm out of the church, lost in a dreamy vision of the countryside, until honking horns shatter their idyl; they are in the middle of the street, causing a traffic jam. They go to an amusement palace and sample the bright lights. Then the trolley to the country. Then the boat back home. But a storm rises, and the wife is lost when they capsize. It clears; the full moon crosses the sky. The husband searches futilely. He goes home, stands in the doorway of their bedroom, sees her bed, now empty, falls upon it weeping. The city woman whistles from outside. He rises, emerges, she sees his hatred and runs, he pursues and catches her, is choking her when the news is shouted that his wife has been found alive. He runs back to her; all is well; the sun rises; the city woman departs; and with her her evil spirit leaves the countryside.

The point in this summary is that plot, the action itself, determines or directly leads to kinetic or imagistic structure. Most obvious are the parallels which pervade the entire film: the whistle and slow following of the city woman at the start, to the whistle and rapid chase at the end, which stops at the same fence the farmer slowly climbed over before; the moon of that seduction, to the moon after the storm; the visions of city life, to the actuality; the imagined drowning to the attempted and to the actual capsizing; the bedroom with the wife sleeping, to the bedroom empty; the terrible trip of the lake, to the tender one later; the agonizing trolley ride, to the joyful one. Note that this series of parallels, each of which starts with the earlier incident, could be reversed to form an outline of the latter part of *Sunrise*; which is in effect an accelerated retrograde of the first portion.

But it is important to make clear that this powerful binary organization might scarcely be perceived in the picture itself, without the expression which the parallels of scenario receive in analogous camera movements and set-ups. Thus, composition and motions themselves become canonic. Full credit must be given Murnau for realizing Mayer's scenario's highest potential; but, to the extent that his architecture is plot-bound, it is fundamentally literary, and incapable of formal purity.

I might mention the most classic of all examples of such structure, which is, however, less satisfactory than *Sunrise*. This is, of course, *Intolerance*, which has been rather carelessly called fugal in its development. I only wish to point out here that the tempo acceleration Griffith employs in alternating his four stories at lesser and lesser intervals is not nearly matched by the *rhythmic* intensification; and, more pertinent for us, that, in terms of plastic organization, the action itself, linear rather than imitative, affords little opportunity for true visual unity, let alone polyphony. The weaving together of four diverse plot lines implies formal looseness, not strength, unless each line is made in terms of particular visual motifs; which Griffith does not do.

The functional approach is more specific and less total than the narrative. It is more purely formal. Its unit is that of the episode, rather than the story. We have seen this in *Earth*, where out of a series of alternate forms develops one synthetic form, cyclical in nature. Plot here determines little in itself, but is manipulated, segmentized, in order to achieve the desired progression of episodes, set pieces, with their concommitant forms. This constitutes a reversal of the narrative approach, where form is determined by story.

The tendency is the functional genre, indeed the only real necessity, is for the episode itself to take on the logic of a special form; while the film as a whole is integrated through repetitions of the same forms in different episodes. We have seen this principle at work in *Earth*. The silent films of Eisenstein, as well as the others of Dovshenko, are the prime examples of functional or episodic construction. Analyses of Eisenstein's method, some by the artist himself, are too well known and available to go into here.

So in the most fully wrought of classic film, the two principle traditions are: the functional or form-oriented; and the narrative or plot-oriented. The latter is distinguished by a more coherent over-all structure; the former by a more precise relationship of form to expression. The paradox is evident: that, by gaining freedom from plot, a new restriction, of form to segmentized material, was created; and *that* through vigorous analysis and abstraction of forms in terms of function, the totality of form became harder to achieve than in more conventional cinema.

Full architectural realization in cinema is not then even in question in the classics. By such realization I mean, in effect, an amalgam of the total coherence of the narrative film with the formal intensity of the functional. But that is figuratively put, because the coherence and intensity that are now, in fact, developing are of a different order.

And this just means that in the work of Anger, Boultenhouse, Brakhage, Markopoulos, Smith, total unity is achieved *apart from plot*; and full precision of expression is achieved *without the isolation of special forms* to fit particular content.

The new film architecture is either plotless, as in Brakhage and Smith; or breaks up plot into purely formal elements of expression, obviating the narrative sense, as in Markopoulos. On the other hand, forms themselves lose their classic distinction: no longer, for instance, can *choreographic* sections be differentiated from *graphic* sections, as in *Earth*; or set pieces be singled out formally, as the bridge or cream separator sequences in *October* or *Old and New*.

To the best of my knowledge, giving full credit to Maya Deren and Sidney Peterson for advancing the cause of absolute film structure, and to Kenneth Anger for reaching the border, the first work which *may* be claimed as total tectonic is *Anticipation of the Night*, which Brakhage followed with the undoubtable architecture of *The Dead* and *Dog Star Man*.

I do not wish to categorize at greater length what is going on right now. It will not hold still for my pen to fix. Right now, for instance, the première of *Twice a Man* looms imminent, which will mark Markopoulos's step into the realm of fully structured film.

Now we have come to the loose end. And why should criticism seek tectonic perfection? Criticism is not art, it depends on art. It must be unfinished.

Note: I have passed over certain special genres: Expressionism (*Caligari*, Watson's *Fall of Usher*); Surrealism (*Chien Andalou*, *Seashell and Clergyman*); Dada (*Entr'Acte*); as well as animation, abstractionism, impressionism. These all require qualifications besides those of narrative or functional; but seem to me not of sufficient architectural significance to merit consideration in this context.

THE IMAGE OF
THE BODY

BY ROBERT KELLY

No. 31, Winter, 1963–64

All along the film has made little
of the body. Perplexed by images of light and dark, obsessed by the
personal dilemmas of his workings, the film-maker has succumbed
to the easiest Manicheism. Possessed of an instrument that plainly
registers and re-presents bodies in motion, the film-maker has, in
his ambition to make high art, scorned the materials his tools afford
him, has preferred instead to go awhoring after a soul that, by his
hazy hypothesis, must set such bodies in motion. Trapped by the
images from which he mentally flees, needing at length something
to stick up there on the pearly screen, he resorts to one single iconic
gesture, *Ecce Homo*, and from the facility of close-up the anguished
pseudomythology of the *face* is born.

Lascaux, Altamira, Gandhara, Heliopolis, Athens, Ravenna, By-
zantium, Florence, Rome: a visual genetics that has formed our way
of seeing. The film from time to time seeks to imitate the composi-

tional sense of painting or of sculpture, but misses the essential *ground* of such meaningful organization: the body standing fully weighted in the world of the eye. Only via the close-up fragmentations of a Malraux ("detail") is the classic reduced visually to the face-mask-soul progression. Nineteenth-century devotional art (Bavarian or Saint-Sulpice or Pre-Raphaelite) provides the cheap, personalistic pleasure of the obsessive face, the face, closer to home, on the barroom floor. The great originals of film, men of technical virtuosity and defective sensibility, took the easiest way. The golden-ringleted, *putto*-lipped darling, and her sad-eyed lover, appear early enough in film, and stay there, *mutatis mutandis,* as apparently the cinema's only interpretive mode of coping with identity.

Bergman (who battens on cliché and sometimes makes a virtue of shimmering mediocrity) shows us recently in *Winter Light* the face of one of his beloved heroines, scarcely moving, for what seems hours on the screen, speaking her thrilling masochistic letter to her rabbit-faced lover, who, at the end of the grisly *perpetuum stabile* of close-up, quivers his upper lip meaningfully in turn. As flabby as the whole is, the attempt was a daring one, and rather instructive: the film returns to lantern slides accompanied by pretentious patter we're presumably too listless to read for ourselves. I write with some anger; the opening moments of Bergman's *The Naked Night* constituted one of the richest and most complex triumphs I've ever seen on the screen. But visual literature is hard, and magic lantern bromides easy; I lament his fall from vision.

The tragedy of the contemporary film is the utter and frightened distrust film-makers have for the *visual means,* the *prima materia* of their own art. In this context, I am speaking about only one aspect of this distrust, rather than the phenomenon itself. But let me note in passing how close *Last Year at Marienbad* came to magnificence, how it failed in its own terms by lack of confidence in those visual terms themselves. That film, by all rights the opening of a new age in the commercial film, closed an old one, hanging on to the naïveté of plot, close-up, and spectral narration.

My concern here is not, however, with the abuse or unimaginative use of a device (close-up) presumably as interesting as any other device, but with the film's almost total inability to present the form and movement and weight of the human body. I rail at the close-up only because it has been one of the principal means of evasion.

The film has feared the body, avoided it, built all hopes on voice and facial *gestik.* I am not limiting my meaning to camera work itself, nor calling for a moral revolution among cameramen. Even when the camera adequately handles the body, editing perverts, distorts, or simply hides.* I demand re-Vision, a new clarity and purpose in dealing with the body.

In my intense belief in the unity of every man, the unison of forces each man is, I find the film's insistence on the soul-body dichotomy, with synecdoche as its formal expression, an oppressive affliction of the human spirit. And of spirit's flesh.

Man has no Body distinct from his Soul; for that call'd Body is a portion of Soul discern'd by the five Senses, the chief inlets of Soul in this age. Energy is the only life, and is from the Body.

I rejoice in the existence of soul, *ruah, kha,* spirit; I will praise accordingly, but will likewise insist that *Shechinah* walks only in the house of flesh, and that spiritual entities shall be predicated of visible phenomenal bodies.

The film has consistently avoided dealing, then, with the human body, with the wholeness that man is, in the only dimension in which the screen can make that wholeness apparent.

The bodies of actors and actresses are derricks to move the speaking head from one part of the world to another. Except when the woman's body is used as a specific sexual object, the body is seldom even seen, allowed to hold the *center* of the visual presence man is. (Valentino tango'd with his eyes.) The film is occasionally willing to deal with the body in explicit sexual terms, but only as fillip to the plot, and then in a deceitful sleight-of-hand way. Physical sex, the supreme bodily act, is hidden under verbal suggestion, evasively projected in negative, encouraged to escape from focus. (Resnais's timid handling of flesh in *Hiroshima* reaps its bland fruit in *Marienbad*, where the utter lack of physical presence of the characters in the intensely *seen* environment marks the major visual failure of the film.)

It was not always so. Earliest film was alive with bodies in motion. Chaplin (through *Modern Times*) disdaining all but the rarest and hence all the more poignant close-up, allows the humble and arrogant and beautiful and grotesque bodies of his people to speak for themselves to the eye. The body is a subtler instrument than the face, and the great film-makers knew it. The body, as such, constitutes the most potent *vision* of identity, and is accordingly the proper and natural centrum for the film.

I would suspect, and hereby submit, that one most plausible ex-

---

* Maddows's foolish *The Savage Eye* (The Peevish Tongue?) exemplifies; a good stripper, well-photographed, a visually exciting sequence, blasphemed against by capricious and poetasting twaddle on the sound.

planation of the powerful and apparently perennial draw of the Western lies in the fact that, of all our cinema—studio, experimental, academic—the Western alone makes slim use of face-soul, but abundant and necessary use of the body as center of the visual experience and sole conveyor of meaning. The body, clothed in the sacred uniform of cowboy and cowgirl that fits its contours and hides no limb, stands clear against the rock or against the sky. The magnificent and incredible spectacle of a man against the sky, a woman standing in the water, is robbed from us by all but the "lowest" cinematic forms.

I see the Western as a wiser guide to film sense than any other category of American film. The fact that, by and large, Westerns are cliché-ridden and repetitious and ill acted is aesthetically trivial; the fact demonstrates *a fortiori* the visual sanity of the form's principal formal and functional means: the body in motion. Given the power of the body's image, the audience can survive all other weaknesses. I am speaking of the true audience that goes to movies for the eye's delight.

I am suggesting that the film, especially the film that takes itself "seriously," has not yet learned to deal with, much less how to deal with, what I contend is the most necessary visual means in any context involving humans, with certain exceptions less random than they look at first.

Brakhage's beautiful *Dog Star Man* centers, in *Part One*, on a body moving uphill. The tension, the surmise, a sight of the body again! generates a complex richness of imagery and meanings incredible after the slack ennui of most current films. I can see why Brakhage is so concerned with home-movies—the body (untrained, awkward, palpably *present*) engages Mr. Buggins as he runs that expensive film through his Kodak. I am fascinated by the legend that tells me of Chicago amateurs, the Pinkwater brothers, no fetishists, who shot thousands of feet of *feet* back in the 1930's. A corrective to Garbo?

(But that same Brakhage, in the earlier *Wedlock House*, almost broke my heart when, after intense and exciting preliminaries in black and white, the man and woman actually go to bed, and the film switches into vague negative, as if the need were: here comes the body, the body is *something else*, we've got to hide it. Thank God that Brakhage has come to full trust now in his visual means.)

The body is not "something else." It is man, it is woman, it is what we see when we see ourselves; we should see it in the darkness of art. The vitality of the film depends on its ability to break away from the psychological conventions of close-up and all that goes with it of evasion and reticence and vagueness. The film must rediscover the body, and the body's energy.

Dancing is body's vision. The body in motion is the body seeing and the body seen. The movement of human forms in space, in the camera's eye, should be the movement of energy rushing throughout all forms, impelled by matter and matter's laws, forming a world in any field in which it stirs.

The body is ever familiar. The body is ever new. Some film-makers, perhaps unconsciously, have discovered and used the power of body's presence in an art that moves in light. The film's clarity is darkness and opacity, as the body is opaque. Buñuel comes to mind, and Eisenstein in *Strike* and Mexico and *Ivan*, Chaplin, Brakhage, Sennett, very different from one another, but each unforgettably committed, visually, to the suffering or triumphing enduring body of man.

A NOTE ON COMEDY IN EXPERIMENTAL FILM

BY SIDNEY PETERSON

No. 29, Summer, 1963

The more the merrier. The amount of laughter it is possible to extract from an audience is in direct proportion to its size. And it must be together. This is what makes television such a sad affair. It is only by grouping that the presence of those talented Judases who lead us to laughter, much as the trained sheep in slaughterhouses lead other sheep to the killing-floor, can be assured. The point I wish to make is that laughter is not only a reaction. It is a talent. It develops with use. In most of us, the capacity is limited, and no amount of practice will carry us much past the point where we are able to mimic those whose sense of the absurd finds a natural outlet in that explosive sound that a celebrated "soldier of humor" once defined as "the sneeze of the intellect." There are solemn souls who can find nothing in the kind of film ordinarily called experimental to sneeze about. I disagree. Experimental works are often very funny indeed. What is needed is not funnier works but more Judases.

Their absence from film-society gatherings and the like is, I suspect, due to their presence elsewhere. Absurdity is all over the place, and a really talented *dynamiteur* is likely to seek the most rewarding spots in which to explode, places where the size of the audience constitutes some sort of guarantee that he will not be alone. And there is another factor here, which has to do with the rules of the game and the essential ambiguity of laughter, in which a core, so to say, of mockery is ever present and threatening. Your true *dynamiteur* reserves his blasts for targets worthy of destruction. Realizing his own strength, he is more attracted by productions costing ten million than by those costing ten hundred dollars. The implied humility of a lack of production value is likely to put him off. He has an instinct, which he shares with the clown, the comic, and the comic writer, for the vices of the age, and humility, in almost any form, is not, in his book, a vice. The rule is that one may not be quite free to laugh at the erotic idiocy of some heated, but otherwise impoverished youth jellied in 16 millimetered acetate, whereas one is entirely free to guffaw at the pretentious juggle of the fiduciary knockers of a screen personality whose income is equal to the combined salaries of all nine members of the Supreme Court, or the contrived gags of jokesters whose reputations are as hallowed, in their way, as Whistler's portrait of his mother. In short, mockery, in our democratic culture, tends to be a poor man's weapon. There is, of course, another factor: the sanctity of art in a society unconsciously dedicated to its destruction. Americans in general—not to mention Englishmen, Frenchmen, Russians, and Italians, also in general—may be said to have the kind of respect for art that undertakers have for life. They are so respectful that it is enough for a work to be called a work of art for it to be accorded the deference normally reserved for a respectable cadaver. Experimental films are frequently, either by intention or accomplishment, works of art. Thus, they are often dead before they are screened.

One must, I think, distinguish between laughter, which may or may not be sneezing, and comedy, which belongs, almost by definition, to the mind. It is precisely because comedy is intellectual in character, no matter how broad, that so much of it is made hyphenate, sentimental, or the like. As that master of it in its most refined form, farce, Sarcey, once said, the verve of it is *endiablé*: The devil is in it. And the devil, no matter what else he may be, is clearly an intellectual. In the words of Jacob Boehme, he is "rough and hard, also dark, hot, bitter, astringent, and cold," whereas human flesh is normally and comparatively "very young and tender." I think the camera has an affinity for "young and tender" flesh. How else can we explain its preoccupation with it? But it also has an affinity for this other thing, which is "rough and hard . . . dark, hot," and so on. In what is called show business, the presence of such elements is properly described as a lack of heart. One of the outstanding things about experimental film is precisely this lack and no amount of panning over "young and tender" flesh can conceal the absence of this sentimental organ when it simply isn't there.

In reintroducing the devil to film in this way, I am not, I think, following in the footsteps of Jean Epstein, whose *Le Cinéma du Diable* is about something else entirely. What I am doing, I hope, is to call attention to a conception of comedy that, although it is certainly related to the rationale of the stage drama of the absurd, goes back much further. Witness the "ferocious fun" of the comic poetry of Scotland at the close of the Middle Ages, in which, as Lewis says, in his *English Literature in the Sixteenth Century Excluding Drama*, "the comic overlaps with the demoniac and the terrifying." Lewis's advice in regard to the comic poetry of Dunbar, for example, is specific. "If you cannot relish a romp, you had best leave this extravaganza alone; for it offers you no other kind of pleasure." And in regard to such poetry in general, he says, "there is no human comedy; the joke lies in the extravagance." In a poem such as *The Cowkelbie Sow*, "the element of extravagance is supplied not so much by the events as by the preposterous connexions between them." In the tradition of comic poetry, such verse skips Chaucer and Dickens; Rabelais and Lucian, Lear and Carroll are the best introductions. In the same way, the best introductions to the extravagances of the experimental cinema are not the works of Ford, Eisenstein, or de Mille. They are those silent comedies, first French and then American, in which people used to experience, until their ribs ached, the ferocity and heartlessness of the farcical view of things.

I don't mean to suggest that there is the likelihood of much rolling in the aisles in response to the works of independent producers of cinematic extravagance. Something important has been lost or set aside. Like the point, as it were, of a joke. But the comic elements are there—at least most of them. And sometimes there is an even greater ferocity, a really chilling astringency, a black bitterness worthy of Boehme's rough devil. And, in the absence of the *dynamiteurs*, the audience is more likely to be disturbed than to laugh. It misses its Judases. It wants to go home.

Where never is heard,
A disparaging word . . .

So much for the behavior of the general public as an audience. There is another audience for film. It is composed of the people who make it. I can't begin to express the depths of joy with which some such individuals respond to the profoundly comic character of their own works. The most dismal production becomes an inspiring romp when viewed with the eyes and heard with the ears of those whose sensibilities are sharpened not so much by their awareness of what they have done, or by the intentions with which they have done it, as by their keen appreciation of what happens anyway in the film, especially in the earlier stages of a production: "preposterous connexions" and the like. There is something about a rough cut that increases the *endiablément*, that makes it possible to howl with delight over things that would simply outrage a more disinterested spectator. And, by the time the rough cut has been refined, you have already been conditioned.

I remember once being involved in the production of a film that was made to the accompaniment of howls that would have put even the most callous laugh-track to shame. Every bit of film that came back from the lab was enjoyed I won't say hysterically but with remarkable thoroughness. When the result was finally revealed in public, a pin might have been heard dropping. The second night, half the audience got up and left. Again, you could have heard a pin drop. Now, listening for pins to drop is not the most pleasant occupation in the world. It is an indication that something has gone wrong. In the end, of course, in such a situation, you decide that, quite unintentionally, you have produced a serious work and that just as there is unconscious humor, there is unconscious tragedy or, at least in this particular case, unconscious *grand guignol*. The important point, however, is not the reaction of the general audience. The presence of a *dynamiteur* or two might have saved the day. The important point is that there is an element of comedy in film itself, in the very process of film-making, which the general public is quite unable, for whatever reasons, to appreciate. This leads to an *activist* attitude toward film among those who are able to enjoy making it, which is probably why film-makers are so unsatisfactory to critics, whose literary instincts lead them to be more interested in what films are about than in what they are; a distinction very few seem to be capable of making.

Given the *activist* approach, the tendency to exploit the intrinsic and often misleading comical-diabolical attributes of the medium is almost overwhelming. Thus, we get film-makers' films in which the basic elements are as ill-matched as Boehme's flesh and the devil. And because they are ill-matched, the consequences are inevitable. New and perhaps unintended subjects emerge. Narration succumbs to the comic devices of inconsequence and illogic, and story becomes something that should have been lost with *The Great Train Robbery* but wasn't.

Perhaps 90 per cent of all experimental work is, from this point of view, in its very nature, comical. It is unnecessary to mention particular works. Some are funny, some funnier. It is partly a question of when. Inconsequence has a way of becoming consequential, and the most illogical sequences may lose their irrationality by merely becoming familiar. Thus, new unintentions emerge from an original lack of intent, and the process may continue indefinitely, with the same eyes never regarding the same film.

This Heraclitan effect is one of the most conspicuous things about experimental works, but it is not necessarily constant. I have experienced many films that seem to repeat themselves upon *alternate* occasions. I have never been able to persuade myself that this was an entirely subjective thing. Is it possible to speak of schizophrenic objects? Change the size of the picture, one's proximity to the screen, the intensity of the image, any of a dozen other things, and you have changed the picture. This is particularly true of works in which the visual excitement is not related to any sort of narrative obsession.

Is it possible that such alternating responses are a factor in the differences in audience behavior? This would indicate that all previews should be repeat showings behind locked doors, both in order to be fair to the picture and to the viewers. I doubt, however, that this will ever be done.

There is, of course, an element of irresponsibility in joy through production. Film-making seems, at worst, a relatively harmless occupation. It is not to be compared, for example, with the manufacture of nuclear weapons. And yet, because there is laughter in it and because laughter is a kind of ultimate weapon, I think it is not totally irrelevant to recall the extraordinary behavior of the scientists and generals who were present at the birth of an age in which it is becoming increasingly difficult to find reasons for laughter. It was a 5:30 A.M., on the 16th of July in 1945, on a stretch of semidesert about fifty miles from Alamagordo. According to the account published much later in *The New York Times*, after the bomb went off, the little groups of observers jumped up and down and clapped and shook hands and back-slapped, "all laughing like happy children." Obviously this was one of those rare occasions on which the *dynamiteurs* become producers. It should have been a movie.

FILM AND THE RADICAL ASPIRATION

BY ANNETTE MICHELSON

No. 42, Fall, 1966

For Noel Burch

The history of Cinema is, like that of Revolution in our time, a chronicle of hopes and expectations, aroused and suspended, tested and deceived. I came to know and care for film in a city that has traditionally sheltered and animated these hopes and expectations. It is not only the political and intellectual capital of its country, but the film-making capital, as well. Quite simply, the distance between the Place de l'Opéra and the studios at Joinville is a matter of a subway ride, not of a transcontinental jet flight. I shall ask you to bear this elementary fact in mind because it has determined much of what I would ever have to say about most things. More than that, it provides the terms of a general, if somewhat crude, metaphor for my concern today. To speak of Film and the Radical Aspiration is necessarily to evoke instances of convergence and dissociation.

Two statements, first, however: not mine, but drawn from the writings of men of quite dissimilar sensibilities and vocations, living and working at a distance of almost two generations. The first, Benjamin Fondane, a writer and critic, a man of the Left, died, when still young, in a German concentration camp. Writing in 1933, he said:

> We are committed with all our strength to the denunciation of a world whose catastrophic end seems more than ever before inevitable. We demand its rightful liquidation, whether that liquidation produce an irremediable vacuum of nothingness or a sovereign renewal through revolutionary means. Such should be—and this regardless of the deep inner wounds inevitably involved in such an aspiration—the aims of will and consciousness today. . . . As for film, the curve of its development has rapidly ascended, only to sink into an immediate decline. Stuffed to bursting, tricked out with an absurd and meretricious pomp, with every kind of frill imaginable, it has hypertrophied into a monstrous industry. The attraction was merely potential, the magic contained . . . the seeds of an unpardonable decay until, with the abruptness of a volcanic eruption, the huge shambles collapsed beneath the weight of its own emptiness. And yet, the cinema continues to interest us for that which it is not, for that which it failed to become, for its ultimate possibilities. . . . It may be that film is the expression of a society unable to sustain a world . . . of the mind. It may be that this tardily conceived art, child of an aged continent, will perish in its infancy. It may be, too, that the Revolution is not utterly to be despaired of.

The second statement—just one sentence—was written by a movie star and published in *Film Culture* a year or two ago. The movie star in question, a performer of quite extraordinary charm and originality, is Taylor Mead, and I presume that some of you have seen him in independently produced films. Taylor Mead has said, "The movies are a Revolution."

*　　*　　*

Film, our most vivacious art, is young enough to remember its first dreams, its limitless promise, and it is haunted, scarred, by a central, ineradicable trauma of dissociation. The attendant guilt and ambivalence, their repressive effects, the manner above all, in which a dissociative principle has been alternately resisted or assumed, converted into an aesthetic principle, the manner in which this resistance or conversion modified or redefines cinematic aspirations are, like everything concerning film, unique in the history of Western culture.

A dream, a presentiment of the medium traversed the nineteenth century. Almost every form of popular diversion characteristic of the era—the family album, the wax museum, the novel itself, the panopticon in all its forms—can be read as an obscure, wistful prefiguration of cinema. My own revelation of the wax museum as prefiguration came a year or so ago when I chose, as a Christmas treat, to accompany a bright little American, French-educated boy to the Musée Grevin. It struck me, as we went slowly through the long, dark, labyrinthine corridors, punctuated by the rather grand tableaux that chronicle the whole of French history, from the early Gauls until the Gaullist regime, that the wax museum, in its very special, hallucinatory darkness, its spatial ambiguity, its forcing of movement upon the spectator, its mixture of diversion and didacticism, is a kind of protocinema.* And of course the historical mode of discourse is, above all, that of the earliest films, which celebrated state occasions, public festivities, followed monarchs to christenings and assassinations. The extraordinary rapidity of the cinema's growth seemed to confirm this vision of a century's wistful fantasy (only seventy years have passed since Méliès witnessed the Lumières' demonstration and produced his own first reel). So, too, did the general climate of anticipatory enthusiasm and accord that animated film-making and criticism in their early, heroic period. That climate seems, in retrospect, Edenic.

Consider the atmosphere surrounding the early theoretical discussions: the Eisenstein-Pudovkin debate on the nature of montage, involving the conception of images as "cells, not elements" engaged in dialectical conflicts, as opposed to the "linkage of chains." Or the discussion, somewhat less familiar to historians, of the function of the subtitle as it crystallized during the 1920's in France: Kirsanov's

* For this reason, Erwin Panofsky's remarks on the waxworks in *Style and Medium in the Moving Pictures* (Transition magazine, No. 26, New York, 1937) would seem to misinterpret the order and reverse the intention and significance of things. I would argue that film, rather than "adding movement to stationary works of art," fulfilled the desire for movement which informs the conception of the wax museum itself. This becomes apparent, of course, only when one considers the experience, both kinetic and visual, within the whole space and sequence of the spectacle, rather than the aspect of the individual tableau as such. This aspiration toward movement and the heightened immediacy that it confers upon the experience is, I believe, borne out by the additional spectacle provided by the Musée Grevin in "The Chamber of Transformations," a remarkable early instance of an "environmental" fusion of changing light, sound, and *décor*.

elimination of the title in the interest of visual explicitness; René Clair's reduction of the title's role to the strictest minimum; the stress placed by Desnos and the Surrealists on its exclusively poetic use; on the subversion of "sense in the interests of poetry." While the controversy developed—and with the unique intensity and inventiveness that characterize critical discourse in France—technology was preparing to transcend the problem. The claim that the "shriek" or "grinding of brakes" was no less real or "present" for being understood rather than heard was rendered comically irrelevant; the problem was simply canceled by the arrival of sound.

Generally speaking, however, discussion, fruitful or academic, took place within a context of broad agreement as to the probable or desirable directions of the medium. Styles, forms, inventions and theoretical preoccupations were largely complementary, not contradictory. A spectrum, rather than a polarity, of possibilities was involved. The Surrealists' admiration of American silent comedy, reflected in the work of Artaud and Dulac among others, the universal excitement over the achievements of Russian film, Eisenstein's openly acknowledged debt to Griffith and that of the young Dreyer to both, testify to a certain community of aspiration. Eisenstein, in the very beautiful essay on *Griffith, Dickens, and the Film Today* said that "what enthralled us was not only these films, it was also their possibilities." And speaking of montage: "Its foundation had been laid by American film-culture, but its full, completed, conscious use and world recognition was established by our films."

The excitement, the exhilaration of artists and intellectuals not directly involved in the medium was enormous. Indeed, a certain euphoria enveloped the early film-making and theory. For there was, ultimately, a very real sense in which the revolutionary aspirations of the modernist movement in literature and the arts, on the one hand, and of a Marxist or Utopian tradition, on the other, could converge in the hopes and promises, as yet undefined, of the new medium.

There was, among the intellectuals concerned with cinema's revolutionary potential, both social and formal, a general and touching reverence for an idea of its specificity. There was, above all, an immediate apprehension, cutting quite across theoretical differences, of its privileged status, its unique destiny.

In an essay on *The Work of Art in the Era of Reproduction Techniques*, whose influence is so strongly evident in Malraux's aesthetics, Walter Benjamin attacked reactionaries, such as Werfel, who, by relegating the movie to the articulation of fantasy and fairy were engaged in a reduction of its scope, a tactics of repression. The most intensely euphoric expression of the new passion, of the convergence of modernist aesthetics and an Utopian ideology is Elie Faure's *Art of Cineplastics*, really an essay in aesthetics-as-science-fiction that predicts the cinema's radical transformation of the very nature of spatio-temporal perception, of historical consciousness and process.

Anticipations and speculations and, more significantly still, the inventions and achievements of the Americans, Russians, French, Germans, and Scandinavians were predicated, then, upon complementary apprehensions of the morphological and syntactical possibilities of the medium evolving within a framework of concord and mutual recognition, shattered, ultimately, by the growing, the traumatic, awareness of a principle of dissociation inherent in the art and its situation.

The point of shock is easily located in history: that moment, at the end of the 1920's in which the "hermaphroditic" nature of a craft that had already expanded and hardened into an industry, could no longer be ignored. The classical instrument of industrial revolution being division of labor, a generation of hardy adventurers, artist-entrepreneurs, director-producers, such as Griffith, were replaced by paid employees. The ultimate consequences involved something analogous to a dissociation of sensibility. This, in turn, rapidly engendered a register of limits and conventions that have acted to inhibit, divert, and reshape cinematic effort.

We are dealing with a Fall from Grace. For men like Griffith, Eisenstein, von Stroheim, Welles, and many more of the most brilliant and radical talents, it created, as we know, in the gardens of California an irrespirable atmosphere, a corruption that was to impair much of the best work done anywhere.

Intellectuals and film-makers alike, here and abroad, reacted with an immediate tension of distrust and, in many instances, withdrawal. The widespread resistance to the introduction of the soundtrack, for example, could certainly be shown to mask or reflect a hostility to the prospect of the medium's accelerated development into an instrument of mass culture. A French philosopher of my acquaintance claims to have stopped going to the movies in 1929. For Fondane, "the sound film is good only in so far as it is dumb." And for Artaud, "cinematic truth lies within the image, not beyond it." The resistance to sound—and it was a resistance to the Word, not ever to music which had, from the beginning, found a place in cinematic convention—expressed a nostalgia for an era of mute innocence and untested hope. It was, in short, a pastoral attitude.

The disenchantment, the sense of moral and aesthetic frustration expressed by Fondane were general. The history of modern cinema is, nevertheless, to a large degree, that of its accommodation to those very repressive and corrupting forces of the post-1929 situation. A complex register of limits and conventions engendered by that situation has been *productively* used. Historical precedents abound, but few or none have attained a comparable degree of dialectical paradox, intricacy, and scandalousness.

* * *

It is the acceptance of the dissociative principle, its sublimation and ultimate conversion to aesthetic purposes that characterize recent, advanced film-making in France and elsewhere in Europe. It is the almost categorical rejection of that principle and the aspiration to an innocence and organicity that animates the efforts of the "independent" film-makers who compose something of an American avant-garde. All discussion of the nature and possibilities of advanced film-making today, of film aesthetics and of future possibilities must, I believe, take this divergence of radicalisms into account. It must also take into account the fact that the question is, as Walter Benjamin remarked, "not whether we are dealing with an art" (and some, apparently, still ask that question), "but whether or not the emergence of this medium has not transformed the nature of all art."

The general resistance in this country to the notion of this transformation assumes its most crucial aspect, not in circles unconcerned with film, but rather in those presumably animated by a commitment to its development. The discomfort and hostility of many, indeed most, film critics to those aspects of contemporary cinema that bypass, contradict or transcend the modes and values of psychosocial observation is familiar; they provide, in fact, both context and target for this series of occasions known as a "festival." Certainly it is true that the generally *rétardataire* character of our film criticism reflects an anxiety about the manner in which postwar cinema, in Europe and America alike, has, at its best, transcended the conventions of a sensibility formed by the premodernist canon of a primarily literary nineteenth century. Both Amos Vogel and Richard Roud have quite rightly called attention to this fact in texts published on the occasion of the Festival's opening. Sadder and more disturbing still, I think, is the revelation, through this fact, that critical rejection of the formal principles and techniques of disjunctiveness involving sound, cutting, or any of the other parameters of film as represented in the work of Bresson, Resnais, or Godard, on the one hand, or in that of Anger, Breer, and Peter Emanuel Goldman, on the other, is part of a more general, basic, powerful contradiction or regression. One simply has to face the fact that a great part of a generation who came to maturity in the 1920's, who were nourished by and committed to, the formal radicalism of a Pound, a Stein, or a Joyce, are these days concerned—absurd and incredible as it seems—with, let us say, the novels of Saul Bellow and Norman Mailer! If the crux of cinematic development lies—as I think it does—in the evaluation and redefinition of the nature and role of narrative structure, we may say that the history of academicism in film-making and film criticism has been that of the substitution of novelistic forms and values for theatrical ones—and this in a century that saw a flowering of American poetry.

* * *

Critical malaise and contradictions, therefore, quite logically, focused last season on two films of Jean-Luc Godard: *Le Petit Soldat* and *Alphaville,* first presented in New York within the context of the Lincoln Center Festival. I say "logically" because it is precisely in so far as *Alphaville* constitutes a really remarkable instance of a reconsideration of the nature and possibilities of certain narrative conventions that I wish to consider it ever so briefly at this point.

Alphaville is an anxious meditation, in the form of a suspense story, on the agony and death of love, liberty and language in a society trapped in the self-perpetuating dialectic of technological progress. It is about feeling in deep freeze. Now, to argue or contest the validity of that idea as a theme of discourse seems to me somewhat questionable in itself, but to attack the "story" except in so far as it served as a support for a cinematic structure was, above all, to betray insensitivity to the film's central "statement."

The violent rehearsal of the content-versus-style liturgies that greeted *Alphaville* not only testified, in negative fashion, to Godard's central importance. Together with a few of his European contemporaries, he does dominate cinema now, and much of what is done anywhere has to be situated in relation to the work of these men. Above all, however, the complex *statement* of the film in regard to the possibilities of narrative convention transcends, in interest and importance, the nature of its *discourse,* and the hostility displayed toward that *discourse,* I take to represent simply a displacement (or dislocation) of hostility to its formal, cinematic statement.

* * *

François Truffaut, reflecting somewhat casually on the history of film, once divided its protagonists into two sorts: the creators of "spectacle" or entertainment, such as Méliès, and the experimenters or inventors, such as Lumière. To this, Godard replied that he had always tried to make "experimental" films in the guise of entertainments. *Alphaville* is such a film. Its conceptual and formal complexities fuse into an elaborate and precisely articulated metaphor of immanence, of the ambiguity of location and dislocation, in both their spatial and temporal modes.

Paris now, her public buildings, offices, hotels, garages, corridors, staircases, and escalators are revealed to those on intimate terms with her landscape, as invaded by the Future. Frontiers between past, present, and future are—like the distinctions between invention and entertainment—abolished through a series of formal strategies: a *prise de conscience* secured through a *prise de vues*, or revelation through imagination. This film, shot entirely on location, is the film of *Dis-location*. And, as narrative structure, lighting, cutting, produce a visual, temporal, or situational transformation, so a continual play with language transforms things known and seen. Thus, the low-income housing developments of post-1945 Paris, known as *Habitations à Loyers Modiques* are the clinics and insane asylums of the future: *Les Hôpitaux des Longues Maladies*. The city's peripheral avenues, *les boulevards extérieurs*, shift and expand into an irrevocably disquieting suggestion of the routes of interplanetary space. Function and scale of object and place are continuously altered, as image and sound converge upon site and situation in the exploration of the cinematic figuration of dislocation, of the ambiguities of time and history. As Gertrude Stein said, "Composition is not there, it is going to be there and we are here. *This is some time ago for us naturally*." The shifting—within—simultaneity of sameness and difference, of being and going-to-be, while we *are*, "some time ago, naturally," structures the time-space within which the mind (and *Alphaville* is "*about*" the birth of mind and sensibility, the rebirth of language *as* a rebirth of love) is constrained to function: that of a dislocation with respect to time. The "past-future" tense of which Godard speaks is our *present situation*.

The progress or plot of *Alphaville*, is, therefore, the passage from one revelation to another; its peripeties are perceptions, structured by the pace and tension of a detective story, of "finding truth." In the face of this, the accusations of "triviality" or "pretentiousness" became embarrassingly irrelevant. The film "states" its concern with the creation of a morphology; the concentration is on pace, tension, weight, and syntactic coherence through narration—narration being in this instance a form of "relating" in the fullest possible sense of the word: a manner of creating *relational* strategies through *telling*.

Alphaville stands, then, as a remarkable instance of a *critical* allegiance, shared by the major European film-makers, to the conventions of Hollywood's commercial cinema, and of the conversion of those conventions to the uses of advanced cinema. For the allegiance *has* acted as context and precondition of formal radicalism. [And it is interesting to consider that Godard's attachment to the Monogram film, the "B series" production, is paralleled, or anticipated by, Eisenstein's life-long affection for the early films that began to come to Russia when he was a boy. He speaks with tenderness of films like *The House of Hate* and *The Mark of Zorro*.] The importance of the suspense story, as refined by Hitchcock for the further use of men such as Resnais and Godard, lies in its paradigmatic character as narrative form, as a "vehicle" of dramatic and formal invention. Perfected in the Hollywood of an era following upon the Crash, it was adopted and refined, sublimated in the interests of a formal radicalism.

The earliest and certainly the most sumptuous, anticipation of this strategy is Feuillade's *Vampires*, shown in its entirety here for the first time during last year's festival. Together with *Alphaville*, it dominated the occasion. Made by a man of utterly intrepid imagination, its formal inventiveness is supported by a firm commitment to a notion of film as a technique of narrative for a mass public. I have discussed elsewhere the manner in which *Vampires* not only sets forth the themes developed in *Alphaville*, and the way in which the cinema of Méliès and Feuillade adumbrated, within the context of the medium's earliest stages, the principles and strategies of which Surrealist art and film provided a subsequent résumé.

"Please believe me," said Feuillade, "when I tell you that it is not the experimenters who will eventually obtain film's rightful recognition, but rather the makers of melodrama—and I count myself among the most devoted of their number. . . . I won't in the least attempt to excuse (this view). . . . I believe I come closer to the truth." It was strict adherence to the logic of this view that guaranteed, for Feuillade, a margin of improbability, of openness, of that oneiric intensity that gives *Vampires* a place among the masterworks of cinema.

Predicated on the development of a narrative convention both strict and elastic enough to accommodate a tension between dramatic probability and fantasy, between the continuity of suspense and the discontinuity of structure—between discourse and poetry, in short—Feuillade's work relates more to the future of film than to its past. Which is to say, as Robbe-Grillet has said, that "Imagination, when really alive, is always of the present." Alain Resnais's fascination with Feuillade might partly confirm this. Resnais's work, like that of his European contemporaries perpetuates the commitment to the constraints and stimuli of a given form; above all, in its straining of the limits of that form, it exemplifies a commitment to the value of Form, as such, which animates the best of advanced European cinema today.

* * *

Now, if we assume, as I shall, that the revolutionary aspiration, both *formal and political,* achieved a moment of consummation in the Russian film of the 1920's and early 1930's, we know, too, that the paradigmatic fusion was dissolved by the counterrevolution of Stalinism. As this happened (and the installation of Stalinism in its more or less definitive form, dates from 1927, the year of Trotsky's expulsion from the Soviet Union, only two years before the introduction of sound into film), European cinema and European art as a whole, abandoned a certain totality of aspiration. The process of dissociation, the split between formal and political aspects of radical or revolutionary efforts was created, irremediably so—at least through our time. The result was either reaction or a sublimation of the revolutionary aspiration into a purely formal radicalism. The vestiges of the politically revolutionary experience and tradition are henceforth expressed in the form of nostalgia and frustration. Politically oriented art at its best became a chronicle of absence, of negation, an analysis of dissociation, and, in the best modernist tradition, a *formal statement of the impossibility of discourse.*

The nostalgia and frustration are explicitly stated in Godard's *Le Petit Soldat,* by Michel, the hero: "In the early thirties, young people had the revolution. Malraux, for example, Drieu la Rochelle and Aragon. We don't have anything any more. They had the Spanish Civil War. We don't even have a war of our own." The formal articulation of this nostalgia for a revolutionary impulse and hope involves a succession of fascinating paradoxes and failures. The case of Resnais, who, almost alone of his particular generation, has attempted to articulate a strong personal political commitment, is particularly fascinating. I have in mind not only *Hiroshima* but *Muriel.* In both films, he has visible difficulty in *situating* the commitment within the total structure of his work, in finding a visual trope that will not inflect the style, or distend the structure. The result in a rhythmical, dramatic, and visual caesura, the stylistic articulation of aphony.

The two explicitly political passages in these films are both distanced, bracketed as spectacles or diversions. In *Hiroshima*, the antiwar demonstration is inserted as a film sequence enacted within the film, while, in *Muriel*, the Algerian war is evoked, not shown, in an amateur movie, by an agonized verbal commentary (the account of a young girl's torture by French soldiers) in counterpoint to the series of innocuous amateur shots that parody the myth of barracks-life hilarity.

This sequence constitutes the most brilliant, the definitive articulation of the disintegration of a cinematic arena for political discourse. The despair over that disintegration is the film's central political "statement." The "statement's" intensity, however, is further amplified through the further distancing of bracketed statement from *itself* (the distance between image and commentary). Its isolation within the texture of the total work, its particular, stylistic disjunctiveness, its own colorless color, are slightly at odds with the disjunctiveness and invented color of the whole. Through a speculative and stylistic refraction, Resnais proposes an image of the shameful scandal that generated the Fifth Republic. His trope is that of the caesura. The crack, the flaw, the rhythmic, visual gap or caesura created by this interlude or "diversion" is the *form* of Resnais's declaration of aphony. It declares his nostalgia for the film that could *not* be made; it incarnates the artist's struggle with the dissociative principle and the politics of dissociation.

And it is fascinating, but distressing beyond telling, to see, in *La Guerre Est Finie*, Resnais's ultimate attempt to assume what he obviously regards as the discursive responsibility of his position, the diabolical logic of that principle in operation. Like *Alexander Nevsky*, *La Guerre Est Finie* is the chronicle of an artist's defeat; it represents a total inversion, the most concrete negation, of a form and a style. In this film, it is the erotic sequences that assume the aspect of interludes or diversions within the total structure and the reversion to a hieraticism of style we have, of course, known and loved: that of *Hiroshima* and, above all, of *Marienbad*. These passages now produce the caesuras that arouse our nostalgia. Far more painfully, however, they declare Resnais's *own* nostalgia for his past achievements. *Vivement Harry Dickson!*

Lucien Goldmann, writing a few years ago in *Les Temps Mod-*

ernes of the supposed atrophy of historical and social consciousness in the New Wave directors, remarked, with a sigh, that political energy and vitality seemed concentrated in the Left, while cinematic talent was reserved for the Right. Goldmann's characteristically Marxist conservative taste and aesthetics aside, the problem needs to be restated—and far more explicitly than is possible on this particular occasion. Most briefly put, however, one might formulate it in the following manner: If, for the young Russians of the immediately post-Revolutionary period, the problem was, as Eisenstein said, "to advance toward new and as yet unrealized qualities and means of expression, to raise form once more to the level of ideological content," the problem for Resnais and his peers is to raise, or rather accommodate, ideological content to the formal exigencies of a modernist sensibility. Ultimately, ideology of any kind—whether that of Surrealism, Marxism, or the antihumanism of the New Novel —provides, at best, a fruitful working hypothesis for the artist. Eisenstein's conception of montage, derived from the orthodoxy of the Dialectic is not really so theoretically convincing as it was aesthetically regenerative. The energy, courage, and intellectual passion that sustained both theory and work were, of course, among the noblest of our century. Eisenstein is a model of the culture of our era—in his defeat as in his achievement, and down to the very fragmentary quality of his work!

One's sense of his defeat, visible in *Alexander Nevsky,* is so particularly agonizing because it constitutes a unique example of what one might call the pathos of dissociation pushed to an extremity of academic style. This pathos writers like Babel and Mayakovsky were spared—through death or suicide. What remained of the aspiration toward a revolutionary art in the Soviet Union after the defeat of Eisenstein had thenceforth to capitulate. In Europe, that aspiration was eventually, in the cinema that interests us, to be sublimated into a concentrated formal radicalism; elsewhere, it assumed the aspect of subversion. This brings us to American film of the "independent" persuasion.

*   *   *

Though generalization about American film is subject to the usual objections, one must, as I briefly indicated at the beginning of this talk, begin one's consideration of this film-making with a recognition of its almost categorical rejection of the aesthetic grounded in the conventions hitherto discussed. The film-makers with whom we are concerned have, in fact, been lead to abandon the tactics of reconciliation basic to European film as a whole. Most importantly, this rejection is in turn predicated on a negation, critical or apocalyptic, of the middle-class society that supported Hollywood, its aesthetic, industry, and art, and that *continues* to sustain—however precariously and capriciously—the activity of most major European directors. This basic dissimilarity of commitment is beginning, moreover, to make itself felt in discussions between French and American film-makers and critics. When Louis Marcorelles of the *Cahiers du Cinéma* claimed, as he did this last spring while addressing a group of independent film-makers and critics, that American films are unprofessional, unconcerned with the problems of mass communication, and, therefore, negligible, he is, of course, indulging in the polemical luxury of ignoring the immense difficulties confronted by artists who, working in a society that, unlike that of many European countries (and especially his own), preserves the sanctity of "free enterprise" by withholding the state subsidies that create a more open situation for the young European. He betrays, however, an extraordinary insensitivity to the pressures that force artists into an artisanal relationship to a powerful industry. He mocks, above all, the steadfastness with which they have undertaken to re-create cinematic language for themselves and their contemporaries.

Many of our best independent film-makers, such as Kenneth Anger, Robert Breer, Peter Emmanuel Goldman, Jonas Mekas, Shirley Clarke, are committed to an aesthetic of autonomy that by no means violates or excludes their critical view of the society in which they manage, as they can, to work.

There is, within "independent" circles another direction or style of effort which I now want to consider, as it represents a militant aspect of a radical aspiration in American film. It is postulated on a conception of film as being, in the very broadest sense, redemptive of the human condition itself. This attitude, however estimable, generates the most difficult and inhibiting contradictions for contemporary radicals. Beneath the burden of redemption, the formal integrity that safeguards that radicalism must and does, ultimately dissolve. I am referring to a cinema represented by the work of Stan Brakhage, and, to some extent, by the criticism of Jonas Mekas—who is sitting in the first row with a tape recorder. I would have wanted, of course, to screen some films or sequences to illustrate this consideration, but must content myself with some quotations from critical writings—and from Brakhage's voluminous correspondence.

"What's the use of cinema if man's soul goes rotten?" says Mekas. "It is not a question of film being good or bad artistically. It is a question of . . . a new understanding of Life."

Brakhage, speaking before a gathering in Berlin in December, 1965 (and this passage, somewhat longer, is extracted, unlike the preceding ones, not from *Film Culture*, but from a report on that Berlin occasion in an article published, according to my recollection, last year in *The Village Voice*).

"This camera," said Brakhage,

I take with me everywhere now. . . . I took it last night into East Berlin. I was, from the very entrance, in a state of terror that I had not imagined existed before. Finally the tension mounted till I felt compelled to take an image, which is the only time when I do work, when that compulsion or need arises directly from something in living. I had nothing to work with but empty streets and a few lights, and as I worked with those, with a fast-speed color film, and I tried to make an impression of my feelings from just those lights as I was there, inside, that which was an incredible experience for me. I have always taken seeing to be anything that comes to me in the form of an image, whether it be closed-eye vision, the dots and whirls and shapes that come when the eyes are closed and that can be seen when they are open. Memory, the remembering of images or the in-gathering of light in the immediacy of the eyes opening. I took images as I could, according to feeling. So that as I've trained myself to hold this camera so that it will reflect the trembling or the feeling of any part of the body; so that it is an extension, so that this becomes a thing to in-gather the light . . . I do not know what I will need to do when I get home in editing to capture the quality of that feeling and to say something of that experience.

Now for many of us, I imagine, and particularly for those who, like myself, have been for some time concerned with contemporary painting and sculpture and the problems of critical method deriving from this development, this statement has a very familiar ring indeed—and highly problematic implications. If, for men like Anger and Breer, or for Resnais and Godard, art and the radical aspiration supply a ground for an ethos, art really does become, for Brakhage, "nothing but a construction in ethics," and the artist a tintype of the "moral hero." The rhetoric is that of abstract expressionism, and I dare say that the Rosenberg pages of *Film Culture* represent in the New York of 1966 the last precinct of the action painter's active authority.

As a prelude to a brief consideration of the nature and consequences of this authority, here is a passage from an essay on de Kooning by Harold Rosenberg:

> Since, for de Kooning, art must discover its form in the actuality of the artist's life, it cannot impose itself upon its practitioner as other professions do upon theirs. Art becomes a way by which the artist can avoid a way. . . .
>
> By a mutual indetermination, art and the artists support each other's openness to the multiplicity of experience. Both resist stylization and absorption into a type. The aesthetic aim to which de Kooning applied the label, "no style," derives from and is the experience of this philosophy of art and of the self.
>
> In conceiving of art as a way of life, de Kooning makes his engagement in his profession total in the sense of the absorption of a priest or saint in his vocation. The idea is faulty. Painting lacks the structure of values by which ethical or religious systems can sustain the individual.

This lucid expression of reserve from the theoretician of action painting with regard to an aesthetic-as-morality is not ultimately surprising; it is the inevitable recognition of the perils and limits of a certain radicalism and its rhetoric.

Here, however, are Godard's thoughts on the matter (and we must have some day a *Wit and Wisdom of J. L. Godard*; he is an aphorist in the grand tradition of Chamfort): "Between aesthetics and ethics, a choice must be made, of course. However, it also goes without saying that each word contains a bit of the other." "Trusting to luck means listening to *voices*." "If the ways of art are unpredictable, this is because the ways of chance are not." And finally, "Making films resembles modern philosophy, Husserl, let's say . . . an adventure, plus the philosophy of that life, and reflecting on life."

* * *

Painters, sculptors, and their critics are involved, at this very moment, in a kind of chastening reappraisal of a rhetoric that passed for the thought of action painting, in a critical surveyal of the arena whose space measures the relation of its philosophical assumptions to its metaphors. It may be premature too soon to demand from the independent or underground film-maker (confined, as he is, to an even more marginal position in society) the critical stringency now beginning to inform the reassessment of action painting and its aesthetics.

To return, briefly but more specifically, to the work and thought of Brakhage, I would argue that the notion of the camera as an extension of the body or its nervous system seems to me highly questionable, and that, ultimately it limits and violates the camera's function. Certainly, this way of thinking calls into question the instrument's fundamental power as expressed in the metaphor of the camera as eye, a marvelously sensitive and flexible one to be sure, that supreme instrument of *mediation*, which is also the "mind's eye," whose possibilities infinitely transcend the limitations of a crude automatism. If cinema is to embody, as according to this aesthetic, it does, the drama and pathos of creation itself, then one may ask whether the history of academicism in film—which, as I have already suggested, proposed the substitution of novelistic forms for the theatrical ones—is not thereby simply extended by the uncritical parody of abstract expressionist orthodoxy.

My own feeling is that the work of Resnais and Godard (to mention only artists represented at this festival) constitute renderings of the agonistic dimension which are infinitely more radical and powerful; their "statements" proclaim the recognition of the dynamics of the medium—and this in the most open and least prescriptive manner possible.

These "statements" by no means necessarily exclude the possibility of stimulus or nourishment from other, developing arts. In America, the work of Robert Breer, for example, has an immediacy produced by the elimination of narrative as plot, or plot re-conceived as pro-gress, involving a complex visual logic, high speed of images, the use of subliminal vision. All these factors articulate a cinematic aspiration toward the condition of the "object" instantly apprehended, an aspiration shared by our most advanced painting today. Rather than fusing in a con-fusion, this work proposes a situation in which film and painting may converge within a tradition of formal radicalism. These films, in their intransigent autonomy, make an almost wholly plastic use of reference and allusion, by no means excluding extra plastic resonances, but animated by a sense of structure as progress-in-time so absolute and compelling that very little else has room or time enough in which to "happen."

The extraordinary advantage of American cinema today does lie partly in the possibilities of these convergences and cross-fertilizations. It may be that American film is unique in its access to a multiplicity of vital efforts unprecedented since the immediately post-Revolutionary situation in Russia. One thinks of its already established, though still embryonic, contacts with a new music, dance, theater, painting, and sculpture. And all these are, in turn, of course, heightened, and perhaps somewhat endangered, by a forced confrontation with technology in its most paroxysmic and pervasive form.

It is precisely at this point that one may anticipate the difficulties that may soon confront the great figures of European cinema, most particularly in France. If cinema and literature have so wonderfully nourished and sustained each other in postwar France (and this within the context of an antiliterary ontology of film), this is, I believe, in so far as they were both involved in a refining of their *respective* ontologies: The Robbe-Grillet–Resnais collaboration is, of course, a supreme instance of this kind of intimacy of independent forces.

Interestingly enough, however—and disquietingly, too—the extra-cinematic, the intellectual context of French film has been (with the exception of Resnais and Bresson) and continues to be, almost exclusively those of Romanticism and Surrealism. In the entire corpus of postwar film, I would cite offhand only four examples of the really significantly composed musical or sound track, and this during France's remarkable post-Webernian renewal of music: Michel Fano's serially composed soundtrack for *L'Immortelle,* Henze's score for *Muriel,* Barbaud's interestingly conceived, though questionable, score for Varda's *Les Créatures,* and above all the utterly remarkable spoken soundtrack of Jacques Tati's *Les Vacances de Monsieur Hulot*—certainly, the most deeply Webernian of all in its exquisite economy, in its inventive use of silence!

In our country, the questioning of the values of formal autonomy has led to an attempted dissolution of distinctions or barriers between media. Perhaps, however, this is because our social and economic hierarchies and distinctions remain pretty well impervious to the radical aspiration of film-makers and of artists in general. The hierarchical distinctions, the barriers between forms are, of course, infinitely more vulnerable. Cinema, on the verge of winning the battle for the recognition of its specificity—and every major film-maker and critic the last half-century has fought that battle—is now engaged in a reconsideration of its aims. The Victor now questions his Victory. The emergence of new "intermedia," the revival of the old dream of synaesthesia, the cross-fertilization of dance, theater, and film, as in the theater pieces of Robert Whitman, the work of Ken Dewey (and both are, significantly, represented in this year's festival) constitute a syndrome of that radicalism's crisis, both formal and social.

In a country whose power and affluence are maintained by the dialectic of a war economy, in a country whose dream of revolution has been sublimated in reformism and frustrated by an equivocal prosperity, cinematic radicalism is condemned to a politics and strategy of social and aesthetic subversion.

"To live," as Webern, quoting Hölderlin, said, "is to defend a form." It is from the strength of its forms that cinema's essential power of negation, its "liquidation of traditional elements in our culture," as Benjamin put it, will derive and sustain its cathartic power.

Within the structure of our culture, ten-year-olds are now filming 8mm serials—mostly science fiction, I am told—in their own backyards. This, perhaps is the *single most interesting fact* about cinema. Given this new accessibility of the medium, anything can happen. Astruc's dream of the camera as fountain pen is transcended, the camera becomes a toy, and the element of play is restored to cinematic enterprise. One thinks of Méliès, both Child and Father of cinema, and one rejoices in the promise of his reincarnation in the generation of little Americans making science-fiction films after school in those backyards. Here, I do believe, lies the excitement of cinema's future, its ultimate radical potential. And as André Breton, now a very venerable radical, has said, "The work of art is valid if, and only if, it is aquiver with a sense of the future."

APPENDIX

THE INDEPENDENT FILM AWARD

To point out original and unique American contributors to the cinema, *Film Culture* establishes the INDEPENDENT FILM AWARD.

FIRST INDEPENDENT FILM AWARD

Since John Cassavetes's film *Shadows*, independently produced by Maurice McEndree and Seymour Cassel, more than any other recent American film, presents contemporary reality in a fresh and unconventional manner, it rightly deserves the first Independent Film Award.

Cassavetes in *Shadows* was able to break out of conventional molds and traps and retain original freshness. The improvisation, spontaneity, and free inspiration that are almost entirely lost in most films from an excess of professionalism are fully used in this film.

The situations and atmosphere of New York night life are vividly, cinematically, and truly caught in *Shadows*. It breathes an immediacy that the cinema of today vitally needs if it is to be a living and contemporary art.

January 26, 1959, New York

SECOND INDEPENDENT FILM AWARD

To point out original and unique American contributions to the cinema *Film Culture* is awarding its second Independent Film Award to

Robert Frank and Alfred Leslie's film
Pull My Daisy

(The first Independent Film Award, January, 1959 was given to John Cassavetes's film *Shadows*.)

Looking back through our last year's film production, we have found a sad and infested landscape, with our official cinema still perpetuating long-dead styles and long-dead subjects. Our official cinema is completely out of tune with the times. We however believe that no art in modern times has any value if it is not modern. Only modern art can be creative, and only modern can be moral, since it does not place obstacles of clichés of life and art between man and the immediacy of life.

Pull My Daisy has all these qualities. Its modernity and its honesty, its sincerity and its humility, its imagination and its humor, its youth, its freshness, and its truth is without comparison in our last year's pompous cinematic production. In its camera work, it effectively breaks with the accepted and 1,000-years-old official rules of slick polished Alton Y Co. cinematographic schmaltz. It breathes an immediacy that the cinema of today vitally needs if it is to be a living and contemporary art.

April 26, 1960, New York

THIRD INDEPENDENT FILM AWARD

To point out original and unique American contributions to the cinema, FC is awarding its third Independent Film Award to

Ricky Leacock—Don Pennebaker—Robert Drew—Al Maysles for the film

Primary

Looking back through our last year's film production, we have found that *Primary*, more than any other film, reveals new cinematic techniques of recording life on film. Whereas the usual fiction film is drowned in heavy theatrics, and the usual theatrical and television documentary has become a pallid and dehumanized illustration of literary texts, in *Primary*, as well as in their film *Cuba Sí, Yankee No*, Ricky Leacock, Don Pennebaker, Robert Drew, and Al Maysles have caught scenes of real life with unprecedented authenticity, immediacy, and truth. They have done so by daringly and spontaneously renouncing old controlled techniques; by letting themselves be guided by the happening scene itself; by concentrating themselves only on man himself, without imposing on him any preconceived "form" or "idea" or "importance." We see *Primary* as a revolutionary step and a breaking point in the recording of reality in cinema. We further believe that the fiction film, too, could intelligently profit from *Primary*'s techniques.

Shadows and *Pull My Daisy* have indicated new cinematic approaches stylistically and formally. *Primary* goes one step further: By exploring new camera, sound, and lighting methods, it enables the film-maker to pierce deeper into the area of new content as well. The main handicap of cinema has been its expensiveness and its need for team work. Since most of human creation is a private personal action, the most sensitive artists have avoided cinema. The techniques of *Primary* indicate that we are entering a long-awaited era, when the budget for a sound film is the same as that of a book of poems, and when a film-maker can shoot his film with sound, alone and by himself and unobtrusively, almost the same way as a poet observing a scene. Thus, heralded by *Primary*, we see another turning point in cinema.

There is a feeling in the air that cinema is only just beginning. 1961

FOURTH INDEPENDENT FILM AWARD

To point out original and unique American contributions to the cinema, FC is awarding its fourth Independent Film Award to

Stan Brakhage
for his films
The Dead and *Prelude*

Looking back through last year's film production, we have found that Stan Brakhage's films, *The Dead* and *Prelude*, stand out as works of exquisite beauty; they point to the unexplored possibilities of the poetic cinema.

Singlemindedly and persistently, during the last ten years, Stan

Brakhage has been pursuing his own personal vision. He has developed a style and a filmic language that is able to express with utmost subtlety the unpredictable movements of his inner eye. He has mastered silence as no other film-maker has done, he has made it an integral part of his films. He has eliminated from his work all literary elements, making it a unique and pure cinematic experience.

Whereas the bulk of the independent film-making in America and elsewhere follows the documentary and the dramatic film traditions, Brakhage has chosen poetry for his artistic self-expression. He has directed his eye inwards, into man's subconscious, wherefrom he draws snatches of the beauty and the meaning of man and the world. He has kept away from the obvious, the explainable, the banal, giving the cinema an intelligence and a subtlety that is usually the province of the older arts. And he has done this with fanatical consistency, upholding—and setting an example for others—the absolute independence of the film artist.
1962

FIFTH INDEPENDENT FILM AWARD

To point out original American contributions to the cinema, FC is awarding its fifth Independent Film Award to

Jack Smith
for his film
Flaming Creatures

In *Flaming Creatures*, Smith has graced the anarchic liberation of new American cinema with graphic and rhythmic power worthy of the best of formal cinema. He has attained for the first time in motion pictures a high level of art that is absolutely lacking in decorum; and a treatment of sex that makes us aware of the restraint of all previous film-makers.

He has shown more clearly than anyone before how the poet's license includes all things, not only of spirit, but also of flesh; not only of dreams and of symbol, but also of solid reality. In no other art but the movies could this have so fully been done; and their capacity was realized by Smith.

He has borne us a terrible beauty in *Flaming Creatures*, at a time when terror and beauty are growing more and more apart, indeed are more and more denied. He has shocked us with the sting of mortal beauty. He has struck us with not the mere pity or curiosity of the perverse, but the glory, the pageantry of Transylvania and the magic of Fairyland. He has lit up a part of life, although it is a part which most men scorn.

No higher single praise can be given an artist than this, that he has expressed a fresh vision of life. We cannot wish more for Jack Smith than this: that he continues to expand that vision, and make it visible to us in flickering light and shadow, and in flame.
1963

SIXTH INDEPENDENT FILM AWARD

To point out original American contributions to the cinema, FC is awarding its sixth Independent Film Award to

Andy Warhol for his films
Sleep, Haircut, Eat, Kiss, and *Empire*

Andy Warhol is taking cinema back to its origins, to the days of Lumière, for a rejuvenation and a cleansing. In his work, he has abandoned all the "cinematic" form and subject adornments that cinema had gathered around itself until now. He has focused his lens on the plainest images possible in the plainest manner possible. With his artist's intuition as his only guide, he records, almost obsessively, man's daily activities, the things he sees around him.

A strange thing occurs. The world becomes transposed, intensified, electrified. We see it sharper than before. Not in dramatic, rearranged contexts and meanings, not in the service of something else (even Cinéma Vérité did not escape this subjection of the objective reality to ideas) but as pure as it is in itself: eating as eating, sleeping as sleeping, haircut as haircut.

We watch a Warhol movie with no hurry. The first thing he does is that he stops us from running. His camera rarely moves. It stays fixed on the subject like there was nothing more meaningful and nothing more important than that subject. It stays there longer than we are used to. Long enough for us to begin to free ourselves from all that we thought about haircutting or eating or the Empire State Building; or, for that matter, about cinema. We begin to realize that we have never, really, seen haircutting or eating. We have cut our hair, we have eaten, but we have never really seen those actions. The whole reality around us becomes *differently* interesting, and we feel like we have to begin filming everything anew. A new way of looking at things and the screen is given through the personal vision of Andy Warhol; a new angle, a new insight—a shift necessitated, no doubt, by the inner changes that are taking place in man.

As a result of Andy Warhol's work, we are going to see soon these simple phenomena, like Eating, or Trees, or Sunrise filmed by a number of different artists, each time differently, each time a new Tree, a new Eating, a new Sunrise. Some of them will be bad, some good, some mediocre, like any other movie—and somebody will make a masterpiece. In any case, it will be a new adventure; the world seen through a consciousness that is not running after big dramatic events but is focused on more subtle changes and nuances. Andy Warhol's cinema is a meditation on the objective world; in a sense, it is a cinema of happiness.
1964

SEVENTH INDEPENDENT FILM AWARD

To point out original American contributions to the cinema, *Film Culture* is awarding its seventh Independent Film Award to

Harry Smith

Harry Smith's creative work reaches across two important fields of film:

His abstract works, both in color and black and white are among the most complex and rich, among the most beautiful, yet to come out of cinema. The modulations of color and form are so certain and subtle, delicate and bold, that these films rank among the very few where attempt is absolutely realized in attainment.

As an animator, Harry Smith is remarkable in perfection of technique, and in intensity of vision, unique. To the decorative wasteland of contemporary animation, he has brought fantastic opulent growth and orgiastic opiate undergrowth, the purest ritual, the most direct uncompromising magic—whether viewed as enchantment, beguilement, invocation; or as a Boschian document of possibilities of Earth, Heaven, and Hell in our world and time.

For a generation, Harry Smith has been creating unquestionable masterworks. Now his films have come to light, and we are delighted to give them and their maker this recognition so long and well deserved.
1965

EIGHTH INDEPENDENT FILM AWARD

To point out original American contributions to the cinema, *Film Culture* is awarding its eighth Independent Film Award to

Gregory Markopoulos

It is now almost twenty years that Gregory Markopoulos has been perfecting that quality so unlikely in the avant-garde, in the independent film—an imagistic elegance, a measured eloquence of editing, a delicate balance of all elements of plot, character, theme—a harmony as classic as the Greek myths of his major works.

At the same time, he has constantly been at the forefront among innovators, developing techniques of rapid cutting and subjective treatments of narrative time that were more than experimental, that were and remain truly new.

Such is the achievement of Gregory Markopoulos, from *Psyche* and *Swain* through *Twice a Man* and his latest completed work *Galaxie*, an achievement in which the traditions of classic and romantic are fused with the most modern art in the roundedness and lucidity of crystal.

1966

NINTH INDEPENDENT FILM AWARD

To point out original contributions to the cinema, *Film Culture* is awarding its ninth Independent Film Award (for the year 1967) to

Michael Snow
for his film
Wavelength

1968

TENTH INDEPENDENT FILM AWARD

To point out original contributions to the cinema FILM CULTURE is awarding its tenth Independent Film Award (for the year 1969) to

Kenneth Anger

for his film *Invocation of My Demon Brother* specifically, and for his entire creative work in general; for his unique fusion of magick, symbolism, myth, mystery, and vision with the most modern sensibilities, techniques, and rhythms of being; for revealing it all in a refreshed light, persistently, constantly, and with a growing complexity of means and content; at the same time, for doing it with an amazing clarity, directness and sureness; for giving to our eye and our senses some of the most sensuous and mysterious images cinema has created; for being the Keeper of the Art of Cinema as well as the Keeper of the Eternal Magick Directions.

1969

INDEX

Italicized numbers represent direct quotations.
Asterisks indicate illustrations.
Films are listed under their directors; books and articles, under their authors.

Dante Alighieri, 8, 282–83
D'Avino, Carmen, 102
Dean, James, 106
De Antonio, Emile, 79, 81
De Broca, Philippe: *The Seven Capital Sins*, 135
De Kooning, Willem, 88, 106, 290, 418
Delluc, Louis, 18
De Maria, Walter, 317–18, 349
Demchenko, Marya, 369
De Mille, Cecil B., 129, 291, 400
Demy, Jacques, *The Seven Capital Sins*, 135
Deren, Maya,* 6, 7, 19, 23–25, 50, 72, 84–86, 89, 137, 139, 171–86, 253, 378, 392; *At Land*, 6; *Choreography for Camera*,* 10, 188–90, 194, 199; *Meshes of the Afternoon*,* 6, 84; *Ritual in Transfigured Time*, 6
De Seta, Vittorio: *Banditi a Orgosolo*, 93
De Sica, Vittorio, 319, 381–82; *The Bicycle Thief*, 47, 50; *Boccaccio 70*, 135
Desnos, Robert, 407
Dewey, Ken, 420
Dhomme, Sylvain: *The Seven Capital Sins*, 135
Dietrich, Marlene, 67
Domarchi, Jean, 126
Dostoyevsky, Fyodor, 24, 70, 361; *The Gambler*, 123
Dovzhenko, Alexandre: *Earth*,* 387–9, 391–92
Drasin, Dan: *Sunday*, 94–95, 98
Dreiser, Theodore: *An American Tragedy*, 322
Drew, Robert, 424–25
Dreyer, Carl Th., 13, 119, 134, 141–59, 328, 377, 382–83, 407; *The Bride of Glomdale*, 144–45; *Day of Wrath*,* 141–43, 145–46, 149–56, 158; *Gertrud*,* 141, 157–59; *Leaves from Satan's Book*, 142; *Love One Another*, 143; *The Master of the House*, 144, 157; "Metaphysic of Ordet," 27–28; *Mikael*, 143–44; *Once Upon a Time*, 143; *Ordet (The Word)*,* 13–14, 27–28, 141–46, 151–58; *The Parson's Widow*, 141–45; *The Passion of Joan of Arc*, 48–49, 143–50, 152–56; *The President*, 142; *Vampyr*,* 143–50, 154–56
Duchamp, Marcel, 18; *Anemic Cinema*, 19, 329

Dulac, Germaine, 407; *The Seashell and the Clergyman*, 392n.
Duncan, Robert, 10, 251–53, 256–57, 336; *Adam's Way*, 253
Duvivier, Julien: *La Bandera*, 6

Eggeling, Viking, 8, 18–19; *La Symphonie Diagonale (Diagonal Symphony)*, 7, 19
Ehrenburg, Ilya, 364
Einstein, Albert, 14, 27–28
Eisenstein, Sergei, 16, 66, 128, 130, 134, 139, 172–73, 182, 292, 341, 380–81, 391, 400, 406, 408, 412, 415; *Alexander Nevsky*, 383, 414–15; *Film Sense*, 77; "Griffith, Dickens and the Film Today," 407; *Ivan the Terrible*, 127, 129, 228, 382, 397; *October*, 128, 392; *The Old and the New*, 392; *Potemkin*, 17, 76–77, 127, 371; *Que Viva Mexico*, 397; *Strike*, 371, 397
Eisner, Lotte, 38–39
Eliot, T. S., 110, 177, 311; *Murder in the Cathedral*, 173; *The Waste Land*, 112
Engel, Morris, 90–92; *The Little Fugitive*, 81, 89–90; *Lovers and Lollipops*, 90; *Weddings and Babies*, 74, 90
Enkidu, 249
Epstein, Jean, 18; *Le Cinéma du Diable*, 400
Ernst, Max, 19
Expressionism, 48, 392n.

Faure, Elie: *The Art of Cineplastics*, 408
Feldman, Morton, 228
Fellini, Federico, 130, 139, 381–82; *Boccaccio 70*, 135; *Nights of Cabiria*, 47, 50; *La Strada*, 50
Feuillade, Louis, 412–13; *Vampires*, 412
Feyder, Jacques, 377; *La Kermesse Héroïque*, 66
Film-Makers Cinematheque, 339, 349
Film-Makers Cooperative, 5, 17, 71–72, 241, 349; Catalogue, 260, 266, 288
Fischinger, Oskar, 303, 305
Flaherty, Robert, 134, 172; *Nanook of the North*, 76, 78, 96
Fleischman, Peter, 275
Fleischner, Bob: *Blonde Cobra*, 281, 317, 322

Fleming, Victor, 66; *Gone with the Wind,* 66
Flynt, Henry, 349
Fondaine, Benjamin, *405, 408–9*
Ford, Charles Henri, 108
Ford, John, 66, 122, 134, 377, 400; *Flesh,* 122; *Grapes of Wrath,* 30, 66; *The Informer,* 66; *Stagecoach,* 66
Foster, Dick, 261, 267
Frampton, Hollis, 11, 327, 329; *Artificial Light,** 346–48
Franju, Georges, 74; *Le Sang des Bêtes (Blood of the Beasts),* 173
Frank, Robert, 71, 80, 275; *Pull My Daisy,* 9, 74, 79, 81, 95–96, 101, 109–12, 115, 137, 424–25; *The Sin of Jesus,* 9, 79, 81, 96
Freud, Sigmund, 6, 99, 208, 221–22
Frier, Bruce, 240
Fuller, Samuel, 126
Futurism, 48, 134

Gance, Abel: *La Roue,* 134
Garbo, Greta, 132, 396
Gauguin, Paul, 125, 242
Gehr, Ernie, 327–28, 337, 349; *Moments,* 334; *Reverberation,* 334–35; *Wait,* 334
Geldzahler, Henry: "Some Notes on Sleep," 300–301
Gide, André, 126
Gildea, John Rose, 111
Gillespie, Dizzy, 270; "Gaucha Guero," 268–69; "Manteca," 269
Ginsberg, Allen, 103, 109–11, 272
Giraudoux, Jean, *126*
Godard, Jean-Luc, 134, 410, 412, 417, *418, 419;* *Alphaville,* 410–12; *À Bout de Souffle (Breathless),* 93; *Le Petit Soldat,* 410, 413; *The Seven Capital Sins,* 135
Goldman, Peter E., 410, 416
Goldmann, Lucien, 414–15
Gombrich, E. H., 303
Gracq, Julien: *The Castle of Argol,* 342
Graves, Robert, 136, 245; *The Greek Myths,* 218; *King Jesus,* 241; *The White Goddess,* 224, 241
Griffith, D. W., 16, 128, 130, 134, 341, 377, 407–8; *Abraham Lincoln,* 127; *The Birth of a Nation,* 127–28, 379–80; *A Corner in Wheat,* 149; *Intolerance,* 142, 380, 391; *Way Down East,* 145
Griffith, Richard, 127
Grosser, Maurice, 380–81
Guitry, Sacha: *Napoléon,* 69
Guthrie, Tyrone, 46
Gutman, Walter, 80

Harlow, Jean, 164–67
Harrington, Curtis, 19, 22–23, 50, 172; *Night Tide,* 102; *On the Edge,* 188
Harris, Hilary, 102; *Polaris Action,* 98
Hawks, Howard, 124, 134; *Gentlemen Prefer Blondes,* 127; *Scarface,* 127
Heister, Stuart: *The Bisquit Eater,* 66
Hemingway, Ernest, 109, 112; *For Whom the Bell Tolls,* 245
Henze, Hans Werner, 420
Higgins, Dick: *Invocation,* 317
Hill, Jerome: *The Sand Castle,* 74, 102
Hirsh, Hy, 271
Hitchcock, Alfred, 124, 129–30, 134, 377; *To Catch a Thief,* 62–63
Hugo, Ian, 22–23, 173; *Jazz of Lights,* 24
Hulme, T. E., 243
Humes, Harold: *Don Peyote,* 80–81
Huston, John, 377; *Moby Dick,* 125–26; *Moulin Rouge,* 242; *The Red Badge of Courage,* 47–48

Independent Film Awards, 72, 423–29
Indiana, Robert, 331
Ionesco, Eugène, 135

Jacobs, Henry, 305
Jacobs, Kenneth, 9, 320, 337; *Blonde Cobra,* 281, 317, 322; *Little Stabs at Happiness,* 280, 317–19, 324; *Soft Rain,* 336; *Star Spangled to Death,* 336; *Tom, Tom, the Piper's Son,** 335–37, 346
Jarry, Alfred, 110
Joffen, Jerry, 331
Jones, Joe, 317
Joyce, James, 7, 22, 297, 410
Jung, C. G., 6, 271, 306, 308

Kafka, Franz, 24, 50
Kaprow, Allen, 101
Kass, Peter: *Time of the Heathen,* 102
Kaufman, Bob, 94
Kazan, Elia, 380
Keaton, Buster, 364; *The General,* 265, 269–70

Pop Art, 138, 328
Porter, Edwin: *The Great Train Rob-bery*, 402
Pound, Ezra, 10, 183, 410; *Gaudier-Brzeska*, 187–88, 194–95, 198, 227, 243
Preminger, Otto, 129, 133; *The Man with the Golden Arm*, 129
Preston, Richard, 8, 97–98, 104
Proust, Marcel, 232, 241
Pudovkin, V., 15–16, 77, 406; *Film Technique*, 77; *Mother*, 146

Rabelais, François, 400
Raft, George, 135
Rainer, Yvonne, 334
Ramuz, C. F.: *La Séparation des Races*, 38
Ray, Man, 18, 48; *Emak Bakia*, 7, 19; *Return to Reason*, 7
Ray, Nicholas, 124; *Party Girl*, 127
Reich, Wilhelm: *Character Analysis*, 279; "Orgonomic Functionalism," 107
Reinhardt, Max, 45
Rembrandt, 126, 339
Renoir, Jean, 66, 78, 112, 124, 126, 127, 134, 377; *Les Bas-Fonds*, 66; *La Chienne*, 66; *La Grande Illusion*, 66–67, 127; *Le Déjeuner sur l'Herbe (Picnic on the Grass)*, 127; *La Règle du Jeu*, 133
Resnais, Alain, 382, 410, 412, 413, 415, 417, 419–20; *La Guerre Est Finie*, 414; *Hiroshima Mon Amour*, 394, 413–14; *L'Année Dernière à Marienbad (Last Year at Marien-bad)*, 377–78, 382, 394, 414–15; *Muriel*, 413–14, 420
Rice, Ron, 9, 101–2; *Chumlum*, 317; *The Flower Thief*, 101, 280; *Queen of Sheba Meets the Atom Man*, 280–81; *Senseless*, 317
Richardson, Samuel, 128
Richter, Hans, 4, 8, 13, 89, 303; *Dreams That Money Can Buy*, 19, 377; "The Film as an Original Art Form," 15–19; *Ghosts Before Break-fast*, 19; *Rhythmus 21*, 7
Rilke, Rainer Maria, 342
Rimbaud, Arthur, 24; *Les Illumina-tions*, 101
Rivette, Jacques, 127; *Paris Nous Ap-partient*, 123

Robbe-Grillet, Alain, 382, 413, 420; *L'Immortelle*, 420
Rochlin, Sheldon, 80
Rogosin, Lionel, 79–80, 90–91; *Come Back, Africa*, 79, 82, 90; *On the Bowery*, 79, 90
Rohmer, Eric, 126
Romney, Henry, 343
Rosenberg, Harold, 417–18
Rossellini, Roberto, 77, 124, 134; *The Miracle*, 46; *Paisan* (Br. *Paisà*), 17
Rouch, Jean, *Chronique d'un Eté*, 93
Roud, Richard, 31, 409; "The French Line," 123
Rubin, Barbara, 323; *Christmas On Earth*, 317, 322–24
Ruttman, Walter, 18; *Berlin, Sym-phony of a City*, 48

Sanders, Denis and Terry: *Crime and Punishment, U.S.A.*, 80, 102; *A Time out of War*, 80, 102
Santayana, George, 126
Sarris, Andrew,* 13, 119; "*Citizen Kane*: The American Baroque," 29–36; "Notes on the *Auteur* Theory in 1962," 121–35
Satie, Erik: "Vexations," 300
Schneemann, Carole, 207; "Kenneth Anger's *Scorpio Rising*," 277–79
Schneider, Betty, 123
Sedgwick, Edie, 331
Sennett, Mack, 397
Serios, Ted, 313
Serra, Richard, 346
Seurat, Georges, 336
Shakespeare, William, 122, 173–74, 178, 180, 181, 380–81, 383, 386; *Hamlet*, 179; *Julius Caesar*, 30; *King Lear*, 242, 385; *Pericles*, 123; *Timon of Athens*, 123; *Troilus and Cres-sida*, 46
Sharits, Paul, 327, 329; *N:O:T:H:I:N:G*, 338, 344–45; *Piece Mandala*, 344; *Ray Gun Virus*, 327, 344–45, 349
Shelley, Percy Bysshe, 10, 88; "Are-thusa," 336
Sherwood, Barbara, 95
Shiomi, Cheiko: *Disappearing Music for Face*, 346–47, 349
Shklovsky, Victor: *Art as Technique*, 335–36

Sibelius, Jean, 128
Singer, Alexander, *A Cold Wind in August,* 102
Singletory, Charles, 310
Sirk, Douglas, 133
Sitney, P. Adams,* 236, 239, 242–43, 349; "Harry Smith Interview," 260–76; "Imagism in Four Avant-garde Films," 187–200; "Interview with Stan Brakhage," 201–29; "Introduction," 3–11; "Structural Film," 326–48
Sjöberg, Alf: *Torment* (Br. *Frenzy*), 382
Sloane, Everett, 35
Smart, Christopher, 242
Smith, Bessie, 270
Smith, Harry,* 7–8, 260–76, 338, 428; #1, 260–61, 267–68; #2, 268–69; #4, 269, 271; #5 (*Circular Tensions*), 269, 271; #10, 271; #11 (*Misterioso*), 271; #12 (*Heaven and Earth Magic: The Magic Feature*),* 8, 269, 271–75; #13 (*Oz*), 269, 273–74; #14 (*Late Superimpositions*), 8, 275
Smith, Jack, 9, 275, 284, 289, 323, 392; *Flaming Creatures,** 10, 281–84, 426–27; *Scotch Tape,* 317, 324, 426–27
Smith, John Corson, 262
Smith, R. J., 264
Snow, Michael, 11, 327–30, 337, 344, 349; ◄───►,* 333-34, 429; *New York Eye and Ear Control,* 333–34; *One Second in Montreal,* 333–34; *Wavelength,** 331, 332–34, 338
Sorrentino, Gilbert, 243
Spottiswoode, Raymond, *A Grammar of the Film,* 43
Stauffacher, Frank, 19, 261, 271
Stein, Gertrude, 109, 212, 224, 380–81, 410, 411; *Four Saints in Three Acts,* 380–81; *Mother of Us All,* 380–81; *Picasso,* 244, 245
Stern, Bert: *Jazz on a Summer's Day,* 80, 102
Sternberg, Josef von, 66, 134, 377; *Anatahan,* 381–82
Stettheimer, Florine, 381
Stevens, Leslie: *Private Property,* 102
Stevens, Wallace, 140
Stone, David C., 80

Stoney, George: *All My Babies,* 102
Strand, Paul, 89
Stravinsky, Igor, 126, 128, 336
Strindberg, August, 24; *Dance of Death,* 379
Stroheim, Erich von,* 13, 52–70, 134, 288, 377, 381–82, 408; *Blind Husbands,* 63, 67, 69; *The Devil's Passkey,* 63, 67, 69; *Foolish Wives,* 59–64, 67–9; *Greed,** 38, 47–48, 53–54, 59–60, 67, 69, 397; *The Marriage of the Prince,* 59; *Merry-Go-Round,* 59, 63; *The Merry Widow,** 52–56, 63, 67–69; "The Merry Widow: Introduced by Stroheim," 52–56; *Paprika,* 66; *Poto-Poto,* 67; *Queen Kelly,* 63; *Walking Down Broadway,* 66–67; *The Wedding March,** 60–61, 63, 67, 69
Surrealism, 7, 48, 110, 222, 272, 275, 392, 407, 412, 415, 420

Talbot, Dan, 80, 384
Tati, Jacques: *Les Vacances de M. Hulot,* 420
Taylor, Elizabeth, 274
Teilhard de Chardin, Pierre, 302, 304
Telberg, Val, 366, 369
Tenney, James, 207, 234, 238
Thomajan, Guy, 80
Thomas, Dylan,* 171–86, 243
Thompson, D'Arcy: *Growth and Form,* 246
Thomson, Virgil, 380
Thoreau, Henry David, 160–63; *Walden,* 166
Tissé, Edward, 382
Toland, Gregg, 33–34
Tolkein, J. R. R., 255
Tolstoy, 76–77, 122–23; *Anna Karenina,* 369
Trotsky, Leon, 413
Truffaut, François, 74, 126, 131, 133, 383, 411; *Jules and Jim,* 99
Tyler, Parker,* 5, 24, 72, 137, 147, 171–86, 211, 337, 351; "For Shadows, Against *Pull My Daisy,*" 108–17; "Orson Welles and the Big Experimental Film Cult," 376–86; "A Preface to the Problems of the Experimental Film," 42–51; *Three Faces of the Film,* 13

Upanishads, 341

Vadim, Roger, 74; *Blood and Roses*, 149; *The Seven Capital Sins*, 135
Vanderbeek, Stan, 8–9, 97–98, 276; *Science Friction*, 8
Van Dyke, Willard, 89
Van Gogh, Vincent, 125
Varda, Agnès: *Les Créatures*, 420
Vasari, Giorgio, 236
Vautier, Ben, 349
Vertov, Dziga,* 92, 341, 351, 353–75; *The Action of Mirnov*, 363; *Battle of Tsaritsyn*, 363–64; *Calendar of Goskinof*, 370; *Chevronets*, 364; *Cine-Translations*, 370; *The Discovery of Sergei Radonezshky's Remains*, 363; *The Eleventh Year*, 363–64, 370, 372, 375; *Enthusiasm*, 363–64; *For the Harvest*, 370; *Forward, Soviets!*, 363–64, 370; *Grimaces of Paris*, 364; *History of the Civil War*, 363–64, 370; *A Holiday for Millions*, 370; *The Kino Eye*, 363–64; *The Kino Eye in the Ukraine*, 363; "Kinoks Revolution," 351, 354; *Kino-Pravda (Film Truth)*, 358, 363–64, 367; *Lenin's Truth*, 370; *Life Caught Unaware*, 370; *Man with a Movie Camera*,* 363–64, 370, 372, 375; *Moscow Nursery*, 370; *The October March*, 363; *The Sixth Part of the World*, 363–64, 370, 372; *Soviet Toys*, 364; *The Struggle Under Tzarism*, 370; *Three Songs of Lenin*, 363–66; *Today*, 364; *The VITK Train*, 363; *Weekly Reels*, 370; "The Writings of . . . ," 353–75
Vessely, Herbert: *No More Fleeing*, 377
Vidor, King, 377
Vigo, Jean, 134, 172; *Zéro de Conduite*, 101
Visconti, Luchino, 134; *Boccaccio 70*, 135
Vogel, Amos,* 171, 409
Voltaire, 126, 128
Vortex, 305–6
Vorticism, 194, 198–99, 227

Wagner, Richard, 342

Walsh, Raoul: *Every Night at Eight*, 135; *High Sierra*, 135
Warhol, Andy, 275–76, 317–18, 328, 338, 341, 343, 349, 427–28; *Beauty #2*, 328, 331; *Blow Job*, 331; *The Chelsea Girls*, 332; *Eat*,* 11, 317–18, 328, 331, 427; *Empire*, 427; *Haircut*, 427; *Harlot*, 328; *Kiss*, 11, 427; *Poor Little Rich Girl: Party Sequence*, 332; *Sleep*, 11, 286, 300–301, 329, 427
Watson, James S.; and Webber, Melville: *Fall of the House of Usher*, 392n.; *Lot in Sodom*, 50, 172, 377
Webern, Anton von, 212, 243, 420–21
Weinberg, Herman G.: "Coffee, Brandy, & Cigars XXX," 65–70; "A Footnote to *Foolish Wives*," 62–64
Weine, Robert: *The Cabinet of Dr. Caligari*, 48–49, 147, 368, 392n.
Welles, Orson, 74, 112, 134, 139, 376–86, 408; *Citizen Kane*, 29–36, 127, 379, 384; *Macbeth*, 383; *Mr. Arkadin*, 127, 384–85; *Othello*, 383–84; *A Touch of Evil*, 73, 384; *The Trial*, 379
Whitman, Robert, 420; *Shower*, 317
Whitney brothers, 19, 172, 261, 303
Whitney, James: *Lapis*, 316
Wieland, Joyce, 327, 329–30, 349; *Catfood*, 337; *1933*, 337; *Reason over Passion*, 337; *Sailboat*, 337
Wilder, Billy, 133; *Sunset Boulevard*, 129, 385
Wilfred, Thomas, 310
Williams, Tennessee, 380; *The Roman Spring of Mrs. Stone*, 23, 47
Wilner, Burton, 22
Wittgenstein, Ludwig: *Tractatus Logico-Philosophicus*, 219
Wurtzel, Sol, 66–67; *Hello Sister*, 66

Young, La Monte, 343, 349
Youngblood, Gene: "The Cosmic Cinema of Jordan Belson," 302–16

Zavattini, Cesare, 50, 381–82
Zen, 9, 101, 216, 331, 349
Zimmerman, Vernon, 9, 176; *Lemon Hearts*, 101